ADVANCES IN QUANTITATIVE ANALYSIS OF

# FINANCE AND ACCOUNTING

Volume **4**

University of
Hertfordshire

College Lane, Hatfield, Herts. AL10 9AB

Learning and Information Services

For renewal of Standard and One Week Loans,
please visit the web site **http://www.voyager.herts.ac.uk**

This item must be returned or the loan renewed by the due date.
The University reserves the right to recall items from loan at any time.
A fine will be charged for the late return of items.

ADVANCES IN QUANTITATIVE ANALYSIS OF

# FINANCE AND ACCOUNTING

**Volume 4**

Editor

# Cheng-Few Lee

Rutgers University, USA

 **World Scientific**

NEW JERSEY · LONDON · SINGAPORE · BEIJING · SHANGHAI · HONG KONG · TAIPEI · CHENNAI

*Published by*

World Scientific Publishing Co. Pte. Ltd.

5 Toh Tuck Link, Singapore 596224

*USA office:* 27 Warren Street, Suite 401-402, Hackensack, NJ 07601

*UK office:* 57 Shelton Street, Covent Garden, London WC2H 9HE

**British Library Cataloguing-in-Publication Data**
A catalogue record for this book is available from the British Library.

ADVANCES IN QUANTITATIVE ANALYSIS OF FINANCE AND ACCOUNTING
Advances in Quantitative Analysis of Finance and Accounting — Vol. 4

ISBN  981-270-021-8

Typeset by Stallion Press
Email: enquiries@stallionpress.com

Printed in Singapore by World Scientific Printers (S) Pte Ltd

# Preface to Volume 4

*Advances in Quantitative Analysis of Finance and Accounting* is an annual publication designed to disseminate developments in the quantitative analysis of finance and accounting. The publication is a forum for statistical and quantitative analyses of issues in finance and accounting as well as applications of quantitative methods to problems in financial management, financial accounting, and business management. The objective is to promote interaction between academic research in finance and accounting and applied research in the financial community and the accounting profession.

The papers in this volume cover a wide range of topics, including earnings management, management compensation, option theory and application, debt management and interest rate theory, and portfolio diversification.

In this volume, there are 14 papers, seven of them apply accounting information to earnings management and management compensation: *1. Firm Performance and Compensation-Based Stock Trading by Corporate Executives; 2. Management Compensation, Debt Contract, and Earnings Management Strategy; 3. Estimated Operating Cash Flow, Reported Cash Flow from Operating Activities, and Financial Distress; 4. Earnings Surprise and the Relative Information Content of Short Interest; 5. Group Types and Earnings Management; 6. The Tendency of Firm Managers to Avoid Small Losses; 7. Beating or Meeting Earnings-Based Target Performance in CEOs' Annual Cash Bonuses.*

Two of the remaining seven papers are related to option theory and application: *1. Real Option Based Equity Valuation Models: An Empirical Analysis; 2. The Shift Function for the Extended Vasicek Model.* Three of the remaining five papers are related to debt management and interest rate theory: *1. Risky Debt-Maturity Choice under Information Asymmetry; 2. A Bayesian Approach for Testing the Debt Signaling Hypothesis in a Transitional Market: Perspectives from Egypt; 3. Taking Positive Interest Rates Seriously.* The remaining two papers are related to portfolio diversification: *1. Do Winners Perform Better Than Losers? A Stochastic Dominance Approach; 2. Corporate Diversification and the Price-Earnings Association.*

# Contents

# List of Contributors

*Chapter 1*

**A. William Richardson**
DeGroote School of Business
McMaster University
1280 Main Street
Hamilton, Ontario L8S 4M4, Canada
Tel.: 905-525-9140 Ext. 23993
Fax: 905-521-8995
Email: awrich@mcmaster.ca

**Raafat R. Roubi**
Department of Accounting
Brock University
Faculty of Business, Taro Hall 225
500 Glenridge Avenue
St. Catharines, Ontario L2S 3A1, Canada
Tel.: 905-688-5550 Ext. 4186
Fax: 905-688-9779
Email: rroubi@brocku.ca

**Hemantha S. B. Herath**
Department of Accounting
Brock University
Faculty of Business, Taro Hall 240
500 Glenridge Avenue
St. Catharines, Ontario L2S 3A1, Canada
Tel.: 905-688-5550 Ext. 3519
Fax: 905-688-9779
Email: hemantha.herath@brocku.ca

*Chapter 2*

**Zahid Iqbal**
School of Business
Texas Southern University
Houston, TX 77004
Tel.: 713-313-7737
Fax: 713-313-7722
Email: Iqbal_zx@tsu.edu

*Chapter 3*

**Chia-Ling Lee**
Department of Accounting and Information Technology
National Chung Cheng University
168 University Rd., Min-Hsiung
Chia-Yi 621
Taiwan, R.O.C.
Tel.: 886-5-2720411 Ext. 34502
Fax: 886-5-2721197
Email: actcll@ccu.edu.tw

**Victor W. Liu**
Department of Business Management
National Sun Yat-sen University
70 Lien-hai Rd.
Kaohsiung 804, Taiwan, R.O.C.
Tel.: 886-7-5254661
Fax: 886-7-5254662
Email: vwliu@mail.nsysu.edu.tw

*Chapter 4*

**Sheen Liu**
Williamson College of Business Administration
Youngstown State University
Youngstown, OH 44504, USA
Tel.: 330-941-7149
Fax: 330-941-1459
Email: sheenxliu@yahoo.com

**Chunchi Wu**
Lee Kong Chian School of Business
Singapore Management University
Singapore 178899
Tel.: 65-6828-0158
Fax: 65-6828-0427
Email: cwu@syr.edu

*Chapter 5*

**Terry J. Ward**
Department of Accounting
PO Box 50
Middle Tennessee State University
Murfreesboro, TN 37132, USA
Tel.: 615-898-2341
Fax: 615-898-5839
Email: tward@mtsu.edu

**Benjamin P. Foster**
University of Louisville, USA
Tel.: 502-852-4826
Email: bpfost01@gwise.louisville.edu

**Jon Woodroof**
The University of Tennessee, USA
Tel.: 865-974-1762
Email: jwoodroof@utk.edu

*Chapter 6*

**Jose Mercado-Mendez**
Department of Economics and Finance
Central Missouri State University
Warrensburg, MO 64093, USA
Tel.: 660-543-8650
Email: mercado@cmsu1.cmsu.edu

**Roger J. Best**
Department of Economics and Finance
Central Missouri State University
Warrensburg, MO 64093, USA
Tel.: 660-543-4246
Email: best@cmsu1.cmsu.edu

**Ronald W. Best**
Department of Accounting and Finance
University of West Georgia
Carrollton, GA 30118, USA
Tel.: 678-839-4812
Email: rbest@westga.edu

*Chapter 7*

**Min-Jeng Shiue**
Department of Accounting
National Taipei University, Taiwan
Tel.: 886-2-2502-4654 Ext. 18412
Fax: 886-2-2506-0730
Email: smj@mail.ntpu.edu.tw

**Chan-Jane Lin**
Department of Accounting
National Taiwan University
1 Roosevelt Rd. Sec. 4
Taipei, Taiwan 106
Tel.: 886-2-3366-1115
Fax: 886-2-2363-3640
Email: cjlin@ntu.edu.tw

**Chi-Chun Liu**
Department of Accounting
National Taiwan University, Taiwan
Tel.: 886-2-3366-1119
Fax: 886-2-2363-8038
Email: ccliu@mba.ntu.edu.tw

*Chapter 8*

**Tarek I. Eldomiaty**
United Arab Emirates University
P.O. Box 17555, UAE
Tel.: 9713-7133405
Fax: 9713-7624384
Email: T.eldomiaty@uaeu.ac.ae

**Mohamed A. Ismail**
United Arab Emirates University
P.O. Box 17555, UAE
Tel.: 9713-7133342
Fax: 9713-7622944
Email: m.ismail@uaeu.ac.ae

*Chapter 9*

**Yi-Tsung Lee**
Department of Accounting
National Chengchi University
64, Tz-nan Rd., Sec. 2, Wenshan
Taipei 11623, Taiwan, R.O.C.
Tel.: 886-2-29393091 Ext. 81027
Fax: 886-2-29387113
Email: actytl@nccu.edu.tw

**Ging-Ginq Pan**
Graduate Institute of Finance
National Pingtung University of Science and Technology
1, Hseuh Fu Road, Neipu Hsiang
Pingtung, Taiwan, R.O.C.
Tel.: 886-8-7703202 Ext. 7818
Fax: 886-8-7703202 Ext. 7833
Email: ggpam@mail.npust.edu.tw

*Chapter 10*

**Wing-Keung Wong**
Department of Economics
National University of Singapore
1 Arts Link, Singapore 117570
Tel.: 65-6874-6014
Fax: 65-6775-2646
Email: ecswwk@nus.edu.sg

**Howard E. Thompson**
Department of Finance, Investment and Banking
University of Wisconsin-Madison
975 University Avenue
Madison, WI 53706, USA
Tel.: 608-831-2456
Fax: 608-262-6378
Email: hthompson@bus.wisc.edu

**Steven X. Wei**
School of Accounting and Finance
The Hong Kong Polytechnic University
Hung Hom, Hong Kong
Tel.: 852-2766-7056
Fax: 852-2330-9845
Email: afweix@inte.polyu.edu.hk

**Ying-Foon Chow**
Department of Finance
Chinese University of Hong Kong
Shatin, New Territories
Hong Kong
Tel.: 852-2609-7638
Fax: 852-2603-6586
Email: yfchow@baf.msmail.cuhk.edu.hk

## Chapter 11

**Shyan Yuan Lee**
Department of Finance
National Taiwan University
Room 1012, 10F, 50, Sec. 4, Keelung Rd.
106, Taipei, Taiwan
Tel.: 886-2-2362-1845
Fax: 886-2-2362-1845
Email: shyanlee@ccms.ntu.edu.tw

**Cheng Hsi Hsieh**
Department of Finance
National Taipei College of Business
321, Sec. 1, Jinan Rd.
Jungjeng Chiu, 100, Taipei, Taiwan
Tel.: 886-2-2916-2133
Fax: 886-2-2232-6378
Email: chhsieh@mail.ntcb.edu.tw

## Chapter 12

**Simon S. M. Yang**
School of Business, Adelphi University
One South Avenue
Garden City, NY 11530, USA
Tel.: 516-877-4618
Fax: 516-877-4607
Email: yang@adelphi.edu

## Chapter 13

**Ben-Hsien Bao**
School of Accounting and Finance
Hong Kong Polytechnic University, Hong Kong
Tel.: 852-2766-7078
Email: afbhbao@inet.polyu.edu.hk

**Da-Hsien Bao**
Accounting and Finance Department
College of Business
Rowan University
New Jersey, USA
Tel.: 856-256-4500 Ext. 3031
Email: bao@rowan.edu

*Chapter 14*

**Enlin Pan**
Chicago Partners, LLC
123 N Waukegan Road, Suite 207
Lake Bluff, IL 60044, USA
Tel.: 847-863-4747
Email: enlin@earthlink.net

**Liuren Wu**
Zicklin School of Business
Baruch College
One Bernard Baruch Way
Box B10-225
New York, NY 10010, USA
Tel.: 646-312-3509
Fax: 646-312-3451
Email: Liuren_Wu@baruch.cuny.edu

Chapter 1

# —— Real Option Based Equity Valuation Models: An Empirical Analysis ——————————————

A. William Richardson
*McMaster University, Canada*

Raafat R. Roubi and Hemantha S. B. Herath
*Brock University, Canada*

This paper provides empirical evidence in support of real option based equity valuation models that relate share price to accounting earnings and book value. Our empirical results are generally consistent with the predictions of several models, all of which are based on real options theory. However, we find that the basic model, which includes components related to put and call options, fits the data more efficiently and parsimoniously than do models modified for the level of firm efficiency (i.e., accounting profitability measured as the return on common equity book value). We also find that the fit of the basic model and the derived coefficients vary with firm efficiency as measured by accounting profitability. We also test for the impact of capital structure on equity valuation and find some evidence for the relevance of debt for loss firms (i.e., low efficiency firms) and growth firms. We find anomalous results for loss firms, consistent with previous research, and provide an explanation for them. Our research contributes to the valuation literature by studying the empirical validity of a general real option based model and thus extends previous empirical studies that were based more or less on an options approach. Our contribution is significant in that there have been many theoretical papers on real options, but few empirical studies of the predictions of these models.

**Keywords:** Real options; valuation; equity valuation; clean surplus.

## 1. Introduction

The valuation of equity securities is of fundamental importance in accounting and finance, and has been the subject of theoretical and empirical study over many years. There have been a considerable number of papers that have examined the relationship between the market value of equity and various accounting numbers reported in the financial statements. For example, Landsman (1986), Barth (1991), and Shevlin (1991) examine the role of balance sheet measures in equity valuation. Other studies such as Ball and Brown (1968), Barth, Beaver, and Landsman (1992), Collins and Kothari (1989), and Collins, Maydew, and Weiss (1997) examine an alternative income statement approach to equity valuation based on earnings. In a more complete framework, Ohlson (1995)

1

and Feltham and Ohlson (1995) combine the two approaches and show that, under a certain reasonable set of assumptions, a firm's value can be modeled as a function of both the book value of equity and the level of earnings.

Although considerable progress has been made, there remain some fundamental questions that have still not been completely resolved. These include (1) the real option fraction of equity value to expand or contract the scale of operations; (2) financial implications of measures such as dividend payout, capital structure, and capital expenditure (Rees, 1997); and (3) to a lesser extent, the negative price-earnings anomaly observed for loss firms in the current paper and in Jan and Ou (1995), Burgstahler and Dichev (1997), and Kothari and Zimmerman (1995). Collins, Pincus, and Xie (1999) provide a reasonable explanation and suggest adding the book value of equity to the simple earnings model.

Ι In his seminal paper, Myers (1977) conceptualized the idea of viewing a firm's growth opportunities as real options. He provides the theoretical framework to value a firm as income generating assets-in-place plus the value of growth opportunities arising from future discretionary investments\Although there has been extensive research on theoretical real option models and applications since Myers' (1977) article, there have been only a few empirical studies in the real options literature. More specifically, Paddock, Siegel, and Smith (1988), Bailey (1991), Quigg (1993), and Moel and Tufano (2002) compare the net present value (NPV) with real options models. McConnell and Muscarella (1985) investigate market reaction to positive NPV projects, and Belkaoui (2000) uses a general regression model with corporate reputation, multinationality, size, profitability, leverage, and systematic risk as variables to estimate growth opportunities. In addition, Burgstahler and Dichev (1997) include an adaptation option (i.e., the value of the option to convert a firm's resources to more productive alternatives) in an equity valuation model and Berger, Ofek, and Swary (1996) consider an abandonment option.

The basic purpose of this paper is to extend our knowledge of the relationship of accounting numbers, specifically book value and earnings, to the market value of equity using real option based valuation models. Following Zhang (2000), this empirical study tests the predictions of a number of valuation models derived by supplementing standard valuation models with real options theory. We run regressions of the various valuation models for our full sample and several sub-samples stratified based on profitability levels. We show that the predictions of the various models hold generally for our sample but that Zhang's (2000) basic valuation model seems superior to his modified models. Because of apparent empirical anomalies in some situations, we have examined the assumptions and predictions of the real option based models more closely. In addition, we consider the financial implications of capital structure by modifying the operational version of Zhang's (2000) basic model to test the value relevance of debt for our sample stratified on profitability. Finally, we show that, although a sub-sample of firms' (i.e., loss firms) coefficients have a negative sign, our empirical findings are not anomalous but rather quite consistent with the more detailed expectations from the model.

The current paper makes several contributions to the valuation literature. First, it provides empirical evidence to support theoretical results based on real options theory. Prior empirical findings are based on the earnings capitalization model and the more complete, but intuitive, valuation models that include earnings and book value as explanatory variables. This contribution is significant since there have been few empirical studies that have tested predictions rooted in real options theory. Second, we incorporate capital structure considerations that are ignored in Zhang's (2000) basic model and discuss the value relevance of debt in equity valuation for cross-sectional stratified sub-samples. Third, despite apparent anomalies, our empirical results are consistent with those of previous research and provide further evidence on the variability of coefficients in valuation models and suggest that Collins, Pincus, and Xie's (1999) warning on the interpretation of the coefficient of earnings be extended. This coefficient appears to depend not just on whether earnings are positive or negative but also on the profitability of the firm. Finally, the current research contributes to the valuation literature by illustrating the convergence of two different theoretical valuation approaches that explain the value relevance of earning and book value.

The rest of this paper is organized as follows: Section 2 provides the theoretical background of the basic valuation model, derives predictions, and discusses prior research. Section 3 discusses real option based equity valuation models for analyzing the cross-sectional behavior of the properties of the valuation function. It also develops predictions for the signs of the coefficients of the operational regression models. Section 4 provides details of the samples used in the study. Section 5 describes statistical analyses and discusses the major findings and results. Section 6 discusses and provides empirical evidence on the relevance of capital structure in equity valuation. Section 7 resolves the anomalous relationship between earnings and equity valuation. Finally, Section 8 provides conclusions and discusses the limitations of this study.


## 2. Background and Prior Research

Recent research has shown that the basic earnings capitalization model to estimate a firm's value is not satisfactory because it yields anomalous empirical results for companies with negative earnings (loss firms) (Hayn, 1995; Jan and Ou, 1995). Burgstahler and Dichev (1997) developed and empirically tested an option-style valuation model, and showed that both book value and earnings contribute to explaining equity value. They also show that the relationship is convex in both earnings and book value, and that the relative explanatory power of earnings and book value vary with accounting profitability. Collins, Pincus, and Xie (1999) supplement the basic earnings capitalization model with book value in order to address the loss firm anomaly. With their revised model, they show that the anomalous results disappear and that the earnings coefficient of the basic capitalization model is biased upward (downward) for profit (loss) firms when the beginning of the period book value of net assets is not included in the empirical tests (Collins, Pincus, and Xie, 1999).

Burgstahler and Dichev (1997) introduce the notion that market value comprises two elements of value. These are adaptation value, which exemplifies the potential use of existing resources for alternative purposes, and recursion value, which assumes the continued use of existing resources for current purposes. They model market value as a function of a fixed adaptation value plus a call option on the recursion value. Collins, Pincus, and Xie (1999) specifically address the anomalous negative coefficient of earnings in the basic earnings capitalization model and motivate the addition of book value by appealing to Ohlson's (1995) valuation model and the clean surplus relation. Their model suggests that earnings be supplemented by book value because it serves as a proxy for expected future normal earnings and abandonment value, i.e. a put option.

More recently, Zhang (2000) developed a formal theoretical model for equity valuation in a real options framework. Zhang (2000) makes quite reasonable assumptions and shows that the Ohlson (1995) and Feltham and Ohlson (1995, 1996) valuation approach can be modified to incorporate the options to either abandon or grow a business, i.e. to include both put and call options.

His model shows that the basic earnings capitalization model may be complemented by an abandonment (put) option or a growth (call) option, depending on the efficiency of the business. In addition, Zhang (2000) shows how the basic model can be modified for different levels of efficiency and derives several specific additional models for relating equity value to accounting numbers.

In Zhang's (2000) basic model, the equity value depends on anticipated future actions, specifically abandonment or discretionary additional investments. The decision as to which action to take depends on a firm's efficiency and growth potential. In conservative accounting settings, equity value is shown to be a function of two accounting variables (earnings and book value) and measurement bias. If accounting measures are assumed to be free from bias, the model produces the following valuation function:

$$V_t = B_t P_d(q) + k X_t + G C_e(q), \tag{A}$$

where $V_t$ is the market value of equity at time $t$; $B_t$, the book value of equity at time $t$; $X_t$, the accounting earnings for the current period ending at time $t$; $G$, the amount invested in new opportunities because of growth potential; $k$, the capitalization factor $= 1/(R-1)$; $R$, 1 plus the risk-free rate of interest; $q$, the operational definition of firm efficiency level;

$$P_d(q) = \frac{1}{R(R-1)} \int\limits_{\underline{v}}^{q_d^* - q_t} [q_d^* - q_t - v_{t+1}] f(v_{t+1}) - \mathrm{d}v_{t+1}$$

is the value of the put option set, that is, to discontinue operations; and

$$C_e(q) = \frac{1}{R(R-1)} \int\limits_{q_e^* - q_t}^{\overline{v}} [v_{t+1} + q_t - q_e^*] f(v_{t+1}) - \mathrm{d}v_{t+1}$$

is the value of the call option set, that is, to expand operations.

In the mathematical expressions for a firm's call and put options, $q_t$ and $q_{t+1}$ are the internal rates of return of cash investment at time $t$ and $t+1$, which represents a firm's operating efficiency; $q_d^*$ is the lower bound of operating efficiency that will trigger discontinuation of the firm's operation (i.e., $q_{t+1} < q_d^*$); $q_e^*$ is the upper bound of operating efficiency that will trigger an expansion of the firm's operation (i.e., $q_{t+1} > q_e^*$); $v_{t+1}$ is a zero mean noise term pertaining to operational efficiency that cannot be predicted; $f(v_{t+1})$ is the probability density function of operational efficiency defined over the region $v_{t+1} \in [\underline{v}, \overline{v}]$

with a zero mean noise term given by $\int_{\underline{v}}^{\overline{v}} vf(v) - dv = 0$. The variable $q_t$ is analogous to the underlying asset in option terminology and has a time series behavior $q_{t+1} = q_t + v_{t+1}$, i.e. it follows a random walk.

In order to investigate the cross-sectional differences in the behavior of the valuation function, Zhang (2000) considers three types of firms that differ in efficiency and/or growth potential:

(i) *Low efficiency firms* have a high probability of discontinuing and a low probability of growth. For these firms, the put option $P_d(.)$ is valuable, and so $BP_d(q)$ accounts for a significant portion of the total value, whereas the call option $C_e(.)$ is negligible.

(ii) *Steady state firms* have a sufficiently high efficiency that the probability of discontinuing is low, but there is no growth potential. They are expected to stay on the current course of operations, i.e., current earnings will continue in perpetuity, and both $P_d(.)$ and $C_e(.)$ are negligible.

(iii) *High efficiency firms* have a high growth potential. For these firms, the call option $C_e(.)$ is valuable, and so the value due to current earnings is supplemented by $GC_e(.)$, which makes up a significant portion of the total value, whereas $P_d(.)$ is negligible.

## 3. Real Option Based Equity Valuation Models

### 3.1. *Model 1*

We transform Zhang's (2000) basic valuation Model A for any firm $i$, which assumes that accounting measures are free of bias, to the following regression model (Model 1):

$$V_{it} = \alpha_1 + \beta_1 B_{it} + \gamma_1 X_{it} + \varepsilon_{it}, \tag{1}$$

where $V_{it}$, $B_{it}$, and $X_{it}$ are the same as defined before, $\alpha_1 = GC_e(q)$, $\beta_1 = P_d(q)$, $\gamma_1 = 1/r_f$, and $\varepsilon_{it}$ is the error term.

Since $G \geq 0$, $r_f = R - 1 > 0$ and the put and call options cannot take negative values, we have the following predictions for the sign of the parameters:

- The coefficient related to the call option will be zero or positive for all firms $(\alpha_1 \geq 0)$.
- The coefficient related to the put option will be positive for all firms $(\beta_1 > 0)$.

- The coefficient related to the current earnings will be positive and equal for all firms ($\gamma_1 > 0 = $ constant).

The form of Model 1 suggests that the contribution of various terms of the valuation function will vary with the efficiency of operations, as proxied by profitability, $q$, of the firm. Analysis of the dependence of the coefficients of Model 1 on profitability based on the properties summarized in Appendix A shows that the following relations hold:

- $\partial \alpha_1 / \partial q = GC'_e(q)$,
- $\partial \beta_1 / \partial q = P'_d(q)$,
- $\partial \gamma_1 / \partial q = 0$.

From the aforementioned terms, we make the following predictions of the relative magnitude of the coefficients in Model 1 at different levels of efficiency[1] ($q$):

- The coefficient of the call option term ($\alpha_1$) will be largest for growth firms and smallest for low efficiency firms.
- The coefficient of the put option term ($\beta_1$) will be largest for low efficiency firms and smallest for growth firms.
- The coefficient of the current earnings term ($\gamma_1$) will be the same for all firms.

## 3.2. *Models 2–4*

Zhang (2000) suggests that it would be appropriate to examine separately sub-samples that are homogeneous with respect to firm efficiency. Zhang (2000) uses $X_t / B_{t-1}$, i.e., the firm's current period profitability (return on equity) as measured by accounting numbers, as a proxy for $q_t$ and makes a number of other assumptions to derive from Model 1 plausible regression models for firms with different levels of efficiency. To derive his models, Zhang (2000) assumes that the book value is the same at the beginning and end of the year ($B_t = B_{t-1}$). Although this is a reasonable assumption in most cases, it may cause some empirical problems if the earnings represent a large percentage of the book value, which could happen if the book value is small.

---

[1]The predictions made here are consistent with predictions 1, 3, 5–7 in Zhang (2000).

For low efficiency firms, the following regression model (Model 2) is derived:

$$V_{it} = \alpha_2 + \beta_2 B_{it} + \gamma_2 X_{it} + \delta_2 \left( \frac{X_{it}^2}{B_{it}} \right) + \varepsilon_{it}, \tag{2}$$

where[2]

$$\alpha_2 = \left[ \frac{1}{1+r_f} + C_c'(r_f) - C_c''(r_f)r_f \right] (\Delta u);$$

$$\beta_2 = \left[ \frac{1 - c_d}{1+r_f} + C_c(r_f) - C_c'(r_f)r_f + \frac{C_c''(r_f)r_f^2}{2} \right] \left( 1 + \frac{u}{B} \right);$$

$$\gamma_2 = \left[ \frac{1}{1+r_f} + C_c'(r_f) - C_c''(r_f)r_f \right];$$

$$\delta_2 = \frac{C_c''(r_f)}{2};$$

$0 < c_d < 1$ is the cost of discontinuation; $u$, the accounting bias between the accounting and economic values; $\Delta u = u_t - u_{t-1}$, the bias between accounting and economic earnings; and, $\varepsilon_{it}$ is the error term.

Since it is assumed that accounting measures are free of bias, $\Delta u = 0$ and $u = 0$. Note that

$$C_c(q) = \frac{1}{R(R-1)} \int_{q_d^* - q_t}^{\bar{v}} [v_{t+1} + q_t - q_d^*] f(v_{t+1}) - dv_{t+1}$$

is the call option to continue operations for low efficiency firms obtained using the put-call parity condition.

Based on the properties of the valuation function developed by Zhang (2000), which are summarized in Appendix A, plus the fact that options cannot take a negative value, the following signs are predicted for the regression parameters of Model 2[3]:

- $\alpha_2 = 0$.
- The sign of $\beta_2$ cannot be determined ($\beta_2 > 0$ or $\beta_2 < 0$ depending on the magnitudes of $C_c(.)$, $C_c'(.)$, and $C_c''(.)$).

---

[2]Note that the expressions for the coefficients here involve $C_c(r_f)$ rather than $C_e(q)$ as in Model 1.

[3]Note that these predictions are based on the assumption that accounting numbers are unbiased. If there is a bias, the major change is that $\alpha_2$ and $\alpha_3$ may be $< 0$ or $> 0$. See Zhang (2000, pp. 281–282) where $u > 0$ but $\Delta u$ may be $< 0$ or $> 0$.

- The sign of $\gamma_2$ cannot be determined ($\gamma_2 > 0$ or $\gamma_2 < 0$ depending on the magnitudes of $C_c'(.)$ and $C_c''(.)$).
- $\delta_2 > 0$.

For steady state firms, the following regression model (Model 3) is derived:

$$V_{it} = \alpha_3 + \gamma_3 X_{it} + \varepsilon_{it}, \tag{3}$$

where $\alpha_3 = \Delta u / r_f$, $\gamma_3 = 1/r_f$, and $\varepsilon_{it}$ is the error term.

The properties referred to the preceding terms yield the following predictions for the signs of the regression parameters of Model 3:

- $\alpha_3 = 0$,
- $\gamma_3 > 0$.

For high efficiency firms, the following regression model (Model 4) is derived:

$$V_{it} = \alpha_4 + \gamma_4 X_{it} + \theta_4 \left(\frac{X_{it}}{B_{it}}\right) + \lambda_4 \left(\frac{X_{it}}{B_{it}}\right)^2 + \varepsilon_{it}, \tag{4}$$

where

$$\alpha_4 = G\left[C_e(r_f) - C_e'(r_f)r_f + \frac{C_e''(r_f)r_f^2}{2}\right] + \frac{\Delta u}{r_f},$$

$$\gamma_4 = \frac{1}{r_f}, \quad \theta_4 = G\left[C_e'(r_f) - C_e''(r_f)\right], \quad \lambda_4 = \frac{G}{2}C_e''(r_f),$$

and $\varepsilon_{it}$ is the error term.

The properties referred to the aforementioned terms plus the fact that $G \geq 0$ yield the following predictions for the signs of the regression parameters for Model 4:

- The sign of $\alpha_4$ cannot be determined ($\alpha_4 > 0$ or $\alpha_4 < 0$ depending on the magnitude of $C_e(.)$, $C_e'(.)$, and $C_e''(.)$).
- $\gamma_4 > 0$.
- The sign of $\theta_4$ cannot be determined ($\theta_4 > 0$ or $\theta_4 < 0$ depending on the magnitude of $C_e'(.)$ and $C_e''(.)$).
- and $\lambda_4 \geq 0$.

In Table 1, we summarize the sign predictions for the four models.

**Table 1.**   Predictions for all models used in the study.

| Model type | $\alpha_i$ | $\beta_i$ $B$ | $\gamma_i$ $X$ | $\delta_i$ $X^2/B$ | $\theta_i$ $X/B$ | $\lambda_i$ $(X/B)^2$ |
|---|---|---|---|---|---|---|
| **Model 1** | | | | | | |
| Low efficiency firms | $\cong 0$ | $> 0$ | $> 0$ | | | |
| Steady state firms | $> 0$ | $\geq 0$ | $> 0$ | | | |
| Growth firms | $> 0$ | $> 0$ | $> 0$ | | | |
| **Model 2** | | | | | | |
| Low efficiency firms | $\cong 0$ | $> 0$ or $< 0$ | $> 0$ or $< 0$ | $> 0$ | | |
| **Model 3** | | | | | | |
| Steady state firms | $\cong 0$ | | $> 0$ | | | |
| **Model 4** | | | | | | |
| Growth firms | $> 0$ or $< 0$ | | $> 0$ | | $> 0$ or $< 0$ | $> 0$ |

*Notes*:

Model 1: $V_{it} = \alpha_1 + \beta_1 B_{it} + \gamma_1 X_{it} + \varepsilon_{it}$.

Model 2: $V_{it} = \alpha_2 + \beta_2 B_{it} + \gamma_2 X_{it} + \delta_2 (X_{it}^2/B_{it}) + \varepsilon_{it}$.

Model 3: $V_{it} = \alpha_3 + \gamma_3 X_{it} + \varepsilon_{it}$.

Model 4: $V_{it} = \alpha_4 + \gamma_4 X_{it} + \theta_4 (X_{it}/B_{it}) + \lambda_4 (X_{it}/B_{it})^2 + \varepsilon_{it}$.

## 4. Sample and Variables

The sample is drawn from the COMPUSTAT database of active US firms over the period 1988–2002 inclusive (i.e., 15 years of annual data for 10,357 companies representing 155,355 firm-year observations included in the active COMPUSTAT US file). The following data items are collected for each firm from the COMPUSTAT database:

(1) The stock price at the fiscal year end adjusted for stock splits and stock dividends occurring during the fiscal year (COMPUSTAT item number A199; mnemonic PRCCF). This variable is coded "$V$" in the current study.

(2) The total common equity interest in the company, including common stock outstanding adjusted for treasury stocks, capital surplus, and retained earnings (COMPUSTAT item number A60; mnemonic CEQ).

(3) The number of common shares outstanding at the year end, excluding treasury stocks and scrip (COMPUSTAT item number A25; mnemonic CSHO).

(4) The income before extraordinary items and discontinued operations available for common equity net of preferred stock dividend requirements and

before adding savings due to common stock equivalents (COMPUSTAT item number A237; mnemonic IBCOM).

(5) Total Debt (TD) = [total long-term debt, plus current liabilities (COMPU-STAT mnemonic DT; no item number exists for this variable)] + preferred stocks (COMPUSTAT item number A130; mnemonic PSTK) + minority interest (COMPUSTAT item number A38; mnemonic MIB).

Data items 2–5 are used to calculate the following variables (all on a per share basis):

- $B_{it}$ = CEQ/CSHO is the book value per share for firm $i$ at time $t$.
- $X_{it}$ = IBCOM/CSHO is the earnings per share before extraordinary items and before discontinued operations for firm $i$ at time $t$.
- $X_{it}/B_{it-1}$ is the accounting return on the beginning book value, which is used as a proxy for profitability $q$.
- TDBV$_{it}$ = (CEQ + TD)/CSHO is the total of the book value of common equity plus debt per share for firm $i$ at time $t$.
- TD$_{it}$ = TD/CSHO is the total debt per share for firm $i$ at time $t$.

After excluding firm-years that have missing data and negative book values plus outliers [boundaries for inclusion are $\pm 3$ standard deviations from the median for the variables earnings ($X_{it}$) and profitability ($X_{it}/B_{it-1}$)], the final sample consists of 64,796 firm year observations, of which 20,100 (31.0%) have negative earnings.[4] To test for capital structure considerations (i.e., relevance of debt), the sample size is further reduced to 63,026 firm-years due to missing values for debt and debt-related variables.

## 5. Analyses and Results

### 5.1. *Descriptive statistics*

The mean, median, and standard errors for the variables used in Models 1 through 4 are given in Table 2. The median and mean values are noticeably different for all variables, and the standard errors are relatively small compared to the mean values for all variables.

---

[4]This proportion is somewhat higher than the value of 22.8% in the final sample of Collins, Pincus, and Xie (1999). This is presumably because our sample includes firm-years from years around the turn of the millennium when there was generally poor economic performance.

**Table 2.**   Descriptive statistics — full sample.

| Variable/statistic | Mean | Median | Standard error |
|---|---|---|---|
| $V$ | 14.36 | 9.50 | 0.06 |
| $B$ | 7.60 | 5.07 | 0.03 |
| $X$ | 0.23 | 0.35 | 0.01 |
| $X/B$ | −0.12 | 0.08 | 0.00 |
| $X^2/B$ | 0.90 | 0.10 | 0.03 |
| $(X/B)^2$ | 0.68 | 0.02 | 0.02 |

**Table 3.**   Correlation coefficients — full sample.

| Item | $V$ | $B$ | $X$ | $X/B$ | $X^2/B$ | $(X/B)^2$ |
|---|---|---|---|---|---|---|
| $V$ | 1 | | | | | |
| $B$ | 0.63* | 1 | | | | |
| $X$ | 0.10* | 0.10* | 1 | | | |
| $X/B$ | 0.14* | 0.15* | 0.37* | 1 | | |
| $X^2/B$ | 0.08 | 0.04 | −0.66* | −0.37* | 1 | |
| $(X/B)^2$ | −0.06 | −0.10* | −0.20* | −0.76* | 0.38* | 1 |

*The correlation coefficient is significant at the 0.01 level.

The correlation coefficients among the six variables for the full sample used in this study are given in Table 3. For the full sample, there is a significant correlation at the 1% level between share price and book value per share (63%) as expected, but the correlations between share price and earnings per share (10%) and book value per share and earnings per share (10%) respectively are relatively low. The correlation coefficients for positive and negative earnings firms in Tables 4 and 5, respectively, provide more insight into the association of stock price and book value with earnings per share. For profitable firms, the results in Table 4 show that share price is positively and significantly correlated with book value per share (64%) and with earnings per share (62%); i.e., each of the two independent variables displays the same level of correlation with stock price. The results for low efficiency (loss firms), in Table 5, show a different correlation pattern; stock price is positive and significantly correlated with book value per share (53%), but negative and significantly correlated with earnings per share (−37%). Also, the results of Table 5 indicate a negative significant correlation between book value per share and earnings per share (−45%). Tables 3–5 also report significant correlations among other independent variables $X_{it}/B_{it}$, $X_{it}^2/B_{it}$, and $(X_{it}/B_{it})^2$, which are expected to be fairly highly correlated. The correlation coefficients between variables with the same

**Table 4.**  Correlation coefficients — positive earnings firms.

| Item | $V$ | $B$ | $X$ | $X/B$ | $X^2/B$ | $(X/B)^2$ |
|---|---|---|---|---|---|---|
| $V$ | 1 | | | | | |
| $B$ | 0.64* | 1 | | | | |
| $X$ | 0.62* | 0.67* | 1 | | | |
| $X/B$ | 0.03 | −0.12* | 0.15* | 1 | | |
| $X^2/B$ | 0.18* | 0.12* | 0.53* | 0.47* | 1 | |
| $(X/B)^2$ | −0.01 | −0.04 | 0.03 | 0.85* | 0.34* | 1 |

*The correlation coefficient is significant at the 0.01 level.

**Table 5.**  Correlation coefficients — negative earnings firms.

| Item | $V$ | $B$ | $X$ | $X/B$ | $X^2/B$ | $(X/B)^2$ |
|---|---|---|---|---|---|---|
| $V$ | 1 | | | | | |
| $B$ | 0.53* | 1 | | | | |
| $X$ | −0.37* | −0.45* | 1 | | | |
| $X/B$ | 0.06 | 0.19* | 0.23* | 1 | | |
| $X^2/B$ | 0.17* | 0.11* | −0.75* | −0.39* | 1 | |
| $(X/B)^2$ | −0.04 | −0.12* | −0.15* | 0.91* | 0.37* | 1 |

*The correlation coefficient is significant at the 0.01 level.

power of earnings (e.g., $X_{it}$ with $X_{it}/B_{it}$ and $X_{it}^2/B_{it}$ with $(X_{it}/B_{it})^2$ are positive, while those between variables having even and odd powers of earnings (e.g., $X_{it}$ with $X_{it}^2/B_{it}$ and $X_{it}/B_{it}$ with $(X_{it}/B_{it})^2$) are negative, which suggests the need for further investigation.

Of utmost importance in these results is the correlation between share price and earnings per share, which is positive for positive earnings firms, but negative for negative earnings firms, while both are far removed from those for the full sample in Table 3. These correlation results, thus, indicate that examining only the correlation coefficients for the full sample masks the differences that show clearly in the positive and negative earnings sub-samples. This suggests some fundamental difference between the positive and negative earnings firms that may impact the results for regression Models 1 through 4.

## 5.2. *Diagnostic statistics*

In this section, we assess our sample data to explore for the presence of serial/autocorrelation and heteroscedasticity problems. Our analysis of full and sub-samples reported in the results section reveals that our data are free from autocorrelation as the Durbin–Watson $d$ statistic is always close to 2; the lowest value of $d$ is 1.86; the highest value of $d$ is $2.01^5$ (Gujarati, 1992). In addition, we tested the data used in this study using Park's test (see Gujarati, 1992) and found no evidence of heteroscedasticity. The results of our tests indicate an $R^2$ of 0.00 and a $t$-value of 0.00 for the variables $(X_{it})$ and $(B_{it})$, an indication of homoscedasticity.

### 5.3. *Results from Model 1*

Firms in the full sample were ranked according to accounting profitability $(X_{it}/B_{it-1})$, the proxy for firm efficiency $(q)$, and separated into three approximately equal-sized sub-samples. The low efficiency sub-sample consisted of 20,100 firm-years with negative earnings (loss firms), whereas the steady state and high growth sub-samples each consisted of 22,348 firm-years reporting positive earnings. The full sample plus the three sub-samples were fitted separately to the regression equation for Model 1, with the results as reported in Table 6.

**Table 6.**   Estimated regression coefficients ($t$-statistics are listed below the coefficients) for Model 1.

| Profitability ($q$): full sample and sub-samples | $\alpha$ | $\beta$ $B_i$ | $\gamma$ $X_i$ | Model $F$-value | Prob. of $F$-value | Model adjusted $R^2$ |
|---|---|---|---|---|---|---|
| Full Sample: 64,796 firm-years | 5.57 84.10 | 1.15 202.27 | 0.20 12.15 | 20,957 | 0.00 | 39% |
| Low efficiency-loss firms: 20,100 firm-years | 3.79 34.62 | 0.90 68.10 | −0.58 −26.02 | 4,332 | 0.00 | 30% |
| Steady state: 22,348 firm-years | 3.62 37.65 | 0.75 68.25 | 4.45 33.89 | 13,392 | 0.00 | 55% |
| Growth: 22,348 firm-years | 7.34 61.37 | 1.08 54.69 | 2.52 26.56 | 9,207 | 0.00 | 45% |

*Notes*: Model 1: $V_{it} = \alpha_1 + \beta_1 B_{it} + \gamma_1 X_{it} + \varepsilon_{it}$. All coefficients are significant at the 0.00 level.

---

[5]In general, based on Gujarati (1992), the presence or absence of positive or negative autocorrelation depends on the calculated $d$ statistics. Positive or negative autocorrelation is said to be present if the value of $d$ is close to zero or 4, respectively. As the value of the $d$ statistic inches close to 2, the more likely it is that autocorrelation is not present.

The fit of Model 1 to the data for the full sample and the three sub-samples is quite good as shown by the reasonable $R^2$ values and the large $F$ values, all significant at the 0.00 level. The fit is clearly poorest, although statistically significant, for the low efficiency sub-sample, that is, the negative earnings (loss) firms.

The coefficients for all four regressions in Table 6 are significant at the 0.00 level. In addition, the $t$-values of the intercept ($\alpha$) for the three sub-samples are all statistically significant. For the full sample, all coefficients are significant and consistent with the predicted signs. For the three sub-samples, all coefficients are also significant and consistent with the predicted signs except for the coefficient of earnings ($\gamma$) for the low efficiency (loss) firms, which is negative and significant rather than positive as predicted. These regression results are consistent with the correlation coefficients that are given in Tables 3–5.

The coefficient for the intercept ($\alpha$) for the growth firms (7.34) is larger than those for the low efficiency (3.79) and steady state firms (3.62), which are close to each other in value. This is consistent with the prediction that the call option is most valuable for the growth firms but not for the other firms. The coefficients of the book value ($\beta$) are close to 1 for the full sample and for the three sub-samples. The coefficient for the book value ($\beta$) is larger for the low efficiency firms than for the steady state firms, consistent with the expectation that the put option should be more important for low efficiency firms. However, it is unexpectedly large for growth firms.[6] Contrary to expectations, the coefficients of earnings ($\gamma$) are not the same for the three sub-samples. The results in Table 6 show that the earnings coefficients increase quite markedly from the low efficiency firms to the steady state firms and then decrease for the growth firms, rather than being the same for all sub-samples as predicted. The fact that the coefficient of earnings ($\gamma$) is larger for the steady state firms is consistent with the expectation that current earnings are more important for them than for growth firms.

At this stage, several points should be noted: First, it seems clear that analysis of the full (pooled) sample masks important differences among the firms.

---

[6]Although the magnitude is unexpected according to the predictions of the model, it may be rationalized as follows: First, there is no reason that a growth firm cannot have a put value. Second, it may be argued that a growth firm is perceived more favorably than low efficiency and steady state firms so that the put value of its assets exceed their accounting book value, whereas the put values of low efficiency and steady state firms are less than their accounting book values.

Stratification by profitability shows important differences that go beyond differences in earnings and so can be usefully incorporated in empirical analyses. Second, the effect of differences in profitability on the coefficient of the book value ($\beta$) is not completely consistent with the predictions of the basic options based valuation model. Third, the coefficient of earnings ($\gamma$) not only differs among sub-samples of firms but is significantly negative for the low efficiency firms ($-0.58$ with a $t$-value of $-26.02$, significance: 0.00), contrary to prediction.

### 5.4. *Results from Models 2–4*

The results of fitting the low efficiency, steady state and growth sub-samples described earlier separately to Zhang's (2000) modified Models 2–4, respectively, are presented in Table 7. The results in Table 7 show the adjusted $R^2$ values of 30% for low efficiency, 45% for steady state, and 38% for growth

**Table 7.** Estimated regression coefficients ($t$-statistics are listed below the coefficients) for Models 2–4.

| Profitability ($q$) sub-samples | $\alpha$ intercept | $\beta$ $B_i$ | $\gamma$ $X_i$ | $\delta$ $X^2/B$ | $\theta$ $X_i/B_i$ | $\lambda$ $(X_i/B_i)^2$ |
|---|---|---|---|---|---|---|
| Low efficiency-loss firms (Model 2): 20,100 firm-years; adjusted $R^2$ = 30%; | | | | | | |
| $F$-value = 2,892 | 3.80 | 0.89 | $-0.66$ | $-0.03$ | | |
| (0.00) | 34.72 | 61.64 | $-18.16$ | $-2.84$ | | |
| Steady state (Model 3): 22,348 firm-years; adjusted $R^2$ = 45%; | | | | | | |
| $F$-value = 18,309 | 5.99 | | 11.65 | | | |
| (0.00) | 60.88 | | 135.31 | | | |
| Growth (Model 4): 22,348 firm-years; adjusted $R^2$ = 38%; | | | | | | |
| $F$-value = 4,663 | 11.18 | | 6.88 | | $-9.01$ | 1.10 |
| (0.00) | 66.72 | | 118.24 | | $-14.51$ | 10.25 |

*Notes*
Model 2: $V_{it} = \alpha_2 + \beta_2 B_{it} + \gamma_2 X_{it} + \delta_2 (X_{it}^2/B_{it}) + \varepsilon_{it}$.
Model 3: $V_{it} = \alpha_3 + \gamma_3 X_{it} + \varepsilon_{it}$.
Model 4: $V_{it} = \alpha_4 + \gamma_4 X_{it} + \theta_4 (X_{it}/B_{it}) + \lambda_4 (X_{it}/B_{it})^2 + \varepsilon_{it}$.

firms. A comparison of data in Tables 6 and 7 shows that $R^2$ is the same for low efficiency firms, and lower for the other two sub-samples.

The predictions for the coefficients from fitting Model 2 for the low efficiency (loss) firms are not very specific so that testing them extensively is not possible. Contrary to predictions, the intercept coefficient ($\alpha$) is non-zero and the return coefficient ($\delta$) is negative. The coefficient for the book value ($\beta$) for Model 2 is positive and significant (0.89, $t$-value: 61.64), consistent with the book value being a primary determinant of the value for loss firms. The coefficient of earnings ($\gamma$) is negative and significant ($-0.66$, $t$-value: $-18.16$), which seems surprising. Both of these observations are consistent with what was found using Model 1. The results of fitting Model 3 for the steady state firms are consistent with the prediction for the coefficient of earnings ($\gamma$), which is positive and significant (11.65, $t$-value: 135.31). This shows that earnings are very important in determining the share price for steady state firms as expected. But the intercept coefficient ($\alpha$) is positive rather than zero as predicted.

The results of fitting Model 4 for the growth firms are also consistent with predictions in that the only two specifically predicted signs, for ($\gamma$) and ($\delta$), are correct. The coefficient of earnings ($\gamma$) is positive and significant (6.88, $t$-value: 118.24) showing that earnings are very important in determining the market value of growth firms also. The magnitude and the significance of the intercept term ($\alpha$) (11.18, $t$-value: 66.72) suggest that the call option is also very important in determining the market value of these firms, as expected. The profitability coefficient ($\theta$) is negative and significant ($-9.01$, $t$-value: $-14.51$) and significantly contributes to valuation. Also, the square of the profitability coefficient ($\lambda$) is positive and significant (1.10, $t$-value: 10.25). Both of these results are consistent with predictions.

## 5.5. *Comparison of results from Model 1 to results from Models 2–4*

The values of the various coefficients and $R^2$ obtained from fitting the three sub-samples to Model 1 and separately to Models 2–4 are summarized in comparative format in Table 8. A comparison of the results from Models 1 and 2 for the low efficiency firms shows that Model 2 has the same explanatory power as Model 1 even though it has an additional explanatory variable. Further, the coefficients ($\alpha$), ($\beta$) and ($\gamma$) in these two models are quite close. The negative value for the return coefficient ($\delta$) is opposite to the predicted value, and its

**Table 8.** Summary comparison of estimated regression coefficients and $R^2$ for low efficiency, steady state, and high efficiency sub-samples using Models 1–4.

| Profitability ($q$) sub-samples | Model | $\alpha$ | $\beta$ | $\gamma$ | $\delta$ | $\theta$ | $\lambda$ | $R^2(\%)$ |
|---|---|---|---|---|---|---|---|---|
| Low efficiency (loss firms) | 1 | 3.79 | 0.90 | −0.58 | – | – | – | 30 |
| | 2 | 3.80 | 0.89 | −0.66 | −0.03 | – | – | 30 |
| Steady state | 1 | 3.62 | 0.75 | 4.45 | – | – | – | 55 |
| | 3 | 5.99 | – | 11.65 | – | – | – | 45 |
| Growth | 1 | 7.34 | 1.08 | 2.52 | – | – | – | 45 |
| | 4 | 11.18 | – | 6.88 | – | −9.01 | 1.10 | 38 |

magnitude is small, suggesting that it does not make a great contribution to valuation.

A comparison of the results of Models 1 and 3 for the steady state firms shows that Model 3 has a noticeably lower explanatory power than does Model 1. Although earnings makes a very important contribution to valuation in Model 3, the large changes in the intercept and earnings coefficients ($\alpha$) and ($\gamma$) from those in Model 1 suggest that the former Model 3 is not properly specified. The behavior here parallels that observed by Collins, Pincus, and Xie (1999) in that book value appears to be a correlated omitted variable in Model 3, leading to an upward bias in the coefficient of earnings ($\gamma$).

A comparison of the results of Models 1 and 4 for the growth firms shows that Model 4 also has a noticeably lower explanatory power than does Model 1, even though it has two terms in place of the book value in Model 1. In addition, the coefficients ($\alpha$) and ($\gamma$) differ between the two models, suggesting that Model 4 is also not well specified.

One reason for the poor performance of Models 2 and 4 may be the assumption that the book value is the same at the beginning and the end of the year ($B_t = B_{t-1}$) as was mentioned earlier. But both Models 3 and 4 do not appear to be well specified, i.e., the omitted variable problem leads to biased coefficients. In particular, the book value term, which is related to a put option, plays an important role for both steady state and growth firms and should not be omitted. This suggests that the absence of the variable "book value" is the major problem, not whether the book value is measured at the beginning or the end of the year in Models 2 and 4. The overall conclusion is that the basic valuation Model 1 captures the information relevant for valuation in a more efficient and parsimonious manner than do Models 2–4 and should be the basis for any further analysis.

## 5.6. *Further analysis of full sample*

A further analysis of the sample data was undertaken in order to investigate the apparently anomalous behavior of the low efficiency firms identified before. The sample was ranked from the lowest to the highest accounting profitability $(X_t/B_{t-1})$ and split into deciles. (Note that the first three deciles, i.e., those with the lowest profitability, include all the loss firms that gave the anomalous results identified earlier). This procedure was motivated by the predictions made earlier that the coefficients $\alpha$ and $\beta$ should vary with profitability. The formation of deciles that are more homogeneous in profitability should fit the data more efficiently and parsimoniously.

The results of fitting Model 1 for deciles are presented in Table 9. The fit to Model 1 for all deciles is quite good as measured by the $R^2$ and $F$ values, although they vary noticeably among deciles. Also, all coefficients are significant at the 0.00 level, except for the coefficient of earnings $(X_{it})$ for decile 2, which is not significantly different from zero.

As stated in Section 3, this study predicts that the intercept coefficient $(\alpha)$ (i.e., call option) should be positive and increase with profitability. The results in Table 9 show that $\alpha$ is positive in all deciles and generally increases as expected with profitability. The results in Table 9 also support this paper's prediction that the coefficient for the book value $(\beta)$ is positive for all deciles and shows a general decrease with profitability although the actual results reveal that the trend is not completely clear or smooth. The results in Table 9 do not support our prediction that the coefficient of earnings $(\gamma)$ is positive and is the same for all deciles. As the data in Table 9 indicate, the coefficient of earnings $(\gamma)$ is positive as predicted only for the seven highest profitability deciles. Conversely, the coefficient $(\gamma)$ is negative and significant for deciles 1 and 2, while not being significantly different from zero for decile 3. The results, however, show a generally increasing trend with profitability. These results are consistent with the negative sign found for the coefficient of earnings $(\gamma)$ for the analysis of the low efficiency (i.e., loss) firms using Model 2 and with the correlation coefficients in Table 5.

The stratification implemented in Table 9 may lead to two problems: First, it may not create homogeneous strata due to the fact that the stratification is based

**Table 9.**   Estimated regression coefficients ($t$-statistics are listed below the coefficients) for Model 1 — full sample split into deciles on profitability ($q$).

| Profitability ($q$) deciles | Firm-years | $\alpha$ Intercept | $\beta B_i$ | $\gamma X_i$ | Model adjusted $R^2(\%)$ | Model $F$-value |
|---|---|---|---|---|---|---|
| Full sample | 64,796 | 5.57 | 1.15 | 0.20 | 39 | 20,957 |
| | | 84.10 | 202.27 | 12.15 | | |
| 1 (Lowest) | 6,480 | 4.61 | 1.67 | −0.11 | 33 | 1,627 |
| | | 21.32 | 37.80 | −2.89 | | |
| 2 | 6,480 | 3.68 | 0.97 | −0.21 | 27 | 1,182 |
| | | 20.18 | 26.77 | −2.29(0.02) | | |
| 3 | 6,480 | 3.31 | 0.86 | −0.01 | 36 | 1,852 |
| | | 20.87 | 53.90 | −0.07(0.94) | | |
| 4 | 6,480 | 3.38 | 0.86 | 1.65 | 46 | 2,743 |
| | | 19.68 | 48.03 | 3.07 | | |
| 5 | 6,480 | 3.25 | 0.80 | 3.46 | 56 | 4,178 |
| | | 19.10 | 22.43 | 6.37 | | |
| 6 | 6,480 | 4.15 | 0.85 | 3.14 | 53 | 3,624 |
| | | 21.35 | 14.53 | 5.26 | | |
| 7 | 6,480 | 4.18 | 1.08 | 2.09 | 60 | 4,909 |
| | | 22.64 | 15.94 | 3.84 | | |
| 8 | 6,480 | 4.78 | 0.48 | 7.21 | 58 | 4,514 |
| | | 24.72 | 6.58 | 14.81 | | |
| 9 | 6,480 | 6.12 | 0.21 | 8.90 | 55 | 3,912 |
| | | 28.76 | 2.57(0.01) | 20.98 | | |
| 10 | 6,476 | 10.08 | 1.56 | 0.48 | 31 | 1,455 |
| | | 41.65 | 26.79 | 2.92 | | |

*Notes*: Model 1: $V_{it} = \alpha_1 + \beta_1 B_{it} + \gamma_1 X_{it} + \varepsilon_{it}$. Coefficients are significant at the 0.00 level except as indicated in brackets.

on a sample split into 10 equally sized groups and does not, accordingly, result in a homogeneous profitability in, or a smooth change in profitability between, strata. Second, each of the 10 strata may not represent a homogeneous pool of firm-years. It is possible that the empirical results in Table 9 are influenced by a high level of intra-decile variability in profitability ($q$). As a result, an alternative approach to stratification of the full sample is also employed. Firms with profitability less than −1.00 and greater than +1.00 were put into separate sub-samples for further analysis. The firms with a profitability in the range −1.00 to +1.00 were divided into 10 sub-samples, each with a profitability range of 0.20. The results of fitting each of these sub-samples to Model 1 are reported in Table 10.[7]

The data in Table 10 indicate that the number of observations in each new stratum varies considerably among the strata, with the highest number in the stratum 0.00–0.20 (32,434 firm-years) and the lowest in the stratum 0.80–1.00 (274 firm-years). In addition, the empirical results in Table 10 reveal that Model 1 fits the data quite well as measured by $R^2$ and $F$ values, although they also vary noticeably among strata. The coefficients $(\alpha)$ and $(\beta)$ are positive and statistically significant for all sub-samples. They also show the expected variation with profitability, although the trends are once more not completely smooth. The earnings coefficient $(\gamma)$ is seemingly erratic in behavior. For the sub-samples with a profitability above +0.40, it is insignificant. For the sub-samples with a negative profitability, the behavior is mixed. It is not significant in the range −0.40 to 0.00, positive and significant in the range −0.80 to −0.40, and negative and significant in the range below −0.80. The results for the negative profitability strata are consistent with the results in Table 9. The fact that the model produces poor results for large negative and positive profitabilities is not unreasonable as it is unlikely that Model 1, or any relatively simple model, would fit well over a wide range of profitability. Rather, it is reasonable to expect Model 1 to fit the data over a "reasonable" or "narrower" range of profitability. The empirical results in Table 10 indicate that Model 1 produces better results in the range between −0.20 and +0.20.

Based on the aforementioned remarks, we re-examine the Model 1 fit for a narrower profitability range (−0.20 to +0.20), which is actually quite a wide range of profitability $(q)$ as it is unlikely that a firm would consistently have a profitability outside that range in the normal course of events. The observations in the profitability range −0.20 to +0.20 were separated into 10 sub-samples, each covering a profitability range of 0.04. The observations in each of these sub-samples were fitted to Model 1, yielding the results reported in Table 11. The number of observations varies a fair amount among the sub-samples, from a low of 1,214 firm-years (−0.20 to −0.16 profitability range) to a high of 7,734 firm-years (0.12–0.16 profitability range). The fit of the data is quite reasonable for all deciles as measured by the $R^2$ and $F$-values, and is much

---

[7]We refitted Model 1 for nine industry groups based on the first digit SIC code. The results of the analysis indicate some industry effect since few independent variables are positive and significant for some industry groups.

**Table 10.**  Estimated regression coefficients (*t*-statistics are listed below the coefficients) for of Model 1: Full sample split on profitability (*q*) range −1.00 to +1.00.

| Profitability (*q*) deciles | Firm-years | $\alpha$ Intercept | $\beta B_i$ | $\gamma X_i$ | Model adjusted $R^2$(%) | Model *F*-value |
|---|---|---|---|---|---|---|
| Full sample | 64,796 | 5.57 84.10 | 1.15 202.27 | 0.20 12.15 | 39 | 20,957 |
| < −1.00 | 1,769 | 6.82 13.57 | 1.77 18.31 | −0.50 −6.70 | 32 | 415 |
| −1.00 to −0.80 | 791 | 3.80 5.97 | 1.78 13.69 | −0.29 −3.43 | 31 | 176 |
| −0.80 to −0.60 | 1,603 | 3.96 11.51 | 1.82 20.55 | 0.19 2.99 | 37 | 465 |
| −0.60 to −0.40 | 2,558 | 3.38 11.60 | 2.44 30.88 | 1.11 11.70 | 44 | 997 |
| −0.40 to −0.20 | 4,309 | 3.63 16.33 | 1.00 18.58 | −0.18 −1.59(0.11) | 26 | 749 |
| −0.20 – 0.00 | 9,070 | 3.46 24.44 | 0.88 57.92 | −0.03 −0.30 (0.77) | 34 | 2,360 |
| 0.00 – 0.20 | 32,434 | 4.00 48.85 | 0.66 69.92 | 5.73 63.44 | 56 | 20,838 |
| 0.20 – 0.40 | 9,044 | 7.33 37.66 | 0.72 11.87 | 5.59 19.70 | 47 | 3,964 |
| 0.40 – 0.60 | 1,571 | 10.82 20.25 | 1.46 6.14 | 1.00 1.50(0.13) | 25 | 266 |
| 0.60 – 0.80 | 571 | 12.08 14.79 | 0.55 2.42 | 1.60 2.73(0.01) | 24 | 93 |
| 0.80 – 1.00 | 274 | 8.39 7.58 | 2.30 7.16 | 0.15 0.25(0.81) | 46 | 119 |
| >1.00 | 802 | 9.24 18.24 | 1.47 10.50 | 0.03 0.14(0.89) | 25 | 131 |

*Notes*: Model 1: $V_{it} = \alpha_1 + \beta_1 B_{it} + \gamma_1 X_{it} + \varepsilon_{it}$. Coefficients are significant at the 0.00 level except as indicated in brackets.

better for the positive profitability sub-samples than for the negative profitability sub-samples. The coefficients ($\alpha$) and ($\beta$) are all positive and significant, and in general terms, show, the expected variation with changing profitability. The earnings coefficient ($\gamma$) varies with profitability. It is positive and significant for a positive profitability, not significantly different from zero near zero profitability, negative for a somewhat negative profitability and positive for a more negative profitability.

**Table 11.** Estimated regression coefficients (*t*-statistics are listed below the coefficients) for of Model 1: Sample split on profitability (*q*) range −0.20 to +0.20.

| Profitability (*q*) ranges | Firm-years | $\alpha$ Intercept | $\beta B_i$ | $\gamma X_i$ | Model adjusted $R^2$(%) | Model *F*-value |
|---|---|---|---|---|---|---|
| −0.20 to −0.16 | 1,214 | 3.46 8.58 | 1.22 10.21 | 1.03 2.01(0.04) | 33 | 300 |
| −0.16 to −0.12 | 1,458 | 4.04 10.86 | 1.45 12.42 | 3.79 5.74 | 27 | 271 |
| −0.12 to −0.08 | 1,678 | 2.84 8.92 | 1.04 28.86 | 0.41 3.61 | 37 | 497 |
| −0.08 to −0.04 | 2,113 | 2.80 10.03 | 0.75 17.70 | −2.84 −5.87 | 39 | 665 |
| −0.04–0.00 | 2,607 | 3.83 14.78 | 0.77 33.05 | −1.13 −2.21(0.03) | 37 | 767 |
| 0.00–0.04 | 4,982 | 3.45 17.99 | 0.83 39.15 | 1.70 2.40(0.02) | 46 | 2,096 |
| 0.04–0.08 | 6,389 | 3.13 18.04 | 0.84 24.66 | 2.86 5.08 | 56 | 3,990 |
| 0.08–0.12 | 7,732 | 4.05 23.15 | 0.81 16.56 | 3.56 7.03 | 53 | 4,431 |
| 0.12–0.16 | 7,734 | 4.14 24.33 | 0.85 13.64 | 4.19 8.56 | 60 | 5,912 |
| 0.16–0.20 | 5,597 | 5.22 25.09 | 0.36 4.56 | 7.79 15.36 | 58 | 3,855 |

*Notes*: Model 1: $V_{it} = \alpha_1 + \beta_1 B_{it} + \gamma_1 X_{it} + \varepsilon_{it}$. Coefficients are significant at the 0.00 level except as indicated in brackets.

It appears that the fit of Model 1 to the sample and the various sub-samples is quite good over the profitability range of −0.20 to +0.20 and the coefficients ($\alpha$) and ($\beta$) are generally as expected. The negative coefficient of earnings ($\gamma$) is the only major source of inconsistency with predictions.

## 6. Financial Management Considerations[8]

Zhang's (2000) model is based on a set of assumptions similar to those of the Ohlson (1995) and Feltham and Ohlson (1995, 1996) valuation models.

---

[8]We thank two anonymous referees for pointing this out, which improved an earlier version of this paper.

These models rely on some form of the Miller and Modigliani (1961) discount dividend model which assumes that current earnings are an adequate characterization of future earnings and dividends and assumes capital structure irrelevancy (Modigliani and Miller, 1958). According to Rees (1997), there are several theoretical and empirical research studies (e.g., Ross, 1977; Leland and Pyle, 1977; Ashton, 1991; McConnell and Muscarella, 1985) that argue for financial management considerations such as dividend payout, debt levels, and capital expenditure in equity valuation. In this section, we relax the debt irrelevancy assumption in Zhang's (2000) basic model to examine the relevance of debt for cross-sectional samples.

Our approach is similar to the approach used by Rees (1997) where we modify (Model 1) the operational version of Zhang's (2000) basic theoretical model given in Model A.[9] In order to examine the value relevance of debt, we restate the book value of equity of a firm $i$ as total capital ($C_i$) less total debt ($D_i$) given by

$$B_{it} = C_{it} - D_{it}.$$

Substituting the value of ($C_i$), we get

$$B_{it} = (B_{it} + D_{it}) - D_{it}.$$

We next substitute the value for ($B_i$) in Model 1 to obtain the following regression model with debt (Model 5):

$$V_{it} = \alpha_1^1 + \beta_1^1(B_{it} + D_{it}) + \beta_1^2 D_{it} + \gamma_1^1 X_{it} + \varepsilon_{it}. \tag{5}$$

When $\beta_1^2 = -\beta_1^1$, Model 5 reduces to Model 1. Therefore, in order to test for the relevant role of debt, we predict that $|\beta_1^1| = |\beta_1^2|$ and $\beta_1^1 > 0$ and $\beta_1^2 < 0$ if the amount of debt is irrelevant to the market value of equity.

## 6.1. *Results from Model 5*

The results of fitting regression equation for Model 5 to the full sample plus the three profitability sub-samples of low, steady state, and growth are given in Table 12. The coefficients for all four regressions are all significant at the 0.00 level. As predicted, for the full sample and the three sub-samples, the coefficients of debt are negative ($\beta_1^2 < 0$) and of total capital (debt plus the book value of equity) are positive ($\beta_1^1 > 0$). For the full sample of 63,026

---

[9]Note that we do not develop a theoretical model.

**Table 12.**  Estimated regression coefficients (*t*-statistics are listed below the coefficients) for Model 5.

| Profitability ($q$): full sample and sub-sample | $\alpha$ | $\beta^1 B_i + D_i$ | $\beta^2 D_i$ | $\gamma X_i$ | Model $F$-value | Prob. of $F$-value | Model adjusted $R^2$(%) |
|---|---|---|---|---|---|---|---|
| **Full Sample:** | | | | | | | |
| 63,026 | 4.77 | 1.33 | −1.327 | −0.695 | 10,519 | 0.0 | 33 |
| firm-years | 54.60 | 165.33 | −147.85 | −34.64 | | | |
| **Low efficiency-loss** | | | | | | | |
| firms: 18,530 | 1.97 | 1.212 | −1.291 | −1.49 | 2435 | 0.0 | 28 |
| firm-years | 10.34 | 50.05 | −47.11 | −43.60 | | | |
| **Steady state:** | | | | | | | |
| 22,248 | 3.34 | 0.803 | −0.791 | 4.34 | 8525 | 0.0 | 54 |
| firm-years | 33.62 | 69.90 | −64.26 | 32.97 | | | |
| **Growth:** | | | | | | | |
| 22,248 | 6.812 | 0.956 | −0.966 | 3.567 | 6083 | 0.0 | 45 |
| firm-years | 53.29 | 50.21 | −49.67 | 37.24 | | | |

*Notes*: Model 5: $V_{it} = \alpha_1^1 + \beta_1^1(B_{it} + D_{it}) + \beta_1^2 D_{it} + \gamma_1^1 X_{it} + \varepsilon_{it}$. All coefficients are significant at the 0.00 level.

firm-years, the two coefficients are equal ($|\beta_1^1| = |\beta_1^2| = 1.33$) in value but opposite in sign. We observe similar interpretation for steady state firms where $|\beta_1^1| \approx |\beta_1^2| = 0.803 \approx 0.791$. Therefore, for both the full sample and steady state firms, our results indicate that debt is irrelevant to firm value. However, the results indicate that debt plays some role in equity valuation for both low efficiency (loss firms) and growth firms. For both these sub-samples, the coefficient of debt is larger than the coefficient for the total capital (debt plus the book value of equity) $|\beta_1^2| > |\beta_1^1|$ (i.e., a low efficiency: 1.291 > 1.212 and a high efficiency: 0.966 > 0.956), an indication of debt relevance. However, judging by the absolute magnitude of the difference of $\beta_1^1$ and $\beta_1^2$, debt is more relevant for loss firms than for growth firms.[10] While the role of debt in equity valuation is mixed, the empirical evidence indicates that debt is more likely to play a role as a quality indicator in equity valuation at the extremes: loss firms and growth firms.

We performed a further analysis by fitting Model 5 to sub-samples based on deciles. The results are presented in Table 13. The coefficients for all regressions

---

[10]Rees (1997) looked only into the direction of the difference. He has not tested for a significant difference between regression coefficients.

**Table 13.** Estimated regression coefficients ($t$-statistics are listed below the coefficients) for Model 5: Full sample split into deciles on profitability ($q$).

| Profitability ($q$) deciles | Firm-years | $\alpha$ Intercept | $\beta^1 B_i + D_i$ | $\beta^2 D_i$ | $\gamma X_i$ | Model adjusted $R^2$(%) | Model $F$-value |
|---|---|---|---|---|---|---|---|
| Full sample | 63,026 | 4.768 54.604 | 1.33 165.33 | −1.327 147.85 | −0.695 −34.64 | 33 | 10,519 |
| 1 (Lowest) | 6,303 | 2.078 4.994 | 2.182 28.11 | −2.348 −27.963 | −1.096 −17.317 | 31 | 930 |
| 2 | 6,303 | 1.803 6.314 | 1.138 19.698 | −1.233 −20.282 | −1.675 −12.04 | 26 | 729 |
| 3 | 6,303 | 2.966 16.148 | 0.993 53.958 | −0.994 −47.195 | 0.167 1.58(0.11) | 37 | 1,231 |
| 4 | 6,303 | 3.148 16.425 | 0.826 43.811 | −0.768 −34.74 | 3.012 7.04 | 44 | 1,632 |
| 5 | 6,303 | 3.052 17.874 | 0.741 27.243 | −0.712 −25.053 | 4.313 11.062 | 57 | 2,790 |
| 6 | 6,303 | 3.757 18.36 | 1.002 20.02 | −1.006 −19.958 | 2.465 4.927 | 53 | 2,381 |
| 7 | 6,303 | 3.83 19.892 | 0.919 14.936 | −0.937 −15.228 | 4.405 9.095 | 62 | 3,410 |
| 8 | 6,303 | 4.96 24.232 | 0.421 6.698 | −0.438 −6.936 | 8.287 20.748 | 59 | 3,044 |
| 9 | 6,303 | 5.852 23.286 | 0.628 8.998 | −0.639 −9.131 | 7.534 21.579 | 51 | 2,147 |
| 10 | 6,299 | 8.966 35.685 | 0.647 19.729 | −0.663 −19.054 | 2.857 22.351 | 30 | 896 |

*Note*: Model 5: $V_{it} = \alpha_1^1 + \beta_1^1(B_{it} + D_{it}) + \beta_1^2 D_{it} + \gamma_1^1 X_{it} + \varepsilon_{it}$. Coefficients are significant at the 0.00 level except as indicated.

are significant at the 0.00 level. As previously observed, the coefficient for total capital (debt plus the book value of equity) is larger than the coefficient for debt in deciles 4 and 5, which are steady state firms indicating value irrelevancy. The coefficient of debt is larger than the coefficient of total capital (debt plus equity) for deciles 1–3, which pertain to loss firms, indicating that debt plays some role as a measure of risk in equity valuation. A similar result is observed for growth firms (deciles 6 through 10), which indicate its value relevance for high profitability firms. Therefore, we can conclude that, similar to previous empirical research (Ross, 1977; Leland and Pyle, 1977; Rees, 1997), debt is relevant with regard to equity valuation in a real option setting.

## 6.2. *Impact of bias in accounting measures*

We noted earlier that the major difficulty with the coefficients from fitting the three sub-samples to Model 1 reported in Table 6 is with the coefficient of earnings ($\gamma$), which is not constant at different profitability levels as predicted by the basic theory, but is, in fact, negative for the low efficiency firms and shows a generally increasing trend with profitability. This same behavior is shown for the results based on different stratification approaches in Tables 9–13. In this section, we provide an explanation for the variation of the coefficients.

Zhang's (2000) basic model shown in Equation (A) was derived under the assumption that accounting measures are unbiased.

$$V_t = B_t P_d(q) + k X_t + G C_e(q). \tag{A}$$

Zhang's more complete model based on economic measures (Zhang, 2000, pp. 278–279) includes the effects of accounting bias as shown in Equation (B):

$$V_t = \frac{1}{R-1}(X_t + \Delta u_t) + P_d \left( \frac{X_t + \Delta u_t}{B_{t-1} + u_{t-1}} \right) (B_t + u_t) +$$
$$+ G C_e \left( \frac{X_t + \Delta u_t}{B_{t-1} + u_{t-1}} \right). \tag{B}$$

The specific biases are as follows:

- Bias in book value = Economic value − Accounting book value = $u_t$.
- Bias in earnings = $\Delta u_t = u_t - u_{t-1}$.

Zhang argues that the following relationships hold under the assumption that accounting is conservative:

- The bias in book value $u_t$ is always positive ($u_t > 0$).
- The bias in earnings $\Delta u_t$ has the following behavior:

  - $\Delta u_t < 0$ following periods of investment decline, i.e., for low efficiency firm-years;
  - $\Delta u_t \cong 0$ following periods of constant recent investment, i.e., for steady state firm-years;
  - $\Delta u_t > 0$ following periods of investment expansion, i.e., for growth firm-years.

Applying these expectations to Equation (B) allows some inferences about the relative magnitudes of the coefficients. For the first term in Equation (B), there should be no effect for the steady state firms because $\Delta u_t \cong 0$, whereas there should be a decrease/increase for the low efficiency/growth firms

**Table 14.**    Effects of accounting bias on regression coefficients.

| Profitability ($q$) sub-samples | $\alpha$ [Call option] | $\beta$ [Put option] | $\gamma$ [Current earnings] |
| --- | --- | --- | --- |
| Low efficiency firms (loss firms) | Smaller | Larger | Smaller [possibly negative] |
| Steady state firms | No effect | No effect | No effect |
| Growth firms | Larger | Smaller | Larger |

because $\Delta u_t < 0/\Delta u_t > 0$, respectively. This means that the coefficient $\gamma$ in Model 1 should be smaller/larger for the low efficiency/growth firms relative to the steady state firms. For the second term in Equation (B), the effect of the bias in book value $u_t$ will be to increase the term. There will be no effect on the argument of $P_d(.)$ for the steady state firms from $\Delta u_t$, but it will be decreased/increased for the low efficiency/growth firms leading to a larger/smaller value for $P_d(.)$, respectively. This means that the coefficient $\beta$ in Model 1 should be larger/smaller for the low efficiency/growth firms relative to the steady state firms. The third term in Equation (B) will have the same effect on the argument of $G_e(.)$ from the bias in earnings $\Delta u_t$. But because this is the call option term, this means that the coefficient $\alpha$ in Equation (B) should be smaller/larger for the low efficiency/growth firms relative to the steady state firms. These predictions are summarized in Table 14.

A re-examination of Table 7 shows that the magnitude of the coefficient $\alpha$ is consistent with the predictions in Table 14 in that it is essentially the same for the low efficiency and steady state firms and much larger for the growth firms, reflecting the value of the call option. The coefficient $\beta$ is consistent with the predictions of Table 14 for the low efficiency and steady state firms. Note that the negative value of the coefficient $\beta$ for loss firms may result from the bias of accounting earnings for the low efficiency sub-sample. Similarly, the coefficient $\gamma$ is consistent with the predictions of Table 14 for the low efficiency and steady state firms. But they are not as predicted for the growth firms. The behavior of the three coefficients over the three profitability sub-samples is largely but not entirely consistent with the expectations derived from accounting bias.

## 7. Loss Firms

An examination of the results in Tables 6, 7, 9–13 shows that the coefficient of earnings ($\gamma$) often takes a negative value for observations with a negative profitability, which results from firms with negative earnings, i.e., the loss firms. At first glance, this appears to conflict with the results of Collins, Pincus, and Xie (1999) who showed that inclusion of the book value in the simple earnings capitalization model removed the negative coefficient of earnings for loss firms. However, there is a fundamental difference between their model and Model 1 used in the current study, namely, that their model uses the book value at the beginning of the year, whereas Zhang's (2000) model uses the book value at the end of the year. We reconcile the two models in Appendix B and show that our results are consistent with their results for loss firms.

## 8. Conclusions and Limitations

The results from this study lead to a number of conclusions that have implications for empirical studies and raise issues that may be addressed in further theoretical analyses. Our results extend the finding of variability of the coefficients of earnings and book value in regression models reported by Burgstahler and Dichev (1997) and reinforce the observation by Collins, Pincus, and Xie (1999) about the downward and upward biases of the coefficient of earnings for negative and positive earnings firms, respectively, if the book value is omitted from the regression model.

Our results show that Zhang's (2000) formal model that supplements the basic capitalization model by put and call option components has an empirical validity for valuation studies. We further show that his basic model (Model 1) provides a more efficient and parsimonious explanation than his modified models (Models 2–4). The results support the expectations of value for a put option, current earnings, and a call option at different profitability levels. Our results also show that there is an effect of accounting bias on the empirical results. This leads to a variation of the values of the coefficients of the three terms in the model with profitability. There is a particular impact for loss firms in that the coefficient of earnings becomes negative.

It is clear from the results found here that an analysis of the full sample masks differences that show up in analyses of the sub-samples. It seems clear that stratification of samples on some basis, profitability here, is necessary in deriving regression coefficients and in the interpretation of empirical results.

In addition, our empirical results indicate that debt is relevant to equity valuation for the low efficiency (loss) firms and growth firms. Debt is not relevant to profitable steady state firms. As a result, one can conclude that the level of debt of loss and high growth firms plays a significant role in equity valuation of these firms.

The results in this study are limited by the fundamental assumption in deriving the basic model that accounting measures are unbiased. There is also a question of whether accounting profitability is the best measure of firm efficiency to stratify the sample. Obviously, a given value of accounting profitability could be obtained from low earnings and a low book value, high earnings and a high book value, or from some intermediate combination of earnings and book value. It may also be that some measure other than accounting profitability may be useful in stratification, although the use of accounting profitability is attractive in that the data are available on a regular and reliable basis. Finally, it should be noted that regression Model 1, derived from the basic valuation model, is linear in earnings and book value, which suggests that it should only be used over a limited range of profitability as observed.

There is obviously much scope for further research. Zhang's (2000) model has been developed using firm profitability as a proxy for firm efficiency and leads naturally to stratification of samples for empirical analysis. The use of accounting profitability for stratification has shown that this is an important consideration. However, other bases for sample stratification might be more useful and merit theoretical consideration. From our study, it is also clear that further theoretical study of the impact of the bias of accounting measures on firm valuation models would be useful. Finally, the development of models that go beyond linear terms in earnings and book value may be useful in resolving some of the apparently anomalous behavior that we observed. Furthermore, these models may also provide a better explanation of firm value over a wider range of the independent variable of earnings and book value and of firm efficiency as proxied here by accounting profitability.

## Appendix A. Some Basic Properties of Options

Zhang (2000) showed that the following properties, where $(.)'$ and $(.)''$ indicate the first order and the second order partial derivatives of $C_e(.)$ and $P_d(.)$ with respect to efficiency $q$ must hold:

$$P_d'(q) = -\frac{1}{R(R-1)}\text{Prob}(v_{t+1} \leq q_d^* - q_t) < 0,$$

$$P_d''(q) = \frac{1}{R(R-1)} f(q_d^* - q_t) > 0,$$

$$C'_e(q) = \frac{1}{R(R-1)}[1 - \text{Prob}(v_{t+1} \leq q^*_e - q_t)] > 0,$$

$$C''_e(q) = \frac{1}{R(R-1)} f(q^*_e - q_t) > 0,$$

$$\frac{1}{R-1} + P'_d(q) > 0.$$

## Appendix B. Reconciling the Apparent Negative Earnings Anomaly

A number of studies have shown that the basic earnings capitalization model is not satisfactory when earnings are negative because the coefficient of earnings observed empirically is negative in such cases. Collins, Pincus, and Xie (1999) demonstrated that the anomalous negative coefficient of earnings for loss firms disappears when the book value of net assets is included in the empirical tests, that is, it appears that the book value is a correlated omitted variable in the basic earnings capitalization model. Yet we observe a significantly negative coefficient of earnings for loss firms in our empirical results.

The regression model that was used by Collins, Pincus, and Xie (1999, p. 44) in their empirical analysis was derived from the Ohlson (1995) and Feltham and Ohlson (1995) models and is given in Equation (B.1)[11]:

$$P_t = \alpha + \beta'X_t + \gamma'\text{BV}_{t-1}, \tag{B.1}$$

where $P_t$ is the cum-dividend stock price; $X_t$ the current period earnings per share; and $\text{BV}_{t-1}$ is the book value per share at the end of year $t - 1$.

The general form of their equation is presented in Equation (B.2) (Collins, Pincus, and Xie, 1999, Equation (2), p. 39)

$$P_t + d_t = \delta_0 + \delta_1 X_t + \delta_2 y_{t-1} + \varepsilon_t, \tag{B.2}$$

where $P_t$ is now the ex-dividend price; $d_t$, the dividends per share; $P_t + d_t$, the cum dividend price; $y_{t-1}$, the beginning year book value per share; and $\varepsilon_t$ is the noise term.

The models in Collins, Pincus, and Xie, (1999) are expressed in terms of earnings for the year and *beginning* of the year book value, whereas

---

[11] Note that Collins, Pincus, and Xie (1999) have interchanged the notation for the coefficients $\beta$ and $\gamma$ in their model relative to the usage in our models. Therefore, we designate their coefficients with a to distinguish them from ours. Also Collins, Pincus, and Xie (1999) use the book value (BV) at time $t - 1$ rather than time $t$ as in our models.

**Table 15.**   Estimated coefficients of Model 1 for loss firms derived from empirical results of Collins, Pincus, and Xie, (1999).

| Collins et al. | Coefficient of earnings $X_t$ $\delta_1 [\beta']$ | Coefficient of book value $B_{t-1}$ $\delta_2 [\gamma']$ | Difference $\delta_1 - \delta_2$ |
|---|---|---|---|
| Current Study | | Coefficient of book value $B_t$ $\beta$ | Coefficient of earnings $X_t$ $\gamma$ |
| 75 | −0.02 | 0.29 | −0.31 |
| 76 | −0.09 | 0.15 | −0.24 |
| 77 | 0.11 | 0.36 | −0.25 |
| 78 | 0.35 | 0.34 | 0.01 |
| 79 | 1.1 | 0.47 | 0.63 |
| 80 | −0.01 | 0.38 | −0.27 |
| 81 | 0.18 | 0.38 | −0.20 |
| 82 | −0.81 | 0.24 | −1.05 |
| 83 | 0.24 | 0.54 | −0.30 |
| 84 | 0.22 | 0.54 | −0.32 |
| 85 | 0.38 | 0.70 | −0.32 |
| 86 | 0.38 | 0.76 | −0.38 |
| 87 | 0.16 | 0.69 | −0.53 |
| 88 | −0.12 | 0.54 | −0.66 |
| 89 | 0.20 | 0.49 | −0.29 |
| 90 | 0.25 | 0.41 | −0.16 |
| 91 | 0.23 | 0.56 | −0.33 |
| 92 | 0.06 | 0.68 | −0.62 |
| Mean | 0.16 | 0.47 | −0.31 |

*Notes*

Collins *et al.*'s model: $P_t = \alpha + \beta' X_t + \gamma' B V_{t-1} + \varepsilon_t$.

Model 1: $V_{it} = \alpha_1 + \beta_1 B_{it} + \gamma_1 X_{it} + \varepsilon_{it}$, $\beta = \delta_2 = \gamma'$, $\gamma = \delta_1 - \delta_2 = \beta' - \gamma'$.

Zhang's (2000) models (Equations (1)–(4) in the paper) are expressed in terms of earnings for the year and *end* of the year book value. To reconcile these two variations of the valuation model, we use the clean surplus relationship given in Equation (B.3)

$$y_t = y_{t-1} + X_t - d_t. \tag{B.3}$$

Substituting the expression for $y_{t-1}$ from Equation (B.3) in Equation (B.2), we obtain the following relationship of cum-dividend price $P_t + d_t$ to earnings and book value at time $t$:

$$P_t + d_t = \delta_0 + \delta_2 d_t + (\delta_1 - \delta_2)X_t + \delta_2 y_t + \varepsilon_t. \tag{B.4}$$

Equation (B.4) is the equivalent to regression Model 1, with

$$\alpha = \delta_1 + \delta_2 d_t = \alpha,$$
$$\beta = \delta_2 = \gamma',$$
$$\gamma = \delta_1 - \delta_2 = \beta' - \gamma'.$$

In Table 15, we reproduce the coefficient estimates for the earnings and the book value of loss firms obtained by Collins, Pincus, and Xie, (1999, Table 4, p. 44). We then show how the results of Collins, Pincus, and Xie, (1999) appear when transformed to Model 1. After transformation, the coefficient of book value has a positive sign for the mean value and for all 18 years studied, and the coefficient of earnings has a negative sign for the mean value and for 16 of the 18 years studied. The results in Table 15 show that the coefficient of book value $\beta$ found empirically for loss firms by Collins, Pincus, and Xie, (1999) is consistent with our results. More importantly, their coefficient of earnings $\gamma$ for loss firms is also quite consistent with those found here for the low efficiency (loss) firms that appear in the first three deciles.

## References

Ashton D. J., "Corporate Financial Policy: American Analytics and UK Taxation." *Journal of Business Finance and Accounting* 18, 465–482 (1991).

Bailey, W., "Valuing Agricultural Firms: An Examination of the Contingent Claims Approach to Pricing Real Assets." *Journal of Economic Dynamics and Control* 15, 771–791 (1991).

Ball, R. and P. Brown, "An Empirical Evaluation of Accounting Numbers." *Journal of Accounting Research* 6, 159–178 (1968).

Barth, M., "Relative Measurement Errors Among Alternative Pension Assets and Liability Measures." *Accounting Review* 66, 433–463 (1991).

Barth, M., W. Beaver and W. Landsman, " Market Valuation Implications of Net Period Pension Cost." *Journal of Accounting and Economics* 15, 22–62 (1992).

Belkaoui, A. R., *Accounting and the Investment Opportunity Set.*, Westport, Connecticut: Quorum Books (2000).

Berger, P., E. Ofek and I. Swary, "Investor Valuation of the Abandonment Option." *Journal of Financial Economics* 42, 257–287 (1996).

Burgstahler, D. and I. Dichev, "Earning, Adaptation and Equity Value." *The Accounting Review* 72, 187–215 (1997).

Collins, D. and S. P. Kothari, "An Analysis of Intertemporal and Cross-Sectional Determinants of ERCs." *Journal of Accounting and Economics* 11, 143–183 (1989).

Collins, D. W., E. Maydew and I. Weiss, "Changes in the Value-Relevance of Earnings and Book Value Over the Past Forty Years." *Journal of Accounting and Economics* 24, 39–67 (1997).

Collins, D. W., M. Pincus and H. Xie, "Equity Valuation and Negative Earnings: The Role of Book Value of Equity." *The Accounting Review* 74, 29–61 (1999).

Feltham, G. and J. A. Ohlson., "Valuation and Clean Surplus Accounting for Operating and Financial Decisions." *Contemporary Accounting Research* 11, 689–731 (1995).

Feltham, G. and J. A. Ohlson., "Uncertainty Resolution and the Theory of Depreciation Measurement." *Journal of Accounting Research* 34, 209–234 (1996).

Gujarati, D., *Essentials of Econometrics*, New York: McGraw-Hill, Inc (1992).

Hayn, C., "The Information Content of Losses." *Journal of Accounting and Economics* 20, 125–153 (1995).

Jan, C. L. and J. Ou, "The Role of Negative Earnings in the Valuation of Equity Stocks." *Working paper*, New York University and Santa Clara University (1995).

Kothari, S. P. and J. L. Zimmerman, "Price and Return Models." *Journal of Accounting and Economics* 20, 155–192 (1995).

Landsman W., "An Empirical Investigation of Pension Fund Property Rights." *The Accounting Review* 61, 44–68 (1986).

Leland, H. and D. Pyle, "Information Asymmetries, Financial Structure, and Financial Intermediation." *Journal of Finance* 32, 371–387 (1977).

McConnell, J. and C. Muscarella, "Corporate Capital Expenditure Decisions and Market Value of the Firm." *Journal of Financial Economics* 399–422 (1985).

Miller, M. and F. Modigliani, "Dividend Policy, Growth and the Valuation of Shares." *Journal of Business* 34, 411–433 (1961).

Modigliani, F. and M. Miller, "The Cost of Capital, Corporation Finance and the Theory of Investment." *American Economic Review* 48, 261–297 (1958).

Moel, A. and P. Tufano, "When are Real Options Exercised? An Empirical Examination of Mine Closings." *Review of Financial Studies* 15, 35–64 (2002).

Myers, S. C., "Determinants of Corporate Borrowings." *Journal of Financial Economics* 5, 147–175 (1977).

Ohlson. J. A., "Earnings, Book Values and Dividends in Security Valuation." *Contemporary Accounting Research* 11, 661–687 (1995).

Paddock, J., D. Siegel and J. Smith, "Option Valuation of Claims on Physical Assets: The Case of Offshore Petroleum Leases." *Quarterly Journal of Economics* 103, 479–508 (1988).

Quigg, L., "Empirical Testing of Real Option Pricing Models." *Journal of Finance* 48, 621–640 (1993).

Rees, W. P., "The Impact of Dividends, Debt and Investment on Valuation Models." *Journal of Business, Finance and Accounting* 24, 1111–1140 (1997).

Ross, S., "The Determination of Financial Structure: The Incentive Signaling Approach." *Bell Journal of Economics* 8, 23–40 (1977).

Shevlin T., "The Valuation of R&D Firms with R&D Limited Partnerships." *The Accounting Review* 66, 1–21 (1991).

Zhang, G., "Accounting Information, Capital Investment Decisions, and Equity Valuation: Theory and Empirical Implications." *Journal of Accounting Research* 38, 271–295 (2000).

Chapter 2

# Firm Performance and Compensation-Based Stock Trading by Corporate Executives

Zahid Iqbal
*Texas Southern University, USA*

Many firms increase equity-based compensation during poor performance to strengthen managerial incentives. Increasing equity-based compensation may, however, trigger stock selling by high-ownership executives who diversify their investment portfolios. In this study, we examine whether such compensation-based stock sales depend on a firm's financial performance. Our findings show that executives do not sell stock in response to stock option awards during declining earnings. This is true even for the high ownership executives. These findings suggest that increasing equity-based compensation during poor performance seems to achieve the incentive-alignment goal for the managers. Our findings show that the high ownership managers sell shares for diversification only when the firm's earnings are rising.

**Keywords:** Firm performance; executive stock trading; stock options; managerial ownership.

## 1. Introduction

Agency conflicts arise in public firms because of separation of ownership and control. Opportunistic managers often do not act in the best interest of the shareholders. To minimize agency conflicts, many firms award stock-based compensation such as stock options and restricted stocks to the executives. Equity-based compensation aligns managers' interest with those of the shareholders and rewards managers for maximizing firm value. Since managers who receive stock options tend to think like shareholders, they have the incentive to improve firm performance and maximize shareholder value (e.g., Jensen and Meckling, 1976; Jensen and Murphy, 1990; Mehran, 1995).

In a recent study, Ofek and Yermack (2000) claim that equity-based pay fails to achieve its incentive-alignment goal when managers already own a high percentage of the firm's stock. Since the value of human capital of managers is already tied to firm performance, any new equity-based compensation increases the risk level of those managers who have a large personal investment in the firm's stock. To hedge risk, these high-ownership managers sell their previously owned firm's stock once they receive equity-based pay. Ofek and Yermack (2000) observe that executive stock selling occurs at the optimal hedge ratio of 0.60, indicating sale of 600 shares of a firms' stock for every 1,000 shares of stock options awarded. Also, executives sell shares equal to 94% of the restricted shares awarded. Overall, the findings in Ofek and Yermack (2000) are at odds with the goal of the board of directors who grant managers stock-based awards to align managerial incentives with those of the shareholders.

Firms often take actions during declining performance that tie managers' wealth more closely to shareholder value. In Gilson and Vetsuypens' (1993) study, 83% of the financially distressed firms are engaged in such actions as lowering exercise price of existing stock options and awarding new stock options. These and other changes in the compensation policy to improve poor performance will not be effective if managers start selling previously owned shares of the firm as part of their own risk-reduction strategy.

The primary purpose of this study is to examine the extent to which firm performance impacts executive stock sales that are related to equity-based compensation. Our evidence indicates that managers do not sell their own stocks in response to stock options awarded during declining earnings. This is true even for the high-ownership executives who are likely to diversify after receiving the stock-based awards. Our results also show that high-ownership managers sell stock only when the firm's earnings are rising and that such selling takes place around the optimal hedge ratio.

Why does the executive forego diversification benefits and refrain from stock selling during poor earnings? We offer the following explanations. First, stock selling may provide signal to the board of directors that the manager is bailing out due to poor performance. This may weaken his relationship with the board and stockholders of the firm. Second, stock selling by the executive during declining earnings warns the financial market that the firm's performance is indeed poor. Third, the manager may prefer high stock ownership during poor performance in order to deter external acquisition (Mikkelson and Partch, 1989; Song and Walkling, 1993) and his replacement by the acquiring firm (Walsh, 1988; Walsh and Ellwood, 1991; and Martin and McConnell, 1991). Also, internal replacement by the board of directors is less likely to occur when the executive has high ownership in the firm (Allen, 1981; Allen and Panian, 1982; Boeker, 1992; Denis, Denis, and Sarin, 1997). To avoid such internal and external replacements which occur when earnings are poor, the executive may avoid selling shares for diversification and may even accumulate shares. Fourth, managers of a poorly performing firm may want to hold on to their stocks to capitalize on future returns. They may implement various operational and financial measures to capitalize on a significant rebound in earnings and stock price.

The paper is organized as follows: The data and sample selections are described in the next section. Section 3 presents the empirical results. The concluding remarks are given in Section 4.

## 2. Data and Sample

We collect data on executive compensation and share ownership from the *Standard and Poor's Corporation's ExecuComp* database. The release of the database that we use has 2,402 firms with at least a stock option award, a restricted stock award, or a stock option exercise from 1992 to 2000. Table 1 provides sample and data descriptions for our study. There are 75,751 person-year observations in the initial sample which has 800 more firms and 57,193 more observations than those reported in Ofek and Yermack (2000).[1] All share quantities are adjusted for stock splits and are stated in common year 2000 units in our study.

Of the 75,751 observations, 67,189 observations are new stock options, 25,473 observations are exercise of existing stock options, and 16,453 observations are restricted shares.[2] The percentage of new stock options in our sample is 88.7% (67,189 divided by 75,751), which is substantially higher than the 67.9% reported in Ofek and Yermack (2000). This indicates the popularity of stock options in the latter half of the 1990s when the stock market experienced astronomical growth. Panel A also provides a percentage breakdown of the sample for individual years from 1992 to 2000. For the total sample, the percentage of stock-based compensation increased every year from 1992 to 1998 and then decreased in the last two years. The percentages for each of the stock-based compensation types also increased through 1998 and declined subsequently. These data on annual percentages indicate that equity-based compensation was most popular around the mid-1990s. Also, a closer look into these figures show that options exercises in the last two years, in 1999 and 2000, did not decrease at the same rate as new stock options and restricted stocks.

---

[1]We delete roughly 2% observations that are reloads.

[2]As in Ofek and Yermack (2000), the sum of new stock options, options exercise, and restricted shares in our study exceeds 100% because many firms have more than one type of equity-based compensation. There are 37,767 cases with stock options only, 4,508 cases with options exercise only, 2,874 cases with restricted shares only, 3,865 cases with all three types of transactions, 9,086 cases with new options and restricted stock, 16,472 cases with new options and options exercise, and 626 cases with restricted stock and options exercise.

**Table 1.**  Descriptive statistics.

| | | Total | 1992(%) | 1993(%) | 1994(%) | 1995(%) | 1996(%) | 1997(%) | 1998(%) | 1999(%) | 2000(%) |
|---|---|---|---|---|---|---|---|---|---|---|---|
| *Panel A: Sample frequencies* | | | | | | | | | | | |
| Number of observations | | 75,751 | 7.90 | 10.08 | 10.90 | 11.62 | 12.52 | 12.99 | 13.38 | 11.81 | 8.81 |
| New stock options | | 67,189 | 7.73 | 9.75 | 10.86 | 11.55 | 12.61 | 13.01 | 13.39 | 12.07 | 9.01 |
| Options exercise | | 25,473 | 7.40 | 10.60 | 9.58 | 10.85 | 12.13 | 13.48 | 13.32 | 11.87 | 10.77 |
| Restricted shares | | 16,453 | 7.40 | 9.63 | 10.62 | 11.96 | 12.72 | 12.96 | 13.66 | 11.89 | 9.17 |
| *Panel B: Annual changes in shares owned and compensation statistics* | | | | | | | | | | | |
| Changes in shares | Mean | −7.20 | −7.20 | −11.20 | −17.05 | −7.62 | −7.64 | −6.98 | −24.30 | −7.10 | 27.13 |
| (thousands of shares) | Median | 1.16 | 1.16 | 0.99 | 0.93 | 0.9 | 1.19 | 0.99 | 1.62 | 1.75 | 1.11 |
| | SD | 964.41 | 964.41 | 625.29 | 683.22 | 531.30 | 688.58 | 681.99 | 1,054.47 | 1,105.60 | 1,717.35 |
| | N | 36.45 | 36.45 | 3.34 | 4.38 | 4.43 | 4.71 | 4.96 | 5.21 | 5.12 | 4.32 |
| New stock options | Mean | 121.94 | 121.94 | 86.93 | 87.11 | 112.03 | 116.71 | 134.18 | 139.80 | 139.66 | 147.50 |
| (thousands shares) | Median | 34.80 | 34.80 | 23.00 | 25.00 | 28.63 | 31.60 | 35.00 | 40.00 | 48.50 | 50.00 |
| | SD | 517.14 | 517.14 | 408.58 | 291.01 | 467.88 | 516.34 | 676.10 | 683.23 | 435.71 | 444.04 |
| | N | 69.24 | 69.24 | 7.62 | 8.21 | 8.77 | 9.45 | 9.72 | 9.94 | 8.86 | 6.67 |
| Black–Scholes value | Mean | 859.57 | 859.57 | 301.45 | 401.85 | 404.59 | 598.95 | 786.12 | 873.51 | 1,448.88 | 2,331.89 |
| (thousands of dollars) | Median | 161.33 | 161.33 | 79.29 | 106.91 | 95.96 | 134.53 | 161.47 | 198.72 | 314.67 | 480.97 |
| | SD | 4,666.62 | 4,666.62 | 876.61 | 1,132.62 | 1,340.07 | 2,669.01 | 3,779.87 | 3,566.35 | 5,662.49 | 9,215.03 |
| | N | 69.77 | 69.77 | 7.63 | 8.25 | 8.80 | 9.49 | 9.84 | 10.14 | 8.95 | 6.67 |
| Options exercise | Mean | 51.79 | 51.79 | 55.20 | 35.90 | 42.02 | 47.00 | 51.14 | 68.18 | 51.19 | 61.38 |
| (thousands of shares) | Median | 0.00 | 0.00 | 0.00 | 0.00 | 0.00 | 0.00 | 0.00 | 0.00 | 0.00 | 0.00 |
| | SD | 378.45 | 378.45 | 424.42 | 245.82 | 252.16 | 286.57 | 261.65 | 683.33 | 269.38 | 346.56 |
| | N | 57.66 | 57.66 | 6.13 | 6.55 | 6.91 | 7.63 | 7.84 | 8.10 | 7.84 | 6.67 |

(Continued)

**Table 1.** (*Continued*)

| | | 1992(%) | 1993(%) | 1994(%) | 1995(%) | 1996(%) | 1997(%) | 1998(%) | 1999(%) | 2000(%) |
|---|---|---|---|---|---|---|---|---|---|---|
| Restricted shares | Mean | 8.15 | 4.79 | 5.08 | 5.77 | 5.58 | 6.08 | 14.20 | 11.47 | 12.03 |
| (thousands of shares) | Median | 0.00 | 0.00 | 0.00 | 0.00 | 0.00 | 0.00 | 0.00 | 0.00 | 0.00 |
| | SD | 233.40 | 34.88 | 34.38 | 54.07 | 37.09 | 68.05 | 546.84 | 248.68 | 129.26 |
| | N | 69.51 | 7.63 | 8.23 | 8.75 | 9.47 | 9.81 | 10.10 | 8.93 | 6.59 |
| Salary and bonus | Mean | 589.41 | 473.08 | 488.73 | 514.21 | 567.93 | 577.15 | 599.32 | 700.84 | 830.36 |
| (thousands of dollars) | Median | 390.31 | 332.37 | 347.83 | 365.00 | 373.20 | 395.00 | 400.00 | 443.66 | 510.23 |
| | SD | 927.78 | 537.08 | 522.67 | 531.26 | 1,248.24 | 714.89 | 756.55 | 1,000.03 | 1,634.28 |
| | N | 69.77 | 7.63 | 8.25 | 8.80 | 9.49 | 9.84 | 10.14 | 8.95 | 6.67 |
| *Panel C: 3-year growth in operating income* | | | | | | | | | | |
| 3-year average annual | Mean (%) | 24.10 | 18.90 | 24.04 | 24.52 | 27.22 | 28.97 | 24.26 | 21.80 | 20.51 |
| Growth in operating | Median (%) | 14.24 | 10.12 | 13.80 | 14.91 | 15.69 | 15.63 | 15.29 | 13.56 | 13.54 |
| Income | SD (%) | 74.50 | 39.22 | 56.06 | 49.16 | 97.83 | 135.81 | 48.67 | 40.41 | 45.71 |
| | N | 61.93 | 6.83 | 7.39 | 7.93 | 8.54 | 8.83 | 8.90 | 7.86 | 5.66 |

*Note*: Descriptive statistics on annual changes in executive share ownership and stock-based compensations for 2,402 firms in which at least one executive received a stock option or a restricted stock award or exercised a stock option, 1992–2000. All data are obtained from the *Standard & Poor's ExecuComp* database. In Panel A, the sum of observations for new stock options, options exercised, restricted shares is greater than 75,751 because many firms have more than one type of stock-based compensation. In Panel A, the yearly percentage in each row is the percent of the row total. In Panel B, Black–Scholes value is the dollar value of new stock option awards using Black–Scholes method. All share quantities are adjusted for stock splits and are stated in common year 2000. SD is the standard deviation and $N$ is the number of observations in person-year in thousands.

In Panel B, we present statistics on annual changes in executive share ownership and executive compensation. Since our empirical analysis is based on annual changes in share ownership, we lose the 1992 data after taking the first differences.[3] The mean value of changes in shares owned is –7.20 thousand shares, whereas the median value is 1.16 thousand shares. Such changes in shareholdings are small compared to the new stock options awarded to the executives. The mean and median new options awarded are 121.94 thousand shares and 34.80 thousand shares, respectively. Compared to new stock options, the exercise of options occurred in smaller numbers, however. The mean and median values of existing options exercised are 51.86 thousand shares and 0.00 shares, respectively.[4] The mean value of restricted shares is 8.15 thousand shares and the median value is 0.00 shares. Overall, stock-based compensation consists mainly of new stock options.

The yearly statistics indicate that, while annual changes in shares owned by the executives do not follow any identifiable pattern, the mean values of new stock options and restricted shares awarded to the executive increased steadily from 1993 to 2000. The dollar value of new stock options (using the Black–Scholes method) also increased over the years. Unlike stock options and restricted stock grants, options exercises fluctuated from year to year without any discernable pattern. Finally, the dollar value of the salary and bonus earned by the executives increased steadily every year. Overall, the statistics in Panel B indicate that although stock-based and cash compensation increased steadily during the sample period, there are no clear patterns of changes in executive shareholding or options exercise.

Panel C in Table 1 provides information on the earnings performance of our sample firms. Our measure of firm performance is the 3-year annualized growth

---

[3]Of the 75,751 total observations, executive share ownership data are reported for 59,089 cases on the *Standard & Poor's ExecuComp* database. Of the 59,089 cases, 3,846 cases from 1992 could not be used to compute annual changes in executive share ownership thus leaving us with 55,243 cases. Of the 55,243 cases, annual changes in shares could be computed for only 36,446 person-year observations because of missing ownership data. We lost one extra year's of annual change due to missing data. For example, annual changes are not available for both 1995 and 1996 due to missing data share ownership data in 1995.

[4]The median values for options exercises and restricted stock awards are zero because *Standard & Poor's ExecuComp* reports zero values for these two compensation variables for majority of the firms. As in Ofek and Yermack (2000), we report descriptive statistics in Table 1 for all observations including those with zero values for new stock options, option exercise, and restricted shares. For statistical tests in later sections, however, we omit missing and zero values. Hence the statistical inferences in Tables 4 and 5 are based on non-zero values.

rate of operating income before depreciation obtained from the *Standard and Poor's Corporation's ExecuComp* database. We use a 3-year earnings growth to capture trading behavior of managers in relation to long-term performance rather than to a temporary downturn.[5] The data on the 3-year growth rate are available for 61,930 person-year observations. The mean and median growth rates over the period 1993–2000, are 24.10% and 14.24% respectively, suggesting that most firms in our sample experienced strong earnings growth. The yearly breakdown shows that both mean and median firm earnings grew from 1993 to 1997 and then declined through 2000.

## 3. Empirical Results

### 3.1. *Executive compensation and firm performance*

As part of our empirical analysis, we first report data on executive compensation for varying levels of firm performance. We create performance quintiles based on 3-year growth in operating income. The growth rate in quintile 1 is > 36.23%; growth rate in quintile 2 is > 19.45% and ≤ 36.23%; growth rate in quintile 3 is > 9.79% and ≤ 19.45%; growth rate in quintile 4 is > 1.19% and ≤ 9.79%; and growth rate in quintile 5 is < 1.19%. Thus performance quintile 1 includes firms with the highest 3-year growth in operating income and performance quintile 5 includes firms with the lowest 3-year growth in operating income.

The findings presented in Table 2 indicate that executives receive more stock options both in terms of the number of shares and Black–Scholes value when earnings rise. The mean and median number of shares and Black–Scholes value of stock options are significantly greater in the higher performance quintiles than in the lower performance quintiles.[6] For example, the mean value of 206,610 shares in quintile 1 is significantly greater than the mean value in

---

[5]We perform similar empirical analysis using current year's return on assets computed as operating earnings before depreciation divided by assets. Our results and conclusions are somewhat similar to the ones presented in this study.

[6]One concern is that the distribution of some of the variables used in our study is not normal. These variables have substantially different mean and median values with the skewness significantly different from zero. To address this issue of non-normality, we perform additional statistical tests after transforming all the variables in Tables 2 and 3 using the Box–Cox method. The Box–Cox method creates new variable such that its skewness is close to 0. The statistical results for the transformed data are qualitatively similar to the results for the raw data reported in Tables 2 and 3. This is especially true for the nonparametric Wilcoxon $Z$-values.

**Table 2.**   Executive compensation and firm performance.

| Quintiles based on 3-year growth in operating income (growth rates in parenthesis) | | New Options (thousands of shares) | Black–Scholes Value (thousands of dollars) | Option Exercise (thousands of shares) | Restricted Shares (thousands of shares) | Salary& Bonus (thousands of dollars) |
|---|---|---|---|---|---|---|
| Performance quintile 1 | Mean | 206.61 | 1,198.05 | 221.51 | 32.57 | 552.88 |
| (>36.23%) | Median | 51.00 | 220.05 | 50.00 | 9.19 | 355.37 |
| | SD | 943.48 | 5,885.59 | 947.47 | 124.11 | 794.52 |
| | N | 10.98 | 12.38 | 4.95 | 1.94 | 12.38 |
| Performance quintile 2 | Mean | 138.08 | 915.48 | 137.56 | 30.07 | 674.11 |
| (>19.45 to ≤ 36.23%) | Median | 44.00 | 183.22 | 31.69 | 9.38 | 418.29 |
| | SD | 438.07 | 3,956.82 | 588.40 | 62.94 | 1,317.85 |
| | N | 11.03 | 12.39 | 4.80 | 2.69 | 12.39 |
| Performance quintile 3 | Mean | 111.81 | 733.72 | 91.40 | 35.15 | 655.67 |
| (>9.79% to ≤ 19.45%) | Median | 38.25 | 151.15 | 24.00 | 8.71 | 450.00 |
| | SD | 369.63 | 3,005.21 | 451.59 | 313.32 | 808.97 |
| | N | 11.04 | 12.38 | 4.59 | 3.19 | 12.38 |
| Performance quintile 4 | Mean | 88.87 | 599.14 | 68.46 | 19.54 | 635.09 |
| (>1.19% to ≤ 9.79%) | Median | 33.20 | 127.53 | 19.19 | 5.45 | 440.00 |
| | SD | 213.75 | 2,367.48 | 229.79 | 63.08 | 810.01 |
| | N | 10.84 | 12.39 | 4.08 | 3.63 | 12.39 |
| Performance quintile 5 | Mean | 104.38 | 701.07 | 76.78 | 51.78 | 533.68 |
| (< 1.19%) | Median | 36.20 | 147.24 | 20.00 | 6.50 | 378.20 |
| | SD | 283.29 | 3,294.15 | 308.78 | 981.39 | 577.26 |
| | N | 11.20 | 12.39 | 3.02 | 2.78 | 12.39 |

(Continued)

**Table 2.**   (*Continued*)

| Quintiles based on 3-year growth in operating income (growth rates in parenthesis) | | New Options (thousands of shares) | Black–Scholes Value (thousands of dollars) | Option Exercise (thousands of shares) | Restricted Shares (thousands of shares) | Salary& Bonus (thousands of dollars) |
|---|---|---|---|---|---|---|
| *Text statistics* | | | | | | |
| Quintile 1 vs. Quintile 2 | *t*–statistic | 6.92$^c$ | 4.43$^c$ | 5.24$^c$ | –0.89 | –8.77$^c$ |
| | Wilcoxon Z | –11.37$^c$ | –3.11$^c$ | –12.89$^c$ | –3.05$^c$ | –17.13$^c$ |
| Quintile 1 vs. Quintile 3 | *t*–statistic | 9.83$^c$ | 7.82$^c$ | 8.45$^c$ | –0.35 | –10.09$^c$ |
| | Wilcoxon Z | –19.70$^c$ | –8.73$^c$ | –21.61$^c$ | –0.78 | –21.81$^c$ |
| Quintile 1 vs. Quintile 4 | *t*–statistic | 12.68$^c$ | 10.51$^c$ | 10.07$^c$ | 5.19$^c$ | –8.07$^c$ |
| | Wilcoxon Z | –26.13$^c$ | –14.69$^c$ | –27.42$^c$ | –8.46$^c$ | –20.31$^c$ |
| Quintile 1 vs. Quintile 5 | *t*–statistic | 10.97$^c$ | 8.20$^c$ | 8.13$^c$ | –0.86 | 2.18$^b$ |
| | Wilcoxon Z | –20.53$^c$ | –10.16$^c$ | –23.70$^c$ | –3.55$^c$ | –5.16$^c$ |
| Quintile 2 vs. Quintile 3 | *t*–statistic | 4.82$^c$ | 4.07$^c$ | 4.25$^c$ | –0.83 | 1.33 |
| | Wilcoxon Z | –8.50$^c$ | –6.18$^c$ | –8.94$^c$ | –2.67$^c$ | –4.34$^c$ |
| Quintile 2 vs. Quintile 4 | *t*–statistic | 10.53$^c$ | 7.64$^c$ | 7.05$^c$ | 6.57$^c$ | 2.81$^c$ |
| | Wilcoxon Z | –15.10$^c$ | –12.59$^c$ | –15.40$^c$ | –13.07$^c$ | –2.54$^c$ |
| Quintile 2 vs. Quintile 5 | *t*–statistic | 6.82$^c$ | 4.64$^c$ | 5.24$^c$ | –1.14 | 10.87$^c$ |
| | Wilcoxon Z | –9.16$^c$ | –7.57$^c$ | –12.83$^c$ | –7.14$^c$ | –12.35$^c$ |
| Quintile 3 vs. Quintile 4 | *t*–statistic | 5.61$^c$ | 3.92$^c$ | 2.92$^c$ | 2.94$^c$ | 2.00$^b$ |
| | Wilcoxon Z | –6.61$^c$ | –6.43$^c$ | –6.78$^c$ | –10.93$^c$ | –1.96$^b$ |
| Quintile 3 vs. Quintile 5 | *t*–statistic | 1.68$^a$ | 0.82 | 1.55 | –0.91 | 13.66$^c$ |
| | Wilcoxon Z | –0.49 | –1.26 | –5.09$^c$ | –4.88$^c$ | –17.04$^c$ |
| Quintile 4 vs. Quintile 5 | *t*–statistic | –4.58$^c$ | –2.80$^c$ | –1.30 | –1.97$^b$ | 11.35$^c$ |
| | Wilcoxon Z | –6.23$^c$ | –5.29$^c$ | –1.01 | –4.82$^c$ | –15.36$^c$ |

*Note:* Executive compensation for quintiles based on 3-year growth in operating income. Performance quintile 1 includes firms with the highest growth in operating income and performance; quintile 5 includes firms with the lowest growth in operating income. Black–Scholes value is the dollar value of new stock option awards using Black–Scholes method. SD is the standard deviation and $N$ is the number of observations in person-year in thousands. Missing values and zero values are omitted.
a,b,c denote significant differences in means and median at the 10%, 5%, and 1%, respectively.

any other quintiles as indicated by the $t$-statistic and Wilxocon $Z$-statistic. One exception is the findings for quintile 5 where firm performance is the lowest. When the firm reaches quintile 5, stock option awards increase, and they are significantly higher than stock options in quintile 4. These results support the notion that firms in the lowest level of earnings performance increase stock-based compensation to enhance managerial incentive. In sum, these results indicate that executives are being rewarded with more stock options when earnings increase and that they are also awarded stock options when earnings decline to the lowest level.

Our results on restricted stock awards are somewhat mixed. For example, the median value of restricted stock awards in quintile 1 is lower than the median value in quintile 2, but higher than the median values in quintiles 3–5. In quintile 5, we find a significant rebound in restricted stock awards from quintile 4. In line with stock option awards, this suggests that firms make an attempt to enhance managerial incentives by granting restricted stocks when earnings decline to the lowest level.

With regard to salary and bonus, we do not find any consistent pattern across the different levels of earnings growth. The dollar amounts of salary and bonus increase from quintile 1 to quintile 3 and then start to decline through quintile 5. One possible explanation is that firms pay less salaries and bonuses because they fund investments during periods of high growth and they experience cash flow problems during periods of low growth. It is during the normal growth period that firms can pay high cash salaries and bonuses.

Finally, Table 2 provides results on exercise of existing stock options. The data clearly indicate that executives exercise significantly more stock options when earnings growth is high than when it is low. The executive in performance quintile 1 firms exercise almost twice as many options (mean is 221.51 thousand shares and median is 50.00 thousand shares) than the executive in any other performance quintiles. Similarly, the mean and median values in quintile 2 are significantly higher than those in quintiles 3–5. These results are expected because options are generally exercised following an increase in stock price (Huddart and Lang, 1996; Carpenter and Remmers, 2001), and our sample firms in the higher performance quintiles experience higher stock returns than those in the lower performance quintiles (results not reported). For example, firms in quintile 1 have a median annual stock return of 25.40%, whereas firms in quintile 5 have a median annual stock returns of only 0.99% (results not reported).

Our overall findings in Table 2 suggest that top executives receive a higher stock-based compensation when earnings are rising. However, there is an increase in stock-based compensation when earnings decline to the lowest level. In the next section, we present data on changes in executive shareholdings and percentage ownership.

### 3.2. *Executive share ownership and firm performance*

In Table 3, we report annual changes in shares owned by executives and percentage of executive ownership in the firm for the performance quintiles. The ownership data are reported for the year the executive received equity-based compensation. In general, the findings show that executives reduce their shareholdings when a firm's earnings increase and increase their shareholdings when a firm's earnings fall. Quintile 1 has the lowest mean ($-63, 820$ shares) and median (370 shares) changes in shares than the mean and median changes in any other quintiles. The differences in the mean and median values between quintile 1 and those in other quintiles are all statistically significant. The median value in quintile 2 (920 shares) is significantly less than the median values in quintiles 3–5; and the median value in quintile 3 is significantly less than the median value in quintile 4. Our results that the median value in quintile 5 is significantly less than the median values in quintiles 3 and 4 are at odds with our conjecture, however. We expected that executives are least likely to sell their own shares when earnings declined significantly (quintile 5). We, nevertheless, proceed with our empirical analysis in the next section to examine whether firm performance has any influence on changes in executive shareholdings that are related to stock-based compensation.

The data on percentage share ownership indicate higher executive ownership at higher levels of firm performance. For example, ownership percentage in quintile 1 is significantly higher than that in quintiles 2–5; ownership percentage in quintile 2 is significantly higher than that in quintiles 3–5; ownership percentage in quintile 3 is significantly higher than that in quintiles 4 and 5; and ownership percentage in quintile 4 is higher than that in quintile 5. These results are consistent with the prior findings that firm performance increases with executive ownership (Mehran, 1995; Morck, Shleifer, and Vishny, 1988).

Overall, we find evidence that executives change shareholdings in the year equity-based compensation is awarded. They decrease shareholdings during increasing earnings and increase shareholdings during declining earnings.

**Table 3.**    Executive share ownership and firm performance.

| Quintiles based on 3-year growth in operating income (growth rates in parenthesis) | | Annual changes in shares (thousands of shares) | Share ownership (percentage) |
|---|---|---|---|
| Performance quintile 1 | Mean | −63.82 | 0.994 |
| (> 36.23%) | Median | 0.37 | 0.076 |
| | SD | 1,433.42 | 3.50 |
| | N | 6.09 | 9.66 |
| Performance quintile 2 | Mean | −9.67 | 0.869 |
| (> 19.45% to ≤ 36.23%) | Median | 0.92 | 0.075 |
| | SD | 874.28 | 3.24 |
| | N | 6.91 | 9.98 |
| Performance quintile 3 | Mean | 16.51 | 0.655 |
| (> 9.79% to ≤ 19.45%) | Median | 1.88 | 0.064 |
| | SD | 1,374.29 | 2.71 |
| | N | 7.06 | 9.96 |
| Performance quintile 4 | Mean | 1.75 | 0.540 |
| (> 1.19% to ≤ 9.79%) | Median | 2.11 | 0.048 |
| | SD | 503.99 | 2.59 |
| | N | 6.89 | 9.88 |
| Performance quintile 5 | Mean | 12.37 | 0.527 |
| (≤ 1.19%) | Median | 1.14 | 0.046 |
| | SD | 354.95 | 2.80 |
| | N | 6.15 | 9.77 |
| *Test statistics* | | | |
| Quintile 1 vs. Quintile 2 | $t$–statistic | −2.63[c] | 2.59[c] |
| | Wilcoxon $Z$ | −4.75[c] | −0.30 |
| Quintile 1 vs. Quintile 3 | $t$-statistic | −3.28[c] | 7.59[c] |
| | Wilcoxon $Z$ | −9.77[c] | −3.21[c] |
| Quintile 1 vs. Quintile 4 | $t$-statistic | −3.56[c] | 10.33[c] |
| | Wilcoxon $Z$ | −12.40[c] | −10.63[c] |
| Quintile 1 vs. Quintile 5 | $t$-statistic | −4.04[c] | 8.52[c] |
| | Wilcoxon $Z$ | −8.66[c] | −12.75[c] |
| Quintile 2 vs. Quintile 3 | $t$-statistic | −1.34 | 5.06[c] |
| | Wilcoxon $Z$ | −5.32[c] | −3.21[c] |
| Quintile 2 vs. Quintile 4 | $t$-statistic | −0.94 | 7.91[c] |
| | Wilcoxon $Z$ | −7.88[c] | −11.44[c] |
| Quintile 2 vs. Quintile 5 | $t$-statistic | −1.85[a] | 6.08[c] |
| | Wilcoxon $Z$ | −3.64[c] | −13.55[c] |

(*Continued*)

**Table 3.** (*Continued*)

| Quintiles based on 3-year growth in operating income (growth rates in parenthesis) | | Annual changes in shares (thousands of shares) | Share ownership (percentage) |
|---|---|---|---|
| Quintile 3 vs. Quintile 4 | $t$-statistic | 0.84 | 3.06[c] |
| | Wilcoxon Z | -2.24[b] | -8.96[c] |
| Quintile 3 vs. Quintile 5 | $t$-statistic | 0.23 | 1.23 |
| | Wilcoxon Z | -2.27[b] | -11.26[c] |
| Quintile 4 vs. Quintile 5 | $t$-statistic | -1.38 | -1.74[a] |
| | Wilcoxon Z | -5.91[c] | -2.89[c] |

*Notes*: Annual changes in shares owned by the executives and executive share ownership percentage for performance quintiles are based on 3-year growth in operating income. Performance quintile 1 includes firms with the highest growth in operating income and performance quintile 5 includes firms with the lowest growth in operating income. Executive share ownership is expressed as a percentage of shares outstanding. SD is the standard deviation and $N$ is the number of observations in person-year in thousands. Missing values and zero values are omitted.

[a,b,c] denote significant differences in means and median at the 10%, 5%, and 1%, respectively.

Such act of increasing executive shareholdings should help the firm achieve incentive-alignment goal during poor earnings. In the following sections, we investigate whether these changes in shareholdings are related to equity-based compensation awards, and whether such relationships depend on firm performance.

### 3.3. *Compensation-based stock selling by executives*

In this section, we present the results of the impact of stock-based compensation on the changes in shareholdings of executives. Following Ofek and Yermack (2000), we test the null hypotheses that stock option awards have no impact on executive shareholdings and that executives retain as many shares as they receive from options exercises or restricted stock awards. The hypotheses are tested by regressing annual changes in shares owned by the executives on new stock options, options exercise, and restricted shares. Current year's stock return is also included in the regression to control for its effect on shareholdings. The regression is of the following form:

$$\Delta S_t = \beta_0 + \beta_1 C_t + \beta_2 R_t \tag{1}$$

where $\Delta S_t$ = change in shares owned by an executive in year $t$; $C_t$ = new options, options exercised, or restricted stocks awarded in year $t$; $R_t$ = dividend-adjusted stock return in year $t$; and, $\exists s$ are the parameter estimates.

For new stock options awarded to the executives, we test the null hypothesis that $\exists_1 = 0$, and for options exercised and restricted stocks awarded, we test the null hypothesis that $\exists_1 = 1$. A positive value for the compensation variable coefficient $\exists_1$ indicates an increase in executive ownership in the firm and a negative value indicates a decrease in ownership. Since new stock options do not increase shareholdings, the null hypothesis is that there is no change in shareholdings after receiving new stock options. The alternative hypothesis is based on the premise that stock option awards increase the risk of the executive who will hedge the risk through stock selling. To achieve an optimal hedge, the executive will sell shares equal to the number of new stock options times the change in option value per unit change in stock price. Ofek and Yermack (2000) find such a hedge ratio to be 0.60, i.e., the executive sells 600 shares for every 1,000 new stock options.

When the executive exercises existing stock options, he sells shares because the hedge ratio increases to 1 and he may need to finance the exercise price and pay income taxes. Similarly, restricted stock awards trigger stock selling because the portfolio risk of the executive increases. In both cases, the null hypothesis is that the executive retains all the shares received through options exercise and restricted stock awards; and the alternate hypothesis is that the executive sells a significant number of shares upon exercising options and receiving restricted stocks.[7]

Panel A in Table 4 provides regression results for the total sample of 31,692 observations for which necessary regression data are available. The results show that executives sell when new stock options are awarded, with a statistically significant $\exists_1$ value of $-0.365$. That is, the executive sells 365 shares of the firm's common stock that he owns for every 1,000 shares of new stock options that he receives.

To incorporate the position of Ofek and Yermack (2000) that only high ownership executives sell to hedge stock portfolio, we create regression variables by interacting stock-based compensation and 0-1 coded variable based on percentage of executive share ownership. Panel B presents the results of interaction variables using the regression equation given in Appendix A. The $\exists_1$ coefficient of $-0.513$ is close to the 0.60 hedge ratio indicating that high-ownership executives sell 513 shares of common stock for every 1,000 shares of new stock options. In contrast, the low-ownership executives increase their

---

[7] See Ofek and Yermack (2000) for the detailed explanations of the hypotheses.

**Table 4.** Executive share ownership and stock-based compensation.

| | | $H_0: \exists_1 = 0$ (for $i = 1, 2, 3$) New options | $H_0: \exists_1 = 1$ (for $i = 1, \ldots, 3$) Options exercised | $H_0: \exists_1 = 1$ (for $i = 1, \ldots, 3$) Restricted shares |
|---|---|---|---|---|
| *Panel A: Total sample* | | | | |
| Constant | $\exists_0$ | 40.778[b] | −0.030 | 32.746[b] |
| Stock-based compensation | $\exists_1$ | −0.365[b] | −0.038[f] | −0.011 |
| Stock return | $\exists_2$ | −0.009 | −0.001 | −0.002 |
| | $N$ | 31,692 | 16,464 | 8,399 |
| Adjusted $R^2$ | | 0.024 | 0.000 | 0.000 |
| *Panel B: Interactions of stock-based compensation and ownership* | | | | |
| Constant | $\exists_0$ | 28.765[a] | −5.195 | 28.741[a] |
| Stock-based compensation awarded to high-ownership executives | $\exists_1$ | −0.513[b] | −0.066[f] | −0.053[f] |
| Stock-based compensation awarded to low-ownership executives | $\exists_2$ | 0.045[b] | 0.127[b,f] | 0.466[b,e] |
| Stock return | $\exists_3$ | −0.010 | −0.004 | −0.002 |
| | $N$ | 31,666 | 16,451 | 8,392 |
| Adjusted $R^2$ | | 0.036 | 0.002 | 0.000 |

*Notes*: Regressions of annual changes in executive share ownership as a function of stock-based compensation. Panel A reports results for all firms, where, $\exists_0$ is the constant, $\exists_1$ is the coefficient for the stock-based compensation variable, and $\exists_2$ the coefficient for the stock-return variable. Panel B reports results based on interactions of stock-based compensation and 0-1 coded executive share ownership percentage. Executive share ownership percentage is coded 1 if it is greater than or equal to the sample median of 0.643%, and coded 0 if less than 0.643%. In Panel B, $\exists_1$ is the compensation variable coefficient for high-ownership executives, $\exists_2$ is the compensation variable coefficient for low-ownership executives, and $\exists_3$ the coefficient for the stock-return variable. Constants are expressed in thousands of shares. Significance of the coefficients is measured by heteroskedastic $t$-statistic (not reported below).
[a,b,c] denote significant differences from zero at the 10%, 5%, and 1%, respectively.
[d,e,f] denote significant differences from one at the 10%, 5%, and 1%, respectively.

shareholdings by 45 shares for every 1,000 of new stock options. The $\exists_2$ value for these executives is 0.045 which is statistically significant.

The findings on options exercised and restricted shares are similar to those reported in Ofek and Yermack (2000) that executives sell shares at all levels of ownership. For options exercise, the $\exists_1$ value of −0.066 for the high-ownership executives and the $\exists_1$ value of 0.127 for the low-ownership executives are both significantly less than 1. These results indicate that executives do not retain most of the shares received from options exercises and that share retention does not depend on the ownership level. Similar findings are observed for restricted stock awards that executives do not increase shareholdings one-to-one in response to the restricted stock awards. This is true for both the high-ownership and the low-ownership executives.

The findings in Table 4 provide evidence that stock selling by executives is related to equity-based compensation. In the case of new stock options, stock selling occurs when the executive owns a high percentage of the firm's stock. In our next analysis, we examine whether compensation-based stock selling depends on earnings performance.

### 3.4. *Equity-based compensation and executive stock selling by firm performance*

Table 5 reports the main findings of the paper which show whether compensation-related stock selling by executives depends on earnings performance. In Panel A, we report the findings by interacting stock-based compensation and 0-1 coded growth variable. The regression equation for the interaction variables in Panel A is given in Appendix B. In Panel B, annual change in shares owned by each executive is regressed on interaction variables computed as compensation variable times 0-1 coded variable based on 3-year growth in operating income times 0-1 coded variable based on executive share ownership percentage. For example, the interaction variable for $\exists_1$ is compensation variable times 1 if quintile 1 (firms with the highest 3-year growth in operating income) times 1 if executive share ownership percentage is greater than or equal to the sample median of 0.643%, 0 otherwise. The sign and significance of interaction variables will provide evidence on the relationship between equity-based compensation and stock selling at various levels of earnings performance. The regression equation for the interaction variables in Panel B is given in Appendix C.

The findings in Panel A show stock selling by the executives in response to new options only in quintile 1 when the firm has the highest earnings growth. The $\exists 1$ value is $-0.654$, which is very close to the 60% hedge ratio. Executives in this group, sell 654 shares of their own stocks for every 1,000 shares of new stock options awarded to them. The findings on new options in Panel B indicate stock selling by the high-ownership executives only when a firm's earnings are rising. The $\exists_1$ value of $-0.773$ and $\exists_2$ value

**Table 5.**  Firm performance, executive share ownership, and stock-based compensation.

| | | $H_0: \beta_i = 0$ (for $i = 1, \ldots, 5$) New options | $H_0: \beta_i = 1$ (for $i = 1, \ldots, 5$) Options exercised | $H_0: \beta_i = 1$ (for $i = 1, \ldots, 5$) Restricted shares |
|---|---|---|---|---|
| *Panel A: Interactions of compensation variable and earnings growth* | | | | |
| Constant | $\beta_0$ | 14.710 | −3.716 | 25.129[a] |
| Performance quintile 1 (highest income performance) | $\beta_1$ | −0.654[b] | −0.348[a,f] | 0.527[b,e] |
| Performance quintile 2 | $\beta_2$ | −0.144 | 0.228[a,f] | 1.426[b] |
| Performance quintile 3 | $\beta_3$ | −0.064 | −0.025[f] | −0.177[a,f] |
| Performance quintile 4 | $\beta_4$ | 0.211 | 0.231[b,f] | −0.348[f] |
| Performance quintile 5 (lowest income performance) | $\beta_5$ | 0.092 | 0.475[c,f] | 0.001[f] |
| Stock return | $\beta_6$ | −0.007 | 0.001 | −0.002 |
| | $N$ | 31,692 | 16,464 | 8,399 |
| Adjusted $R^2$ | | 0.043 | 0.029 | 0.001 |
| *Panel B: Interactions of compensation variable, executive ownership, and earnings growth* | | | | |
| Constant | $\beta_0$ | 8.618 | −6.812 | 22.685 |
| Stock-based compensation awarded to high-ownership executives in performance quintile 1 (highest performance) | $\beta_1$ | −0.773[b] | −0.449[b,f] | 0.416[a,f] |
| Stock-based compensation awarded to high-ownership executives in performance quintile 2 | $\beta_2$ | −0.280[b] | 0.270[f] | 0.991[a] |
| Stock-based compensation awarded to high-ownership executives in performance quintile 3 | $\beta_3$ | −0.110 | −0.031[f] | −0.182[b,f] |
| Stock-based compensation awarded to high-ownership executives in performance quintile 4 | $\beta_4$ | 0.259 | 0.282[b,f] | −1.154[f] |

(*Continued*)

**Table 5.**  (*Continued*)

| | $H_0: \exists_i = 0$ (for $i = 1, \ldots, 5$) New options | $H_0: \exists_i = 1$ (for $i = 1, \ldots, 5$) Options exercised | $H_0: \exists_i = 1$ (for $i = 1, \ldots, 5$) Restricted shares |
|---|---|---|---|
| Stock-based compensation awarded to high-ownership executives in performance quintile 5 (lowest performance) $\quad \exists_5$ | 0.134 | 0.493[c,f] | 0.086[f] |
| Stock-based compensation awarded to low-ownership executives in performance quintile 1 (highest performance) $\quad \exists_6$ | 0.127[c] | 0.213[b,f] | 0.681 |
| Stock-based compensation awarded to low-ownership executives in performance quintile 2 $\quad \exists_7$ | 0.041[b] | 0.068[c,f] | 2.947 |
| Stock-based compensation awarded to low-ownership executives in performance quintile 3 $\quad \exists_8$ | 0.011 | 0.052[f] | 0.615[b] |
| Stock-based compensation awarded to low-ownership executives in performance quintile 4 $\quad \exists_9$ | 0.147[c] | 0.066[f] | 0.430[c,f] |
| Stock-based compensation awarded to low-ownership executives in performance quintile 5 (lowest performance) $\quad \exists_{10}$ | 0.055 | 0.218[a,f] | 0.061[f] |
| Stock return $\quad \exists_{11}$ | −0.009 | 0.000 | −0.003 |
| $N$ | 31,666 | 16,451 | 8,392 |
| Adjusted $R^2$ | 0.053 | 0.037 | 0.001 |

*Note:* Regressions of annual changes in executive share ownership as a function of stock-based compensation, firm performance, and executive share ownership levels. In Panel A, annual change in shares owned by each executive is regressed on five interaction variables ($\exists_1$, $\exists_2$, $\exists_3$, $\exists_4$, and $\exists_5$) and current year's stock returns ($\exists_6$). The interaction variables are computed as stock-based compensation times 0–1 coded variables based on 3-year growth in operating income. For example, the interaction variable for $\exists_1$ is compensation variable times 1 if quintile 1 (firms with the highest 3-year growth in operating income), 0 otherwise. In Panel B, annual change in shares owned by each executive is regressed on ten interaction variables ($\exists_1$, $\exists_2$, $\exists_3$, $\exists_4$, $\exists_5$, $\exists_6$, $\exists_7$, $\exists_8$, $\exists_9$, and $\exists_{10}$) and current year's stock returns ($\exists_{11}$). The interaction variables are computed as compensation variable times 0–1 coded variable based on executive share ownership percentage times 0–1 coded variable based on 3-year growth in operating income times 0–1 coded variable based on executive share ownership percentage. For example, the interaction variable for $\exists_1$ is compensation variable times 1 if quintile 1, 0 otherwise, times 1 if executive share ownership percentage is greater than or equal to the sample median of 0.643%, 0 otherwise. Constants are expressed in thousands of shares. Significance of the coefficients is measured by heteroskedastic *t*-statistic (not reported below).

a,b,c  denote significant differences from 0 at the 10%, 5%, and 1%, respectively.
d,e,f  denote significant differences from 1 at the 10%, 5%, and 1%, respectively.

of $-0.280$ are significantly different from 0, whereas the $\beta_3$, $\beta_4$, and $\beta_5$ values are not significantly different from 0. For the low ownership executives, we observe an increase in shareholdings during both high and low levels of earnings growth. The coefficients $\beta_6$, $\beta_7$, and $\beta_9$ are all positive and statistically significant.

For options exercised and restricted stocks, we find results similar to those reported in Table 4. In Panel A, stock selling is observed at almost all levels of earnings performance. The $\beta$ values for all performance quintiles (except the $\beta_2$ value for restricted shares) are all significantly less than 1 indicating that stock selling in response to options exercise and restricted stock awards does not depend on earnings performance. Similar results are observed in Panel B that executives sell shares in response to options exercise and restricted shares awards, but the stock selling does not depend on earnings growth and executive ownership level. One exception appears to the low-ownership executives during high earnings growth. The $\beta$ values for low-ownership executives in quintiles 1–3 are not significantly less than 1.

In sum, the results in Table 5 provide evidence that executive stock selling in response to new stock options depends on firm's earnings performance. Stock selling is observed by the high-ownership executives when earnings are rising. The results for options exercise and restricted stocks indicate stock selling at all levels of earnings performance and executive ownership.

## 4. Conclusions and Discussions

Stock-based pay is awarded to corporate executives as an incentive to increase firm performance and shareholder wealth. When executives already own a high percentage of the firm's stock, any additional awards may not achieve the intended goal of incentive alignment. The executive may sell his own shares in the firm for portfolio diversification. Since poorly-performing firms grant substantial equity-based awards, stock selling in these firms may not increase managerial incentives and firm performance.

In this paper, we examine the extent to which compensation-based stock sales by corporate executives depend on firm performance. We find that high-ownership managers do not sell shares in response to stock option awards when earnings are declining. They sell shares only when the firm is experiencing a high earnings growth.

Our study addresses the basic question of whether or not the board's effort to improve firm performance through higher managerial ownership is effective. Although Ofek and Yermack's (2000) initial work establishes that stock compensation fails to increase ownership after a threshold level because of the diversification needs of the executives, we show that firm performance plays an important role in the executive's decision about holding shares. Our evidence that the executives hold on to their stocks during poor performance suggests that the increasing equity-based compensation during poor performance is achieving its intended goal.

## Appendix A

$$\Delta S_t = \beta_0 + \beta_1 O_{it} {}^* C_t + \beta_3 R_t \quad \text{for } O_{it} (i = 1, 2),$$ where $\Delta S_t$ is the change in shares owned by an executive in year $t$; $O_{1t} = 1$ if executive ownership percentage in year $t \geq 0.643\%$, 0 otherwise; $O_{2t} = 1$ if executive ownership percentage in year $t < 0.643\%$, 0 otherwise; $C_t$ the new options, options exercised, or restricted stocks awarded in year $t$; $R_t$ the current year's dividend-adjusted stock returns; and $\exists s$ are the parameter estimates.

Executive share ownership percentage is coded 1 if greater than or equal to the sample median of 0.643%, and coded 0 if less than 0.643%. $\exists_1$ is the compensation variable coefficient for high-ownership executives, $\exists_2$ is the compensation variable coefficient for low-ownership executives, and $\exists_3$ is the coefficient for the stock-return variable.

## Appendix B

$$\Delta S_t = \beta_0 + \beta_i P_{it} {}^* C_t + \beta_6 R_t \quad \text{for } P_{it} (i = 1, \dots, 5),$$ where $\Delta S_t$ is the change in shares owned by an executive in year $t$; $P_{1t} = 1$ if performance quintile 1 in year $t$, 0 otherwise; $P_{2t} = 1$ if performance quintile 2 in year $t$, 0 otherwise; $P_{3t} = 1$ if performance quintile 3 in year $t$, 0 otherwise; $P_{4t} = 1$ if performance quintile 4 in year $t$, 0 otherwise; $P_{5t} = 1$ if performance quintile 5 in year $t$, 0 otherwise; $C_t$ the new options, options exercised, or restricted stocks awarded in year $t$; $R_t$ the current year's dividend-adjusted stock returns; and $\exists s$ are the parameter estimates.

The annual change in shares owned by each executive is regressed on five interaction variables ($\exists_1, \exists_2, \exists_3, \exists_4,$ and $\exists_5$) and current year's stock returns ($\exists_6$). The interaction variables are computed as stock-based compensation times 0-1 coded variables based on 3-year growth in operating income. For example, the interaction variable for $\exists_1$ is compensation variable times 1 if quintile 1 (firms with the highest 3-year growth in operating income), 0 otherwise.

For new stock options, we test the null hypothesis that $\exists_i = 0$ (for $i = 1, \ldots, 5$), and for options exercised and restricted stocks awarded, we test the null hypothesis that $\exists_i = 1$ (for $i = 1, \ldots, 5$).

## Appendix C

$\Delta S_t = \beta_0 + \beta_i O_{it} * P_{it} * C_t + \beta_{11} R_t$    for $O_{it} (i = 1, 2)$ and for $P_{it} (i = 1, \ldots, 5)$, where $\Delta S_t$ is the change in shares owned by an executive in year $t$; $O_{1t} = 1$ if executive ownership percentage in year $t \geq 0.643\%$, 0 otherwise; $O_{2t} = 1$ if executive ownership percentage in year $t < 0.643\%$, 0 otherwise; $P_{1t} = 1$ if performance quintile 1 in year $t$, 0 otherwise; $P_{2t} = 1$ if performance quintile 2 in year $t$, 0 otherwise; $P_{3t} = 1$ if performance quintile 3 in year $t$, 0 otherwise; $P_{4t} = 1$ if performance quintile 4 in year $t$, 0 otherwise; $P_{5t} = 1$ if performance quintile 5 in year $t$, 0 otherwise; $C_t$ the new options, options exercised, or restricted stocks awarded in year $t$; $R_t$ the current year's dividend-adjusted stock returns; and $\exists s$ are the parameter estimates.

The annual changes in shares owned by each executive are regressed on ten interaction variables ($\exists_1, \exists_2, \exists_3, \exists_4, \exists_5, \exists_6, \exists_7, \exists_8, \exists_9$, and $\exists_{10}$) and current year's stock returns ($\exists_{11}$). For new stock options, we test the null hypothesis that $\exists_i = 0$ (for $i = 1, \ldots, 10$), and for options exercised and restricted stocks awarded, we test the null hypothesis that $\exists_i = 1$ (for $i = 1, \ldots, 10$).

## References

Allen, M. P., "Managerial Power and Tenure in the Large Corporation." *Social Forces* 60, 482–494 (1981).

Allen, M. P and S. Panian, "Power Performance and Succession in the Large Corporation." *Administrative Science Quarterly* 27, 538–547 (1982).

Boeker, W., "Power and Managerial Dismissal: Scapegoating at the Top." *Administrative Science Quarterly* 37, 400–421 (1992).

Carpenter, J. N and B. Remmers, "Executive Stock Option Exercises and Inside Information." *Journal of Business* 74, 513–534 (2001).

Denis, D. J., D. K. Denis and A. Sarin, "Ownership Structure and Top Executive Turnover." *Journal of Financial Economics* 45, 193–221 (1997).

Gilson, S. C. "Management Turnover and Financial Distress." *Journal of Financial Economics* 25, 241–262 (1989).

Gilson, S. C and M. R. Vetsuypens, "CEO Compensation in Financially Distressed Firms: An Empirical Analysis." *Journal of Finance* 48, 425–458 (1993).

Huddart, S and M. Lang, "Employee Stock Option Exercises: An Empirical Analysis." *Journal of Accounting and Economics* 21, 5–43 (1996).

Jensen, M. C and W. H. Meckling, "Theory of the Firm: Managerial Behavior, Agency Costs and Ownership Structure." *Journal of Financial Economics* 3, 305–360, (1976).

Jensen, M. C and K. J. Murphy, "CEO Incentives: It's Not How Much You Pay, But How." *Harvard Business Review* 68, 138–153 (1990).

Martin, K. J and J. J. McConnell, "Corporate Performance, Corporate Takeovers, And Management Turnover." *Journal of Finance* 46, 671–687 (June 1991).

McEachern, W. *Managerial Control and Performance*. Lexington, MA: Heath.

Mehran, H., "Executive Compensation Structure, Ownership, and Firm Performance." *Journal of Financial Economics* 38, 163–184 (1995).

Morck, R., A. Shleifer and R. W. Vishny, "Management Ownership and Corporate Performance." *Journal of Financial Economics* 20, 293–316 (1988).

Mikkelson, W. H and M. M. Partch, "Managers' Voting Rights and Corporate Control." *Journal of Financial Economics* 25, 263–290 (1989).

Ofek, E and D. Yermack, "Taking Stock: Equity-Based Compensation and the Evolution of Managerial Ownership." *Journal of Finance* 55, 1367–1384 (2000).

Song, M. H and R. A. Walkling, "The Impact of Managerial Ownership on Acquisition Attempts and Target Shareholder Wealth." *Journal of Financial and Quantitative Analysis* 28, 439–457 (1993).

Walsh, J. P. "Top Management Turnover Following Mergers and Acquisitions." *Strategic Management Journal* 9, 173–183 (1988).

Walsh, J. P and J. W. Ellwood, "Mergers, Acquisitions, and the Pruning of Managerial Deadwood." *Strategic Management Journal* 12, 201–217 (1991).

Chapter 3

# Management Compensation, Debt Contract, and Earnings Management Strategy

Chia-Ling Lee*
*National Chung Cheng University, Taiwan, R.O.C.*

Victor W. Liu
*National Sun Yat-sen University, Taiwan, R.O.C.*

Positive accounting theory hypothesizes that certain economic and contracting variables (such as earnings-based compensation and debt contracts) provide a manager with incentives to obtain his own self-interest by managing reported earnings. A separating equilibrium at stage 1 is developed in which the manager of a good firm selects an income-increasing strategy and the manager of a bad firm selects an income-decreasing strategy. We point out that the strategic use of a debt-contract, comprised of repayments and costly distress financing, can induce the manager to reveal his firm type by an earnings management strategy at stage 1. However, in the final stage a pooling equilibrium and a separate equilibrium can be obtained at the same time. In a pooling equilibrium the managers of two types both choose an income-increasing strategy to increase their compensation. However, if the manager of the bad firm takes his reputation into consideration, then he may have an incentive to choose the income-decreasing method. We can hence derive a separate equilibrium at stage 2.

**Keywords:** Debt contract; compensation; earnings management strategy; information asymmetry.

## 1. Introduction

A growing number of studies provide evidence supporting that earnings management is a widespread phenomenon (Healy, 1985; Merchant, 1990; Bruns and Merchant, 1990; Defond and Jiambalvo, 1994; Richardson, 2000). The theoretical literature related to earnings management has discussed the motivation and result behind earnings management under the condition of information asymmetry between the manager and the owner (Dye, 1988; Tureman and Titman, 1988; Hughes and Schwartz, 1988; Chaney and Lewis, 1995). Managers choose accounting procedures and accruals or change the accounting method in order to increase or decrease reported earnings. Positive accounting

---

*Corresponding author.

theory hypothesizes that economic and contracting variables induce the manager to manage reported earnings, e.g. increasing a manager's compensation or reducing the possibility of violating any provisions of debt covenants, and to smooth out reported earnings (see Healy, 1985; Schipper, 1989; Watts and Zimmerman, 1978, 1990). However, in this paper we demonstrate that the strategic use of a debt-contract and managerial compensation can motivate the choice of reporting earnings and reveal a manager's true type about the prospects under the existence of information asymmetry.

We review the literature related to the issue that discusses the effects of compensation and debt-contracts on creating incentives for earnings management. Several articles examine the effects of compensation contracts on earnings management incentives. Watts (1977) and Watts and Zimmerman (1978) point out that bonus schemes create an incentive for managers to select accounting policies that boost the value of their award. Healy (1985) and Holthausen, Larcker, and Sloan (1995) find a strong association between accruals and managers' income-based incentives under a bonus contract. Dechow and Sloan (1991) show that a CEO may reduce research and development spending in his final years in office in order to increase the reported earnings. This kind of CEO behavior is consistent with the short-term nature of many CEOs' compensation.

In addition to these empirical studies, several theoretical papers address managerial compensation and earnings management. Lambert (1984) and Dye (1988) demonstrate that risk-averse managers have an incentive to smooth earnings so as to smooth their compensation. Elitzur and Yaari (1995) show that the choice of a compensation scheme by owners affects earnings management. Chaney and Lewis (1995) consider managerial compensation to analyze how the strategic management of reported earnings influences investors' assessments of a firm's market value.

Aside from evidence which reveals the relation between compensation and earnings management, academic accountants have devoted much effort to obtain empirical evidence on the importance of debt agreements in determining accounting policy (see the reviews of Watts and Zimmerman (1990) and Christie (1990)). According to the Watts and Zimmerman (1990) survey, earlier empirical research studies generally support that the closer the firm is to violating accounting-based debt covenants, the more likely the firm will be in selecting an income-increasing strategy. DeFond and Jiambalvo (1994) and Sweeney (1994) examine debtors' manipulative behavior. They find that violations of accounting covenants are expensive to debtors and hence debtors will try to manipulate accounting numbers to avoid or defer defaults. Healy and Palepu (1990) and DeAngelo, DeAngelo and Skinner (1994) all indicate that firms in financial difficulty tend to place more emphasis on managing cash flows by reducing dividend payments and restructuring their operations and contractual relations.

The evidence provided by the above studies indicates that managers may manage earnings to increase bonus awards or to avoid debt covenant violations. In order to receive higher managerial compensation, managers with higher cash flows are more likely to choose an income-increasing method. Following the debt monitoring assumption provided by Jensen (1986, 1989), managers with higher debt are less likely to choose an income-increasing method. Although prior studies provide the effect of debt and compensation on earnings management, a manager's reporting choice is still unclear when we simultaneously consider the case of debt and compensation incentive. The manager is likely to increase reported earnings to increase bonus awards, but the size of a manager's compensation affects the ability of repaying. If the firm cannot repay, then its managers should be replaced.

What we are concerned with is how a manager decides an earnings management strategy given the trade-off between increasing bonus awards and increasing job security. Studies by Ross (1977), Ravid and Sarig (1991), and Brick, Frierman, and Kim (1998) have demonstrated that using financial policies, including the level of debt and dividends, can signal a firm's quality (e.g. cash flow and variance of cash flow) and help achieve a separating equilibrium. The main difference between our work and these three works is that this paper focuses on a manager's choice of earnings reporting based on the consideration of debt and managerial compensation.

This paper introduces the reaction of creditors to establish the debt-contract in a two-period setting. At the end of period 1, the manager's reported earnings influence the manager's awards. The paper then introduces the possibility of liquidation in a debt-contract. The manager considers that earnings are reported to ensure that no liquidation appears at the end of period 1. How a firm's true earnings and debt-contract influence the manager's earnings management strategy is also explained.

The approach adopted in this paper differs in two ways from previous earnings management studies. Firstly, we consider compensation and debt variables simultaneously to analyze a manager's earnings management strategy when he has private information about his firm's cash flow. This paper considers a debt-contract, which includes the possibility of reducing the borrowing based on a two-period model. Such a debt-contract is sufficient to induce the privately-informed manager to adopt different earnings management methods. Our arguments should view debt as an incentive in financial reporting. Secondly, prior studies indicate that a firm's private information about future profit influences the firm's earnings management strategy. Thereafter, we set the firm's prospect of true earnings to be the firm's private information. Our model indicates that the manager of a bad firm facing a trade-off between debt-contract covenant and managerial compensation would less likely select an income-increasing method. This result is also consistent with empirical evidence provided by Gul (2001), which indicates that the level of debt decreases the likelihood that managers have an incentive to choose an income-increasing method.

The remainder of this paper is organized as follows. In Section 2, we establish the economic setting of the basic model. In Section 3, a variant of the basic model is analyzed. We show the equilibrium of the earnings management strategy for different types of firms. The conclusions are summarized in Section 4.

## 2. The Basic Model

This section introduces a model that focuses on the manager's earnings management strategy for his/her compensations in a debt-contract setting. The model in this study applies versions of Gilles and Antoine (1998) for the debt-contract in a two-period setting. The owner of the firm hires a manager to operate the project and the manager has to choose a reporting system at the beginning of each period. In order to realize how debt-contracts affect the manager's reporting strategy, we outline what debt-contracts, earnings reporting strategy, and manager's compensation are in the following section.

### 2.1. *The debt-contract*

The firm has an initial wealth of $w$ and needs more capital to have access to a positive net cash flow project, which requires finance capital to undertake a project. Assume that the project is a two-period investment. The firm needs an issuance of debt at amount $B$ to undertake the two-period project. The firm has to repay $P_t$, at the end of stage $t$ whenever possible, $t = 1, 2.$[1] Here, $P_t$ includes the interest payment for period $t$ and the period $t$ repayment required by the creditor. The issuance of debt may incur some cost of financial distress. As cash flows are non-verifiable, feasible contracts can only specify that the firm repays the promised amounts, or otherwise the firm must raise additional funds to meet the repayment by using short-term financing or the creditor has the right to liquidate the assets.

Due to some transaction cost in the financial markets, distress financing is more costly than ordered financing. Thus, a financial shortfall incurs costs (e.g., Altman, 1984; Ravid and Sarig, 1991). When the credit, including the original debt financing and distress financing at the end of stage 1, is not paid at stage 2, the firm faces bankruptcy.[2] The firm will face the cost of distress financing and bankruptcy and will either raise debt at the end of stage 1 or not. Hence, this paper considers the condition of the probability of asset liquidation to proxy for the cost of distress financing. The firm generates $X_t$ at the end of stage $t$ when the assets are liquidated. The assets depreciate, and so we know $X_1 < B$. For simplicity, we assume $X_2 = 0.$[3]

## 2.2. *True earnings and reported earnings*

We attempt to model the sensibility and desirability of an earnings management strategy in a two-period setting. Consider a two-period, two-date setting with dates indexed by $t = 1, 2$. Productive activity takes place in each of the two periods. There are two types of firms in the economy, indexed by $i = L, H$. The firm with the higher true earnings from the project is referred to as the good firm (H-type firm). The company that yields the lower true earnings from the project is referred to as the bad firm (L-type firm). The manager has perfect knowledge of the firm's type $i \in \{H, L\}$, but potential creditors and the owner do not have.

The true income of firm $i$ from the project in each period is $\pi_{it}$, $i = H, L$; $t = 1, 2$. We refer to the firm's true income from the project as its type, and

---

[1]Think, for instance, of stages 1 and 2 as being the short-run stage and long-run stage, respectively.

[2]While the firm cannot repay the promised amount at stage 2 even if the firm issues new debt, the firm cannot raise debt at the end of stage due to a bad reputation.

[3]At the end of stage 2, the value of asset liquidation is very low due to asset depreciation. In a past version of Gilles and Antoine (1998), the analytical results were not affected by this assumption.

thus $\pi_{Ht} > \pi_{Lt}$. Here, $\pi_{it}$ is according to the following process: $\pi_{it} = \mu_i - e_{it}$. The true income in each period is affected by some random noise term $e_{it}$ and we assume that $e_{it}$ is stochastically independent with an identical normal distribution with variance $\sigma_i^2$ and zero mean and is stationary over time. The distribution of $\pi_{it}$ takes either a low value ($\mu_L$, $\sigma_L^2$) or a high value ($\mu_H$, $\sigma_H^2$).

After observing the true earnings, the firm chooses the reporting strategy. We suppose the manager has two strategies of earnings reporting. One is an income-increasing strategy, and the other is an income-decreasing strategy. The manager of an i-type firm reports earnings, $R_{it}^m$, if he/she chooses the $m$ reporting method, $m = D, I$. Symbol $I(D)$ is denoted to represent the reporting strategy of the income-increasing (income-decreasing) method. The earnings report consists of true income plus or minus an available earnings manipulation. Denote $\varepsilon^i$ to be the earnings manipulation accrual of an i-type firm. The manager's reported earnings are defined as:

$$R_{it}^m = \begin{cases} \pi_{it} + \varepsilon_{it} & \text{if } m = I \\ \pi_{it} - \varepsilon_{it} & \text{if } m = D \end{cases}; \quad i = H, L. \tag{1}$$

## 2.3. *Management compensation*

The manager is compensated in two periods. The manager's compensations are based on the reported earnings. This compensation scheme is analogous with the manager's compensation function set up by Elitzur and Yarri (1995). Furthermore, the measure of reported earnings used in a manager's compensation is consistent with empirical literature.

Many in the empirical literature have indicated evidence that managerial compensation is closely related to accounting measures of earnings and may even be more closely related to accounting measures of performance than to a stock market measure of performance (e.g., Antle and Smith, 1986; Lambert and Larcker, 1987; Kostiuk, 1989; Jensen and Murphy, 1990; Rosen, 1992). In addition, Rogerson (1997) shows that the other reason for managerial compensation based on accounting earnings is to provide a robust solution to the investment incentive problem. Rogerson (1997) also indicates that we can observe compensation contracts in the real world that are much more closely tied to stock market performance than to an accounting performance measure.

In an i-type firm, the manager chooses an $m$ accounting method to report earnings. The manager's compensations, $W_{it}^m$, can then be expressed as follows:

$$W_{it}^m = a + bR_{it}^m ,$$

where $a$ is the base salary, not contingent on earnings; and $b$ is the bonus rate, or the slope of a linear sharing rule.

After paying $W_{it}^m$ to the manager, an i-type firm can obtain $\pi_{it} - W_{it}^m$. The surplus cash flow $\pi_{it} - W_{it}^m$ is available for repaying creditors. The manager's compensations can affect the ability of the firm's repayments. However, the manager's reporting method influences his/her compensations. The manager will adopt an income-increasing method that enables him/herself to obtain a higher compensation, but it reduces the firm's ability to repay. The manager has to consider the trade-off when selecting the reporting method.

As described above, the sequence of the events is as follows:

- In stage 1:
  - ($A_1$) The owner of the firm signs the debt-contract. The firm borrows \$B from the creditor against a pledge to repay $\{P_t\}$, $t = 1, 2$.
  - ($A_2$) The cash flow is realized at the end of period 1, if the creditor accepts the debt-contract.
  - ($A_3$) The true cash flow is observed by the manager. The manager reports financial earnings according to the earnings management strategy.
  - ($A_4$) The manager is compensated based on reported earnings.
  - ($A_5$) The firm obtains cash flow from the project and repays $P_1$ to the creditor after payment compensation. If an i-type firm after choosing an $m$ reporting strategy cannot repay $P_1$, then a fraction $f_i^m$ of the assets is liquidated. Re-negotiation may occur until the firm is satisfied.

- In stage 2:
  - ($A_6$) The cash flow is realized if the firm still carries on in stage 2.
  - ($A_7$) The manager observes the true earnings and reports according to the reporting strategy.
  - ($A_8$) The manager is compensated based on reported earnings.
  - ($A_9$) The firm pays $P_2$ to the creditor.

In the case of default, the result of a re-negotiation implies that a fraction $f_i^m$ of the asset is liquidated given an $m$ reporting strategy of firm $i$. The operation capacity at stage 2 is then $1 - f_i^m$. Alternatively, $1 - f_i^m$ may be considered as a possibility for liquidation following a default. Assume the expected cash flow of the good firm is enough to repay at stages 1 and 2.

For a given debt-contract, a Perfect Bayesian Equilibrium in the finance market is defined by:

- Given a creditor's beliefs regarding the firm's type, the creditor decides a sequence of payments $\{P_1, P_2\}$ from the firm and a fraction of the asset being liquidated ($f_i^m$) to maximize his profit.
- According to the type of the firm, the manager reports his optimal earnings. A sequence of reported earnings describes the manager's earnings management strategy. Let $R_{it}^m(P_t)$ be the reported earnings at payment $P_t$, $t = 1, 2$.
- The creditor updates a probability distribution regarding his belief obtained by Bayes' rule and the manager's reporting equilibrium strategies.

The equilibrium in this paper is derived by reverse induction. The following section describes the manager's reporting strategy and the payment covenants.

## 3. Earnings Management Strategy and Debt Covenants

The manager's reports affect his/her compensations. The surplus' true earnings after deducting managerial compensation are available for repayment. In stage 2, the relationship between the surplus true earnings and the promised repayment of the debt-contract can influence the manager's reporting method. The manager's earnings management strategy in an i-type firm at stage 2 is as follows[4]:

$$R_{i2}^m(P_2) = \begin{cases} R_{i2}^I & \text{if } \pi_{i2} - W_{i2}^I \geq P_2, \\ R_{i2}^D & \text{otherwise.} \end{cases} \tag{2}$$

Using $R_{it}^m$ from Equation (1), we know that the promised repayment in the debt-contract will be:

$$P_2 = \begin{cases} \pi_{L2} - W_{L2}^D & \text{if } \lambda \left(\pi_{L1} - W_{L1}^D\right) \geq \pi_{L1} - W_{L1}^I, \\ \pi_{L2} - W_{L2}^I & \text{otherwise.} \end{cases} \tag{3}$$

---

[4]In stage 2 the earnings management strategy of a manager of an i-type firm could be initially expressed as:

$$R_{i2}^m(P_2) = \begin{cases} \pi^{iI} & \text{if } \left(1 - f_i^I\right) X_2 + \pi_2 - W_{i2}^I \geq P_2, \\ \pi^{iD} & \text{otherwise,} \end{cases}$$

where $f_i^I$ is the fraction of liquidation of the assets when the manager of an i-type firm adopts the I reporting strategy. However, we assume $X_2 = 0$, and the manager's earnings management strategy can be rewritten as Equation (2).

Here, $\lambda$ is the probability that the L-type firm knows that the manager does adopt an income-increasing strategy in stage 1.

In stage 1 the manager's reporting strategy can be expressed as follows:

$$R_{i1}^m(P_1) = \begin{cases} \pi_{i1}^I & \pi_{i1} - W_{i1}^I \geq P_1, \\ \pi_{i1}^D & \text{otherwise.} \end{cases} \tag{4}$$

From Equation (4), we know that if $\pi_{i1} - W_{i1}^I < P_1$, then the manager adopts an income-decreasing method in order to repay the debt, irrespective of the firm's type. However, we consider the case of $\pi_{i1} - W_{i1}^I \geq P_1$. When $\pi_{H1} - W_{H1}^I \geq P_1$ and $\pi_{L1} - W_{L1}^I < P_1$, the manager of an H-type firm would like to adopt an income-increasing strategy to report earnings, whereas the manager of an L-type firm would like to adopt an income-decreasing strategy. Thus, the maximum repayment for separating the reporting in stage 1 is: $P_1 = \pi_{H1} - W_{H1}^I$.

From $\pi_{H1} - W_{H1}^I \geq P_1 > \pi_{L1} - W_{L1}^I$, we derive the separating equilibrium that the manager of the bad firm chooses an income-decreasing strategy and the manager of the good firm chooses an income-increasing strategy. When the repayment of period 1 is set in the range of $\pi_{H1} - W_{H1}^I \geq P_1 > \pi_{L1} - W_{L1}^I$, the manager of an L-type firm expects a fraction $f_L^D$ of assets to be liquidated in case he adopts an income-increasing strategy. A fraction $f_L^D$ of liquidation of assets reduces the operation capacity, and the manager's compensation would then be reduced by the fraction.

When the creditor liquidates a fraction $f$ of the assets in stage 1, the manager looses at least $f_L^D \pi_{L2}$. Thus, the manager will prefer to repay in cash first and liquidate as little as possible. Once the manager is compensated based on reported earnings, the amount of cash left plus the return of liquidation are enough to repay $P_1$. Whenever the manager adopts an I strategy or D strategy, he has to accept the liquidation of a fraction $f$ of the assets such that:

$$\pi_{L1} - (a + bR_{L1}^I) + f_L^I \cdot X_1 = \pi_{L1} - (a + bR_{L1}^D) + f_L^D \cdot X_1 = P_1.$$

Thus, we can obtain that

$$f_L^I = \frac{f_L^D + 2b\varepsilon_{L1}}{X_1}. \tag{5}$$

**Lemma 1**

*There exists an optimal debt-contract in which the fraction of liquidation is satisfied: $f_L^I = f_L^D + 2b\varepsilon_{L1}/X_1$.*

Lemma 1 is a typical feature of a debt-contracting problem. Let us now describe the reason to explain why the manager of the bad firm adopts an income-decreasing strategy. The manager avoids losing compensation at stage 2 due to liquidation. Assume that the discount rate is zero. Thus, given that the manager adopts an income-decreasing method at stage 2, the manager of the $L$ firm is willing to adopt an income-decreasing strategy and obtain less compensation at period 1 if and only if he gets at least what he obtains by an income-increasing strategy. That is:

$$a + bR_{L1}^D + \left(1 - f_L^D\right)(a + b(\pi_{L2} - \varepsilon_{L2}))$$
$$\geq a + bR_{L1}^I + \left(1 - f_L^I\right)(a + b(\pi_{L2} - \varepsilon_{L2})). \tag{6}$$

The inequality in Equation (6) induces the manager of the bad firm to choose the income-decreasing strategy at $t = 1$. Thus, it follows from the inequality in Equation (6) binding that:

$$f_L^I(a + b(\pi_{L2} - \varepsilon_{L2})) = 2b\varepsilon_{L2} + f_L^D(a + b(\pi_{L2} - \varepsilon_{L2})). \tag{7}$$

Lemma 1 can simply be equality (7), we can rewrite (7) to be:

$$b = \frac{(X_1 - a)}{(\pi_{L2} - \varepsilon_{L2})}. \tag{8}$$

If the manager adopts an income-increasing method at stage 2, the manager of an $L$ firm is willing to adopt an income-decreasing strategy at period 1, and it will be set as:

$$a + bR_{L1}^D + (1 - f_L^D)(a + b(\pi_{L2} + \varepsilon_{L2}))$$
$$\geq a + bR_{L1}^I + (1 - f_L^I)(a + b(\pi_{L2} + \varepsilon_{L2})). \tag{9}$$

This implies that the bonus rate induces the manager of the bad firm to choose the income-decreasing strategy at period 1, which should be set as:

$$b = \frac{(X_1 - a)}{(\pi_{L2} - \varepsilon_{L2})} \tag{10}$$

The set of bonus rates available to managers (which are given by (8) and (10) with a parameter $X_1$) induces the manager of the bad firm to choose the income-decreasing strategy. The value of the bonus rate increases with the value of liquidation. This implies that the owner should provide a higher bonus rate when the value of liquidation increases. If the liquidation is inefficient, then the owner could avoid liquidation by setting a bonus rate. The threat of bad consequences associated with liquidation makes the owner provide higher incentives in the compensation contract. Thus, it can be said that in a separating equilibrium, the manager of the bad firm adopts an income-increasing method, as the left cash flow is not enough for repayment.

The possibility of liquidation decreases stage 2's payoff. A combination of the possibility of liquidation and the bonus rate in the compensation contract makes the income-increasing strategy unfavorable to the manager of the bad firm. It is now shown that under asymmetric information, with regards to the firm's true earnings, from the two-period project the debt-contract and bonus rate induce the manager of the bad firm to adopt an income-decreasing strategy.

## Proposition 1
*At stage 1, a separating equilibrium, in which the manager of the good firm chooses an income-increasing strategy and the manager of the bad firm chooses an income-decreasing strategy, is obtained if and only if: $\pi_{H1} - W_{H1}^{I} \geq P_1 > \pi_{L1} - W_{L1}^{I}$. Hence, the value of the bonus rate increases with the value of liquidation.*

We know that $P_1 > \pi_{L1} - W_{L1}^{I}$. If $f_L^I \neq 0$, then $P_1 = \pi_{L1} - W_{L1}^{I} + f_L^I X_1$ can hold. In a separating equilibrium at stage 1, the manager of the bad firm gives up some compensation in order to maintain the size of operation in stage 2. At this time, the owner should set the optimal bonus rate of the manager's compensation in order to influence the manager's reporting strategy.

The expectation of liquidation induces the manager of the bad firm to adopt an income-decreasing method. For the parameter value of repayment, the owner makes sure that the manager of the bad firm chooses the income-increasing method to enjoy higher compensation, which will trigger liquidation. The manager of the bad firm prefers a reduction of compensation to a liquidated loss. Thus, the manager of the bad firm prefers the income-decreasing strategy rather than the income-increasing strategy.

A good firm is identified as one that expects to achieve a higher profit from the project. A good firm has the ability to repay the creditor. The compensation is based on the reported earnings. The manager has an incentive to make an increase in the reported earnings in order to be paid a higher compensation.

At stage 1 the manager of the good firm chooses an income-increasing strategy and the manager of the bad firm chooses an income-decreasing strategy.

The implication is that the strategic use of a debt-contract and compensation-contract induces the manager to reveal the firm's type in stage 1 by earnings management strategies. If the repayment is too high for the manager of the bad firm when he/she chooses an income-increasing strategy, then the firm expects a low cash flow and the owner should set the covenant of early repayment and increase the bonus rate. Thus, when the manager considers the earnings reporting strategy, he/she will not only care about capturing benefits for himself, but also keep the firm away from being liquidated.

At stage 1 the strategic use of debt and compensation can induce the manager to reveal his firm type. However, whether the separating equilibrium of the manager's earnings management strategy can be achieved or not depends on the degree of the manager's reputation. The following proposition summarizes the argument at stage 2.

**Proposition 2**

*At stage 2, there exists a separating equilibrium and a pooling equilibrium regarding the manager's earnings management strategy. A separating equilibrium exists, in which the manager of the good firm chooses the income-increasing strategy and the manager of the bad firm chooses the income-decreasing strategy, when the manager indeed does not want to cause default. A pooling equilibrium, in which the managers of the good firm and the bad firm choose the income-increasing strategy, can possibly be obtained, if the manager of the bad firm prefers high compensation to avoidance of default.*

According to Proposition 1, we know that the manager of the bad firm chooses the income-decreasing strategy $t$. The ex-post belief of the owner regarding $\lambda$ is $\lambda = 1$, i.e., the manager of the bad firm does not adopt the income-increasing method. Hence, by Equation (3), we obtain $P_2 = \pi_{L2} - W^D_{L2}$. Therefore, $P_2 \leq \pi_{L2} - W^D_{L2}$, and we then know that the manager of the good firm will choose the income-increasing strategy at stage 2. In order to avoid default at stage 2, the manager of the bad firm will choose an income-decreasing strategy. However, the project is only for two periods. At stage 2, the liquidation of assets does not have an impact on the sequential compensation of the manager of the bad firm. Choosing the income-increasing method increases the earnings report. Hence the manager can obtain higher compensation by choosing the income-increasing method rather than the income-decreasing method. Thus, the manager of the bad firm has the incentive to adopt the income-increasing strategy at stage 2 for higher compensation in period 2.

If the event of liquidation of assets has an impact on the manager's reputation, then it may force the manager of the bad firm to choose the income-decreasing method. When the manager of the bad firm is concerned about his/her reputation, he/she may protect the firm and cover the firm's repayment at the expense of his/her compensation. This may be the reason why some bad firms report high earnings and some provide low earnings. Their managers have different considerations.

In the above equilibrium, both the available reporting discretion and the fraction of liquidation influence the repayment of the debt-contract. In order to make a manager of the bad firm reveal the firm's type at an early stage, the repayment of stage 1 should be set higher when the value of liquidation of the assets is higher. Since the project is a two-period investment in our setting, the fraction of liquidation would be useful in separating the types of firms at stage 2. This implies that the possibility of liquidation induces the manager to adopt an income-decreasing strategy at the end of the debt-contract when the manager is concerned about his/her reputation or because of the bad consequences associated with liquidation.

## 4. Conclusions

In a firm, the owner hires the manager to operate the business and the manager's compensation is partly based on the reported earnings. The manager can secretly observe the future cash flow from the given projects. If the manager chooses the income-increasing method, then he/she would be paid more compensation. However, this will result in a reduction of the available amount of cash flow for the repayment, and hence the firm might possibly face liquidation. This paper constructs a two-period debt-contract to analyze how compensation and debt-covenants influence the firm's earnings management strategy, when the firm possesses private information regarding the expected cash flow. This paper demonstrates that a debt-contract can be thought of as an incentive scheme for firms choosing an earnings management strategy. Furthermore, long-term debt can induce the firm to reveal its private information regarding the expected cash flow at the initial stage.

This paper assumes that the firm's expectation of cash flow is either high or low and introduces the possibility of liquidation into modeling the debt-contract. We describe how the possibility of liquidation induces the manager of the bad firm not to maximize his/her own self-interests by increasing the reported earnings. The left-over cash flow of the bad firm will not be enough to make the repayments if the manager increases the reported earnings for his/her own self-interests. On the other hand, the good firm will produce enough cash flow irrespective of the chosen reporting strategy. In such a case, there will be a separate equilibrium at stage 1. The manager of the bad firm will then adopt the income-decreasing strategy to escape liquidation. Hence, the manager of the good firm will adopt an income-increasing strategy to increase his/her own interests. The higher the expectation is for being liquidated at the end of period 1, the more the manager of the bad firm will be induced to adopt the income-decreasing strategy. In a separate equilibrium, the results indicate that the owner should provide a higher bonus rate when the value of liquidation increases. The owner could adjust the bonus rate to avoid liquidation.

The debt-contract is a two-period contract. The threat of liquidation may not be a useful incentive in influencing the manager's choice of earnings management strategy. At stage 2, a pooling equilibrium and a separate equilibrium may exist at the same time. In a pooling equilibrium, managers of the two types of firms choose the income-increasing strategy, because they would like to increase their own self-interests. However, liquidation breaks down the manager's reputation. When the manager of the bad firm is concerned about his/her reputation, he/she may have an incentive to choose the income-decreasing method. We can then derive a separate equilibrium in which the manager of the bad firm adopts an income-decreasing strategy and the manager of the good firm adopts an income-increasing strategy at the final stage.

This paper studies how the liquidation of the debt-contract affects a manager's earnings management strategy. A situation in which the firm faces a threat of liquidation is like the situation of a takeover. Future research may include the study of the choice of reported earnings when the firm faces a friendly and/or hostile takeover.

## References

Altman, E. I., "A Further Empirical Investigation of the Bankruptcy Cost Question." *Journal of Finance* 39, 1067–1089 (1984).
Antle, R. and A. Smith, "An Empirical Investigation of the Relative Performance Evaluation of Corporate Executives." *Journal of Accounting Research* 24, 1–39 (1986).

Brick, I. E., M. Frierman and Y. K. Kim, "Asymmetric Information Concerning the Variance of Cash Flows: The Capital Structure Choice." *International Economic Review* 39, 745–761 (1998).

Bruns, W. J. and K. A. Merchant, "The Dangerous Morality of Managing Earnings." *Management Accounting* 72, 22–25 (1990).

Chaney, P. K. and C. M. Lewis, "Earnings Management and Firm Valuation Under Asymmetric Information." *Journal of Corporate Finance* 1, 319–345 (1995).

Christie, A., "Aggregation of Test Statistics: An Evaluation of Evidence on Contracting and Size Hypotheses." *Journal of Accounting and Economics* 12, 15–36 (1990).

DeAngelo, H., L. DeAngelo and D. J. Skinner, "Accounting Choice in Troubled Companies." *Journal of Accounting and Economics* 17, 113–144 (1994).

Dechow, P. M. and R. G. Sloan, "Executive Incentives and the Horizon Problem: An Emperical Investigation." *Journal of Accounting and Economics* 14, 51–90 (1991).

Defond, M. and J. Jiambalovo, "Debt Covenant Violation and Manipulation of Accruals" *Journal of Accounting and Economics* 17, 145–176 (1994).

Dunk, J. C., D. P. Franz and H. G. Hunt III, "An Examination of Debt-Equity Proxies V.S. Actual Debt Covenant Restrictions in Accounting Choice Studies." *Journal of Business Finance and Accounting* 22, 615–635 (1995).

Dye, R., "Earnings Management in Overlapping Generations Model." *Journal of Accounting Research* 26, 195–235 (1988).

Elitzur, R. R. and V. Yaari, "Executive Incentive Compensation and Earnings Manipulation in a Multi-period Setting." *Journal of Economic Behavior and Organization* 26, 201–219 (1995).

Gilles, C. and F. G. Antoine, "Dynamic Adverse Selection and Debt." Working Paper, Les Financial Markets Group (1998).

Gul, F. A., "Free Cash Flow, Debt-monitoring and Manager's LIFO/FIFO Police Choice." *Journal of Corporate Finance* 7, 475–492 (2001).

Healy, P. M. and K. G. Palepu, "Effectiveness of Accounting-based Dividend Covenants." *Journal of Accounting and Economics* 12, 97–124 (1990).

Healy, P., "The Effect of Bonus Schemes on Accounting Decision." *Journal of Accounting and Economics* 7, 85–107 (1985).

Holthausen, R. W., D. F. Sloan and G. Richard, "Annual Bonus Schemes and the Manipulation of Earnings." *Journal of Accounting and Economics* 19, 29–75 (1995).

Hughes, P. J. and E. S. Schwartz, "The LIFO/FIFO Choice: An Asymmetric Information Approach." *Journal of Accounting Research* 26, 41–58 (1988).

Jensen, M. C., "Agency Costs of Free Cash Flow, Corporate Finance and Takeovers."*American Economic Review* 76, 323–339 (1986).

Jensen, M. C., "Eclipse of Public Corporation." *Harvard Business Review* 5, 61–74 (1989).

Jensen, M. C. and K. J. Murphy, "Performance Pay and Top-Management Incentives." *Journal of Political Economy* 98, 225–264 (1990).

Kostiuk, P. F., "Firm Size and Executive Compensation." *Journal of Human Resources* 25, 90–105 (1989).

Lambert, R. A. and D. F. Larcker, "An Analysis of the Use of Accounting and Market Measures of Performance in Executive Compensation Contracts." *Journal of Accounting Research* 25, 85–125 (1987).

Lambert, R., "Income Smoothing As Rational Equilibrium Behavior." *Accounting Review* 59, 604–618 (1984).

Merchant, K. A., "The Effects of Financial Controls on Data Manipulation and Management Myopia." *Accounting, Organizations and Society* 15, 297–314 (1990).

Ravid, S. A. and O. H. Sarig, "Financial Signalling by Committing to Cash Outflows." *Journal of Financial and Quantitative Analysis* 26, 165–180 (1991).

Richardson, V. J., "Information Asymmetry and Earnings Management: Some Evidence." *Review of Quantitative Finance and Accounting* 15, 325–347 (2000).

Rogerson, W. P., "Intertemporal Cost Allocation and Managerial Investment Incentives: A Theory Explaining the Use of Economic Value Added as a Performance Measure." *Journal of Political Economy* 105, 770–795 (1997).

Ross, S. A., "The Determination of Financial Structure: The Incentive-Signalling Approach." *The Bell Journal of Economics* 8, 23–40 (1977).

Schipper, K., "Earnings Management," Accounting Horizons, Dec. 1989, pp. 91–102.

Sweeney, A., "Debt-covenant Violation and Managerial Participation." *Journal of Accounting Research and Economics* 17, 281–308 (1994).

Trueman, B. and S. Titman, "An Explanation for Accounting Income Smoothing." *Journal of Accounting Research* 26, 127–139 (1988).

Watts, R. and J. L. Zimmerman, "Towards a Positive Theory of the Determination of Accounting Standards." *Accounting Review* 53, 112–134 (1978).

Watts, R. and J. L. Zimmerman, "Positive Accounting Theories: A Ten Perspective." *Accounting Review* 65, 131–156 (1990).

Watts, R., "Corporate Financial Statements: Product of the Market and Political Processes." *Australian Journal of Management* 2, 53–75 (1977).

Chapter 4

# Risky Debt-Maturity Choice Under Information Asymmetry

Sheen Liu

*Youngstown State University, USA*

Chunchi Wu*

*Singapore Management University, Singapore and*
*Syracuse University, USA*

The traditional equilibrium models of signaling with debt-maturity require transaction costs by firms when raising new capital. In this paper, we propose a new model that has no such requirement. We demonstrate that a separating equilibrium of debt-maturity choice exists under a much more general condition, once accounting for the interactions between borrowers and lenders. The model is able to explain the observed complex financial structure. It is found that callable debt functions much like short-term debt, and serial debt similar to long-term debt. In equilibrium, high-quality firms issue short-term debt, and low-quality firms issue long-term debt.

**Keywords:** Bond maturity; information asymmetry; signaling; sequential games.

## 1. Introduction

Under information asymmetry, firm insiders with better information than outside investors will choose to issue those securities the market appears to value most. Knowing this, rational investors will try to infer insider information from firms' financing strategies. Signaling theory contends that under certain conditions firms' choice of risky debt-maturity can convey the insider information about firm quality.[1] Plausible signaling equilibria often require transaction costs by firms when raising capital (see, e.g., Bhattacharya, 1979; Flannery, 1986). In particular, for firms to signal their true quality to the market effectively, transaction costs of issuing or retiring debts must be high enough to deter low-quality firms from mimicking high-quality firms.[2] Conversely, when

---

*Corresponding author.

[1] See Ravid (1996) for a review of debt-maturity signaling literature.

[2] See Flannery (1986) and Wu (1993).

financial market transactions are costless and changes in firm value are independent over time, firms' debt-maturity structure may fail to provide a credible signal. Kale and Noe (1990) examine the decision of debt-maturity choice using precise equilibrium refinements. They demonstrate that in the absence of transaction costs, there is no separating Nash sequential equilibrium since low-quality firms always have an incentive to mimic high-quality firms. Under this condition, both short- and long-term debt poolings are Nash sequential equilibrium outcomes, but only the short-term debt pooling equilibrium is universally divine.[3] On the other hand, a separating equilibrium exists if there are transaction costs and investment outcomes are correlated. Diamond (1991, 1993) shows that liquidity risk may force low-quality firms to use short-term debt, leaving only intermediate-quality firms to issue long-term debt.[4] Using a different approach, Titman (1992) shows that a separating debt-market equilibrium can be obtained if swap agreements are allowed to resolve the problem of interest rate uncertainty.

The requirement of transaction costs for a separating equilibrium may be due to the underlying assumptions in signaling models, some of which are arguably refutable. For example, previous studies often contend that without transaction costs, there is only one plausible outcome for firms' debt-maturity choice ($M$): both "Good" (G) and "Bad" (B) firms choose to issue short-term debt, $M = \{S, S\}$. A critical assumption behind these models is that investors will price risky debt at the average quality of firms where the distribution of quality is prior knowledge. This assumption results in a pooling equilibrium in which the value of Bad firms increases at the expense of Good firms (see Rothschild and Stiglitz, 1976; Ross, 1977; Campbell and Kracaw, 1980). The separating equilibrium is not forthcoming because Bad firms can always mimic Good firms in the absence of transaction costs.

However, the outcome of pooling may not be incentive-compatible. It is not necessarily costless for Bad firms to mimic Good firms. When the time comes for Bad firms to refinance their debt, they will more likely be in a worse

---

[3]Note that when the assumption of independent changes in firm value is relaxed, Kale and Noe (1990) demonstrate that a separating equilibrium may exist, in which high-quality firms issue short-term debt and low-quality firms issue long-term debt.

[4]Diamond (1991) does not explicitly assume transaction costs. In his model, forced liquidation results in a loss of management's control rent. In a sense, lost control rent is an opportunity cost of signaling. It can be shown that an absence of the control rent would result in a pooling equilibrium. Guedes and Opler (1996) and Stohs and Mauer (1996) find results consistent with Diamond's predictions.

state and to pay a much higher premium to refinance short-term debt. Bad firms ought to consider this consequence when deciding whether they should mimic Good firms. Even without transaction costs, mimicking may not be the best strategy for Bad firms because they may be penalized upon refinancing their short debt.[5]

A simple example may help illustrate this point. Two applicants apply for the same job, and the employer offers two contracts, short- and long-term. The short-term contract offers a higher annual salary than does the long-term contract, and there are no other costs for renewing the contracts. Knowing her own productivity, the "Good" applicant does not worry about the renewal of her contract and so prefers the short-term contract. Although the "Bad" applicant can also get a higher salary by signing the short-term contract, she knows that she may not be able to renew her contract after it expires. Thus, mimicking the "Good" applicant is not costless. If the cost of mimicking is greater than the gain from the higher salary of the short-term contract, the "Bad" applicant will prefer the long-term contract. If the employer can somehow design the contract optimally to allow each candidate to differentiate herself, a separating equilibrium can arise.

One serious drawback of traditional debt-maturity models is that they assume investors are not actively involved in the signaling game. A direct consequence is that the pricing mechanism of debts is exogenously given, instead of being endogenously derived from investors' rational choices. In this setting, investors wait passively for the outcome of the game between Good and Bad firms. If both firms choose to issue short-term debt, investors will price this debt at the average quality of firms, resulting in a pooling equilibrium. Conversely, if Good firms borrow short and Bad firms borrow long, investors will price short debt at the quality of Good firms and long debt at the quality of Bad firms, resulting in a separate equilibrium. Either the pooling or the separating equilibrium is the outcome of the game solely between Good and Bad firms, and investors cannot influence their financing strategy. For example, Good firms will choose to issue short-term debt only if the added refinancing cost of a rollover strategy is smaller than their misinformation value in the pooling equilibrium. A separating equilibrium can occur when at the same time the gain that Bad firms achieve from issuing short-term debt is less than the flotation cost

---

[5]The recent events of Enron, Tyco, and WorldCom are excellent examples of how market discipline is enforced. After investors discover that truthful information was not disclosed, these firms can no longer have normal access to debt-markets.

incurred. When these conditions are not met, both firms will issue the same debt and a pooling equilibrium occurs. Firms optimally (or suboptimally) choose a debt-maturity structure based on market conditions, and investors play little role in this process.

The assumption that investors are inactive is rather unrealistic. In reality, investors (particularly institutional investors) in the debt-market often interact with the issuers or investment bankers to come to an agreement with the terms of debts. Market equilibrium is typically an outcome of interactions between suppliers and demanders. Investors can change their pricing strategy to affect the firm's debt choice and ultimately alter the equilibrium outcome. Like the aforementioned example of labor contracts, investors may set different terms for borrowers so that they will reveal their true credit quality.

In this paper, we propose an alternative model of debt-maturity choice that accounts for the interactions between borrowers and lenders. In this model, both firms and investors play an important role in the determination of a debt-market equilibrium. Good firms have an incentive to differentiate themselves from Bad firms to reduce their debt financing costs. Investors have an incentive to identify Bad firms to reduce their investment risk associated with adverse selection. Good firms use different debt instruments to signal their credit quality to the market. Investors actively search for an optimal pricing scheme to induce firms to differentiate among themselves by choosing different debt instruments. Including investors as active strategic players in the game produces an equilibrium outcome dramatically different from previous ones. We show that a separating equilibrium of debts with different maturities exists under a much more general condition. In particular, flotation costs are no longer required for the existence of a separating equilibrium.

The model is capable of explaining the complicated debt structure observed in the financial world. It is found that bond covenants are useful for resolving the problem of asymmetric information. For example, the call provision can reduce the misinformation value (dead-weight cost) or the cost of signaling in achieving the informational equilibrium. Similarly, the sinking-fund provision conveys the quality of the bond issuers. The sinking-fund call feature is shown to reinforce the effect of the amortization scheme in resolving the problem of asymmetric information faced by the issuers. In contrast, serial debt with no sinking-fund calls behaves much like long-term debt. Thus, bond covenants may either enhance the maturity effect or simply serve a function similar to debt-maturity in corporate financing decisions.

The remainder of this paper is organized as follows: Section 2 presents a pricing model of debts with asymmetric information. Section 3 discusses investors' pricing strategies and derives the equilibrium of a sequential game including the investor as a player. Section 4 provides numerical examples to illustrate the separating equilibrium with and without flotation costs. Finally, Section 5 concludes the paper.

## 2. The Model

This section sets up a valuation model of long- and short-term bonds under information asymmetry. The key assumptions underlying this model are summarized as follows:

(A.1)  There are two periods in the model. Each firm invests in a single project at the beginning of period 1, $t_0$. The project is liquidated at the end of period 2, $t_2$, and the distribution of its liquidation value is common knowledge. The liquidation values are $M_3$, $M_4$, and $M_5$, where $M_3 > M_4 > M_5$. The probabilities of reaching different states and final liquidation values are displayed in Figure 1.[6] The firm does not default at any state except $S_5$. At state $S_5$, $M_5$ is zero; that is, there is no residual value, or the recovery rate of the debt is zero upon default.[7] At $t_0$, the firm must borrow an exogenous amount of debt $D$ to finance the project, which generates no cash flow before its liquidation at $t_2$.

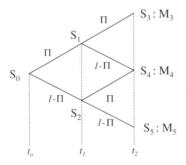

**Figure 1.**   The two-period binomial tree of the firm's project.

---

[6]The setup of this probability structure is similar to Flannery (1986).

[7]To simplify the problem, $M_5 = 0$ is assumed. This assumption can be easily relaxed to consider the seniority of debts.

(A.2)  Two types of debt instruments are considered for financing the project: long-term and short-term debts. Long-term debt lasts for two-periods, whereas short-term debt lasts only for one-period.

(A.3)  When a short debt is retired at the end of the first period, $t_1$, it is refinanced with another short debt maturing at $t_2$. We refer to the combination of two short debts as the "short-term" financing strategy and the issuance of long debt as the "long-term" strategy.

(A.4)  In the discrete case, we assume two types of firms: "Good" firms have projects with an "up" probability $p = p_G$, and "Bad" firms have projects with $p = p_B < p_G$. Investors know the fact that $\theta$ percent of firms (projects) are "Good," but they cannot identify a particular firm's quality. In the continuous case, the true "up" probability, $p$, for each firm is unobservable and distributed on $p \in L = (0, 1)$, according to a strictly increasing function $f(p) \in C^\infty$. We use the discrete case to illustrate the fundamental principle of choice between long and short debts. The discrete case is then extended to a continuous distribution of credit quality to generalize the results to multiple debt instrument choice.

(A.5)  There is information asymmetry in the sense that the management's information set is different from outside investors'. Consequently, the management's perception of the "up" probability ($\Pi = p$) differs from investors' ($\Pi = \pi$). Investors have homogeneous expectations and adopt the same rule of valuation on risky claims.

(A.6)  Firm managers and investors are risk-neutral, expected wealth maximizers.

Given the estimate of "up" probability, $\pi$, risk-neutral investors require an interest factor (one plus the coupon rate) on the long-term debt issued at $t_0$, $R_L^\pi$, such that the expected payoff on risky debt equals the principal amount lent:

$$F = \pi F R_L^\pi + (1 - \pi)\pi F R_L^\pi. \tag{1}$$

This equality yields an interest factor for the long-term debt

$$R_L^\pi = \frac{1}{2\pi - \pi^2}. \tag{2}$$

The risk-neutral manager's valuation of equity when pursuing a long-term borrowing strategy is

$$V_L = p\{p\lfloor M_3 - R_L^\pi F\rfloor + (1 - p)\lfloor M_4 - R_L^\pi F\rfloor\} + (1 - p)p\lfloor M_4 - R_L^\pi F\rfloor. \tag{3}$$

Substituting Equations (2) into (3) and rearranging yields

$$V_L = V^i + V_L^{mis} \tag{4}$$

where the firm's value is composed of an intrinsic value

$$V^i = p^2 M_3 + 2p(1-p)M_4 - F \tag{5}$$

and a misinformation value

$$V_L^{mis} = F \frac{2(\pi - p) + (p^2 - \pi^2)}{2\pi - \pi^2}, \tag{6}$$

which is caused by asymmetric information. The misinformation value is represented by the difference between the value viewed by the outside investor (reflected in his $\pi$ estimate) and its fair value based on the insider's information (for $p$).

The firm issuing short-term debt retires it at $t_1$. By (A.1), no default occurs at $t_1$ and so the entire principal $F$ is retired (the coupon rate is zero) and the same amount of short debt is reissued. At state $S_1$, investors require an interest factor $(R_1^\Pi | S_1)$ for short debt. Similarly, at state $S_2$, given investors' estimate of "up" probability $\Pi = \pi$, investors require an interest factor $(R_1^\pi | S_2)$ for short debt. Thus, for the short debt issued at $t_0$, risk-neutral investors will require one-period interest factors such that

$$F = \pi F(R_1^\pi | S_1) + (1 - \pi)F\pi(R_1^\pi | S_2) \tag{7}$$

Lemma 1 establishes the values of the short-term interest factors $(R_1^\Pi | S_i)$, $i = 1, 2$ at different states.

**Lemma 1**

The short-term interest factor for refinancing at $t_1$ is given by

$$(R_1^\pi | S_1) = 1, \qquad (R_1^\pi | S_2) = \frac{1}{\pi}. \tag{8}$$

**Proof.** At state $S_1$, $F$ amount of short debt is retired, and the same amount of short debt is re-issued. At this state, investors know that short debt is default-free, and thus, they charge an interest factor $(R_1^\Pi | S_1) = 1$. At state $S_2$, given the estimate of "up" probability $\Pi$, investors know that short debt has a default probability of $1 - \Pi$ and a recovery rate of zero. Thus, they require an interest factor

$$(R_1^\pi | S_2) = \frac{1}{\pi}. \tag{9}$$

Alternatively, using $(R_1^\Pi | S_1) = 1$ and Equation (7), we have

$$F = \pi F + (1 - \pi)\pi F (R_1^\pi | S_2)$$

by which we can solve for the one-period interest factor at state $S_2$

$$(R_1^\pi | S_2) = \frac{1}{\pi}$$

Note that we made no assumption before that investors know the true probability of the "up" state for each firm's project. The values of the interest factors in Equations (2) and (9) depend on investors' *estimate* of the "up" probability $\pi$. Setting $\Pi = \pi$, we can obtain the interest factors required by investors for both short and long debts. For ease of notation, we henceforth replace $(R_1^\Pi | S_1)$ with one, and $(R_1^\Pi | S_2)$ with $R_1^\Pi$.

The risk-neutral manager's valuation of equity under the short-term debt financing strategy is

$$V_S = p\{p[M_3 - F] + (1 - p)[M_4 - F]\} + (1 - p)p\lfloor M_4 - F R_1^\pi \rfloor. \quad (10)$$

Substituting Equation (9), with $R_1^\Pi$ evaluated at $\Pi = \pi$, into Equation (10) and rearranging, we have

$$V_S = V^i + V_S^{\text{mis}}, \qquad V_S^{\text{mis}} = F(1 - p)\frac{\pi - p}{\pi}. \quad (11)$$

Previous studies (see, e.g., Flannery, 1986; Kale and Noe, 1990; Diamond, 1991) have implicitly assumed that investors take a passive role in the determination of the signaling equilibrium. We denote the pricing strategy when investors are inactive as *pricing strategy A*. Under this pricing strategy, the values of the "up" probability are determined according to firms' debt-maturity choices ($M$):

1. If $M = \{L, S\}$ or $M = \{S, L\}$, then $\pi_S = p_G$ and $\pi_L = p_B$.[8]
2. If $M = \{L, L\}$ or $M = \{S, S\}$, then $\pi_S$ or $\pi_L$ is chosen so that $\sum_i V_i^{\text{mis}}(q) = 0$,

where $i = S$ (short debt), $L$ (long debt), and $q = G$ (good firm), $B$ (bad firm). In the first case, Good and Bad firms choose different financing strategies, and so the probability of the "up" state is assigned according to the quality of each firm. In the second case, Good and Bad firms choose the same financing

---

[8]Previous studies (Flannery, 1986; Kale and Noe, 1990; Diamond, 1990) show that $M = \{L, S\}$ is not a viable separating equilibrium.

strategy. Since it is not possible to distinguish Good from Bad firms through their financing patterns, an average price is charged to all bonds such that the aggregate misinformation value is equal to zero. On the sell side of the market, Bad firms gain and Good firms lose. On the buy side, those who invest in Bad firms' bonds pay an excessive price.

There are two potential difficulties with this pricing strategy commonly adopted in the existing debt-maturity literature: First, the pricing strategy presumes that investors will accept whatever pricing rules that are given. However, if investors are rational, they should be able to choose a pricing rule that better serves their interests. Second, it assumes no investor learning. In reality, investors may receive a signal, $m \in M$, conveyed by firms or information agencies. They may then estimate $\pi$ based on $m$ and price the debts either under the separating equilibrium or under the pooling equilibrium. In either case, investors' pricing strategy would be based on their best assessment of $\pi$, rather than on a passive reaction to firms' debt choice or an exogenously given pricing rule. The pricing strategy chosen by investors should directly affect the firm's choice of debt or alternatively, the firm's financing decision should take into account the expected pricing strategy of the investors. In the following section, we discuss an alternative pricing strategy and a sequential game in which investors' pricing strategy is explicitly accounted for.

## 3. Debt-Market Equilibrium

Under information asymmetry, investors are uncertain about the quality of Good and Bad firms. This uncertainty could cause a mispricing of bonds with investors paying an excessive price for low-quality bonds. It is therefore in their interest to try to distinguish Good from Bad firms. For example, investors can offer different prices to the bonds issued by firms by assigning different values of $\pi_L$ and $\pi_S$ based on their best judgment. Given the values of $\pi_L$ and $\pi_S$, the firm will compare its equity values under different financing strategies. If $V_L > V_S$, it will issue long-term debt; otherwise, it will issue short-term debt. Thus, the criterion for the firm's financing decision is the value difference:

$$\Delta V = V_L - V_S + c$$
$$= p \frac{(1-p)(2-\pi_L)\pi_L + (2-p-(2-\pi_L)\pi_L)\pi_S}{(2-\pi_L)\pi_L\pi_S} + c, \quad (12)$$

where the flotation cost $c$ is included. If the difference in Equation (12) is greater than zero, the firm chooses to issue long debt; otherwise, it issues short debt.

If investors could somehow find a combination of $\pi_L$ and $\pi_S$ so that Good and Bad firms choose to issue different debts, they would be able to discern the firm type and to price the debt more efficiently. Although investors may not know exactly the initial quality of each firm, they could assign a plausible set of $\pi$ values to the debts issued by firms and observe their response. The response of Good and Bad firms to investors' $\pi$ estimates, or their choice of long or short debt, sends a signal back to investors. Investors refine their estimate for the firm quality based on the feedback signal they receive. They would then change their offer based on their revised probability estimates and observe firms' response in the next round. This learning and adjustment process may continue until precise estimates of $\pi$ are obtained and a market equilibrium is achieved. We define this strategy of actively searching for a better price or a better estimate of $\Pi$ (firm quality) as *pricing strategy B*. We will show that, under pricing strategy B, an optimal combination of $\pi_L$ and $\pi_S$ exists even under zero flotation costs such that the separating equilibrium is always achievable.

### 3.1. *A separating equilibrium without flotation costs*

We first examine the case with $c = 0$, which represents a debt-market with zero flotation costs. It can be shown that a separating equilibrium of the debt-market exists in the absence of flotation costs. We summarize the equilibrium condition as follows.

**Proposition 1**
A separating equilibrium of the debt-market exists if $\pi_L$ and $\pi_S$ satisfy the condition that

$$0 \leq \pi_L \leq \pi_S \leq \frac{(2 - \pi_L)\pi_L}{2 - (2 - \pi_L)\pi_L}. \tag{13}$$

Firms with a quality $p < p^*$ prefer long-term debt, whereas firms with a quality $p > p^*$ prefer short-term debt. Firms with a quality $p = p^*$ are indifferent to long- and short-term debts. The value of the cutoff quality $p^*$ is given by

$$p^* = \frac{(2 - \pi_L)\pi_L - \pi_S[2 - (2 - \pi_L)\pi_L]}{(2 - \pi_L)\pi_L - \pi_S}. \tag{14}$$

**Proof.** See Appendix A.

The inequality in Equation (13) establishes the necessary condition for a separating equilibrium. The sufficient condition further requires that $p_B < p^*$

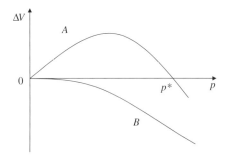

**Figure 2.** Changes in $\Delta V$ with quality $p$ under zero $c$.

and $p_G > p^*$ where $p_i$, $i = $ B, G are the true probability of the "up" state for Bad and Good firms, respectively. Figure 2 gives a graphical presentation of the above results. Assuming that $p = 0$, from Equation (12) we have $\Delta V = 0$ given $c = 0$. But for a separating equilibrium, there must exist a positive $p^*$ that makes $\Delta V = 0$. Curve A in Figure 2 shows one possible path for this condition to be held where the value of the criterion function goes up and then goes down to cross the horizontal axis. Firms prefer long debt when $p < p^*$ but prefer short debt when $p > p^*$. On the contrary, the path depicted by curve B does not cross the horizontal axis, and so no separating equilibrium exists in this case.

Curve A has a positive slope at $p = 0$ and a concave curvature so that the curve crosses $\Delta V = 0$ line at a strictly positive $p$. The comparative statistics of Equation (12) show that when $c = 0$,

$$\left.\frac{\partial \Delta V}{\partial p}\right|_{p=0} = \frac{(1 + \pi_S)(2 - \pi_L)\pi_L - 2\pi_S}{\pi_S(2 - \pi_L)\pi_L}, \tag{15}$$

$$\frac{\partial^2 \Delta V}{\partial p^2} = -2\frac{(2 - \pi_L)\pi_L - \pi_S}{\pi_S(2 - \pi_L)\pi_L}. \tag{16}$$

It is straightforward to show that if

$$\left.\frac{\partial \Delta V}{\partial p}\right|_{p=0} > 0, \tag{17}$$

then the second-order derivative must be negative

$$\frac{\partial^2 \Delta V}{\partial p^2} < 0. \tag{18}$$

Using Equation (15), the condition in Equation (17) can be explicitly expressed as:

$$\pi_S \leq \frac{(2 - \pi_L)\pi_L}{2 - (2 - \pi_L)\pi_L}. \tag{17a}$$

Combining Equations (17a) with (A.5) in Appendix A and noting that $\pi_L > 0$, we can easily obtain the necessary condition in Equation (13). Thus, Equation (17) is a critical condition for a separating equilibrium. Curve B in Figure 2 has a negative value for both the first and second derivatives. Because the condition in Equation (13) is violated, there is no separating equilibrium. As shown, curve B does not cross the horizontal axis ($\Delta V = 0$) at any positive $p$.

Figure 3 gives a graphical representation of the necessary condition for the separating equilibrium. The horizontal axis measures the "up" probability of long-term debt $\pi_L$ and the vertical axis measures that of short-term debt $\pi_S$. The dotted line represents $\pi_L = \pi_S$, and the upper left triangular region consists of $\pi_L \leq \pi_S$. The solid curve represents the boundary for Equation (17) and the dashed curve that for Equation (18). The region to the right of the solid curve satisfies the condition in Equation (17), while the region to the right of the dashed curve satisfies the condition in Equation (18). Hence, the region between the solid line and the dotted line indicates where the separating equilibrium exists under the condition of no flotation costs.

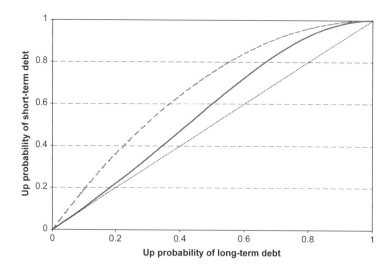

**Figure 3.**   The separating equilibrium region for $\pi_L$ and $\pi_S$.

### 3.2. *A separating equilibrium with flotation costs*

We next consider the case with flotation costs. Previous studies have often relied on a restrictive flotation cost structure to derive a signaling equilibrium. We show that a separating equilibrium always exists in the presence of flotation costs, but this equilibrium is a special case of the more general equilibrium that includes zero floatation costs.

**Proposition 2**

If $c > 0$, and $\pi_L$ and $\pi_S$ satisfy the condition that

$$0 \leq \pi_L \leq \pi_S \leq (2 - \pi_L)\pi_L, \tag{19}$$

then a separating equilibrium exists. Firms with a quality $p < p^*$ prefer the long debt, whereas firms with a quality $p > p^*$ prefer the short debt. Firms with a quality $p = p^*$ are indifferent to long and short debts. The value of the cutoff quality $p^*$ is given by

$$
p^* = \frac{(2 - \pi_L)\pi_L - \pi_S[2 - (2 - \pi_L)\pi_L]}{2[(2 - \pi_L)\pi_L - \pi_S]}
$$
$$
+ \frac{\sqrt{[\pi_S(2 - (2 - \pi_L)\pi_L) - (2 - \pi_L)\pi_L]^2 + 4c\pi_S(2 - \pi_L)\pi_L[(2 - \pi_L)\pi_L - \pi_S]}}{2[(2 - \pi_L)\pi_L - \pi_S]}.
$$
$$\tag{20}$$

**Proof.** See Appendix A.

Figure 4 shows possible functions of $\Delta V$ with respect to $p$ for the cases with (Curve B) and without flotation costs (Curve A). For a positive flotation cost, $c > 0$, $\Delta V$ is simply shifted up in parallel to the zero $c$ curve (Curve A). Because Curve A has a negative first-order derivative of $\Delta V$ with respect to $p$,

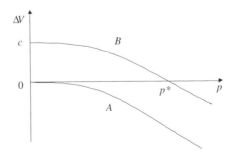

**Figure 4.** A shift in $\Delta V$ given a positive $c$.

$(\partial \Delta V/\partial p)|_{p=0} < 0$, and a negative second-order derivative, $(\partial^2 \Delta V/\partial p^2) < 0$, it does not cross the horizontal axis. However, with a positive value of $c$, $\Delta V$ does cross the horizontal axis (see Curve B), since $(\partial^2 \Delta V/\partial p^2) < 0$. Therefore, for $c > 0$, the condition for the first-order derivative in Equation (17) is no longer required. Combining $(\partial^2 \Delta V/\partial p^2) < 0$, (A.11) in Appendix A, and $\pi_L > 0$, we obtain the condition in Equation (19). As a result, the separating equilibrium region in Figure 3 is expanded since a positive first-order derivative is no longer required. The separating equilibrium region is now located between the dashed curve and the dotted line. Curve A in Figure 4 is drawn purposely to be similar to Curve B in Figure 2. It is shown that for some cases not having a separating equilibrium when flotation costs are zero, a separating equilibrium can be achieved when flotation costs become positive. Thus, the flotation cost differential between long and short debt strategies makes it easier to reach a separating equilibrium.

### 3.3. *Comparison of pricing strategies A and B*

When investors' pricing strategies are taken into consideration, the original game (under pricing strategy A) must be augmented to include investors as an additional player. The setting of the extended game incorporating investors' strategic behavior is shown in Figure 5. This game includes two reduced games: one is under pricing strategy A, and the other is under pricing strategy B. Previous studies (e.g., Flannery, 1986; Diamond, 1991; Kale and Noe, 1990)

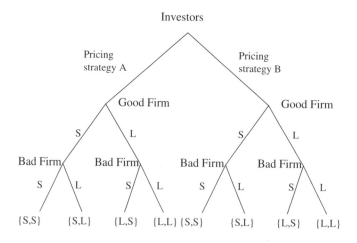

**Figure 5.**   The game involving active investors.

consider only the first reduced game, in which pricing strategy A is the only possibility and investors are passive. The outcome of the first reduced game is either a pooling equilibrium or a separating equilibrium depending on the nature of the flotation cost function.

The second reduced game assumes that investors adopt pricing strategy B and interact with firms to determine equilibrium bond prices. Since investors know the distribution of firm quality, $\theta$, they can select proper probability estimates satisfying $\pi_S > \pi_L$, and search a $p^*$ value such that $p_G > p^* > p_B$. Under this pricing strategy, the sufficient condition of the separating equilibrium is satisfied. Good firms borrow short, whereas Bad firms borrow long, and both firms are better off than in any other choices given investors' estimates of $\pi_S$ and $\pi_L$. Thus, this financing strategy is unequivocally the optimal choice for both types of firms. To resolve the adverse selection problem, investors minimize the total absolute misinformation value,

$$V^{\mathrm{mis}} = |V^{\mathrm{mis}}(G)| + |V^{\mathrm{mis}}(B)|. \tag{21}$$

It can be easily shown that the total absolute misinformation value is always smaller under strategy B than under strategy A.

**Corollary 1**
Under pricing strategy B, there will be a separating equilibrium, in which Good firms borrow short, while Bad firms borrow long.

This result does not depend on the magnitude of flotation cost. If the flotation cost satisfies the condition that $V_L^{\mathrm{mis}}(G) < -c$ and $V_S^{\mathrm{mis}}(B) \leq c$, the two pricing strategies, A and B, lead to the same separating equilibrium. If the flotation cost is not high enough to satisfy this condition, these two pricing strategies lead to different equilibria. Pricing strategy A leads to a pooling equilibrium in short debt, whereas pricing strategy B still leads to a separating equilibrium. Investors' best interest is to minimize the total absolute misinformation value of the debt-market. Since pricing strategy B leads to a lower total absolute misinformation value than does pricing strategy A, it is preferred by investors. Comparing these two cases, we conclude that pricing strategy B dominates pricing strategy A.

**Corollary 2**
Investors always prefer pricing strategy B to strategy A. There is a separating equilibrium under pricing strategy B regardless of flotation costs.

## 4. Numerical Examples

In this section, we provide numerical examples to explain the intuition behind the model. Good and Bad firms' decisions to issue long versus short debt depend on the cost of each debt, which is in turn conditional on $\pi_L$ and $\pi_S$ set by investors. At the beginning of the game, investors do not know the exact value of $p_G$ and $p_B$ for each firm, but they possess a knowledge of the proportion of Good ($\theta$) and Bad ($1 - \theta$) firms and the average quality of firms, $p_{avg}$. At any stage of the game, investors will always balance their estimates of $\pi_S$ and $\pi_L$ such that their combination equals the average quality of firms:

$$p_{avg} = \theta \pi_S + (1 - \theta)\pi_L. \tag{22}$$

Hence, when investors raise the estimate for $\pi_S$, they must lower the estimate for $\pi_L$, given that $p_{avg}$ is known.

Table 1 provides a numerical example for the adjustment process. Here, we assume that $p_G = 0.97$, $p_B = 0.93$, and $\theta = 0.5$. This gives an average "up" probability $p_{avg} = 0.95$. Since initially investors do not know the exact "up" probability of each firm, they may try to price long and short debts based on the average probability $\pi_L = \pi_S = p_{avg} = p^* = 0.95$, and observe the response of each firm. As shown in line one of Table 1, at these values of $\pi_L$ and $\pi_S$, long debt yields a higher firm value for Bad firms than short debt does ($\Delta V_B = 0.093$), while short debt provides a higher value for Good firms ($\Delta V_G = -0.097$). Thus, Bad firms would prefer long debt, and Good firms would prefer short debt. The response of each type of firm tells investors that $p_G > 0.95$ and $p_B < 0.95$, and accordingly, they would reduce $\pi_L$ and increase $\pi_S$. Investors may eventually reduce $\pi_L$ to 0.944 and increase $\pi_S$ to 0.956, and

**Table 1.**  Numerical Example 1 ($c = 0$, $p_G = 0.97$, $p_B = 0.93$, and $\theta = 0.5$).

| $\pi_L$ | $\pi_S$ | $p^*$ | $\Delta V_B$ | $\Delta V_G$ | $V^{mis}$ |
|---|---|---|---|---|---|
| 0.9500 | 0.9500 | 0.9500 | 0.093 | −0.097 | 0.152 |
| 0.9490 | 0.9510 | 0.9466 | 0.076 | −0.111 | 0.145 |
| 0.9480 | 0.9520 | 0.9431 | 0.058 | −0.124 | 0.138 |
| 0.9470 | 0.9530 | 0.9394 | 0.041 | −0.138 | 0.131 |
| 0.9460 | 0.9540 | 0.9354 | 0.023 | −0.152 | 0.125 |
| 0.9450 | 0.9550 | 0.9311 | 0.005 | −0.166 | 0.118 |
| 0.9440 | 0.9560 | 0.9266 | −0.013 | −0.180 | 0.110 |

Note: $p^*$ is calculated from Equation (14), $\Delta V$ from Equation (12), and $V^{mis}$ from Equation (21).

discover that both firms no longer choose different debts but instead both prefer short debt. This outcome convinces investors that the best they can do is to set $\pi_L = 0.945$ and $\pi_S = 0.955$ to keep Bad firms from mimicking Good firms.

The aforementioned example assumes zero flotation costs, $c = 0$. Although there are no flotation costs to prevent Bad firms from mimicking Good firms, the resulting misinformation value serves for this function. The misinformation value in this separating equilibrium is less than that in the pooling equilibrium under pricing strategy A, which is represented in line one of Table 1. It is in investors' interests to prevent the pooling equilibrium from occurring. Investors minimize the sum of misinformation values by choosing $\pi_L = 0.945$ and $\pi_S = 0.955$.

The next example assumes a positive flotation cost $c = 0.001$. As shown in Table 2, at $\pi_L = \pi_S = p_{avg} = 0.95$, long debt yields a higher value than does short debt for both Bad and Good firms ($\Delta V_B = 0.193$, $\Delta V_G = 0.003$), given a positive flotation cost $c$. Thus, both firms would prefer long debt. The response of Good firms is different from the case with $c = 0$ (see Table 1) because flotation costs make short-term debt financing more costly. The existence of flotation costs allows investors to increase the difference between $\pi_L$ and $\pi_S$ to reach the separating equilibrium. For $c = 0.001$, investors can minimize the absolute misinformation value by choosing $\pi_L = 0.94$ and $\pi_S = 0.96$.

It can be shown that an additional increase in flotation costs will further reduce the misinformation value. At a certain level of flotation costs, the perfect revealing separating equilibrium may emerge. This case is illustrated in Table 3

**Table 2.** Numerical Example 2 ($c = 0.001$, $p_G = 0.97$, $p_B = 0.93$, and $\theta = 0.5$).

| $\pi_L$ | $\pi_S$ | $p^*$ | $\Delta V_B$ | $\Delta V_G$ | $V^{mis}$ |
|---------|---------|--------|--------------|--------------|-----------|
| 0.95 | 0.95 | 0.9706 | 0.193 | 0.003 | 0.152 |
| 0.949 | 0.951 | 0.9678 | 0.176 | −0.011 | 0.145 |
| 0.948 | 0.952 | 0.9649 | 0.158 | −0.024 | 0.138 |
| 0.947 | 0.953 | 0.9618 | 0.141 | −0.038 | 0.131 |
| 0.946 | 0.954 | 0.9585 | 0.123 | −0.052 | 0.125 |
| 0.945 | 0.955 | 0.9549 | 0.105 | −0.066 | 0.117 |
| 0.944 | 0.956 | 0.9512 | 0.087 | −0.080 | 0.110 |
| 0.943 | 0.957 | 0.9471 | 0.068 | −0.095 | 0.103 |
| 0.942 | 0.958 | 0.9428 | 0.050 | −0.110 | 0.096 |
| 0.941 | 0.959 | 0.9382 | 0.031 | −0.125 | 0.088 |
| 0.94 | 0.96 | 0.9332 | 0.012 | −0.140 | 0.081 |
| 0.939 | 0.961 | 0.9279 | −0.007 | −0.155 | 0.073 |

**Table 3.** Numerical Example 3 ($c = 0.0029$, $p_G = 0.97$, $p_B = 0.93$, $\theta = 0.5$).

| $\pi_L$ | $\pi_S$ | $p^*$ | $\Delta V_B$ | $\Delta V_G$ | $V^{mis}$ |
|---|---|---|---|---|---|
| 0.95 | 0.95 | 1.0074 | 0.3832 | 0.1928 | 0.201 |
| 0.949 | 0.951 | 1.0056 | 0.3659 | 0.1794 | 0.201 |
| 0.948 | 0.952 | 1.0037 | 0.3484 | 0.1658 | 0.201 |
| 0.947 | 0.953 | 1.0017 | 0.3300 | 0.1520 | 0.201 |
| 0.946 | 0.954 | 0.9995 | 0.3129 | 0.1381 | 0.201 |
| 0.945 | 0.955 | 0.9971 | 0.2948 | 0.1240 | 0.201 |
| 0.944 | 0.956 | 0.9946 | 0.2766 | 0.1096 | 0.201 |
| 0.943 | 0.957 | 0.9919 | 0.2581 | 0.0951 | 0.201 |
| 0.942 | 0.958 | 0.9890 | 0.2395 | 0.0803 | 0.201 |
| 0.941 | 0.959 | 0.9859 | 0.2207 | 0.0654 | 0.201 |
| 0.94 | 0.96 | 0.9826 | 0.2017 | 0.0503 | 0.201 |
| 0.939 | 0.961 | 0.9790 | 0.1825 | 0.0349 | 0.201 |
| 0.938 | 0.962 | 0.9752 | 0.1632 | 0.0194 | 0.201 |
| 0.937 | 0.963 | 0.9710 | 0.1436 | 0.0037 | 0.201 |
| 0.936 | 0.964 | 0.9665 | 0.1238 | −0.0122 | 0.050 |
| 0.935 | 0.965 | 0.9617 | 0.1039 | −0.0284 | 0.042 |
| 0.934 | 0.966 | 0.9564 | 0.0838 | −0.0447 | 0.034 |
| 0.933 | 0.967 | 0.9507 | 0.0634 | −0.0612 | 0.025 |
| 0.932 | 0.968 | 0.9446 | 0.0429 | −0.0779 | 0.017 |
| 0.931 | 0.969 | 0.9378 | 0.0222 | −0.0949 | 0.009 |
| 0.93 | 0.97 | 0.9305 | 0.0013 | −0.1120 | 0 |
| 0.929 | 0.971 | 0.9225 | −0.0197 | −0.1293 | 0.009 |

where we set $c = 0.0029$. At this level of flotation costs, both Good and Bad firms would prefer long debt up to $\pi_L = 0.937$ and $\pi_S = 0.963$. By increasing the difference between $\pi_L$ and $\pi_S$ further, investors would observe that Good and Bad firms start to choose different debts until the perfect revealing separating equilibrium is reached. Investors reduce the sum of absolute misinformation value to zero by choosing $\pi_L = 0.93$ and $\pi_S = 0.97$.

Obviously, higher flotation costs may allow investors to increase the differential between $\pi_L$ and $\pi_S$ further. However, it is not optimal for investors to do so. An increase in the differential between $\pi_L$ and $\pi_S$ beyond the optimal level would only increase the total absolute misinformation value since the perfect revealing condition is optimal for pricing long and short debts.

The preceding examples show that the perfect revealing separating equilibrium is a special case of the general separating equilibrium. As indicated, the perfect revealing separating equilibrium requires the flotation cost to be above a certain level. This result is consistent with previous findings. However, contrary to previous studies, we show that a separating equilibrium can still be achieved when the flotation cost is below this level, or even becomes zero. The separating equilibrium may not be able to eliminate the misinformation value entirely, but its magnitude is always smaller than that in a pooling equilibrium.

## 5. Conclusions

In a market where rational investors are active participants in the signaling game, their pricing strategy leads to a separating equilibrium of debts with different maturity arrangements in the absence of flotation costs. The interaction of borrowers' incentives and investors' inferences about firm quality results in an informational equilibrium under a much more general condition. Firms can effectively signal their true quality to the market even if financial market transactions are costless. Unlike previous studies, we show that a firm's debt-maturity structure can provide a credible signal in the absence of transaction costs.

Information asymmetry can create a rather complex maturity structure. Our analysis can be easily generalized to the case of multiple maturity structure. In equilibrium, higher-quality firms issue shorter-term debt, resulting in a pecking order of debt financing. Firms of the highest quality issue short-term debt, and firms of the lowest quality issue long-term debt or serial debt. Firms of intermediate quality issue debts of intermediate maturity. Thus, bond ratings should be related to the effective bond maturity *ceteris paribus*. Moreover, to the extent that industries are characterized by different degrees of information asymmetry, there should be cross-sectional variations in debt-maturity structure. Industries with higher information asymmetry will tend to use short-term debt. Conversely, industries with lower information asymmetry would be more likely to follow the asset-liability matching principle to determine the maturity structure of debt (see Demirgüç-Kunt and Maksimovic, 1999; Emery, 2001).

## Appendix A

### A.1. *Proof of Proposition 1*

Setting the criterion function for the firm's debt financing decision to be zero,

$$\Delta V = p \frac{(1-p)(2-\pi_L)\pi_L + (2-p-(2-\pi_L)\pi_L)\pi_S}{(2-\pi_L)\pi_L\pi_S} = 0 \qquad (A.1)$$

and solving for $p$, we can obtain the cutoff quality of firm ($p^*$):

$$p^* = 0, \qquad p^* = \frac{(2 - \pi_L)\pi_L - \pi_S[2 - (2 - \pi_L)\pi_L]}{(2 - \pi_L)\pi_L - \pi_S}, \qquad \text{(A.2)}$$

where $p^* = 0$ represents the case that the firm would go bankrupt for certain, and so it should be ruled out. The coexistence of short and long debts requires that

$$0 < p^* < 1. \qquad \text{(A.3)}$$

Imposing the condition in Equation (A.3) on Equation (A.2), we have

$$0 < \pi_S < \frac{(2 - \pi_L)\pi_L}{2 - (2 - \pi_L)\pi_L}. \qquad \text{(A.4)}$$

By definition,

$$\pi_L \le \pi_S. \qquad \text{(A.5)}$$

Combining Equations (A.4) and (A.5) gives

$$0 < \pi_L \le \pi_S < \frac{(2 - \pi_L)\pi_L}{2 - (2 - \pi_L)\pi_L}. \qquad \text{(A.6)}$$

### A.2. *Proof of Proposition 2*

Assume $c > 0$, and set the criterion function for the firm's debt decision to be zero:

$$\Delta V = p \frac{(1 - p)(2 - \pi_L)\pi_L + (2 - p - (2 - \pi_L)\pi_L)\pi_S}{(2 - \pi_L)\pi_L\pi_S} + c = 0. \qquad \text{(A.7)}$$

Solving for $p$, we can obtain the cutoff quality of firms:

$$p^* = 0,$$

$$p^* = \frac{(2 - \pi_L)\pi_L - \pi_S[2 - (2 - \pi_L)\pi_L]}{2[(2 - \pi_L)\pi_L - \pi_S]}$$
$$+ \frac{\sqrt{[\pi_S(2 - (2 - \pi_L)\pi_L) - (2 - \pi_L)\pi_L]^2 + 4G\pi_S(2 - \pi_L)\pi_L[(2 - \pi_L)\pi_L - \pi_S]}}{2[(2 - \pi_L)\pi_L - \pi_S]}. \qquad \text{(A.8)}$$

Again, the case of $p^* = 0$ is discarded. Imposing the condition in Equation (A.3) on Equation (A.8), we have

$$-\frac{2(2 - \pi_L)\pi_L}{3 - 2(1 - G)\pi_L + (1 - G)\pi_L^2} < \pi_S < (2 - \pi_L)\pi_L. \qquad (A.9)$$

By definition,

$$\pi_L \leq \pi_S. \qquad (A.10)$$

Combining Equations (A.9) and (A.10) gives

$$0 < \pi_L \leq \pi_S < (2 - \pi_L)\pi_L. \qquad (A.11)$$

## Acknowledgments

We thank Richard Green, Kose John, and Lemma Senbet for helpful comments.

## References

Bhattacharya, S., "Imperfect Information, Dividend Policy and the "Bird in the Hand" Fallacy." *Bell Journal of Economics* 10, 259–270 (1979).

Campell, T. S. and W. A. Kracaw, "Information Production, Market Signaling and the Theory of Financial Intermediation." *Journal of Finance* 35, 863–882 (1980).

Demirgüc-Kunt, A. and V. Maksimovic, "Institutions, Financial Markets, and Firm Debt Maturity." *Journal of Financial Economics* 54, 295–336 (1999).

Diamond, D. W., "Debt Maturity Structure and Liquidity Risk." *Quarterly Journal of Economics* 106, 709–737 (1991).

Diamond, D. W., "Seniority and Maturity of Debt Contracts." *Journal of Financial Economics* 33, 341–368 (1993).

Emery, G. W., "Cyclical Demand and the Choice of Debt Maturity." *Journal of Business* 74, 557–590 (2001).

Flannery, M. J., "Asymmetric Information and Risky Debt Maturity Choice." *Journal of Finance* 41, 19–37 (1986).

Guedes, J. and T. Opler, "The Determinants of the Maturity Structure of Corporate Debt Issues." *Journal of Finance* 51, 1809–1833 (1996).

Kale, J. R. and T. H. Noe, "Risky Debt Maturity Choice in a Sequential Game Equilibrium." *Journal of Financial Research* 2, 155–165 (1990).

Ravid, S. A., "Debt Maturity — A Survey." *Financial Markets, Institutions & Instruments* 5, 1–69 (1996).

Ross, S. A., "The Determination of Financial Structure: The Incentive-Signaling Approach." *Bell Journal of Economics* 8, 23–40 (1977).

Rothschild, M. and J. E. Stiglitz, "Equilibrium in Competitive Insurance Markets: An Essay on the Economics of Imperfect Information." *Quarterly Journal of Economics* 91, 629–649 (1976).

Stohs, M. and D. Mauer, "The Determinants of Corporate Debt Maturity Structure." *Journal of Business* 69, 279–312 (1996).

Titman, S., "Interest Rate Swaps and Corporate Financing Choices." *Journal of Finance* 47, 1503–1516 (1992).

Wu, C., "Information Asymmetry and the Sinking Fund Provision." *Journal of Financial and Quantitative Analysis* 28, 399–416 (1993).

Chapter 5

# Estimated Operating Cash Flow, Reported Cash Flow From Operating Activities, and Financial Distress

Terry J. Ward*
*Middle Tennessee State University, USA*

Benjamin P. Foster
*University of Louisville, USA*

Jon Woodroof
*The University of Tennessee, USA*

Bahnson, Miller, and Budge (1996) and Krishnan and Largay (2000) discovered differences between net operating cash flow (OCF) as estimated by prior studies and cash flow from operating activities (CFFO) as reported on the cash flow statement. Our study examines whether these differences could impact the results from financial distress models and explains why prior financial distress research generally found that OCF provided little useful incremental information in explaining financial distress. In our study, OCF does not add significant explanatory power to distress models. In contrast, the operating cash flow variable taken directly from the cash flow statement, CFFO, adds significant explanatory power beyond accrual accounting variables and even beyond OCF. We then conduct analyses to help explain these results. Similar to Bahnson *et al.* and Krishnan and Largay, we find significant differences between OCF and CFFO. We also find that the differences are significantly different between the distressed and nondistressed groups of firms. Although the differences between CFFO and OCF are significant for both distressed and nondistressed groups, OCF tends to be overstated in greater magnitudes for the distressed firms than for the nondistressed firms. However, OCF is as likely to be overstated as understated for the nondistressed firms. Previous financial distress research studies estimated net operating cash flow variables similar to OCF. Our findings may explain why these studies generally concluded that operating cash flow did not contain incremental explanatory content above accrual information.

**Keywords:** Estimated operating cash flow (OCF); cash flow from operating activities (CFFO); financial distress.

---

*Corresponding author.

## 1. Introduction

Bahnson, Miller, and Budge (1996) found that cash flow from operations (CFFO) as reported on the Statement of Cash Flows differs from operating cash flow (OCF) as estimated using published accrual data. Our study examines whether the difference could explain why prior financial distress research generally found that OCF provided little useful incremental information in explaining financial distress. Results from our financial distress logistic regression models indicate that CFFO adds significant explanatory power to accrual accounting variables, while OCF does not. CFFO dominates OCF when included in a model with OCF; CFFO even adds significant explanatory power beyond OCF. Finding stronger results for CFFO than OCF presents evidence that prior financial distress research conclusions may be misleading.

We then conduct analyses to attempt to discover what may cause the logistic regression results. We confirm Bahnson *et al.* (1996) findings of differences between CFFO and OCF with our combined sample of distressed and nondistressed firms. In separate analyses, we find that OCF tends to be overstated relative to CFFO and exhibits much more variation than CFFO. Also, the distressed firms experience significantly larger differences between OCF and CFFO than do nondistressed firms. Greater variation in OCF than CFFO and larger differences between OCF and CFFO for distressed firms likely explain our findings from the financial distress models.

This paper is organized as follows. The next section discusses our motivation for the study and relevant prior literature. We then discuss our research methods and present and discuss the statistical results. The paper ends with a discussion of the implications of our findings in light of those found by Bahnson *et al.* (1996).

## 2. Motivation for Study and Relevant Prior Literature

Prior to the issuance of Statement of Financial Accounting Standards No. 95 (SFAS No. 95) that required the cash flow statement, some literature (e.g., Lawson, 1978, 1985; Lee, 1972, 1978) suggested that cash flow information should be superior to accrual income information in distinguishing between nondistressed and distressed firms. This literature, prior financial distress literature, and research with the Statement of Cash Flows provide the motivation for our study.

## 2.1. *Prior research*

Much previous research attempted to determine the incremental usefulness of net operating cash flow over accrual information in explaining financial distress. These studies normally either compared the usefulness of an estimated operating cash flow to other flow variables, particularly income, or tested the usefulness of accrual components used to adjust income to arrive at net operating cash flow.

Many studies used the ability to predict financial distress as the criterion for evaluating the usefulness of cash flow and accrual information (e.g., Lau, 1982; Casey and Bartczak, 1984; Casey and Bartczak, 1985; Gentry, Newbold, and Whitford, 1985, 1987; Gombola, Haskins, Ketz, and Williams, 1987; Aziz, Emanuel, and Lawson, 1988; Aziz and Lawson, 1989; Gilbert, Menon, and Schwartz, 1990; Ward, 1994; Ward and Foster, 1996, 1997). Since these are the studies most relevant to this paper, they are summarized in Table 1.

Other related areas of research also compared the usefulness of accrual and cash flow information. Some studies used share prices as either an implicit or an explicit proxy for future cash flows to compare accruals and cash flows (e.g., Ball and Brown, 1968; Beaver and Dukes, 1972; Rayburn, 1986; Bowen, Burgstahler, and Daley, 1987; Cheng, Liu, and Schaefer, 1996; Barth, Beaver, Hand, and Landsman, 1999). Other studies used future cash flows as the criterion to measure the usefulness of current accounting information (e.g., Greenberg, Johnson, and Ramesh, 1986; Finger, 1994; Lorek and Willinger, 1996; Barth, Cram, and Nelson, 2001). Results of these studies were somewhat mixed, but they generally suggested that cash flows are useful, but not as useful as accrual information. Barth *et al.* (2001) provided a thorough summary of these studies.

The financial distress studies in Table 1 used data prior to SFAS No. 95's requirement that companies issue cash flow statements. Consequently, researchers had to estimate net operating cash flows by adjusting income statement information using changes in balance sheet accounts. Depending on the flows and components tested, the studies in Table 1 started with different funds flow totals to arrive at an estimated net operating cash flow. However, all the studies estimated net operating cash flow in basically the same manner.

Some of the studies, such as Casey and Bartczak (1984, 1985), calculated working capital from operations by first adjusting income for changes in nonworking capital current assets and liabilities other than debt. Next, they eliminated noncash accrual items from working capital from operations to arrive at

**Table 1.**   Studies that tested the ability of estimated operating cash flow (OCF) to explain future financial distress.

| Study | Sample | Variables tested/Methodology | Findings |
|---|---|---|---|
| Lau (1982) | 350,20, 15, 10, and 5 firms in 5 states: nondistressed, omitting or reducing dividends, default of loan interest and/or principal payments, protection under Chapter X or XI, and bankruptcy and liquidation for 1976<br><br>Holdout (separate period–1977) Matched by size | Author generated 5-state multiple discriminant analysis and nominal logistic regression models. Author compared the incremental predictive ability over accrual ratios of various funds-flow variables of which OCF was one.<br>Models were lagged 1, 2, and 3 years. | Results were mixed; however, working capital from operations appeared to be the strongest explanatory variable. |
| Casey and Bartczak (1984) | Samples contained 60 bankrupt (B) and 230 nonbankrupt (NB) firms<br><br>One-half of firms used to develop statistical models, and one-half of firms used as hold-out (same period as models) | Authors compared OCF scaled by various measures with 6 accrual ratios in separate models. Linear multiple discriminant analysis and conditional stepwise logit analysis were used to generate models lagged 1,2,3,4, and 5 years before event. | Neither cash flow variable had higher explanatory rates than the combined model with 6 accrual ratios. |
| Casey and Bartczak (1985) | Same as before | The methods used were the same as before except the authors added OCF to the accrual variables to test the incremental usefulness of OCF over accrual information. | The addition of various operating cash flow variables did not increase explanatory value. |
| Gentry, Newbold, and Whitford (1985) | Sample contained 33 distressed and 33 nondistressed firms<br>No holdout sample, but 2nd sample of weak/nonweak firms | The authors tested 7 cash-based funds flows (each divided by total net flow). They did not test OCF, but tested components of OCF. Multiple discriminant analysis, probit, and logit techniques were used to generate models lagged 1, 2, and 3 years before event. | Some funds flow components have information content, but the flow components of OCF did not improve explanatory value. |

*(Continued)*

**Table 1.**   (*Continued*)

| Study | Sample | Variables tested/Methodology | Findings |
|---|---|---|---|
| Gombola, Haskins, Ketz, and Williams (1987) | 77B/77NB Two separate models: early (1967–1972) and late (1973–1981) | The authors compared OCF, working capital from operations, and income plus depreciation expense, with each flow scaled by total assets. Each model contained the six ratios loading highest on factors as control variables. Linear discriminant analysis was primarily used to generate models lagged 1, 2, 3, and 4 years before the event. | OCF variables were not significant in explaining future bankruptcy. OCF variables were not more useful in late-year models. |
| Aziz, Emanuel, and Lawson (1988) | Sample contained 49B/49NB firms No holdout sample, jackknife technique was used for predictions | The authors tested six estimated cash flow variables, each scaled by book value of firm. The authors did not specifically test the incremental ability of cash flows over accruals in predicting bankruptcy. Multiple discriminant analysis and logistic regression were used to generate models lagged 1, 2, 3, 4, and 5 years before event. The authors compared results to those reported by Altman's Z-score model (1968) and ZETA model of Altman, Haldeman, and Narayanan (1977). | OCF and estimated taxes paid were significant as early as the 5th year before bankruptcy. |
| Aziz and Lawson (1989) | Same as before, except the authors also used a holdout sample of 26B/67NB firms | Same methodology as above, except the authors tested the incremental predictive power of each estimated cash flow variable over the accrual ratios. | Cash flow variables did not improve on existing models' overall ability to explain future bankruptcy. |

(Continued)

**Table 1.** *(Continued)*

| Study | Sample | Variables tested/Methodology | Findings |
|---|---|---|---|
| Gilbert, Menon, and Schwartz (1990) | Two main samples: (1) sample of 76 bankrupt and 304 randomly selected nondistressed firms and (2) sample of 76 bankrupt and 304 distressed firms<br><br>Distressed firms were those which had negative cumulative earnings over a consecutive three-year period<br><br>Holdout sample generated by splitting above sample into two groups | The authors replicated Casey and Bartczak's (1985) and Altman's (1968) studies.<br><br>Logistic regression was used to generate bankrupt versus nondistressed dichotomous models and bankrupt versus distressed dichotomous models. | OCF has incremental usefulness in explaining future distress in the bankrupt versus distressed models.<br><br>However, bankruptcy models performed poorly in distinguishing bankrupt from distressed firms. |
| Ward (1994) | 164, 22, 23, and 18 firms in four states: nondistressed, omitting or reducing dividends, loan principal/interest default or debt accommodation, and protection under Chapter X<br>The holdout sample contained 111, 17, 14, and 16 firms | The author compared OCF, Beavers' (1966) Naive Operating Flow (net income + depreciation), and net income to see whether or not the naive operating flow (NOF) correlated with OCF or net income.<br>All models included seven accrual variables as control variables; one variable controlled for size, while six of the variables were variables used by Casey and Bartczak (1984).<br>Four state ordinal logistic regression was used to generate models lagged 1, 2, and 3 years before the events. | OCF was significant in explaining future distress one of three years before the event. NOF was also significant 1 of the 3 years before distress. NOF appears to be a better measure of economic income than net income but is not a measure of operating cash flow. |

*(Continued)*

**Table 1.** (*Continued*)

| Study | Sample | Variables tested/Methodology | Findings |
|---|---|---|---|
| Ward and Foster (1996) | The developmental sample used to generate the models contained 150, 16, 21, and 17 firms in four ordinal states: nondistressed, omitting or reducing dividends, loan principal/interest default or debt accommodation, and protection under Chapter X The holdout sample contained 103, 12, 13, and 13 firms in four ordinal states | The authors compared the incremental usefulness of various funds flow variables: net income, net income + depreciation expense + deferred tax, Thomas's net quick assets flow, and OCF. All ratios were adjusted to eliminate depreciation expense and deferred tax allocations from the scaling measure. All models included the seven accrual control variables used by Ward (1994). The authors also compared the components of OCF. Ordinal logistic regression was used to generate the four-state models lagged 1, 2, and 3 years before the events. | Net income + depreciation expense + deferred tax was the most important funds flow variable. OCF was significant one of the three years, while net income was also significant one of the three years. |
| Ward and Foster (1997) | 253 nondistressed firms, 29 bankrupt firms, and 35 loan default/accommodation firms Holdout sample = 106 nondistressed firms, 28 bankrupt firms, and 23 loan default firms Authors used the 253 nondistressed firms and 29 bankrupt firms to generate dichotomous bankruptcy models and used the 253 nondistressed firms and 35 loan default firms to generate dichotomous loan default/accommodation models | All models contained OCF, estimated investing cash flow, and financing cash flow variables. All models included the seven accrual control variables used by Ward (1994) and Ward and Foster (1996). Binary logistic regression was used to generate dichotomous models lagged 1, 2, and 3 years before the event. | OCF fit the loan default models better than the bankruptcy models but was still significant only one of three years at a *p*-value less than .05. The authors did not test the incremental explanatory ability of OCF over accrual ratios. |

estimated net operating cash flow. Other studies obtained estimated net operating cash flow by simply starting with income, eliminating all noncash income statement items, and adding or subtracting changes in current assets and liabilities other than investments and debt. Table 1 shows that prior studies found that net operating cash flow estimated by these methods had limited significant explanatory power in explaining financial distress when added to accrual ratios.

## 2.2. *Research related to articulation and the cash flow statement*

Research related to the cash flow statement requires a re-evaluation of conclusions drawn from these studies. Bahnson *et al.* (1996) found evidence that net operating cash flow (OCF) as estimated in prior research studies may vary from cash flow from operating activities (CFFO) as reported on the cash flow statement. They found that 75% of companies reported a CFFO amount that could not be reconciled with net income through noncash expenses and changes in current accounts and other information on the balance sheet. Bahnson *et al.* conclude that this nonarticulation of the cash flow statement "suggest(s) that the results of these (cash flow) studies may be corrupted by errors in their estimates of OCF (net operating cash flow)," (p. 7) and that "it may be imprudent to continue accepting the dominant conclusion that OCF has little information content" (p. 8). In a securities market returns study, Cheng *et al.* (1997) indeed found that CFFO reported on the cash flow statement contained more value-relevant information than estimated net operating cash flow.

Krishnan and Largay (2000) investigated a sample of firms that reported its Statement of Cash Flows under the direct method to determine whether cash flows reported using the direct approach outperformed related flows estimated using indirect approaches. They found that the direct flows out-predicted the estimated flows and that the estimated measures possessed measurement error over the reported measures.

Consequently, in a financial distress context, we address: (1) whether or not CFFO provides more useful information than OCF; and (2) whether or not CFFO and OCF have incremental explanatory power beyond accrual accounting information. Also, because of Bahnson *et al.*'s findings, we compare OCF and CFFO separately for distressed and nondistressed firms in our sample to explore any differences between OCF and CFFO that may affect results. Bahnson *et al.* did not investigate whether or not the magnitude of the differences between OCF and CFFO varied for distressed and nondistressed firms.

## 3. Research Methods

### 3.1. *Sample*

*Compact Disc Disclosure* and the *Wall Street Journal Index* are initially searched to identify firms that declared bankruptcy or defaulted on a loan interest or principal payment or received a favorable debt accommodation in 1991 and 1992. Firms that are not included, or had incomplete data, in the *Compustat PC+* database are eliminated from the sample. We then randomly select nondistressed firms for 1991 and 1992 from the same industries as the distressed firms.

We next examine the annual reports or 10-Ks of all firms included in the sample to identify and verify relevant information about each firm. We eliminate distressed firms for which we could not verify the occurrence and date of the distress event. We also eliminate nondistressed firms for which we could not verify the lack of any distress event within the sample period. Likewise, firms with unaudited statements or with managers under investigation for fraudulent financial reporting are dropped from the sample. Our final sample includes 50 distressed firms and 105 nondistressed firms.

We then obtain data from *Compustat PC+* for these companies' financial statements one, two, and three years prior to their distress. Thus, for the 1991 firms we obtain information from their financial reports for 1990, 1989, and 1988. Companies are first required to issue cash flow statements in 1988.

### 3.2. *Statistical methods and variables*

We use logistic regression to test the incremental explanatory power of the operating cash flow variables above accrual accounting ratios. Logistic regression was used (and discussed) in several prior financial distress studies (e.g., Casey and Bartczak, 1984, 1985; Aziz *et al.*, 1988; Aziz and Lawson, 1989; Gilbert *et al.*, 1990; Ward, 1994; Ward and Foster, 1996, 1997).

The dependent variable in this study is a dichotomous distress variable. The distress variable is defined based on the research by Neill, Schaefer, Bahnson, and Bradbury (1991), Bahnson and Bartley (1992), and Ward and Foster (1997). Both Neill *et al.* and Ward and Foster recommended a financial distress measure more broadly defined than just bankruptcy as the most valid dependent variable when testing the ability of financial information to explain insolvency. Thus, this study's dependent variable is the following dichotomous response coded as follows:

DISTRESS = 0 if company did not become bankrupt or experience a loan default or favorable debt accommodation, and

1 if company became bankrupt or experienced a loan default or favorable debt accommodation.

To develop a model based on accrual accounting ratios, we obtain accrual ratios that were found useful in prior financial distress research. These independent variables are listed below. The first six accrual variables are similar to the ratios used by Casey and Bartczak (1985). Ohlson (1980) recommended that models also include a variable to control for size (the log of total assets). Ward (1994) and Ward and Foster (1996, 1997) used all seven control variables in their studies. The accrual variables are as follows:

INCTA       = net income/total assets,
SALCURA     = sales/current assets,
CURACURL    = current assets/current liabilities,
TLIOEQ      = total liabilities/owners' equity,
CURATA      = current assets/total assets,
CMSTA       = cash plus marketable securities/total assets, and
SIZE        = log (total assets).

The two cash flow variables of interest are

OCF = income before extraordinary items + depreciation and amortization + deferred taxes and investment tax credit (decrease) + equity in net loss (earnings) + loss (gain) from sale of property, plant, and equipment and investments + funds from operations − others + decrease (increase) in inventory + decrease (increase) in accounts receivable + decrease (increase) in other current assets + increase (decrease) in current liabilities other than current debt; and

CFFO = cash flow from operating activities as reported on the Statement of Cash Flows.

OCF is the estimated net operating cash flow measure used in prior financial distress research. The reliability of OCF as a "true" cash flow measure depends both on (1) articulation between the published Income Statement and Balance Sheet and (2) the validity of *Compustat* data derived from the published statements. CFFO is now reported directly on the Statement of Cash Flows. Prior studies scaled OCF by a balance sheet subtotal to control for heteroscedasticity. The most common scaling measures used were total assets, total liabilities, and current liabilities. Thus, we use all three scaling measures in this study.

We first run the logistic regression analysis with the seven accrual accounting variables and obtain the $-2$ log likelihood statistic produced by the model. We then add OCF and CFFO separately to this model, run the logit regression analysis, and obtain a $-2$ log likelihood statistic for each model. We complete our logistic analyses by running a full model with both OCF and CFFO included together to help clarify the relative strength of each variable in explaining financial distress.

We next investigate whether or not differences exist between OCF and CFFO for the sample as a whole and the distressed and nondistressed groups separately. We conduct *t*-tests on mean differences and construct a contingency table to help better understand the data.

## 4. Statistical Results

### 4.1. *Logistic regression models*

We run several logistic regression models to examine whether or not OCF and CFFO produce different statistical results when testing the usefulness of net operating cash flow in explaining future financial distress. Table 2 reports the results of this analysis. For each of the three lagged periods, we develop a logistic model that includes the seven accrual accounting variables used frequently in prior financial distress studies (the accrual model). We then add OCF or CFFO separately to the accrual models. The change in $-2$ log likelihood statistic from the accrual model to each added variable model measures the incremental explanatory power of either OCF or CFFO over the accrual ratios. The change in $-2$ log likelihood statistic follows a Chi-square $(\chi^2)$ distribution with one degree of freedom.

**Table 2.**   Logistic regression analysis: CFFO and OCF added separately to base accrual model including seven accrual variables.

| Year Lagged / Model[1] | Overall Model −2 log likelihood Statistic[2] | Δ in −2 log likelihood[3] | p-Value of Δ in −2 log likelihood |
| --- | --- | --- | --- |
| *Panel A — Scaled by Total Assets* | | | |
| Year 1 | | | |
| Accrual Model | 91.191 (7 df) | NA | NA |
| Accrual + CFFO Model | 95.862 (8 df) | 4.671 | 0.031 |
| Accrual + OCF Model | 92.358 (8 df) | 1.1670 | 0.280 |
| Year 2 | | | |
| Accrual Model | 49.284 (7 df) | NA | NA |
| Accrual + CFFO Model | 52.748 (8 df) | 3.464 | 0.063 |
| Accrual + OCF Model | 49.335 (8 df) | 0.051 | 0.821 |
| Year 3 | | | |
| Accrual Model | 28.914 (7 df) | NA | NA |
| Accrual + CFFO Model | 32.445 (8 df) | 3.531 | 0.060 |
| Accrual + OCF Model | 28.926 (8 df) | 0.012 | 0.913 |
| *Panel B — Scaled by Total Liabilities* | | | |
| Year 1 | | | |
| Accrual Model | 91.191 (7 df) | NA | NA |
| Accrual + CFFO Model | 97.799 (8 df) | 6.608 | 0.010 |
| Accrual + OCF Model | 91.606 (8 df) | 0.415 | 0.519 |
| Year 2 | | | |
| Accrual Model | 49.284 (7 df) | NA | NA |
| Accrual + CFFO Model | 50.757 (8 df) | 1.473 | 0.225 |
| Accrual + OCF Model | 49.310 (8 df) | 0.026 | 0.872 |
| Year 3 | | | |
| Accrual Model | 28.914 (7 df) | NA | NA |
| Accrual + CFFO Model | 38.372 (8 df) | 9.458 | 0.002 |
| Accrual + OCF Model | 30.824 (8 df) | 1.910 | 0.167 |

*(Continued)*

**Table 2.** (*Continued*)

| Year Lagged | Model[1] | Overall Model −2 log likelihood Statistic[2] | Δ in −2 log likelihood[3] | p-Value of Δ in −2 log likelihood |
|---|---|---|---|---|
| *Panel C — Scaled by Current Liabilities* | | | | |
| Year 1 | Accrual Model | 91.191 (7 df) | NA | NA |
| | Accrual + CFFO Model | 95.327 (8 df) | 4.136 | 0.042 |
| | Accrual + OCF Model | 92.152 (8 df) | 0.961 | 0.327 |
| Year 2 | Accrual Model | 49.284 (7 df) | NA | NA |
| | Accrual + CFFO Model | 50.746 (8 df) | 1.462 | 0.227 |
| | Accrual + OCF Model | 49.345 (8 df) | 0.061 | 0.805 |
| Year 3 | Accrual Model | 28.914 (7 df) | NA | NA |
| | Accrual + CFFO Model | 31.163 (8 df) | 2.249 | 0.134 |
| | Accrual + OCF Model | 28.915 (8 df) | 0.001 | 0.975 |

[1] The Accrual Model contains seven accrual variables used in prior cash flow research. The Accrual Model + CFFO Model contains CFFO added to the accrual variables. The Accrual Model + OCF Model contains OCF added to the accrual variables. CFFO = cash flow from operating activities as reported on the Statement of Cash Flows. OCF = income before extraordinary items + depreciation and amortization + deferred taxes and investment tax credit (decrease) + equity in net loss (earnings) + loss (gain) from sale of property, plant, and equipment and investments + funds from operations-others + decrease (increase) in inventory + decrease (increase) in accounts receivable + decrease (increase) in other current assets + increase (decrease) in current liabilities other than current debt. The accrual variables are INCTA = net income/total assets, SALCURA = sales/current assets, CURACURL = current assets/current liabilities, TLIOEQ = total liabilities/owners' equity, CURATA = current assets/total assets, CMSTA = cash plus marketable securities/total assets, and SIZE = log (total assets).

[2] The −2 log likelihood Statistic follows a $\chi^2$ distribution (seven degrees of freedom in the Accrual Model, eight degrees of freedom in the other two Models).

[3] The Δ in −2 log likelihood follows a $\chi^2$ distribution with one degree of freedom. A significant Δ in −2 log likelihood indicates that the added variable has incremental usefulness over the variables included in the Accrual Model in explaining financial distress.

Table 2 shows the −2 log likelihood statistic for each model and the change in −2 log likelihood statistic when OCF or CFFO is added separately to the accrual model. Table 2 contains the results for the three years prior to the distress event; each panel reports results with OCF and CFFO scaled by a different measure. Results show that OCF adds no significant explanatory power in any year with any scaling measure. Finding that OCF does not have incremental usefulness over accrual information is consistent with prior studies' results.

In contrast, CFFO is significant (at $p$-value $< 0.10$) for all three years when scaled by total assets, for two of the three years when scaled by total liabilities, and for one year when scaled by current liabilities. Using actual operating cash flow as reported on the cash flow statement (CFFO) generally produces significant incremental results above accrual ratios.

Table 3 reports results from a full model including the seven accrual variables and both cash flow variables scaled by total assets. Because CFFO and OCF are supposed to measure the same construct, one would expect them to be highly correlated. When two highly correlated variables are included together in a logit model, the correlation creates unstable parameter estimates for the two variables. The more dominant variable will normally maintain the expected sign on its parameter estimate and will also maintain significance if it is sufficiently dominant. However, the weaker variable's parameter estimate will be skewed away from the dominant variable's parameter estimate. In extreme cases, the weaker variable's parameter estimate may even show a sign opposite from expected.

The two operating cash flows should be negatively related to financial distress; financially distressed firms should have lower operating cash flows than nondistressed firms one, two, and three years before the event period. Table 3 results show that the CFFO parameter estimate does exhibit a negative sign all three years. However, OCF has an opposite sign from expected (positive sign) each of the three years. Also, CFFO is still significant in the full model each year, while OCF is not significant any year. These results appear to suggest that CFFO is the dominant variable of the two operating cash flows. This result is further illustrated by looking at the change in −2 log likelihood from adding each operating cash flow to a reduced model that includes the other cash flow variable and the accrual ratios. The change in −2 log likelihood statistic for each lagged period shows that CFFO has significant incremental value over OCF, while OCF does not have significant incremental value over CFFO.

**Table 3.** Logistic regression analysis: CFFO and OCF scaled by total assets added together in a full model.

| Variables[1] | Year 1 | Year 2 | Year 3 |
|---|---|---|---|
| | Parameter estimates | Parameter estimates | Parameter estimates |
| Intercept | 3.4353 | −0.5169 | 0.2772 |
| INCTA | −12.5384*** | −9.5330*** | −5.4168* |
| SALCURA | −0.3911** | −0.0378 | −0.2220 |
| CURACURL | −1.0507*** | −0.1854 | −0.0014 |
| TLIOEQ | 0.0042 | −0.0086 | 0.0203 |
| CURATA | 0.0359 | 1.2308 | 0.3399 |
| CMSTA | −5.1428 | −1.6706 | −1.7328 |
| SIZE | −0.1956 | −0.0364 | −0.0217 |
| CFFO | −8.4974** | −4.4258* | −8.0766** |
| OCF | 3.4473 | 0.6674 | 3.2302 |
| Overall Model −2 log likelihood statistic[2] | 97.144*** | 53.064*** | 35.003*** |
| Δ in −2 log likelihood from adding CFFO to an OCF model[3] | 4.786**** | 3.729** | 6.077** |
| Δ in −2 log likelihood from adding OCF to a CFFO model[4] | 1.786 | 0.316 | 2.558 |

[1]The Combined Full Model contains both cash flow variables, CFFO and OCF, and the seven accrual ratios (INCTA, SALCURA, CURACURL, TLIOEQ, CURATA, CMSTA, and SIZE) regressed on DISTRESS. See Table 2 for definitions of the independent variables.

[2]The Overall Model −2 log likelihood Statistic for each model follows a $\chi^2$ distribution with nine degrees of freedom. This statistic tests the overall strength of the variables in the model. Significance for each parameter estimate is based on a Wald $\chi^2$ Statistic and tests the signaling ability of each individual independent variable.

[3]The Δ in −2 log likelihood from adding CFFO to an OCF model is the change in the −2 log likelihood Statistic for a base model with OCF and the accrual variables (reported in Table 2) to a −2 log likelihood Statistic for a full model with CFFO added to the base model. It exhibits a $\chi^2$ distribution with one degree of freedom. A significant Δ −2 log likelihood indicates that CFFO has incremental usefulness over OCF.

[4]The Δ in −2 log likelihood from adding OCF to CFFO model is the change in the −2 log likelihood Statistic for a base model with CFFO and the accrual variables (reported in Table 2) to a −2 log likelihood statistic for a full model with OCF added to the base model. It exhibits a $\chi^2$ distribution with one degree of freedom. A significant Δ −2 log likelihood indicates that OCF has incremental usefulness over CFFO.

***Significant at $p$-value $\leq$ .01.
**Significant at $p$-value $\leq$ .05.
*Significant at $p$-value $\leq$ .10.

## 4.2. *How CFFO and OCF differ?*

Tables 2 and 3 results suggest that prior cash flow studies may have erroneously concluded that operating cash flow offers no incremental explanatory power over accrual ratios in explaining financial distress. Results suggest that, in explaining financial distress, estimated operating cash flow (OCF) differs from cash flow from operating activities (CFFO) as reported on the current Statement of Cash Flows. Table 3 results suggest that CFFO is likely the better operating cash flow variable for explaining financial distress. Consequently, understanding how the two operating cash flow variables differ is important. Thus, in the light of this study's logit regression results, and of Bahnson *et al.*'s (1996) findings, we conduct further analyses to examine whether the differences between OCF and CFFO can provide some explanation for the logistic regression results of OCF and CFFO.

We begin our analyses by examining the differences between CFFO and OCF scaled by total assets. Table 4 reports the mean and standard deviation of CFFO and OCF by group (distressed and nondistressed). Table 4 also reports the results of *t*-tests for differences between the means of CFFO and OCF for the distressed and nondistressed groups of firms.

Each year prior to distress, the CFFO mean for the nondistressed group is significantly higher than the CFFO mean for the distressed group.

**Table 4.**   Means and standard deviations of CFFO and OCF scaled by total assets with *t*-test of each variable's mean difference for nondistressed and distressed firms.

| Year | Distressed | | | Standard | *T*-Statistic | Prob > \|*T*\| |
| | Group | Variable | Mean | deviation | | |
|---|---|---|---|---|---|---|
| Year 1 | Nondistressed | CFFO | 0.0191 | 0.0918 | 4.970 | 0.0000 |
| | Distressed | CFFO | −0.0313 | 0.2172 | | |
| | Nondistressed | OCF | 0.0932 | 0.1049 | −0.3562 | 0.7222 |
| | Distressed | OCF | 0.1115 | 0.5060 | | |
| Year 2 | Nondistressed | CFFO | 0.0916 | 0.1229 | 4.2552 | 0.0000 |
| | Distressed | CFFO | 0.0040 | 0.1126 | | |
| | Nondistressed | OCF | 0.0874 | 0.1299 | 1.0164 | 0.3110 |
| | Distressed | OCF | 0.0547 | 0.2717 | | |
| Year 3 | Nondistressed | CFFO | 0.0940 | 0.0884 | 4.7408 | 0.0000 |
| | Distressed | CFFO | 0.0094 | 0.1305 | | |
| | Nondistressed | OCF | 0.0956 | 0.1224 | 2.4200 | 0.0165 |
| | Distressed | OCF | 0.0293 | 0.2175 | | |

Table 4 reveals quite different results for OCF. For Years 1 and 2, the OCF means are not significantly different for the two groups. In fact, the OCF mean is larger for the distressed firms than for the nondistressed firms in Year 1.

Because Table 4 revealed group differences for the means of CFFO and OCF, we examined the difference between CFFO and OCF by group. Table 5 reports the mean difference (DIFF) between CFFO and OCF for each group for each year prior to the distress event. Table 5 also reports the results of $t$-tests on DIFF. DIFF tends to be negative each year, suggesting that OCF is overstated, when compared to CFFO. Also, the results show that the overstatement is greater for the distressed firms than for the nondistressed firms. The overstated mean difference is significantly greater for the distressed firms when compared to the nondistressed firms in year 1 ($p$-value $< 0.05$) and year 2 ($p$-value $< 0.075$).

As reported in Table 4, the standard deviations for OCF tend to be larger than the standard deviations for CFFO, especially for the distressed firms. These results indicate that $t$-tests on the means may be somewhat misleading because of the large amount of variation in the data. Consequently, we developed a contingency table to determine whether or not the magnitude and direction of the percentage difference between the distressed and nondistressed firms is significant.

The percentage difference (PER_DIFF) for each firm $= [($CFFO $-$ OCF$)/$ (absolute value (CFFO))] $\times 100$. When investigating directional differences, scaling the differences by CFFO would produce erroneous results when OCF is larger than CFFO and CFFO is negative. Thus, one must scale the differences by the absolute value of CFFO. The Pearson $\chi^2$ significance test for the contingency table is based on the number of occurrences in each category and

**Table 5.**   Means and standard deviations of the difference (DIFF) between CFFO and OCF, with $t$-test of DIFF between distressed groups.

| Year | Distressed group | Mean of DIFF[1] | Standard deviation | $T$-Statistic | Prob $> |T|$ |
|------|------------------|-----------------|--------------------|--------------|-------------|
| Year 1 | Nondistressed | −0.00129 | 0.06379 | 2.1601 | 0.0323 |
|        | Distressed    | −0.14294 | 0.66792 | | |
| Year 2 | Nondistressed | 0.00418  | 0.07346 | 1.8029 | 0.0734 |
|        | Distressed    | −0.05064 | 0.29386 | | |
| Year 3 | Nondistressed | −0.00164 | 0.08089 | 0.9834 | 0.3270 |
|        | Distressed    | −0.01990 | 0.15033 | | |

[1]DIFF = CFFO − OCF.

is not affected by the large variation in data (unlike tests based on means, the contingency table test of significance is not based on continuous data).

Table 6 includes the number of distressed and nondistressed firms observed that possess percentage differences based on three levels of magnitude for each year. Thus, each firm is sorted by the direction and magnitude of the percentage difference between OCF and CFFO. The percentage differences are broken down into: $< -30$, $\geq -30$ and $\leq 30$, and $> 30$. Thus, Table 6 contains a three-by-two, percentage difference by distress, contingency table for each year.

Each cell in Table 6 contains the observed frequency of observations, cell percentage out of the total 155 firms, column percentage (of the particular distress category), and each cell's contribution to the overall $\chi^2$. As indicated by the Pearson $\chi^2$ statistic, results show a significant pattern in the direction and magnitude of the percentage differences between OCF and CFFO and the distress category of firms for all three years.

The cell contributions to the overall $\chi^2$ suggest that the significant difference for each year is primarily caused by differences in the $< -30$ and the $\geq -30$ and $\leq 30$ categories for the distressed firms (the largest cell $\chi^2$ contributions occur in these two cells). The distressed firms have significantly greater large negative differences (exceeding 30%), and fewer small differences (within 30%), than do nondistressed firms. The results are consistent for all three years, although they are strongest for Year 1. Comparing the column percentages for the nondistressed and distressed firms show that the distressed firms have a higher proportion of large negative percentage differences between OCF and CFFO than do the nondistressed firms (e.g., 50% versus 14.29% for Year 1). Thus, Table 6 results indicate that OCF tends to be overstated relative to CFFO in greater magnitudes for distressed firms than for nondistressed firms. For the nondistressed firms, OCF is equally likely to be less than or greater than CFFO.

## 4.3. *Analyses of CFFO and OCF and financial distress research*

Our additional analyses reveal potential reasons prior financial distress research found that estimated net operating cash flow possessed little incremental usefulness. The proxy used for net operating cash flow (OCF) may not adequately capture actual operating cash flow as reported on the cash flow statement. Table 4 reveals significant differences between the groups for the means of CFFO all three years but not for OCF one and two years prior to the distress event. Table 5

**Table 6.**   Three by two contingency table: Percentage difference (PER_DIFF) between CFFO and OCF by DISTRESS.

**Year 1:** *Frequency of observations, cell percentage, column percentage, and cell $\chi^2$ Contribution.*

| | Frequency<br>Percent<br>Column percentage<br>$\chi^2$ cell contribution | DISTRESS | | |
|---|---|---|---|---|
| | | No | Yes | Totals |
| | < −30 | 15<br>9.68%<br>14.29%<br>5.400 | 25<br>16.13%<br>50.00%<br>11.340 | 40<br>25.81% |
| PER_DIFF | ≥ −30 and ≥ 30 | 71<br>45.81%<br>67.62%<br>2.786 | 15<br>9.68%<br>30.00%<br>5.852 | 86<br>55.48% |
| | > 30 | 19<br>12.26%<br>18.10%<br>0.021 | 10<br>6.45%<br>20.00%<br>0.044 | 29<br>18.71% |
| | Total | 105<br>67.74% | 50<br>32.26% | 155<br>100.00% |

Pearson $\chi^2$ (2 df) = 25.446 ( *p*-value = 0.001)
Percentage difference = [(CFFO − OCF)/(absolute value (CFFO))] × 100

**Year 2:** *Frequency of observations, cell percentage, column percentage, and cell $\chi^2$ contribution.*

| | Frequency<br>Percent<br>Column percentage<br>$\chi^2$ cell contribution | DISTRESS | | |
|---|---|---|---|---|
| | | No | Yes | Totals |
| | < −30 | 14<br>9.03%<br>13.33%<br>2.333 | 17<br>10.97%<br>34.00%<br>4.901 | 31<br>20.00% |
| PER_DIFF | ≥ −30 and ≥ 30 | 77<br>49.68%<br>73.33%<br>1.472 | 22<br>14.19%<br>44.00%<br>3.091 | 99<br>63.87% |

*(Continued)*

**Table 6.**   *(Continued)*

| | | | | |
|---|---|---|---|---|
| > 30 | | 14 | 11 | 25 |
| | | 9.03% | 7.10% | 16.13% |
| | | 13.33% | 22.00% | |
| | | 0.509 | 1.068 | |
| | Total | 105 | 50 | <u>155</u> |
| | | 67.74% | 32.26% | 100.00% |

Pearson $\chi^2$ (2 df) = 13.374 (*p*-value = 0.001)
Percentage difference = [(CFFO – OCF)/(absolute value (CFFO))] × 100

**Year 3:** *Frequency of observations, cell percentage, column percentage, and cell $\chi^2$ contribution.*

| | | DISTRESS | | |
|---|---|---|---|---|
| Frequency<br>Percent<br>Column percentage<br>$\chi^2$ cell contribution | | No | Yes | Totals |
| | < −30 | 21 | 19 | 40 |
| | | 13.55% | 12.26% | 25.81% |
| | | 20.00% | 38.00% | |
| | | 1.372 | 2.881 | |
| PER_DIFF | ≥ −30 and ≤ 30 | 65 | 19 | 84 |
| | | 41.94% | 12.26% | 54.19% |
| | | 61.90% | 38.00% | |
| | | 1.152 | 2.419 | |
| | > 30 | 19 | 12 | 31 |
| | | 12.26% | 7.74% | 20.00% |
| | | 18.10% | 24.00% | |
| | | 0.190 | 0.400 | |
| | Total | 105 | 50 | <u>155</u> |
| | | 67.74% | 32.26% | 100.00% |

Pearson $\chi^2$ (2 df) = 8.414 (*p*-value = 0.015)

shows that the mean difference between CFFO and OCF is generally negative, suggesting that, on average, OCF is overstated relative to CFFO. Table 6 results show that when differences between CFFO and OCF exist, OCF is overstated in significant magnitudes for the distressed firms, while OCF is as likely to be understated as overstated for the nondistressed firms.

## 5. Conclusion

This study examines whether CFFO produces more useful information than OCF in explaining future financial distress. When included in financial distress logistic regression models with accrual variables, OCF is not significant (at a $p$-value $< 0.10$) in any year regardless of the scaling measure used. In contrast, CFFO is significant all three years when scaled by total assets, in Years 1 and 3 when scaled by total liabilities, and in Year 1 when scaled by current liabilities. In fact, results suggest that CFFO even adds significant explanatory power to models that include OCF.

Additional analyses confirm Bahnson *et al.*'s (1996) findings that CFFO as reported on the Statement of Cash Flows differs from net operating cash flow as estimated in prior studies (OCF). Results show that large and significant differences exist between OCF and CFFO and more so for the distressed firms than the nondistressed firms. OCF is more likely to exceed CFFO by a large amount for distressed firms than for the nondistressed firms. The increased amount of the differences between OCF and CFFO for the distressed firms likely explains the failure of prior studies to find OCF incrementally significant over accrual variables in distress models.

Finding stronger results for CFFO than OCF has important implications. First, our results suggest that previous cash flow research findings may be misleading because researchers had to estimate the cash flows using accrual data. Thus, prior cash flow research should be replicated using actual cash flows now that the actual cash flows are available. Our results provide evidence supporting the FASB's decision to require a separate cash flow statement. However, like Bahnson *et al.* (1996), our results indicate that the FASB should perhaps issue more explicit directions for reporting cash flow from operations.

## 6. Acknowledgment

This research was partially supported by a Middle Tennessee State University Summer Research Grant and by the Business and Economic Research Center. The authors wish to thank participants at The University of Tennessee Workshop and University of Kentucky Research Workshop for their comments and suggestions on earlier drafts of this paper.

## References

Altman, E. I., "Financial Ratios, Discriminant Analysis and the Prediction of Corporate Bankruptcy." *Journal of Finance* 23, 589–609 (1968).

Altman, E. I., R. G. Haldeman and P. Narayanan, "Zeta Analysis: A New Model to Identify Bankruptcy Risk of Corporations." *Journal of Banking and Finance* 1, 37–72 (1977).

Aziz, A., D. C. Emanuel and G. H. Lawson, "Bankruptcy Prediction—An Investigation of Cash Flow Based Models." *Journal of Management Studies* 25, 419–437 (1988).

Aziz, A. and G. H. Lawson, "Cash Flow Reporting and Financial Distress Models: Testing of Hypotheses." *Financial Management* 18, 55–63 (1989).

Ball, R. and P. Brown, "An Empirical Evaluation of Accounting Income Numbers." *Journal of Accounting Research* 6, 159–178 (1968).

Bahnson, P. R. and J. W. Bartley, "The Sensitivity of Failure Prediction Models to Alternative Definitions of Failure." *Advances in Accounting* 10, 255–278 (1992).

Bahnson, P. R., P. B. W., Miller and B. P. Budge, "Nonarticulation of Cash Flow Statements and Implications for Education, Research and Practice." *Accounting Horizons* 10, 1–15 (1996).

Barth, M. E., W. H. Beaver, J. R. M. Hand and W. R. Landsman, "Accruals, Cash Flows, and Equity Values." *Review of Accounting Studies* 4, 205–229 (1999).

Barth, M. E., D. P. Cram and K. K. Nelson, "Accruals and the Prediction of Future Cash Flows." *The Accounting Review* 76, 27–58 (2001).

Beaver, W. H., "Financial Ratios as Predictors of Failure." *Journal of Accounting Research* (Supplement), 71–127 (1966).

Beaver, W. H. and R. E. Dukes, "Interperiod Tax Allocation, Earnings Expectations, and the Behavior of Security Prices." *The Accounting Review* 47, 320–333 (1972).

Bowen, R. M., D. Burgstahler and A. Daley, "The Incremental Information Content of Accruals versus Cash Flows." *The Accounting Review* 62, 723–747 (1987).

Casey, C. J. and N. J. Bartczak, "Cash Flow — It's Not the Bottom Line." *Harvard Business Review* 62, 61–66 (1984).

Casey, C. J. and N. J. Bartczak, "Using Operating Cash Flow Data to Predict Financial Distress: Some Extensions." *Journal of Accounting Research* 23, 384–401 (1985).

Cheng, C., D. Liu and T. Schaefer, "Earnings Permanence and the Incremental Information Content of Cash Flows from Operations." *Journal of Accounting Research* 34, 173–181 (1996).

Cheng, C. S. A., C-S. Liu and T. F. Schaefer, "The Value Relevance of SFAS No. 95 Cash Flows from Operations as Assessed by Security Market Effects." *Accounting Horizons* 11, 1–15 (1997).

Finger, C. A., "The Ability of Earnings to Predict Future Earnings and Cash Flow." *Journal of Accounting Review* 32, 210–223 (1994).

Gentry, J. A., P. Newbold and D. T. Whitford, "Classifying Bankrupt Firms with Funds Flow Components." *Journal of Accounting Research* 23, 146–160 (1985).

Gentry, J. A., P. Newbold and D. T. Whitford, "Funds Flow Components, Financial Ratios, and Bankruptcy." *Journal of Business Finance and Accounting* 14, 595–606 (1987).

Gilbert, L. R., K. Menon and K. B. Schwartz, "Predicting Bankruptcy for Firms in Financial Distress." *Journal of Business Finance and Accounting* 17, 161–171 (1990).

Gombola, M. J., M. E., Haskins, J. E. Ketz and D. D. Williams, "Cash Flow in Bankruptcy Prediction." *Financial Management* (Winter), 55–65 (1987).

Greenberg, R. R., G. L. Johnson and K. Ramesh, "Earnings versus Cash Flow as a Predictor of Future Cash Flow Measures." *Journal of Accounting, Auditing, and Finance* 1, 266–277 (1986).

Krishnan, G. V. and J. A. Largay III, "The Predictive Ability of Direct Method Cash Flow Information." *Journal of Business Finance & Accounting* (January/March), 215–245 (2000).

Lau, A. H-L., *On the Prediction of Firms In Financial Distress, With An Evaluation of Alternative Funds-Flow Concepts*, Ph.D. Dissertation (Washington University), 1982.

Lawson, G. H., "The Rationale of Cash Flow Accounting." In *Trends In Managerial and Financial Accounting* ed. C. V. Dam, Martins Nijhoff, 1978.

Lawson, G. H., "The Measurement of Corporate Performance on a Cash Flow basis: A Reply to Mr. Egginton." *Accounting and Business Research* (Spring), 99–107 (1985).

Lee, T. A., "A Case for Cash Flow Reporting." *Journal of Business Finance* 4, 27–36 (1972).

Lee, T. A., "The Cash Flow Accounting Alternative for Corporate Financial Reporting." In *Trends in Managerial and Financial Accounting* ed. C. V. Dam, Martins Nijhoff, 1978.

Lorek, K. S. and G. L. Willinger, "A Multivariate Time-Series Prediction Model for Cash-Flow Data." *The Accounting Review* 71, 81–101 (1996).

Neill, J. D., T. F. Schaefer, P. R. Bahnson and M. E. Bradbury, "The Usefulness of Cash Flow Data: A Review and Synthesis." *Journal of Accounting Literature* 10, 117–149 (1991).

Ohlson, J. A., "Financial Ratios and the Probabilistic Prediction of Bankruptcy." *Journal of Accounting Research* 19, 109–131 (1980).

Rayburn, J., "The Association of Operating Cash Flow and Accruals with Security Returns." *Journal of Accounting Research* 24, 112–133 (1986).

Ward, T. J., "An Empirical Study of the Incremental Predictive Ability of Beaver's Naive Operating Flow Measure Using Four-State Ordinal Models of Financial Distress." *Journal of Business Finance and Accounting* 21, 547–561 (1994).

Ward, T. J. and B. P. Foster, "An Empirical Analysis of Thomas's Financial Accounting Allocation Fallacy Theory in a Financial Distress Context." *Accounting and Business Research* 26, 137–152 (1996).

Ward, T. J. and B. P. Foster, "A Note on Selecting a Response Measure for Financial Distress." *Journal of Business Finance and Accounting* 27, 869–879 (1997).

Chapter 6

# ——Earnings Surprise and the Relative Information Content of Short Interest ————————————

Jose Mercado-Mendez
*Central Missouri State University, USA*

Roger J. Best
*Central Missouri State University, USA*

Ronald W. Best
*University of West Georgia, USA*

Restrictions imposed on short selling provides incentive for these traders to be better informed, leading to the use of short interest data as an information measure. We add to the literature on whether short sellers are, indeed, better informed traders by investigating whether there are changes in short interest near-term to extreme earnings surprises. If short sellers are better informed (or better able to anticipate corporate events), short interest data should reflect noticeable changes in advance of these significant announcements. After controlling for company-specific factors, we find only limited evidence that the average short seller trades with superior information.

**Keywords:** Short interest; short selling; earnings surprise.

## 1. Introduction

Diamond and Verrechia (1987) (henceforth DV) model the impact of the imposition of constraints and restrictions on short selling. In the presence of short sale prohibitions, stock prices do not efficiently move to true values through time. When constraints (as opposed to prohibitions) on short selling exist, DV predict that short selling provides information to market participants allowing a more efficient adjustment over time to the fundamental value. An unambiguous implication of the model, therefore, is that announcements of larger levels of short interest will lead to lower stock prices. Indeed, Conrad (1986), Senchack and Starks (1993), Asquith and Meulbroek (1995), and Desai *et al.* (2002) find evidence consistent with the model's predictions. Conrad (1986) and Senchack and Starks (1993) show that announcements of high levels of short interest generate significant negative abnormal returns. Asquith and Meulbroek (1995) find that short interest and stock returns are negatively correlated for NYSE firms, and Desai *et al.* (2002) show that heavily shorted firms listed on NASDAQ experience negative abnormal returns.

As is true with classical models in finance, rational expectations form the basis of the DV model. Further, DV assume that at least some portion of the short sellers in their model represent "informed" traders — that is, these traders possess superior information regarding the true value of the firm. In fact, it is the existence of better informed traders that allows market participants to glean information from the set of trades observed in each period and to update their expectations regarding the true stock price. In this manner, and depending on the degree of constraints or restrictions placed on short selling activities, the stock price will adjust rationally through time towards the correct value.

Recent behavioral-based finance research, however, has challenged the rationality of investors in all circumstances. Cooper *et al.* (2001) show that (during the market bubble of the 1990s) investors significantly increased the stock price of companies that changed to a .com name. This response occurred even for companies that derived little or no revenue from internet-based activities. Rashes (2001) finds that investors' confusion over stocks with similar ticker symbols can drive stock prices from fundamental values. Hirshleifer and Shumway (2003), Kamstra *et al.* (2003), and Saunders (1993) find that the mood of market participants has a significant impact on stock prices. On days when mood is more positive (e.g. on sunny days), stock returns are higher than on negative mood days. Finally, Hirshleifer (2001) provides an overview of numerous cognitive biases that appear to significantly influence individual investors, often leading to irrational behavior.

In the presence of irrationality on the part of (at least some) traders, evidence of stock price changes subsequent to short interest announcements may have an alternative explanation. While the previous empirical findings are consistent with the presence of informed traders who engage in short selling (as in DV), it is also possible that short sellers are no better informed than other traders and that investors simply exhibit "herding" behavior upon the observation of the level of short interest. That is, investors incorrectly infer that short sales represent trades of better informed market participants when these trades merely represent speculative activities. Thus, additional evidence is needed to ascertain whether (at least some) short sellers possess superior information.[1]

---

[1]Additional evidence is also necessitated by the recent use of short interest as an information measure such as in Kadiyala and Vetsuypens (2002).

Because announcement and longer-term returns are subject to the cognitive biases (and incorrect assessments) of typical investors, we propose a more direct test of the informativeness of short interest by examining the change in short interest surrounding earnings surprises. By examining short interest patterns around a predictable event date (i.e. an earnings announcement), we can infer whether informed short selling occurs. Specifically, we use large negative (positive) earnings surprise as a proxy for bad (good) news and determine whether short sellers anticipate this news by observing changes in overall short positions.

In similar research, Gintschel (2001) examines the correlation between the short interest ratios of NASDAQ firms and naive earnings surprise. He finds essentially no correlation between these measures. This result, although contrary to the DV model predictions, is not surprising. Fried and Givoly (1982) and O'Brien (1988) show that analysts' forecasts of earnings are superior to "mechanical" forecasts. Thus, the use of a naive forecast introduces noisy observations into the data set. That is, we would expect little correlation between short interest and earnings changes for firms which have an increase or decrease in earnings from the previous period if investors (and short sellers) have already anticipated this change. These observations are likely to mask any ability to detect informed short selling surrounding firms with *unexpected* changes in earnings. Thus, we use analysts' forecasts of earnings to determine whether firms experience a significant degree of unexpected earnings and examine the behavior of short sellers around the announcement of this surprise.

We also examine the short interest data for stocks traded on the organized exchanges (NYSE and AMEX) and NASDAQ separately to identify whether short sellers are relatively more informed on one of these types of markets. Short sales restrictions (SEC rule 10a-1) applied only to securities listed or traded on an organized exchange (i.e. NYSE/AMEX) until 1994 when NASDAQ adopted similar short sale rules (NASD 3350). We examine short interest data after 1994 (when NYSE/AMEX and NASDAQ impose similar short sales restrictions) to determine whether firms listed on a particular exchange are more sensitive to changes in short interest near an earnings announcement due to different listing restrictions or differential coverage by financial analysts. *Ex ante*, differential levels of information asymmetry or the availability of shares that can be borrowed for shorting may create differences in the ability of short sellers to anticipate information or to exploit superior information for exchange-traded or NASDAQ stocks.

In general, our results provide little support for the hypothesis that short sellers on average trade with superior information. We find that, statistically, there are no changes in short interest ratios preceding earnings announcements for firms with unusually large negative or positive earnings surprises. This result holds whether securities are traded via NASDAQ or on the organized exchanges. When we control for company-specific characteristics (i.e. size and book-to-market ratio), we find some support for informed trading, but only for a subset of NASDAQ firms. These results call into question the assumption that short sellers (on average) are better informed traders and limit the usefulness of the short interest ratio as an information measure.

The remainder of our paper is organized as follows. The next section provides details of the data collection process and a description of the final sample. The third section includes the methodology and a discussion of the results we obtain. In the final section, we provide a summary of our results and some concluding comments.

## 2. Data

We begin our analysis by first calculating earnings surprise for all firms listed on the First Call IBES earnings forecasts database from 1996 through 2000. We use quarterly earnings announcements and calculate earnings surprise as the actual (announced) earnings per share minus the median forecasted earnings for that quarter. Best, Best and Young (1998) show that earnings surprise is best measured as the difference between actual and forecasted earnings divided by stock price. Thus, we standardize unexpected earnings by the firm's stock price prior to the earnings announcement. Based on our calculations, firms that have negative earnings surprises are ones in which actual earnings fall below expected earnings. We then rank firms based on earnings surprise for each calendar year of the sample.[2] To alleviate problems associated with potential outliers, for each year, we remove the most extreme 0.5% of firms in each tail of the distribution of earnings surprise. The elimination of extreme observations

---

[2]The month of the earnings announcement lags the fiscal year ended by a minimum of one month. Thus, for firms with a December fiscal year end, the earnings surprise is measured in the following calendar year. We include these firms in the calendar year prior to the year in which earnings surprise is calculated. We choose the sample based on calendar years to eliminate the possibility of time clustering.

is typical in the earnings announcement literature (see Park and Pincus, 2002), and the use of 0.5% follows from Shin and Soenen (1998).

From the remaining firms, we then select the 1% of firms with the most negative earnings surprise and the 1% of firms with the most positive earnings surprise. This results in 588 firms with "large" negative earnings surprises and 588 firms with "large" positive earnings surprises over our sample period. We use the most extreme earnings surprises because we presume that short sellers would be most interested in shorting stocks with the "worst" earnings news and avoiding (or closing short positions in) stocks with the "best" earnings news.

Next, we match the firms identified from IBES with data from Standard and Poor's *Research Insight* database. Dechow *et al.* (2001) find evidence that short interest may be related to fundamentals-to-price ratios. Thus, we collect market value of equity (MVE) from the month immediately prior to the earnings announcement month and the book-to-market (BM) ratio six months prior to the earnings announcement month, along with the exchange identifier from *Research Insight*. Because the IBES ticker symbols and cusip numbers do not always correspond with those on *Research Insight*, we can correctly match only 432 negative surprise firms and 471 positive surprise firms from our initial sample to the appropriate *Research Insight* data. Using these firms, we then search for the level of short sales in data provided by NASDAQ (for both NASDAQ and AMEX listed stocks) and the *Wall Street Journal* for firms listed by the NYSE. We eliminate from the sample any firms for which we cannot match short sales data. Thus, our final sample includes 325 firms with negative earnings surprise and 334 firms with positive earnings surprise. Of the firms with negative surprises, 276 are listed on NASDAQ, 23 on AMEX and 26 are from the NYSE. For the positive surprises, 245 are on NASDAQ, 17 are AMEX-listed, while 72 are from the NYSE.

Table 1 lists the number of sample firms by year and SIC code. As shown, a relatively larger proportion of our sample comes from the 3000 and 7000 SIC code ranges. It is within these ranges that high-tech (computer technology oriented) firms are classified. The relative proportions (not shown), however, are not substantially different from the universe of firms (as listed on Research Insight) over the same time period. Further, in our subsequent tests, we examine whether time variations or industry effects influence our results. We find no such effects. Thus, all test results are reported for only the aggregate sample.

**Table 1.**   Number of firms by SIC code.

| SIC Code | Year of Earnings | | | | | |
|---|---|---|---|---|---|---|
| | 1996 | 1997 | 1998 | 1999 | 2000 | All |
| 1000–1999 | 6 | 10 | 13 | 9 | 4 | 42 |
| 2000–2999 | 14 | 14 | 16 | 11 | 12 | 67 |
| 3000–3999 | 42 | 34 | 51 | 34 | 22 | 183 |
| 4000–4999 | 11 | 25 | 22 | 20 | 20 | 98 |
| 5000–5999 | 9 | 10 | 11 | 10 | 13 | 53 |
| 6000–6999 | 6 | 5 | 4 | 3 | 6 | 24 |
| 7000–7999 | 16 | 24 | 38 | 25 | 49 | 152 |
| 8000–8999 | 0 | 1 | 4 | 4 | 7 | 16 |
| Total | 104 | 123 | 159 | 116 | 133 | 635 |

## 3. Methodology and Results

In Table 2, we provide summary information for our sample segmented by exchange and earnings surprise (ES). As indicated, the level of negative ES is similar across NASDAQ and NYSE/AMEX firms, with means of −0.0677 and −0.0574 respectively. Positive ES is also similar for NASDAQ (0.0200) and NYSE/AMEX (0.0164) firms in our sample. The average book-to-market (BM) ratio is remarkably consistent for NASDAQ firms segmented by negative and positive ES (0.54 versus 0.52). These are similar to the average BM ratio for the NYSE/AMEX positive ES firms (0.56), but lower than the average NYSE/AMEX BM ratio for firms with negative ES (0.73).[3] Finally, not surprisingly, the typical NASDAQ firm in our sample is significantly smaller than the typical NYSE/AMEX firm. This is potentially problematic for our analysis as the relatively small size of the negative ES firms (for both NASDAQ and NYSE/AMEX) could restrict the activities of short sellers as they attempt to borrow shares.[4] It is possible that we may find no short interest changes for smaller firms, or, alternatively, the best informed short sellers will begin short

---

[3]As shown, the median firms have essentially identical BM ratios for the NYSE/AMEX ES subgroups. The NASDAQ median BM ratio is essentially the same across ES subgroups, but lower than NYSE/AMEX firms.

[4]Smaller firms have fewer shares outstanding, lessening the likelihood that sufficient quantities of shares are available to borrow. In particular, if few shares are available, the expected benefit of shorting may be insufficient for the investor to engage in short selling.

**Table 2.** Summary statistics.

|  | Sample Size | ES | BM | MVE |
|---|---|---|---|---|
| **NASDAQ Firms:** | | | | |
| Negative ES | 276 | −0.0677 | 0.5420 | 171.7121 |
|  |  | (−0.0612) | (0.3960) | (91.3820) |
| Positive ES | 245 | 0.0200 | 0.5157 | 402.3078 |
|  |  | (0.0172) | (0.4040) | (130.0440) |
| **NYSE/AMEX Firms:** | | | | |
| Negative ES | 39 | −0.0574 | 0.7309 | 512.9972 |
|  |  | (−0.0495) | (0.556) | (261.574) |
| Positive ES | 75 | 0.0164 | 0.5629 | 3,116.362 |
|  |  | (0.0140) | (0.5700) | (635.709) |

Notes: ES is the earnings surprise, defined as the difference between forecasted and actual earnings divided by the firm's stock price. BM is the book-to-market ratio six months prior to the earnings announcement month, and MVE is the market value of equity at the end of the month preceding the earnings announcement and is in millions. Median values are in parentheses.

selling activities far in advance of the earnings announcement when shares are still available for shorting.[5]

As previously indicated, our hypothesis is that *if* short sellers are better informed, greater levels of short sales (or alternatively, short interest) will occur for firms with extreme negative earnings surprise and lower levels of short sales will be evident for firms with extreme positive surprises. To ascertain whether support exists for this hypothesis, we first calculate the short interest ratio (short interest divided by average daily volume) for each of the firms in our sample by month. With respect to the denominator of the short interest ratio, NASDAQ reports the average daily share volume for the short interest reporting period, while the NYSE and AMEX reports the average number of shares traded daily in the preceding month (AMEX switched to the average daily volume in February 2001). Thus, to avoid improper comparisons, we segment our sample and report our results for NASDAQ and NYSE/AMEX separately.

We then examine the level of short interest for the months surrounding the earnings announcement month. If short sellers are better informed, on average we expect to see a larger short interest ratio (SIR) in the month including ($SIR_t$) and immediately preceding ($SIR_{t-1}$) the earnings announcement when

---

[5] See Angel, Christophe and Ferri (2003) for a description of short selling activities in the Nasdaq market.

compared to the month immediately following ($SIR_{t+1}$) the earnings announcement for firms with negative ES. That is, better-informed investors would rationally increase short positions prior to the earnings announcement, then close those positions after earnings are announced. We expect to see little activity in the SIR surrounding the earnings announcement for firms with positive ES. If short interest activity does occur for positive ES firms, declines in the SIR prior to the earnings announcement would be consistent with short sellers possessing superior information. Further, we also expect that firms with negative ES will have significantly larger SIRs in the months preceding and including the earnings announcement than the SIRs for firms with positive ES. To help control the potential problems associated with share availability for smaller firms (and the potential that short sellers are trading far in advance of the earnings announcement), we examine the level of short interest two months prior to the earnings announcement in this analysis.

Table 3 lists the average SIR for NASDAQ firms for the months surrounding the earnings announcement. For negative ES firms, the level of SIR steadily declines from 3.543 two months before the earnings announcement to 2.570 one month after the announcement. Although we expect a decline in the month

**Table 3.**   SIR surrounding the earnings announcement for NASDAQ firms.

|  | Month | | | |
| --- | --- | --- | --- | --- |
|  | $SIR_{t-2}$ | $SIR_{t-1}$ | $SIR_t$ | $SIR_{t+1}$ |
| Negative ES | 3.543 | 3.385 | 3.067 | 2.570 |
|  | (1.470) | (1.428) | (1.465) | (1.146) |
| Positive ES | 2.818 | 2.856 | 2.861 | 2.531 |
|  | (1.387) | (1.468) | (1.199) | (1.198) |
| *t*-test for difference (Negative ES − Positive ES) | 1.870** | 1.166 | 0.541 | 0.122 |

Notes: SIR is the short interest ratio for the month relative to the earnings announcement month ($SIR_t$). SIR is calculated as the level of short interest divided by average daily volume for the month over which short interest is determined. ES is earnings surprise and is calculated as the difference between forecasted and actual earnings divided by the firm's stock price. Averages are reported, with median values appearing in parentheses. There are 276 firms with negative ES and 245 with positive ES for each month. The *t*-statistic is calculated assuming unequal variances.
**Significant at 5%.

after the earnings announcement for these firms, a decline in short interest *prior* to the earnings announcement, which we observe in the month immediately prior to the month of the earnings announcement, is surprising if short sellers are better informed traders. Equally puzzling is the average SIR for the positive ES NASDAQ firms. These firms exhibit little change in the SIR surrounding the earnings announcement. Although lack of substantial changes in the average SIR for these firms may not be surprising, the *level* of short interest is. Two months prior to the earnings announcement, the average SIR is statistically smaller for positive ES firms than for negative ES firms. In the months immediately prior to and including the earnings announcement, however, the two months we expect to see large differences across earnings surprise groups, the average SIR is statistically indistinguishable among negative and positive ES firms. Although it is possible that the smaller size of the negative ES NASDAQ firms may limit short selling activity, causing us to fail to detect the "superior information" of short sellers, the relatively large amount of short interest in the positive ES firms cannot be explained by market microstructure. Thus, based on this evidence, it appears that the majority of short selling activity in NASDAQ firms is due less to superior information and more to "herding" behavior (or speculative/hedging activities) on the part of these traders.

We also examine the pattern in SIRs surrounding the earnings announcement month for NYSE/AMEX firms to test for evidence of superior trading by short sellers in these markets. These results, segmented by negative and positive ES, appear in Table 4. For NYSE/AMEX firms that have negative ES, the average SIR increases from 8.679 two months prior to the earnings announcement to 11.292 one month prior to 16.469 in the month of the earnings announcement. The average SIR then drops to 10.489 in the month following the earnings announcement. This pattern is consistent with the hypothesis that short sellers possess superior information, as better-informed investors increase short positions prior to earnings announcements for firms with worse than expected earnings, and close these positions after the earnings are announced. The positive ES firms, however, exhibit a similar pattern in the average SIR. In fact, the average SIR for positive ES firms on NYSE/AMEX is statistically the same as for the negative ES firms in the month before, of and after the earnings announcement. This again suggests that most short sellers are engaging in speculative (or hedging) activities as opposed to trading on superior information,

**Table 4.**  SIR surrounding the earnings announcement for NYSE/AMEX firms.

| | Month | | | |
|---|---|---|---|---|
| | $SIR_{t-2}$ | $SIR_{t-1}$ | $SIR_t$ | $SIR_{t+1}$ |
| Negative ES | 8.679 | 11.292 | 16.469 | 10.489 |
| | (7.216) | (7.942) | (6.418) | (6.682) |
| Positive ES | 12.656 | 12.641 | 14.951 | 12.428 |
| | (7.826) | (7.053) | (7.459) | (6.352) |
| *t*-test for difference (Negative ES − Positive ES) | −1.810** | −0.429 | 0.227 | −0.480 |

Notes: SIR is the short interest ratio for the month relative to the earnings announcement month ($SIR_t$). SIR is calculated as the level of short interest divided by average daily volume for the month over which short interest is determined. ES is earnings surprise and is calculated as the difference between forecasted and actual earnings divided by the firm's stock price. Averages are reported, with median values appearing in parentheses. There are 39 firms with negative ES and 75 with positive ES for each month. The *t*-statistic is calculated assuming unequal variances.
**Significant at 5%.

as better-informed investors would not increase their short positions prior to the announcement of a positive earnings surprise.[6]

To determine whether any of the patterns we find in the average SIR in Tables 3 and 4 represent statistically significant changes, we calculate parametric *t*-tests on the change in SIR by month. For this test, we continue to segment the sample by whether the stock trades over the NASDAQ system or on NYSE/AMEX and by whether the firm experiences a negative or positive ES. These results appear in Table 5. As shown, the decline in SIR for the month following the earnings announcement for NASDAQ firms with negative ES is statistically significant at the 10% level (with a *t*-statistic of −1.336). In light of the (anecdotal) declines in the average SIR leading up to the earnings announcement, however, this statistical evidence does not support the "superior information" hypothesis for short sellers. Further, the changes in the average SIR observed for NYSE/AMEX firms with negative ES, the strongest evidence in favor of informed trading, are, in fact, statistically insignificant. No other changes in the average SIR are significant. Thus, statistically speaking, we

---

[6]To determine whether volume effects are driving our SIR results, we also examine the percentage change in the actual level of short interest. Because of the highly skewed nature of this data, we examine the percentage change for the median firm. These results, available from the authors, do not change the qualitative interpretations we derive from using the average SIR.

**Table 5.**  Change in SIR from previous month.

| Exchange | Month | | |
| --- | --- | --- | --- |
| | $SIR_{t-1}$ | $SIR_t$ | $SIR_{t+1}$ |
| **Panel A**: Negative Earnings Surprise | | | |
| NASDAQ | −0.158 | −0.318 | −0.497 |
| | (−0.321) | (−0.672) | (−1.336*) |
| NYSE/AMEX | 2.613 | 5.178 | −5.980 |
| | (0.894) | (0.781) | (−0.909) |
| **Panel B**: Positive Earnings Surprise | | | |
| NASDAQ | 0.038 | 0.005 | −0.330 |
| | (0.455) | (0.013) | (−0.990) |
| NYSE/AMEX | −0.015 | 2.310 | −2.523 |
| | (−0.006) | (0.714) | (−0.602) |

Notes: SIR is the average short interest ratio. The change in SIR in the table is the difference in the average SIR for the month listed minus the average SIR from the previous month. $SIR_t$ represents the earnings announcement month. Earnings surprise is defined as the difference between forecasted and actual earnings divided by the firm's stock price. $t$-statistics are calculated assuming unequal variances and appear in parentheses.
*Significant at 10%.

detect from the average SIR *no* evidence that short sellers, on average, possess superior information when trading.

As a final test, we employ regression analysis to determine the relationship between the SIR surrounding the earnings announcement and the magnitude of the earnings surprise while controlling for each firm's market value of equity, book-to-market ratio and whether the firm had a negative earnings surprise. We use six regressions, each distinguished by the dependent variable. As the dependent variable in Regressions 1, 2, and 3, we use measures of the SIR for our sample of NASDAQ firms. Specifically, in Regression 1, the dependent variable is the SIR in the month prior to the earnings announcement. The dependent variable in Regression 2 is the change in SIR from two months before to one month before the earnings announcement and in Regression 3, the dependent variable is change in SIR from the month before to the month of the earnings announcement. In Regressions 4, 5, and 6, the dependent variables are defined the same as in Regressions 1, 2, and 3, except that the SIR measures are for our sample of NYSE/AMEX firms. The independent variables in each regression are the earnings surprise, book-to-market ratio, market value of equity, and a dummy variable equal to one if the ES is negative. We use the book-to-market ratio and market value of equity to control for fundamental variables that have been shown to influence short selling activities. The dummy variable is necessary to allow for asymmetric short selling activities across types of earnings surprise. If low levels of short interest exist for firms that experience positive ES, we would see no significant declines in short interest. For negative ES firms, however, there is potential for a much larger change in short interest (in absolute magnitude). Thus, this dummy variable coefficient would indicate whether such relationships exist. The estimated regression coefficients appear in Table 6.

As indicated, there are no statistically significant coefficients in Regressions 2, 5, and 6. In Regression 4, besides the intercept, the only statistically

**Table 6.**   Regression analysis coefficients.

| Regression | NASDAQ Firms (521 observations) | | | NYSE/AMEX Firms (114 observations) | | |
|---|---|---|---|---|---|---|
|  | 1 | 2 | 3 | 4 | 5 | 6 |
| Intercept | 3.56*** | −0.036 | 0.536* | 13.80*** | −0.646 | −2.273 |
| BM | −0.424 | −0.086 | −0.047 | 3.42 | 1.086 | −2.265 |
| MVE | −0.0000 | 0.0000 | 0.0000 | −0.0004* | 0.0000 | 0.0001 |
| ES | −24.05** | 1.317 | −25.88*** | −102.05 | 1.774 | 56.359 |
| D | −1.571 | 0.322 | −1.946*** | −10.629 | −2.663 | 1.935 |
| F-statistic | 1.921 | 0.202 | 3.360** | 1.777 | 0.733 | 0.485 |
| Adj. $R^2$ | 0.007 | −0.006 | 0.018 | 0.027 | −0.010 | −0.019 |

Notes: The dependent variable in Regressions 1 and 4 is the level of the SIR in the month prior to the earnings announcement month. The dependent variable for Regressions 2 and 5 is the change in SIR from two months prior to one month prior to the earnings announcement. The dependent variable for Regressions 3 and 6 is the change in SIR from one month before to the month of the earnings announcement. BM is the book-to-market ratio six months prior to the earnings announcement month, and MVE is the market value of equity at the end of the month preceding the earnings announcement. ES is the earnings surprise, and is calculated as the difference between forecasted and actual earnings divided by the firm's stock price. D is a dummy variable equal to one if the earnings surprise is negative.
*Significant at 10%.
**Significant at 5%.
***Significant at 1%.

significant coefficient is the market value of equity. The negative coefficient for this variable implies that larger firms (NYSE/AMEX) have lower levels of SIR in the month prior to the earnings announcement. Thus, consistent with our previous results, we find no evidence to support superior trading by short sellers in NYSE/AMEX firms. We do, however, find an interesting pattern for the NASDAQ firms in Regressions 1 and 3.

In Regression 1, the estimated coefficient for earnings surprise is negative and significant at the 5% level. This indicates that, after controlling for book-to-market ratio and market value of equity, NASDAQ firms with negative (positive) earnings surprise have marginally higher (lower) SIRs in the month prior to the earnings announcement. Regression 3, with the dependent variable equal to the change in the SIR from the month before to the month of the earnings announcement, provides greater insight into the behavior of short sellers near the earnings announcement. The coefficient for earnings surprise is −25.88 which is significant at the 1% level. Because ES is negative when earnings are less than expected and positive when earnings are greater than expected, this implies that, after controlling for book-to-market ratio and size, NASDAQ firms with negative earnings surprise have significant increases in the SIR immediately prior to the earnings announcement. Further, NASDAQ firms with positive earnings surprise have significant decreases in the SIR prior to the earnings announcement. This finding is consistent with expectations if short sellers are better informed. The significantly negative coefficient (−1.946) on the dummy variable (which equals one if the earnings surprise is negative), however, reveals that this interpretation is erroneous. Indeed, for NASDAQ firms with negative earnings, the typical firm experiences a *decrease* in the SIR immediately prior to the earnings announcement. For example, the average earnings surprise for NASDAQ firms with negative ES is −0.0677 (Table 2). This implies that for the average NASDAQ firm with negative ES, the marginal change in the SIR is $(-25.88) * (-0.0677) - 1.946 = -0.194$ (i.e. for the average negative ES NASDAQ firm, the SIR actually declines immediately prior to the earnings announcement). For NASDAQ firms with more extreme negative earnings surprise (i.e. less than −0.0752), the regression results imply an increase in the SIR immediately prior to the earnings announcement. For NASDAQ firms with positive ES, Regression 3 implies a significant decrease in the SIR immediately prior to the earnings announcement. This is consistent with informed trading by short sellers. Overall, given that there are not significant increases in the SIR for NYSE/AMEX firms with negative ES, and that the SIR changes significantly in the correct direction for only subsets of the NASDAQ firms, the regression results provide only weak evidence that short sellers are better informed traders.

## 4. Conclusions

Using earnings surprise and short interest ratios for a sample of AMEX, NAS-DAQ, and NYSE firms during the period 1996–2000, we find only limited evidence to support the Diamond and Verrecchia (1987) hypothesis that (at least some) short sellers are better informed than the typical investor. We examine the short interest activity of firms that have extreme earnings surprises and find that average short interest ratios are typically the same for firms that experience either a negative or positive earnings surprise. Further, we find that average short interest ratios do not change significantly in the months leading up to and including large positive or negative earnings surprise for either NASDAQ or NYSE/AMEX-traded stocks. After controlling for firm size and book-to-market ratio, however, we find that there are some significant declines in the short interest ratio for NASDAQ firms that experience more extreme negative earnings surprises than our sample average. Given that our sample is chosen such that we include only extreme earnings surprises initially, and given that similar evidence is non-existent for NYSE/AMEX firms, this finding can be considered only weak evidence in support of superior trading by short sellers. We also find evidence of significant declines in the short interest ratio immediately prior to the earnings announcement for NASDAQ firms that experience positive ES after controlling for size and book-to-market ratio.

Based on our collective results, we conclude that most short sales result from "herding" behavior, or speculative/hedging positions, rather than from superior information. This calls into question the use of short interest data as an information measure.

## References

Angel, J., S. Christophe and M. Ferri, "A Close Look at Short Selling on Nasdaq," *Financial Analyst Journal* 59, 66–74 (2003).

Asquith, P. and L. Meulbroek, "An Empirical Investigation of Short Interest," Working paper, Harvard Business School, Harvard University (1995).

Best, R., R. Best and A. Young, "An Examination of Proxies of Information Asymmetry," *Advances in Financial Planning and Forecasting* 8, 17–34 (1998).

Conrad, J., "The Price Effect of Short Sale Restrictions: Some Empirical Tests," Ph.D. Dissertation (Unpublished), University of Chicago, 1986.

Cooper, M., O. Dimitrov and P. R. Rau, "A Rose.com by any other name," *Journal of Finance* 56, 2371–2388 (2001).

Dechow, P., A. Hutton, L. Muelbroek and R. Sloan, "Short-sellers, fundamental analysis and stock returns," *Journal of Financial Economics* 61, 77–106 (2001).

Desai, H., K. Ramesh, R. Thiagarajan and B. Balachandran, "An Investigation of the Information Role of Short Interest in the Nasdaq Market," *Journal of Finance* 57, 2263–2287 (2002).

Diamond, D. and R. Verrecchia, "Constraints on Short Selling and Asset Price Adjustment to Private Information," *Journal of Financial Economics* 18, 277–311 (1987).

Fabozzi F. and F. Modigliani, *Capital Markets–Institutions and Instruments*, Prentice Hall, Englewood Cliffs, NJ, 1992.

Fried, D. and D. Givoly, "Financial Analysts' Forecasts of Earnings: A Better Surrogate for Market Expectations," *Journal of Accounting and Economics* 4, 85–107 (1982).

Gintschel, A., "Short Interest on Nasdaq," Emory University, Working Paper, 2001.

Hirshleifer, D., "Investor Psychology and Asset Pricing," *Journal of Finance* 56, 1533–1597 (2001).

Hirshleifer, D. and T. Shumway, "Good Day Sunshine: Stock Returns and the Weather," *Journal of Finance* 58, 1009–1032 (2003).

Kadiyala, P. and M. Vetsuypens, "Are Stock Splits Credible Signals? Evidence from Short Interest Data," *Financial Management* 31, 31–49 (2002).

Kamstra, M., L. Kramer and M. Levi, "Winter Blues: A Sad Stock Market Cycle," *American Economic Review* 93, 324–343 (2003).

O'Brien, P., "Analysts' Forecasts as Earnings Expectations," *Journal of Accounting and Economics* 10, 53–83 (1988).

Park, C. and M. Pincus, "Internal Versus External Equity Funding Sources and Earnings Response Coefficients," *Review of Quantitative Finance and Accounting* 16, 33–52 (2002).

Rashes, M., "Massively confused investors making conspicuously ignorant choices (mci-mcic)," *Journal of Finance* 56, 1911–1927 (2001).

Reed, A., "Costly Short-Selling and Stock Price Adjustment to Earnings Announcements," University of North Carolina, Working Paper, 2002.

Saunders, E. M. Jr., "Stock Prices and Wall Street Weather," *American Economic Review* 83, 1337–1345 (1993).

Senchack, A. and L. Starks, "Short Sale Restrictions and Market Reactions to Short-Interest Announcements," *Journal of Financial and Quantitative Analysis* 28, 177–194 (1993).

Shin, H. and L. Soenen, "Efficiency of Working Capital Management and Corporate Profitability," *Financial Practice and Education*, Fall/Winter, 37–46 (1998).

Chapter 7

# ——— Group Types and Earnings Management ———

Min-Jeng Shiue
*National Taipei University, Taiwan*

Chan-Jane Lin* and Chi-Chun Liu
*National Taiwan University, Taiwan*

Although a considerable body of research has examined management's incentives to manipulate earnings, relatively little work has examined factors that constrain earnings management. This paper examines the relation between earnings management and one of such important factors — group characteristics in a specific area: business groups in Taiwan. Three hypotheses were derived to test the above connections. Two different regression approaches were employed to conduct our analyses: ordinary least square and two-step regressions. Empirical evidence shows that group member firms with or without a bank and group type are two key factors of a group's organizational structure that explain the extent of discretionary accruals. Sensitivity tests indicate that the results are robust.

**Keywords:** Earnings management; business groups; group types; discretionary accruals.

## 1. Introduction

In the last few decades, the Asian economic miracle stimulated the greatest expansion of wealth in the history of mankind. Many countries in this region, including Taiwan, enjoyed a high growth in real GDP, with relatively little pressure on consumer prices. However, following the Asian financial crisis in 1997, a large number of Taiwanese companies in traditional industries faced many operating and financial difficulties. It seems to have been a sign that Taiwan's economy had a case of the financial flu. Moreover, the financial distress of more than half of those companies was primarily caused by complicated transactions with significantly interlocked affiliates.

To prevent the spread of the troubled conditions, the Taiwan government asked companies to disclose complete information about their related party transactions in financial reports. The government modified and promulgated the specific chapter in the Company Law named "the related enterprises" on June 25, 1997. Furthermore, the Securities and Futures Bureau (SFB) also promulgated the special guidelines for preparation of financial reports

---

*Corresponding author.

by related parties so that these groups would present more detailed financial information.[1,2] Financial reporting problems in a group or a diversified company in emerging markets have also been a major concern of security market participants because of weak disclosure requirements, ineffective governance mechanisms, and a poorly developed market for corporate control.[3] Recently, several researchers suggest that emerging markets such as India have poorly functioning institutions, leading to severe agency and information problems (Khanna and Palepu, 2000). In addition to financial reporting issues, misguided regulations and inefficient judicial systems are another two main sources of market failure (Khanna and Palepu, 1997). The above problems imply that managers of group firms in the emerging markets have more opportunities to manipulate earnings.

Managers or group leaders also have a variety of incentives to manipulate earnings. The group reputation is one of the major concerns of managers as the groups are usually ranked on the group's size, which is measured in total revenues or assets, and operating performance measured in earnings. Next, the need to issue debts or new equities by member firms in the group may offer incentive for earnings manipulation. Incentive may also occur when one or more of the group members have planned to file an initial public offering (IPO). However, in consideration of the group as a whole, different factors, such as group reputation, group and member firm characteristics, tax considerations, and the extent of external finance demand, may influence the incentive to manipulate earnings.

Studies in earnings management can be divided into two categories, event-specific or non-event-specific studies. Examples of event-specific earnings management studies are earnings management around seasoned equity offerings (Teoh, Welch, and Wong, 1998a; Shiah-Hou, 2000), IPOs (Aharony, Lin, and Loeb, 1993; Teoh, Welch and Wong, 1998b), and import relief investigations (Jones, 1991). Examples of general or non-event-specific earnings

---

[1]The Groups will be formally defined in Section 2.

[2]According to the new rules promulgated by the SFC on April 30, 1999, a subordinate company of a public company shall, at the end of each business year, prepare and submit an additional financial report named "Affiliated Enterprises Reports". The controlling company of a public company shall, at the end of each business year, prepare and submit two additional reports, named "Consolidated Business Reports of Affiliated Enterprises" and "Consolidated Financial Statements of Affiliated Enterprises".

[3]See La Porta *et al.* (1998).

management studies include earnings management to increase managerial compensation (Healy, 1985; Guidry, Leone, and Rock, 1999), or to smooth reported earnings (DeFond and Park, 1997). In this paper, we focus on non-event-specific earnings management in a certain area — business groups.

There have been many studies since the 1980s concerning the ways and means of earnings management. The academic evidence on earnings management shows that earnings management occurs for a variety of reasons: to influence stock market perception, to increase management's compensation, to reduce the likelihood of violating debt contracts, and to avoid regulatory intervention (Healy and Wahlen, 1999). Managers have diverse ways to meet their target surplus through earnings management. One of the most effective ways is to change operations, for example, by altering shipment schedules and speeding up or deferring maintenance. Other methods include assets sales, accounting principle changes, and accounting accrual manipulation.

Prior earnings management studies have found that high discretionary accruals indicate earnings manipulations (Healy, 1985; DeAngelo, 1986; Jones, 1991) and audit qualifications (Bartov, Gul, and Tsui, 2000), that is, high discretionary accruals in financial reports are accompanied with poor earnings quality. Managers or leaders in a group have more opportunities to manipulate earnings through complex transactions between the group members. Compared with managers in non-group firms, managers in business groups may have more techniques to manage earnings. Examples of these instruments in Taiwan are trades on non-publicly held securities, direct or indirect financing transactions, estate transactions, and purchase and sales transactions between affiliated corporations (Yang, 1994), and the use of accruals to manipulate earnings. Investors and other users can make better decisions if they can see through the real financial numbers by the connection between group characteristics and earnings management. In addition, business groups are a prominent feature of industrial organization of many emerging economies in Asia, characterized by diversification across a wide range of businesses. Despite the fact that group firms play an important role during the economic development of emerging countries, less attention has been paid to the groups except for a few studies (e.g., Numazaki, 1986; Khanna, 2000; Guillen, 2000; Claessens, Joseph, and Lang, 2002). In addition, empirical research on the earnings manipulation behavior of group firms has not been specifically examined.

This paper, therefore, attempts to add to the literature on earnings management by examining business groups in Taiwan. Analyses are conducted by two different regression approaches: ordinary lease square and two-step regressions to investigate how business group characteristics influence managerial behavior in earnings management. In short, this study contributes to the literature of earnings management in two ways. First, it identifies some important factors such as the group's complexity that may affect earnings management behavior within business groups. Second, findings from this research have implications to both practitioners and regulators on earnings management in business groups.

Empirical evidence shows that group member firms with or without a bank and group type are two key factors of a group's organizational structure that explain the extent of discretionary accruals.

The paper proceeds as follows: Section 2 describes the institutional background of business groups in Taiwan. Section 3 discusses the theoretical connection of earnings management within business groups. Research design including the hypotheses, sample selection, variable measurement, descriptive statistics, and the empirical models is provided in the Section 4. The findings are then presented and summarized in Section 5, and Section 6 consists of concluding remarks.

## 2. Institutional Background

The business group is a widespread phenomenon, known in many countries under various names. In a study of business groups in Taiwan by China Credit Information Service (CCIS)[4] in 2000, a business group is defined as a cluster of three or more related corporations that mutually acknowledge their common membership and have both combined sales and total assets of at least NT $400 million or the sum of combined sales and total assets of more than 1 billion. For each business group, there is usually an identifiable core company and the corresponding core family. For a firm to be considered as a group member, it usually meets one of the following criteria. First, the group's core company or core owner's family owns more than 50% or the majority of the firm's outstanding shares. Second, more than 25% of the firm's outstanding shares

---

[4]China Credit Information Service (CCIS) is one of the leading business information agencies in Taiwan. Since 1971, CCIS has been publishing *"Business Groups in Taiwan"* continually. This publication won the 1997 Golden Tripod Award, the highest honor for publishers in Taiwan, and has become one of the most important research resources of business groups in Taiwan ever since. Most of the academic researches in business groups in Taiwan employed the data by CCIS (e.g., Feenstra *et al.*, 1999; Guillen, 2000; Khanny and Rivkin, 2001).

are mutual-shareholding. Third, more than half of the board members of the firm are the same as those of the core company, or the board members in the firm and in its core company are interlocking or are relatives.

The present structure of business groups in Taiwan is a product of unique historical circumstances. The mutual effects of larger economic and political forces outside the island constructed the environment in which Taiwanese entrepreneurs emerged and developed. The institutional framework for the modern corporate economy was introduced in Taiwan by the Japanese colonial government at the beginning of the 20th century, although by then Taiwanese society was already highly commercialized.[5] The colonial economy was dominated by the Japanese, although a few Taiwanese including large landlords, traditional merchants, and new collaborators were induced to invest in newly established banks and industries and sometimes were granted economic and political advantages.[6] After the Second World War and the "retrocession" of the island to China, most Japanese-owned corporate assets were confiscated and reorganized into state-owned enterprises by the Chinese government. However, due to being economically weakened and politically unorganized, the Taiwanese failed to assume power in decolonized Taiwan. The first landmark in Taiwan's postwar corporate economy was the Land Reform of 1949–1953, in which four state-owned corporations were privatized as their shares were given to former landlords as compensation for their land titles.[7]

During the 1960s, under heavy pressure from the United States, the government started to liberalize Taiwan's economy (Gates, 1981). The private sector continued to expand in the 1960s and 1970s except for a few key industries and public utilities controlled by the government. Three kinds of "capitalists" can be identified since the 1970s: former landowning Taiwanese, emigrant Mainlander industrialists, and the *nouveaux riche*.[8] Apart from the above historical

---

[5]The following description about the evolution of business group in Taiwan is based on Numazaki (1986).

[6]There were five famous family groups during the time of the colonial economy — the House of Lin Benyuan in northern Taiwan, the Lin clan of Wufeng in Zhanghua County, the Gu family from Lugang, the Yans of Keelung, and the largest sugar merchant, the Chens of Tainan.

[7]These four corporations are Taiwan Cement, Taiwan Agricultural and Forestry Products, Taiwan Industrial Machinery and Mining, and Taiwan Pulp and Paper.

[8]A number of successful traders, petty bourgeoisie and peasants made a rapid transition to this capitalist class.

view to explain group formation in Taiwan, several studies present other factors as an explanation to group development such as environmental factors, business operating policy, legal factors, financial planning considerations, and the family effect.

The most recent descriptive statistics about group business in Taiwan can be found from various reports published by CCIS. The total number of groups increased by nearly 100% in the last two decades, and the number of member corporations increased from 651 firms to 4,317 firms, an increment ratio of 563%. Furthermore, the number of groups with more than 20 member corporations had dramatically increased from 2 in 1978 to 65 in 1999.

It seems indisputable that the industrial structure of Taiwan consists primarily of small and medium sized businesses and that this predominance is what distinguishes Taiwan from other industrial societies in the Asian region. However, Hamilton and Ko (1990) show that the matter is not so straightforward. That is, Taiwan does not have more small businesses than other societies in East Asia. In fact, the percentages of both middle-sized firms (30–299 workers) and large-sized firms (300 or more workers) in Taiwan are highest, by comparison with those in Japan and South Korea. Nevertheless, in comparison with Korea and Japan, Taiwan's business groups are considerably smaller overall (Feenstra, Yang, and Hamilton, 1999).

In spite of the relative size of business groups in Taiwan, the revenue and percentage of GDP is notable and shows considerable growth. A report from CCIS, in 2000, stated total operating revenues from 195 business groups were nearly 7.3 trillion NT dollars (CCIS, 2000),[9] which means revenues from business groups accounted for more than 77.89% of Taiwan's GDP in 1999; comparatively, the total was less than 45% of GDP in 1996. Total business group assets expanded by more than 50 times, from 0.33 trillion NT dollars in 1978 to 16.7 trillion NT dollars in 1999. Moreover, in the same period, an average group's total assets rose dramatically from 3.3 billion NT dollars to nearly 86 billion NT dollars.

According to the study of business groups in Taiwan by China Credit Information Service in 2000, there are three basic patterns of such overlapping ownership, which are the "sister" type, the "mother–child" type and the "marriage" type. Figure 1 illustrates the formation of these three types of business groups.

---

[9]As far as this paper is concerned, due to data constraints, the issue published in 1998 was used instead to identify the list of the member corporations.

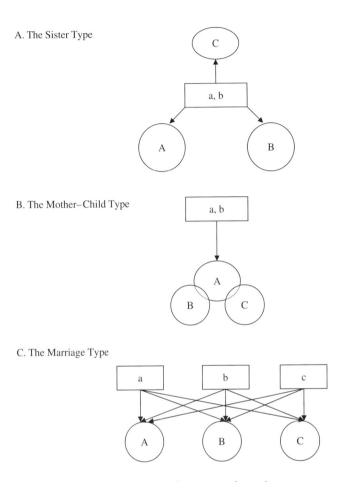

**Figure 1.**  Types of business group formation.

As Figure 1A indicates, when the core persons or corporations a and b jointly or separately invest in companies A, B, and C, the three companies are said to be in a "sister' relationship. Most of the "sister" type groups are family-controlled, such as Taiwan Cement Group, one of the famous five entrepreneurs in the colony, and the Advanced Semiconductor Engineering Group (ASE), a well-known but new business group founded in 1984.

When the core persons or corporations a and b jointly invest in a company A, which in turn holds shares of companies B and C, the relation between A and B or A and C stands as "mother" to "children" (see Figure 1B). In other words, this is a parent-subsidiary relationship. The Yulon Group, a traditional but well-known motor manufacturer, and the Acer Group, a notable global computer-manufacturing group, are two examples of such a business group type.

When the core persons or corporations a, b, and c jointly invest in companies A, B, and C, the relationship between the companies A, B, and C is said to be a "Marriage" pattern (see Figure 1C), united as if one family is sending a bride to another. Additionally, when corporations a and b invest in company A jointly, while b and c invest in another company B, and a and c invest in company C jointly, or other similar share interlocking patterns, this also creates a Marriage-type relationship. An example would be the Tuntex Group, a fast growing and diversified group. But ever since the Asian financial crisis in 1997, the group is trying to cut-down its group coverage.

Among the three basic types, the Mother–Child type accounts for 24.78%; the Sister type, 22.12%; while the Marriage type, only 3.54% in 1997. The remaining more than 40% of the groups were a mix of the Mother–Child and the Sisters types.

## 3. Literature Review

Healy and Wahlen (1999) review the academic evidence on earnings management and its implications for accounting standard setters and regulators. Earnings management occurs for a variety of reasons. Managers can influence market perception (DeAngelo, 1988; Teoh *et al.*, 1998a) through earnings manipulation. Furthermore, managers are also able to increase their own compensation, reduce the likelihood of violating lending agreements (Healy, 1985; DeAngelo, DeAngelo and Skinner, 1994), and avoid regulatory intervention (Beatty, Chamberlain, and Magliolo, 1995; Collins, Snackelford, and Whalen, 1995). In addition, Fudenberg and Tirole (1995) suggest that managers have incentives to distort reported earnings to maximize their expected length of tenure.

Many earnings management tools have been examined by prior literature. Managers can change operations to manipulate the underlying cash flows. Examples of this include altering shipment schedules, offering end-of-period sales, and speeding up or deferring maintenance. However, using operating decisions to manipulate earnings has real economic costs. Another manipulation tool is asset (long-lived assets and investments) sales. Bartov (1993) suggests that the recognized income from disposal of long-lived assets and investments smooth earnings and mitigates accounting-based restrictions in bond covenants. However, this kind of improvement in performance may occur primarily in firms that increase their operating efficiency (John and Ofek, 1995; Beger and Ofek, 1995). A change in accounting principle is also a possible instrument to manipulate earnings — an example of this is a change in the method of depreciation from double-declining to straight-line depreciation of plant assets. But the cumulative effect of the adjustment should be reported in the income statement as a specific and irregular item. The most common tool examined in prior studies is the use of the flexibility allowed in generally accepted accounting procedures to change reported earnings through accounting accruals without changing the underlying cash flow. For example, managers can adjust allowance for losses (inventory obsolescence, bad debt, and product warranty expenses), alter the point at which sales are recognized, or shift costs between expense and capital accounts. They may even select a specific method of depreciation, or choose or change the estimated useful life or the salvage value of the depreciable assets.

Other than the tools mentioned above, managers or leaders in a group might have more chances or opportunities to manipulate earnings through complex transactions between the group members. As reported in Yang (1994), the most common types of non-arm's-length transactions within the business groups in Taiwan are: 1) trades on non-publicly held securities, 2) direct or indirect financing, 3) estate transactions, and, 4) purchase and sales transactions between affiliated corporations. In recent years, some new and more complex transaction patterns have emerged. For example, the manipulation could be done through irregular transactions between overseas subsidiaries and other affiliates.

However, only a few studies examine the opportunistic behavior in business groups in Taiwan. Tsao (1999) examines the relationship of earnings management tools and motivations between conglomerate and non-conglomerate corporations. It was documented that compared with non-conglomerate firms, business groups are more likely to use financial-related party transactions to manipulate earnings while issuing bonds. Huang (1995) studies the earnings manipulation by family businesses in Taiwan. She found that there is a positive, although insignificant, relation between the intensity of family control and the extent of earnings manipulation.

This study examines the phenomenon of earnings management in business groups in Taiwan by observing the behavior of discretionary accruals. Using accounting accruals has an advantage over other earnings manipulation techniques. First, sometimes it is costly for corporations to manipulate earnings through changes in normal operating activities. Second, the impact of accounting principle changes on earnings can be easily detected. Third, the underlying motive (earnings management or improvement of efficiency) of assets sales is usually indistinguishable. Fourth, it is almost impossible to get comprehensive information as to how the groups manipulate earnings by specific instrument, such as foreign subsidiary information and the details of related party transactions. Finally, accounting choices that potentially impact reported earnings include a portfolio of both accruals estimations and specific method choices (Schipper, 1989).

Sheng (1997) simultaneously examined two earnings manipulation tools in Taiwan, accounting policy choice and accruals, and found that political cost is the only earnings manipulation factor that would significantly affect a firm's earnings manipulation behavior. In an attempt to capture the net effect of all accounting choices that impact reported income, this paper follows a number of prior studies and chooses to examine the behavior of total discretionary accruals and their components (DeFond and Jiambalvo, 1994; DeFond and Subramanyam, 1997).

## 4. Hypothesis Development and Research Design

### 4.1. *Hypotheses*

#### 4.1.1. *Organizational complexity*

A large literature has shown that managers can exercise judgment in financial reporting and in structuring transactions to influence perceptions and wealth of stakeholders. Earnings management occurs when managers have incentives to use such discretionary power to benefit specific groups of stakeholders (e.g., managers or stockholders). Motivations for earnings management arise from capital market, contracting, and regulations. Managers' opportunities to manage earnings can be expected to increase with organizational complexity. Business group complexity stems from several sources. Firms in these groups often span numerous industries while linkages across group firms occur at several levels, such as cross shareholdings, commercial ties, personnel sways, joint business, and periodic meetings of the top executives. Kroszner and Rajan (1997) examine banking structure in the US prior to the Glass–Stegall

Act and provide evidence that organizational structure can influence a firm's credibility and effectiveness. Dewenter, Novaes, and Pettway (2001) also find that group membership can affect the cost of issuing new capital through an individual firm's relation with outside investors. As the groups present a more complex organizational structure, it is more difficult to analyze the relation between one firm's actions and the group's overall strategy. From an outsider's perspective, the group's internal workings are opaque and difficult to disentangle. Detection of opportunistic behavior is then more difficult and reputation concerns are less likely to effectively constrain such actions. Leaders or managers in these groups are therefore more likely to use unexpected accruals to manipulate earnings.

We use two different measures to proxy the complexity of organizational structure in group firms. The first proxy is the type of business group (BGTYPE). As demonstrated in Section 2, the Mother–Child type was usually a parent–subsidiary relationship. Group members were expanded through many direct or indirect investments by the controlling company and its subsidiaries. The Marriage type also presents a complex structure because of the mutual investments by group members. Thus, we expect that it would be much more arduous for the public to disentangle the business in these two group types. The second proxy is the presence of an investment company (INVEST) in a group. Nayyar (1993) argues that benefits from a positive reputation in an existing business and from an economics of scope are available from related, but not from unrelated, diversification. On the other hand, groups are reputed to be less transparent if group members include investment companies because it will be difficult for information users to realize the group's operation. Based on the above analyses, the following hypotheses are directional and are stated in the alternative form.[10]

---

[10]Actually, accruals managed upwards in some periods may be offset at some point by accruals managed downwards. However, we are interested in the long-term relation between group characteristics and earnings management. Prior studies have explored this issue using the same research design as ours. For example, Becker *et al.* (1998) examine the relation between the audit quality and the earnings management. They find that clients of non-Big Six auditors reported discretionary accruals that increased income relatively more than the discretionary accruals reported by clients of Big Six auditors. For a sample of NASDAQ firms, Francis, Maydew, and Spark (1999) also show that the Big-Six-audited firms had lower amounts of estimated discretionary accruals.

**H1:** *Ceteris paribus*, members in the Mother–Child type, the Marriage type and a mix of these two types report relatively higher discretionary accruals compared to members in the other groups.

**H2:** *Ceteris paribus*, members in the groups with an investment company are more likely to report relatively higher discretionary accruals compared to members in the groups without an investment company.

### 4.1.2. *Uncertainty of external financing*

Group executives have to cope with business financial demand all the time, which may induce them to present a better financial condition of the group. As group members include a financial institution, the uncertainty or risk of external financing will be lower. Therefore, managers of these group firms have less incentive to manipulate earnings to show the favorable condition in order to keep their credibility. The following hypothesis is directional and stated in the alternative form.

**H3:** *Ceteris paribus*, members in the groups with a financial institution are more likely to report relatively lower discretionary accruals compared to members in the groups without a financial institution.

### 4.2. *Sample selection and data sources*

The initial samples were selected from the 1998/1999 issue of *Business Groups in Taiwan* (CCIS, 1998). From 1996 to 1997, there were 2,430 member corporations including both publicly and non-publicly held companies. The sample is further restricted to member firms with complete data in the Taiwan Economic Journal (TEJ) databases.[11] The financial institutions, "other industry companies", and "composite industry companies" are excluded from the sample since computing discretionary accruals for these firms is problematic. We also eliminate firms with insufficient data to compute discretionary accruals and firms that close their books on dates other than the end of December. Finally, the samples with member firms within a group consisting of less than two are also

---

[11] These databases include three different data sources: the TaiEx listed, over-the-counter (OTC), and other public firms (PUB). We use five-year cross-sectional data (a four-year period for OTC firms only) from 1991 to 1995 to estimate discretionary accruals. While 1991 is the first data year for OTC market, the first estimated year is 1992 due to data requirement for variables deflated by lagged total assets.

**Table 1.** Sample selection procedure.

| Criteria | Firm-year | Percentage |
|---|---|---|
| Initial group's firms (from 1996 to 1997) | 2,430 | 100.00 |
| Data not available in TEJ | (1,556) | 64.03 |
| Financial institution | (46) | 1.89 |
| Other and composite industry | (40) | 1.65 |
| Others* | (269) | 11.07 |
| Final sample | 519 | 21.36 |

*Note*: *These include 36 securities firms, 66 investment companies, and 157 companies with less than 2 member firms or lack of sufficient data.

deleted. These sample selection procedures yielded a final sample of 519 firm-year observations, including 233 traded on the listed market, 35 traded on the OTC market, and 251 not traded on the public markets. Details of the sampling procedure are presented in Table 1.

### 4.3. *Estimation of discretionary accruals*

Given the lack of time-series data, we measure discretionary accruals by the cross-sectional variation of the modified Jones (1991) accruals estimation model reported in Dechow, Sloan, and Sweeney (1995). In addition, Subramanyam (1996) finds that the cross-sectional Jones models are generally better specified than their time-series counterparts.[12] Thus we follow Dechow *et al.* (1995) and Subramanyam (1996) and many other studies employing a two-stage estimation process. First, nondiscretionary accruals for each of 17 industries are estimated by Equation (1a). All terms in this model are scaled by lagged total assets to control for heteroscedasticity.

$$\frac{\text{ACRUS}_{jt}}{A_{jt-1}} = \alpha_0 \left( \frac{1}{A_{jt-1}} \right) + \alpha_1 \left( \frac{\Delta\text{REV}_{jt}}{A_{jt-1}} \right) + \alpha_2 \frac{\text{PPE}_{jt}}{A_{jt-1}} + e_{jt}, \qquad (1a)$$

where $\text{ACRUS}_{jt}$ is the total accounting accruals for firm $j$, at year $t$; $A_{jt-1}$, the total assets for firm $j$, at year $t-1$; $\Delta\text{REV}_{jt}$, the change in revenues from the prior period for firm $j$, at year $t$; $\Delta\text{REV}_{jt} - \Delta\text{AR}_{jt}$, the change in cash-basis revenue for firm $j$, at year $t$; $\text{PPE}_{jt}$, the gross property, plant and equipment for firm $j$, at year $t$; $e_{jt}$ is the error term for firm $j$, at year $t$.

---

[12]We use the cross-sectional modified Jones Model to estimate discretionary accruals not only because this model can better detect earnings management on US firms (see Dechow *et al.*, 1995; Bartov *et al.*, 2000) but also because this model is one of the most popular detecting models in Taiwan (see Shiah-Hou, 2000; Lin, Shine, and Su, 2002).

In stage 2, discretionary (unexpected) component of accruals is measured by the difference between a firm's actual total accruals and non-discretionary (expected) accruals (NDA) based on the parameter estimates of each industry in Equation (1b).

$$\text{NDA} = \hat{\alpha}_0 \left( \frac{1}{A_{jt-1}} \right) + \hat{\alpha}_1 \left( \frac{\Delta \text{REV}_{jt} - \Delta \text{AR}_{jt}}{A_{jt-1}} \right) + \hat{\alpha}_2 \frac{\text{PPE}_{jt}}{A_{jt-1}}, \qquad (1b)$$

where $\Delta \text{AR}_{jt}$ is the change in accounts receivable from the prior period for firm $j$, at year $t$.

As in other studies (Teoh *et al.*, 1998a; Becker, Defond, Jiamobalvo, and Subramanyam, 1998), total accruals (ACRUS) are computed as:

$$\text{ACRUS}_{jt} = \text{NI}_{jt} - \text{OCF}_{jt},$$

where, for firm $j$, at year $t$; $\text{NI}_{jt}$ is the income before extraordinary items; and, $\text{OCF}_{jt}$ the cash flows from operations.

### 4.4. *Measurement of independent variables*

The explanatory variables used in this study are defined as follows:

### 4.4.1. *Test variables*

BANK and INVEST are dummy variables. If group members contain a bank (an investment company), BANK (INVEST) would take on a value 1, and 0 for others. BGTYPE is defined as 1 if the group belongs to Mother–Child, Marriage or a mix of Mother–Child and Marriage type of groups and 0 for others.

### 4.4.2. *Control variables*

The first control variable is pre-managed revenues (CREV). CREV is defined as the difference between the revenues before discretionary current accruals and industry median. Revenues before discretionary current accruals are measured as the change of net operating revenues minus discretionary current accruals.[13] As far back as nearly a half century ago, Hepworth (1953) suggested

---

[13]Similar to discretionary accruals, discretionary current accruals are the difference between current accruals and nondiscretionary current accruals (NDCA). The following regression parameters were estimated.

$$\frac{\text{CACRUS}_{jt}}{A_{jt-1}} = \alpha_0 \left( \frac{1}{A_{jt-1}} \right) + \alpha_1 \left( \frac{\Delta \text{REV}_{jt}}{A_{jt-1}} \right) + \varepsilon_{jt}, \qquad (\text{N1a})$$

that management's objectives should not necessarily be to report maximum profits, but to smooth their income over the years. Managers of business groups or group leaders are concerned about their firm's or group's earning performance while considering the demand for external financing or the group's reputation. When financial institutions review the creditworthiness of the group members, both the stable earnings stream and endorsement of the principal company are important factors. Moreover, several well-known institutions in Taiwan such as, China Credit Information Service and Common Wealth Magazine, periodically disclose to the public the ranking of business groups by their earnings, operating revenues, or total assets. These external financing and reputation incentives induced managers in a group to smooth earnings.

Size and leverage are also control variables that may be associated with discretionary accruals, because size may surrogate for numerous omitted variables and high leverage may be connected with debt covenant violation (DeFond and Park, 1997; Becker *et al.*, 1998). The natural log of sales (SIZE) is included to control for the compounding effect of firm size. Leverage (LEV) is defined as the ratio of debt to total assets. Lastly, EXACRUS is used to control the impact of accrual reversals, which is the deflated amount of prior period total accruals.[14,15] All of these variables have been examined in prior studies and are employed to control for the possible confounding effects of group attributes.

---

where $\text{CACRUS}_{jt}$ is the current accruals, $\Delta$(accounts receivables + inventory + other current assets) $- \Delta$(accounts payable + tax payable + other current liabilities), for firm $j$, at year $t$; $A_{jt-1}$, the total assets for firm $j$, at year $t-1$; $\Delta \text{REV}_{jt}$, the change in revenues from the prior period for firm $j$, at year $t$; and $e_{jt}$ is the error term for firm $j$, at year $t$.

NDCA are computed as the predicted values in Equation (N1b). The difference between a firm's actual current accruals and NDCA is the discretionary component of current accruals.

$$\text{NDCA} = \hat{\alpha}_0 \left( \frac{1}{A_{jt-1}} \right) + \hat{\alpha}_1 \left( \frac{\Delta \text{REV}_{jt} - \Delta \text{AR}_{jt}}{A_{jt-1}} \right), \tag{N1b}$$

where $\Delta \text{AR}_{jt}$ is the change in accounts receivable from the prior period for firm $j$, at year $t$.

[14] Francis, Maydew, and Sparks (1996) argue that firms with greater endogenous accruals-generating potential have greater uncertainty about reported earnings because of the difficulty that outsiders have in distinguishing discretionary and non-discretionary accruals. In this paper, the accruals-generating potential is named by the lagged of total accruals deflated by total assets.

[15] Becker *et al.* (1998) suggest using the absolute amount of total accruals to control a firm's accruals-generating potential. Also, prior discretionary accruals is an alternate variable to control accrual-reversals effect (DeFond and Park, 1997; Young, 1998). Due to data constraints, we use past total accruals as a control variable instead of prior discretionary accruals.

## 4.5. *Testing models*

We run the following Ordinary Least Square (OLS) regression to analyze and test our hypotheses.

$$DA_{jt} = \alpha_0 + \alpha_1 SIZE_{jt} + \alpha_2 CREV_{jt} + \alpha_3 LEV_{jt} + \alpha_4 EXACRUS_{jt}$$
$$+ \alpha_5 BGTYPE_{jt} + \alpha_6 INVEST_{jt} + \alpha_7 BANK_{jt} + \varepsilon_{jt} \qquad (2)$$

where for firm $j$, at year $t$; DA is the discretionary accruals, computed using the cross-sectional modified Jones model; SIZE, the log of sales; CREV, the pre-managed net revenues, the difference between the change of net revenues before discretionary current accruals and industry median; LEV, the total liabilities divided by total assets; EXACRUS, the prior period total accruals deflated by lagged total assets; BGTYPE, the dummy variable, 1 if group types are Marriage, Mother–Child, or a mix of Mother–Child and Marriage types, 0 otherwise; INVEST, the dummy variable, 1 if group members contain one or more investment company, 0 otherwise; BANK, the dummy variable, 1 if group members contain a bank, 0 otherwise; and $\varepsilon$, is the error terms.

From this model, $\alpha_5$ to $\alpha_7$ are planned to test the group's organizational structure hypothesis.

## 5. Empirical Results

### 5.1. *Descriptive statistics*

Descriptive statistics are reported in Table 2. Overall, statistics show that the values of the constructed variables distribute within reasonable ranges.[16] The average size (ASSET) of the sample firms is NT \$12,540 million. The mean and median total accounting accruals (ACRUS) are $-0.001$ and $-0.013$ respectively. The mean value of discretionary accruals (DA) is $-0.03$.

Table 3 describes Pearson correlation coefficients. As expected, DA is negatively correlated with BANK and positively with INVEST and BGTYPE but only with BANK significance at the 0.1 level. Results of OLS regressions are shown in Table 4.

---

[16]The mean and median values of debt ratio (LEV) in our sample firms are nearly 0.5. We also find that several firms have extremely higher LEV. However, the bias is not substantial. As we delete two irregular samples (LEV < 1), the empirical results in the following section are moderately the same.

**Table 2.** Descriptive statistics of group firms in firms year (1996–1997).

| Variable* | Mean | Median | SDV | Min | Max |
|---|---|---|---|---|---|
| ASSET | 12,540 | 5,033 | 21,747 | 53 | 200,999 |
| REV | 7,325 | 2,915 | 12,426 | 1.282 | 97,756 |
| CREV | 0.046 | 0 | 0.417 | −2.120 | 3.81 |
| OCF | 0.044 | 0.051 | 0.144 | −0.711 | 1.350 |
| ACRUS | −0.001 | −0.013 | 0.119 | −0.635 | 0.512 |
| EXACRUS | 0.013 | −0.005 | 0.163 | −0.401 | 2.428 |
| CACRUS | 0.017 | 0.006 | 0.124 | −0.395 | 0.650 |
| LEV | 0.478 | 0.461 | 0.191 | 0.011 | 1.182 |
| DA | −0.030 | −0.020 | 0.197 | −1.540 | 1.007 |
| ROA | 5.007 | 4.97 | 7.193 | −64.22 | 36.69 |
| EPS | 1.123 | 0.97 | 2.088 | −15.14 | 10.85 |
| BGTYPE | 0.370 | 0 | 0.483 | 0 | 1 |
| INVEST | 0.497 | 0 | 0.500 | 0 | 1 |
| BANK | 0.108 | 0 | 0.311 | 0 | 1 |

*Notes*: *ASSET is the total assets in millions of NT dollars; REV, the net operating revenues in millions of NT dollars; CREV, the pre-managed net revenues before extraordinary items and taxes, the change of net income before extraordinary items and taxes minus discretionary current accruals and industry median; OCF, the operating cash flows deflated by lagged total assets; ACRUS, the total accounting accruals deflated by lagged total assets; EXACRUS, the prior period ACRUS; CACRUS, the current accruals, computed as $\Delta$(accounts receivables + inventory + other current assets) − $\Delta$(accounts payable + tax payable + other current liabilities) and deflated by lagged total assets; LEV, the total liabilities divided by total assets; DA, the disiscretionary accruals, computed using the cross-sectional modified Jones Model; ROA, the return on total assets (in percentages); EPS, the earnings per share; BGTYPE = 1 if group types are Mother–Child, Marriage, or a mixed of Mother–Child and Marriage types, 0 otherwise; INVEST = 1 if group members contain an investment company or more, 0 otherwise; and, BANK = 1 if group members contain a bank, 0 otherwise.

## 5.2. *OLS regressions*

Hypothesis 1–3 predicted that the extent of discretionary accruals reported does depend on the extent of the complexity of a group's organizational structure and the uncertainty or risk of external financing. From Table 4, the coefficient of BGTYPE is positive and significant at the 0.10 level. The coefficient of BANK is significantly negative (BANK = −0.058 and $p = 0.001$), indicating that member firms are less likely to use discretionary accruals to manipulate earnings while there is a financial company in the group, that is, Hypothesis 1 and 3 are supported. These findings are consistent with the

**Table 3.**   Correlation analysis of some key variables.[a]

| | SIZE | CREV | LEV | EXACRUS | BGTYPE | INVEST | BANK | DA |
|---|---|---|---|---|---|---|---|---|
| SIZE | 1 | | | | | | | |
| | (0.000) | | | | | | | |
| CREV | 0.103 | 1 | | | | | | |
| | (0.019) | (0.000) | | | | | | |
| LEV | 0.044 | 0.137 | 1 | | | | | |
| | (0.312) | (0.002) | (0.000) | | | | | |
| EXACRUS | 0.063 | 0.128 | 0.136 | 1 | | | | |
| | (0.153) | (0.004) | (0.002) | (0.000) | | | | |
| BGTYPE | 0.055 | 0.074 | −0.093 | 0.003 | 1 | | | |
| | (0.207) | (0.091) | (0.034) | (0.939) | (0.000) | | | |
| INVEST | −0.034 | 0.019 | −0.101 | −0.054 | 0.196 | 1 | | |
| | (0.445) | (0.668) | (0.021) | (0.218) | (0.001) | (0.000) | | |
| BANK | 0.053 | −0.012 | 0.116 | 0.002 | 0.042 | 0.176 | 1 | |
| | (0.227) | (0.778) | (0.008) | (0.967) | (0.337) | (0.001) | (0.000) | |
| DA | 0.011 | −0.328 | −0.065 | 0.010 | −0.076 | 0.028 | 0.062 | 1 |
| | (0.798) | 0.001 | (0.138) | (0.812) | (0.086) | (0.527) | (0.161) | (0.000) |

*Notes*: [a]Two-sided *p*-values in parentheses. SIZE is the log of sales. CREV, the pre-managed net revenues before extraordinary items and taxes, the change of net income before extraordinary items and taxes minus discretionary current accruals and industry median; LEV, the total liabilities divided by total assets; EXACRUS, the Lagged total accruals deflated by total assets; BGTYPE = 1 if group types are Mother–Child, Marriage, or a mixed of Mother–Child and Marriage types, 0 otherwise; INVEST = 1 if group members contain an investment company or more, 0 otherwise; BANK = 1 if group members contain a bank, 0 otherwise; and DA is the discretionary accruals, computed using the cross-sectional modified Jones Model.

argument by Kroszner and Rajan (1997) that organizational structure can influence a firm's credibility and effectiveness. The coefficient of INVEST is positive in Table 4, but not significantly.

In Table 4, consistent with prior research findings, the coefficient estimate on SIZE is generally positive, while the coefficients estimate on LEV are generally negative (Both the coefficient of SIZE and LEV are not significantly at the conventional level). The negative coefficient on the extent of leverage variable is consistent with an association of high leverage and financial distress, with distress leading to contractual renegotiations that provide incentives to reduce earnings (DeAngelo *et al.*, 1994). As expected, firms having higher prior period total accruals have more discretionary accruals in the following year. The coefficient of EXACRUS is positive but not significantly at the conventional level. The coefficient of CREV is negative and significant at the 1% level.

**Table 4.** OLS regression of discretionary accruals and group firm characteristics[a] — Separated Estimating Model.

| Variable[b] | Pred. | Coeff | $t^c$ |
|---|---|---|---|
| INTERCEPT | +/− | −0.121 | −1.649 |
| SIZE | + | 0.014 | 1.269 |
| CREV | − | −0.164 | −3.234*** |
| LEV | − | −0.005 | −0.091 |
| EXACRUS | − | 0.066 | 0.724 |
| BGTYPE | + | 0.033 | 1.792* |
| INVEST | + | 0.015 | 0.893 |
| BANK | − | −0.058 | −2.806*** |
| Adj-$R^2(N = 519) = 0.117$ | | | |

*Notes*: [a]$DA_{jt} = \alpha_0 + \alpha_1 SIZE_{jt} + \alpha_2 CREV1_{jt} + \alpha_3 LEV_{jt} + \alpha_4 EXACRUS_{jt} + \alpha_5 BGTYPE_{jt} + \alpha_{12} INVEST_6 + \alpha_7 BANK_{jt} + \varepsilon_{jt}$.
[b] All variables are defined as in Table 3.
[c]$t$-statistics are adjusted for heteroskedasticity following the method suggested in White (1980).
*Significant at the 10% level.
***Significant at the 1% level.

## 5.3. *Additional tests*

This section reports the results of a series of tests designed to assess the sensitivity of the above findings to alternative model specifications.

### 5.3.1. *Pooled estimating model*

To collect more sample firms for model estimation, we pool publicly traded and non-publicly traded companies by industry to estimate discretionary accruals and discretionary current accruals and rerun the regression model 2. Consistent with our earlier results, BGTYPE and BANK are two key factors to explain the earnings management behavior on group firms (see Table 5).

### 5.3.2. *The group characteristics and the absolute value of discretionary accruals*

Warfield, Wild, and Wild (1995) show that the absolute value of discretionary accruals is a good proxy for the combined effect of upward and downward earnings management decisions. In addition, Barton (2001) presents evidence that managers using derivatives and discretionary accruals as partial

**Table 5.** OLS regression of discretionary accruals and group firm characteristics[a] — Pooled Estimating Model.

| Variable[b] | Pred. | Coeff | $t$[c] |
|---|---|---|---|
| INTERCEPT | +/− | −0.090 | −1.206 |
| SIZE | + | 0.009 | 0.782 |
| CREV1 (?) | − | −0.139 | −2.855*** |
| LEV | − | −0.005 | −0.098 |
| EXACRUS | − | 0.064 | 0.765 |
| BGTYPE | + | 0.038 | 2.159** |
| INVEST | + | 0.004 | 0.221 |
| BANK | − | −0.043 | −2.038** |
| Adj−$R^2(N = 519) = 0.085$ | | | |

*Notes:* [a]$DA_{jt} = \alpha_0 + \alpha_1 SIZE_{jt} + \alpha_2 CREV1_{jt} + \alpha_3 LEV_{jt} + \alpha_4 EXACRUS_{jt} + \alpha_5 BGTYPE_{jt} + \alpha_6 INVEST_{jt} + \alpha_7 BANK_{jt} + \varepsilon_{jt}$.

[b]DA1: Discretionary accruals, computed using the cross-sectional modified Jones model by pooled estimating approaches. Other variables are defined as in Table 3.
[c]$t$-statistics are adjusted for heteroskedasticity following the method suggested in White (1980).
**Significant at the 5% level.
***Significant at the 1% level.

substitutes for smoothing earnings. The author emphasizes his interest in the magnitude, not the direction, of discretionary accruals. His analysis is based on the absolute value of the proxy for discretionary accruals(|DAC|). Barton predicts and finds a significant negative association between derivatives' notional amounts and proxies for the magnitude of discretionary accruals. More recently, Klein (2002) uses the absolute values of adjusted abnormal accruals to examine whether audit committee and board characteristics are related to earnings management. Klein (2002) shows that board or audit committee independence and abnormal accruals are negatively correlated. Group characteristics are long-term determinants of discretionary accruals. We ran another regression model using absolute discretionary accruals as a dependent variable instead of discretionary accruals. However, some of the factors, for example, CREV and EXACRUS variables were short-term or directional measures. In contrast, the other member firm's characteristics and group characteristics were long-term or non-directional measures. So, we used a two-step procedure to analyze the regression. Using short-term determinants of discretionary accruals as independent variables, we ran the following OLS regression first and kept its residuals.

$$\text{DA}_{jt} = \alpha_0 + \alpha_1 \text{SIZE}_{jt} + \alpha_2 \text{CREV}_{jt} + \alpha_3 \text{EXACRUS}_{jt} + \varepsilon_{jt}. \quad (3a)$$

Next, we applied the absolute residuals from the above regression as a dependent variable and ran the following regression.

$$|\varepsilon_{jt}| = \beta_0 + \beta_1 \text{LEV}_{jt} + \beta_2 \text{BGTYPE}_{jt} + \beta_3 \text{INVEST}_{jt}$$
$$+ \beta_4 \text{BANK}_{jt} + e_{jt} \quad (3b)$$

In Equation (3b), $(\beta_2$ through $\beta_4)$ are designed to examine the group characteristics effects on the use of the absolute value of discretionary accruals. Results from regression tests using this alternative approach are robust (see Table 6). For example, the coefficient of BGTYPE is significantly positive at the 0.05 level and the coefficient of BANK is significantly less than 0 at the 0.05 level.

**Table 6.** Two-step OLS regression of discretionary accruals and group firm characteristics.

| *The First Step*[a] Variable[b] DEP = DA | Coeff | $t$ [c] |
|---|---|---|
| INTERCEPT | −0.106 | −1.488 |
| SIZE | 0.013 | 1.185 |
| CREV | −0.161 | −3.103*** |
| EXACRUS | 0.062 | 0.689 |
| Adj-$R^2$($N = 519$) = 0.017 | | |
| *The Second Step*[d] Variable[a] DEP = ABS (RESI) | Coeff | $t$ [b] |
| INTERCEPT | −0.006 | −0.331 |
| LEV | 0.245 | 5.733*** |
| BGTYPE | 0.027 | 2.039 ** |
| INVEST | −0.008 | −0.630 |
| BANK | −0.029 | −2.101** |
| Adj-$R^2$($N = 519$) = 0.098 | | |

*Notes:* [a]$\text{DA}_{jt} = \alpha_0 + \alpha_1 \text{SIZE}_{jt} + \alpha_2 \text{CREV1}_{jt} + \alpha_3 \text{EXACRUS}_{jt} + \varepsilon_{jt}.$
[b]All variables are defined as in Table 3.
[c]$t$-statistics are adjusted for heteroskedasticity following the method suggested in White (1980).
[d]$|\varepsilon_{jt}| = \beta_0 + \beta_1 \text{LEV}_{jt} + \beta_2 \text{BGTYPE}_{jt} + \beta_3 \text{INVEST}_{jt} + \beta_4 \text{BANK}_{jt} + e_{jt}.$
*Significant at the 5% level.
***Significant at the 1% level.

## 6. Summary and Conclusions

This study focuses on earnings management behavior in a specific area — business groups in Taiwan. Earnings management is measured in terms of discretionary accruals estimated using a cross-sectional version of the modified Jones (1991) model. Two different methods of regression analysis, OLS and two-step regression models were conducted to examine our arguments.

We examined the proposition that the characteristics of group membership can influence a firm's credibility and the cost of issuing new capital. We hypothesize that the extent of discretionary accruals reported will depend on the extent of complexity of a group's organizational structure and the uncertainty of external financing. This study presents evidence that group types and member firms with or without a financial company are two key factors of a group's characteristics to explain the extent of discretionary accruals. Sensitivity tests indicate that the results are robust to our choice of estimating approaches of discretionary accruals and current accruals.

While we document a negative association between discretionary accruals and the number of financial companies in a group and a positive association between discretionary accruals and group types conditional on external financing and group complexity, much about this relation is unknown. One extension of this research is to further refine the measures of firm and group characteristics such as the impact of family groups. Additional considerations related to group and member firm characteristics may include formation pattern of the groups such as horizontal, vertical or conglomerate groups, and the different influence between upper hierarchy and lower level members in the group, each of these reveal different earnings management incentives. Finally, it would be interesting to see the differing extent of manipulation between group firms and non-group firms if the manipulative behavior is more prevalent within group firms.

## Acknowledgments

The authors appreciate the useful comments from Cheng-Few Lee (the Editor) and two anonymous referees. We also thank the participants at the Accounting Association of Australia & New Zealand (AAANZ) 2001 Annual Conference and the workshop participants at the National Taipei University, Taiwan.

# References

Aharony, J., C. J. Lin and M. P. Loeb, "Initial Public Offerings, Accounting Choices and Earnings Management." *Contemporary Accounting Research* 10, 61–81 (1993).

Barton, J., "Does the Use of Financial Derivatives Affect Earnings Management Decisions?" *The Accounting Review* 76, 1–26 (2001).

Bartov, E., "The Timing of Asset Sales and Earnings Manipulation." *The Accounting Review* 68, 840–855 (1993).

Bartov, E., F. A. Gul and J. Tsui, "Discretionary-Accruals Models and Audit Qualifications." *Journal of Accounting and Economics* 30, 421–452 (2000).

Beatty, A., S. Chamberlain and J. Magliolo, "Managing Financial Reports of Commercial Banks: The Influence of Taxes, Regulatory Capital and Earnings." *Journal of Accounting Research* 33, 231–261 (1995).

Becker, C., M. DeFond, J. Jiamobalvo and K. Subramanyam, "The Effect of Audit Quality on Earnings Management." *Contemporary Accounting Research* 15, 1–24 (1998).

Beger, P. G. and E. Ofek, "Diversification's Effect on Firm Value." *Journal of Financial Economics* 37, 39–65 (1995).

China Credit Information Service, LTD, *Business Groups in Taiwan 1998/1999*, Taipei, Taiwan (1998).

China Credit Information Service, LTD, *Business Groups in Taiwan 2001*, Taipei, Taiwan (2000).

Claessens, S., P. H. Joseph and L. Lang, "The Benefits and Costs of Group Affiliation: Evidence from East Asia." Working paper, University of Amsterdam and CEPR (2002).

Collins, J., D. Shackelford and J. Wahlen, "Bank Differences in the Coordination of Regulatory Capital, Earnings and Taxes." *Journal of Accounting Research* 33, 263–291 (1995).

DeAngelo, E., H. DeAngelo and D. Skinner, "Accounting Choices of Troubled Companies." *Journal of Accounting and Economics* 17, 113–143 (1994).

DeAngelo, L., "Accounting Numbers as Market Valuation Substitutes: A Study of Management Buyouts of Public Shareholders." *The Accounting Review* 61, 400–420 (1986).

DeAngelo, L., "Managerial Competition, Information Costs, and Corporate Governance: The Use of Accounting Performance Measures in Proxy Contests." *Journal of Accounting and Economics* 10, 3–36 (1988).

Dechow, P. M., R. Sloan and A. Sweeney, "Detecting Earnings Management." *The Accounting Review* 70, 193–225 (1995).

DeFond, M. L. and C. W. Park, "Smoothing Income in Anticipation of Future Earnings." *Journal of Accounting and Economics* 23, 115–139 (1997).

DeFond, M. L. and J. Jiambalvo, "Debt Covenant Effects and Manipulation of Accruals." *Journal of Accounting and Economics* 17, 145–176 (1994).

DeFond, M. L. and K. R. Subramanyam, "Restrictions to Accounting Choice, Evidence from Auditor Realignment." Working paper, University of Southern California (1997).

Dewenter, K., W. Novaes and R. H. Pettway, "Visibility versus Complexity in Business Groups: Evidence from Japanese *keiretsu*." *The Journal of Business* 74, 79–100 (2001).

Feenstra, R., T. H. Yang and G. Hamilton, "Business Groups and Product Variety in Trade: Evidence from South Korea, Taiwan and Japan." *Journal of International Economics* 48, 71–100 (1999).

Francis, J. R., E. Maydew and H. C. Sparks, "Earnings Management Opportunities, Auditor Quality, and External Monitoring." Working paper, University of Missouri Columbia (1996).

Francis, J. R., E. L. Maydew and H. C. Spark, "The Role of Big 6 Auditors in the Credible Reporting of Accruals." *Auditing: A Journal of Practice & Theory* 18, 17–34 (1999).

Fudenberg, K. and J. Tirole, "A Theory of Income and Dividend Smoothing Based on Incumbency Rents." *Journal of Political Economics* 103, 75–93 (1995).

Gates, H. *Ethnicity and Social Class, Anthropology of Taiwanese Society*, Stanford, CA: Stanford Univ. Press, 241–281 (1981).

Guidry, F., A. J. Leone and S. Rock, "Earnings-Based Bonus Plans and Earnings Management by Business-Unit Managers." *Journal of Accounting and Economics* 26, 113–142 (1999).

Guillen, M. F. "Business Groups in Emerging Economies: A Resource-Based View." *Academy of Management Journal* 43, 362–380 (2000).

Hamilton, G. G. and C. S. Ko, "The Institutional Foundations of Chinese Business: The Family Firm in Taiwan." *Comparative Social Research* 12, 135–157 (1990).

Healy, P., "The Effect of Bonus Schemes on Accounting Decisions." *Journal of Accounting and Economics* 7, 85–107 (1985).

Healy, P and J. Wahlen, "A Review of the Earnings Management Literature and its Implications for Standard Setting." *Accounting Horizons* 13, 365–383 (1999).

Hepworth, S. R., "Periodic Income Smoothing." *The Accounting Review* 28, 32–39 (1953).

Huang, S. C., *A Study of Earnings Manipulation on Family Business* , Master Theses, National Chung Cheng University (in Chinese) (1995).

John, K. and E. Ofek, "Asset Sales and Increase in Focus." *Journal of Financial Economics* 37, 105–126 (1995).

Jones, J. J., "Earnings Management During Import Relief Investigations." *Journal of Accounting Research* 29, 193–228 (1991).

Khanna, T., "Business Groups and Social Welfare in Emerging Markets: Existing Evidence and Unanswered Questions." *European Economic Review* 44, 748–761 (2000).

Khanna, T. and K. Palepu, "Why Focused Strategies May Be Wrong for Emerging Markets." *Harvard Business Review* 75, 41–51 (1997).

Khanna, T. and K. Palepu, "Is Group Affiliation Profitable in Emerging Markets: Analysis of Diversified Indian Business Groups." *The Journal of Finance* 55, 867–892 (2000).

Khanna, T. and J. W. Rivkin, "Estimating the Performance Effects of Business Groups in Emerging Markets." *Strategic Management Journal* 22, 45–74 (2001).

Klein, A., "Audit Committee, Board of Director Characteristics, and Earnings Management." *Journal of Accounting and Economics* 33, 375–400 (2002).

Kroszner, R. S and R. G. Rajan, "Organization Structure and Credibility: Evidence from Commercial Bank Securities Activities Before the Glass-Steagall Act." *Journal of Monetary Economics* 39, 475–516 (1997).

La Porta, R., F. Lopez-de-Silanes, A. Shleifer and R. Vishny, "Law and Finance." *Journal of Political Economy* 106, 1113–1155 (1998).

Lin, C. J., M. J. Shiue and Y. Y. Su, "A Study of Future Earnings and Earnings Smoothing: Empirical Evidence from Taiwan." Review of Securities & Futures Markets 14, 139–148 (in Chinese) (2002).

Nayyar, P. R., "Stock Market Reactions to Related Diversification Moves by Service Firms Seeking Benefits from Information Asymmetry and Economies of Scope." *Strategic Management Journal* 14, 469–491 (1993).

Numazaki, I., "Networks of Taiwanese Big Business: A Preliminary Analysis." *Modern China* 12, 487–534 (1986).

Schipper, K., "Commentary on Earnings Management." *Accounting Horizons* 3, 91–102 (1989).

Sheng, W. W., "Firms' Earnings Management: An Investigation of Accounting Policy Choices and Accruals." *Management Review* 16, 11–38 (in Chinese) (1997).

Shiah-Hou, S. R., "The Long-Run Performance of Season Equity Offering in Taiwan." *Management Review* 19, 1–33 (in Chinese) (2000).

Subramanyam, K. R., "The Pricing of Discretionary Accruals." *Journal of Accounting and Economics* 22, 249–282 (1996).

Teoh, S. H., I. Welch and T. J. Wong, "Earnings Management and the Underperformance of Seasoned Equity Offerings." *Journal of Financial Economics* 50, 63–99 (1998a).

Teoh, S. H., I. Welch and T. J. Wong, "Earnings Management and the Long-Term Market Performance of Initial Public Offerings." *The Journal of Finance* 53, 1935–1974 (1998b).

Tsao, C. F., *The Relationship Between Conglomerate Corporations and Earnings Management*, Master Theses, Soochow University (in Chinese) (1999).

Warfield, T., J. Wild and K. Wild, "Managerial Ownership, Accounting Choices, and Informativeness of Earnings." *Journal of Accounting and Economics* 20, 61–91 (1995).

White, H., "A Heteroskedasticity-Consistent Covariance Matrix Estimator and a Direct Test for Heteroskedasticity." *Econometrica* 48, 817–838 (1980).

Yang, W. C., "The Types of Non-Arm-Length Transactions in Business Groups." *Taipei Bar Journal* 174, 48–54 (in Chinese) (1994).

Young, S., "The Determinants of Managerial Accounting Policy Choice: Further Evidence for the UK." *Accounting and Business Research* 28, 131–143 (1998).

Chapter 8

# A Bayesian Approach for Testing the Debt Signaling Hypothesis in a Transitional Market: Perspectives from Egypt

Tarek I. Eldomiaty and Mohamed A. Ismail
*United Arab Emirates University, UAE*

This paper examines the effects of determinants of capital structure on firm's equity market value. The underlying assumption is that when a firm changes its capital structure, it actually changes the relative position and the market values of its securities' holders. This is the signaling hypothesis of capital structure changes. The financial signaling hypothesis is examined in two adaptive stages. The first stage is concerned with determining the relevant determinants of capital structure. The second stage is concerned with examining the signaling effect of the relevant determinants of capital structure. As for the determinants of capital structure, the paper examines a comprehensive number of factors that have been examined in the literature of the three theories of capital structure; trade-off theory, pecking order theory and free cash flow theory. The methodology addresses modeling the determinants capital structure and their signaling effect employing the Bayesian approach.The final results, which are a good match to research results of other developing countries, show that two determinants of capital structure are the most relevant and significant determinant of financial signaling. The two determinants are firm's size and profitability. The contribution of this paper is that the results provide support to other research in capital structure in developing countries although this paper follows different analytical tool that works under different assumptions. This provides validity to research on capital structure in developing countries.

**JEL Classifications:** G32, C21.

**Keywords:** Capital structure; financial signaling hypothesis; modelling; Bayesian.

## 1. Introduction

When a firm changes its capital structure, it actually changes the relative position and the market values of its capital suppliers' securities holdings. To the extent the capital suppliers are interested in their securities' market value, the firm's market value changes. The two dimensions considered in this paper are changes in firm's capital structure and its market value. Firm's market value is to be considered a criterion that provides a positive role to firm's manager to lessen the agency problems with outsiders. In this sense, the relationship between firm's capital structure and its market value can provide a reward to the manager on the basis of competence while signaling through finance the framework of choice faced by the managers (Ross, 1978). In addition, the problems of moral hazard and adverse selection can be avoided to some extent (Darrough and Stoughton, 1986). By enhancing firm's market value, the manager is in position to clarify his/her actions to the outsiders, thus mitigating the problem of moral hazard. At the same time, it is unlikely for the manager to adverse a financing choice that can strengthen the firm's market value. Therefore, the relationship between firm's capital structure and its market value can provide a monitoring function to such models of incentive–signaling–financial with agency relationships.

This study employs the Bayesian approach to determine the most important capital structure-related factors that affect firm's market value. The basic objective of the paper is to choose the highly likely group of factors (or determinants) that are associated with firms' market value the most. The factors in that group can be taken as the most influential factors that helps signal firm's market value. The novelty of the paper is that it is the first attempt to employ the Bayesian approach for examining the financial signaling hypothesis in a transitional market.

The rest of the paper is organized as follows. Section 2 discusses the theoretical underpinnings of the financial-agency signaling theory. Section 3 outlines the research variables/proxies examined in the study. Section 4 describes the data used in the paper and a detailed discussion of the Bayesian technique and its implementation used for the modelling purpose. Section 5 discusses the results and Section 6 concludes.

## 2. The Financial-Agency Signaling Hypothesis: A Review of the Literature

Changes in a firm's capital structure bring about changes in the relative position and/or power of capital providers (e.g., stockholders and debtors). When they are aware enough of the effects of changing capital structure, they presumably react accordingly. This is the main point of the theory of signaling. Masulis (1983) studied the relationship between changes in capital structure and firm value. The results indicate that both stock prices and firm values are positively related to changes in debt level and leverage. The theory of signaling states that information asymmetry between a firm and outsiders leads the former to make certain changes in its capital structure. Ross (1977), Myers and Majluf

(1984) and John (1987) have shown that under asymmetric information, firms may prefer debt to equity financing. In other cases, the asymmetric information may leave corporate insiders with a degree of residual uncertainty leading to the pecking order effect, i.e., the relative preference of equity financing (Noe, 1988). In the early beginnings, Modigliani and Miller (1958) presented their first model of firm capital structure that assumes that the market value of a firm is independent of its capital structure. They based that relationship on certain assumptions (e.g., market imperfections) that include the absence of taxes; transaction costs, and bankruptcy costs are called the irrelevance proposition. Stiglitz (1969), Hamada (1969), Mossin (1969) and Fama and Miller (1972) have reached part of Modigliani and Miller's (1958) conclusion that the value of the firm would be invariant to its capital structure even when there is a positive probability of bankruptcy, but only as long as there are no transactions costs associated with bankruptcy. However, Miller and Modigliani (1966) presented another model as a criterion of the optimality phase of capital structure. The model has shown a positive relationship between the value of the firm and its leverage due to a debt tax shield effect. Boness, Chen, and Jatusipitak (1974), Kim, McConnel, and Greenwood (1977) and Masulis (1980) found significant relationships between leverage changes and stock price changes. Taggart (1977) developed a model of corporate financing patterns that shows the effects of the market value of firm's securities on its capital structure. He reached a conclusion that movements in the market values of long-term debt and equity are important determinants of corporate security issues. Myers (1977) found a positive association between part of firm's capital structure, e.g., debt financing, and profitability measured in terms of expected future value of the firm's assets. Harris and Raviv (1990) show that leverage-increasing changes in capital structure are accompanied by increases in firm value. Kjellman and Hansen (1995) provided another evidence that most of the listed firms in Finland seek to maintain a target capital structure in order to maximize firm value by minimizing the costs of prevailing market imperfections. In the financial signaling models, the relationship between firm's capital structure and its market value is eventual. That is, the ultimate objective of the firm's insiders is to enhance its market value to solve the agency problems (i.e., minimize the agency costs) associated with the prevailed asymmetric information. Consequently, in terms of financial signaling, when insiders are trying to raise external finance by selling securities, they have to signal to outsiders the expected value of the their holdings. Since insiders must ultimately bear all agency costs, that situation describes a 'financial agency-signaling model,' in which insiders choose their firm's capital structure to minimize agency costs and, at the same time, enhance its market value. McConnell and Muscarella (1985) and John (1987) have reached an implication that firms which have precommitted to invest in their projects either through contractual restrictions or through announcements of capital expenditure plans should elicit positive stock and bond prices increases. This means that firms' capital structure should be altered according to the best market value of the firm's securities. Heinkel (1982) developed a signaling equilibrium model showing that investor expectations about individual firms do depend upon the capital structure of the firms. John (1987) describes the signaling effect that outsiders depend on their conjectures about the relationship between firm' actions, i.e., capital structure and true market value, to bid competitively for firm's securities. Moreover, the signaling effect of a firm's capital structure and its relation to the market value can limit insiders' opportunistic behavior. Firms' managers would choose the financing package (or capital structure) that enhances the value of the outsiders' holdings. Hovakimian, Opler, and Titman (2001) find that firms issue equity after stock price increases. This implies simultaneous changes in the firm's capital structure and its market value. Moreover, the firm can use its capital structure to signal the prospects of its investment decisions and growth opportunities thus support and enhance its market value. In this sense, Myers (1977), Froot, Scharfstein, and Stein (1993) and Graham (1996) indicate that investment decisions, especially among growth firms, are inversely related to the presence of long-term debt in a firm's capital structure. In addition, firms need to maintain financial flexibility to avoid the costs of underinvestment. In sum, these works indicate that a firm can plan and use its capital structure to exploit growth opportunities, avoid the problem of underinvestment and thus enhance its market value.

## 3.  Variables and Research Proxies

### 3.1. *Dependent variables*

The dependent variable examined in this study is firms' market value (MV) defined as the number of shares outstanding times the current closing price per share on the date of financial statement preparation. This variable is to measure firm's adjustment to a target value; therefore it is measured as the changes in market value $\Delta Y_t = \Delta MV_t = MV_t - MV_{t-1}$.

### 3.2. *Independent variables*

The change in a firm's capital structure is measured by the debt-ratio (Total debt/Total assets). The debt-ratio is measured in book rather than market value. Two studies have presented theoretical and empirical justification for the use of book value. Myers (1977) argues that the debt book value is related to the value of assets in place. Taggart (1977) finds that there is very little to choose between the book and market value formulations.

The signaling effect of debt on firm's market value is measured by taking into account that the amount of changes in market value in a certain period $[(t) - (t-1)]$ is affected by the amount of changes $[(t) - (t-1)]$ in debt in the same period. The debt ratio is denoted to as (DR). The $\Delta DR_t$ is to measure firm's adjustment to a target value. Therefore, the changes in (DR) variable is $\Delta Y_t = \Delta DR_t = DR_t - DR_{t-1}$ and the changes in the market value (MV) variable is $\Delta Y_t = \Delta MV_t = MV_t - MV_{t-1}$.

The factors that affect firm's debt policy are referred to in the literature as the determinants of capital structure. This study examines as many comprehensive number of determinants of capital structure as possible. The determinants cover the basic variables and/or proxies for the three theories of capital structure: trade-off, pecking order and free cash flow.

The measurement of the time effects for each of the variables examined in this paper varies from variable to another. According to the literature review, it has been realized that examining the changes (in the form of $\Delta X_t = X_t - X_{t-1}$) in the level of an explanatory variable(s) may address and/or result in some new insights. In addition, some variables are examined in lag effects in this paper to address the dynamic effects of changes in the level of the determinants of firm's debt. This presents one of the usefulness of such studies to corporate managers when they need to plan for some changes in the capital structure.

It is worth referring to the possible signaling effect of the three theories of capital structure. The three theories involve a signaling effect taking into account that, when making capital structure decisions, managers are bounded by the assumptions of either one or more theory (theories) at a time. The signaling effect of the three theories can be realized when managers obtain financing mix — following the assumption of the theory or theories — that improves the firm's market value. For example, the trade-off theory assumes that the optimal debt is realized when bankruptcy costs or risks equal the tax savings of debt. In this case, an optimal debt does not result in extra costs to pay which improves firm's profitability leading eventually to improve firm's stock price (signaling effect). As for the pecking-order theory and free cash flow theory, the common factor between both is that the firm seeks financing from internal sources of financing when available, which increases the equity-financing part of firm's capital structure. In this case, the benefits from equity financing can be realized when employing it for financing the prospected profitable projects (signaling effect).

Table 1 summarizes the capital structure determinants examined in this study, the ratio(s) or proxy for each determinant and the previous studies related to each determinant.

**Table 1.**    List of the factors examined in the study. The $\Delta$ is measured as $t - t - 1$ except for DR where $\Delta DR_t$ is measured as $\Delta DR_t = DR_{t+1} - DR_t$.

| Factors (Determinants of capital structure) | Variables (Ration/Proxy) | Theoretical/Empirical underpinnings |
| --- | --- | --- |
| Target debt ratio[1] | $DE_{t+1}$ | Debt-equity ratio in a next period (Marsh, 1982; Auerbach, 1985; Graham and Harvey, 2001) |
| Average industry leverage | $ADR_{AVG}$ | An indicator to the average leverage level of other firms in the same industry (Bowen, Baley, and Huber, 1982; Castanias, 1983) |
| Structure of tangible assets | $FATA_t$ — Ratio of Fixed Assets/Total Assets | An indicator to the structure of tangible assets (Martin and Scott, 1974; Jensen and Meckling, 1976; Schmidt, 1976; Myers, 1977; Ferri and Jones, 1979; Grossman and Hart, 1982; Myers and Majluf, 1984; Harris and Raviv, 1991; Rajan and Zingales, 1995; Ghosh, Cai, and Li, 2000) |
| Relative tax effects | $\Delta NDTAX$ (The ratio of depreciation to total assets) | A proxy for non-debt tax shields (DeAngelo and Masulis, 1980; Bowen *et al.*, 1982; Bradley, Sarrell, and Kim, 1984; Ross, 1985; Kim and Sorensen, 1986; Titman and Wessels, 1988; Harris and Raviv, 1991; Homaifar *et al.*, 1994; Ghosh *et al.*, 2000; Ozkan, 2001) |
| Growth | $GTA_t$ (Growth of Total Assets = percentage change in total assets) | Proxies for firm's future growth rate (Myers, 1977; Harris and Raviv, 1991; Ghosh *et al.*, 2000) |

*(Continued)*

**Table 1.** (*Continued*)

| | | |
|---|---|---|
| Investment growth opportunities | Market-Book Ratio $MB_t$ (Dummy variables for High, average, and low MB) | Firm's growth options (Myers, 1984; Williamson, 1988; Titman and Wessels, 1988; Haris and Raviv, 1990; Lasfer, 1995; Loughran and Ritter, 1995; Rajan and Zingales, 1995; Ozkan, 2001; Hovakimian *et al.*, 2001) |
| Bankruptcy risk | $DCR_t$ (Debt Coverage Ratio) | A proxy for firm's failure (Castanias, 1983; Harris and Raviv, 1990) |
| Agency costs | $ER_t$ (Expense Ratio = Operating expenses scaled by annual sales$^2$) | A measure of how effectively the firm's management controls operating costs, including excessive prerequisite consumption, and other direct agency costs (Jensen, 1986; Stulz, 1990; Ang, Cole, and Lin, 2000) |
| Industry classification | $IC_t$ (Dummy variables for different types of non-financial industries) | The industry effects on firm's capital structure (Schwarz and Aronson, 1967; Gupta, 1969; Scott, 1972; Scott and Martin, 1975; Schmidt, 1976; Ferri and Jones, 1979; Titman and Wessels, 1988; Graham and Harvey, 2001) |
| Size | In *Assets$_t$*, the natural logarithm of total assets (Dummy variable for larger, moderate, and small size firms) | The effects of firm's size on the composition of capital structure (Gupta, 1969; Toy, Stonehill, Remmeis, Wright, and Beekhuisen, 1974; Schmidt, 1976; Ferri and Jones, 1979; Titman and Wessels, 1988; Chung, 1993; Homaifar, Zeitz, and Benkato, 1994; Rajan and Zingales, 1995; Ozkan, 1996, 2001; Ghosh *et al.*, 2000) |
| Profitability | Δ EBITDA (Earnings Before Interest, Taxes, and Depreciation over total) assets | Firm's profitability ratio's which indicate the relationship between firm's profitability and leverage (Toy *et al.*, 1974; Martin and Scott, 1974; Schmidt, 1976; Carleton and Silberman, 1977; Marsh, 1982; Long and Maltiz, 1985; Titman and Wessels, 1988; Raviv, 1991; White, 1974; Rajan and Zingales, 1995; Ghosh *et al.*, 2001; Ozkan, 2001) |
| Financial flexibility | $REA_t$ + 1 (The expected effect of 'Retained Earnings Ratio' as a proxy for the retention rate) | The relationship between retention ratio and target debt-equity ratio, which has its own ground in the 'pecking order theory.' (Marsh, 1982; Pinegar and Wilbricht, 1989; Opler, *et al.*, 1999) |
| Liquidity position | $\Delta CashR_t$ (Cash Ratio) | The relationship between assets' liquidity and the use of debt (Ozkan, 2001) |

(*Continued*)

**Table 1.**   (*Continued*)

| Interest rate | IR$_t$ (Interest Rate on bank loans). | The relationship between market interest rate and issuing debt (Bosworth, 1971; White, 1974; Solnik and Grall, 1975; Taggart, 1977) |
|---|---|---|
| Timing effect | $\Delta$PE$_t$ (Price/Earnings Ratio). | The relationship between stock prices and issuing equity (Bodenhammer, 1968; Baxter and Cragg, 1970; Bosworth, 1971; Marsh, 1977, 1979; Taggart, 1977; Lucas and McDonald, 1990; Hovakimian *et al.*, 2001) |
| Transaction costs | DPR$_t$ (Dividend Payout Ratio) | The effects of transaction costs of issuing or retiring debt on the choice of capital structure (Martin and Scott, 1974; Marsh, 1982; Fischer, Heinkel and Zechner, 1989; Gilson, 1997) |
| Free cash flow | FCF$_t$ | Direct estimate of the free cash flow operational perspective (Keown Martin, Petty, and Scott, 2002) |

[1] There are alternative approaches to calculate the target ratios such as (1) the average over certain number of years; (2) by fitting an autoregressive function; (3) by taking the maximum debt ratio in the past (Marsh, 1982). However, the three approaches result in one estimate for the target ratio which gives the impression that firms look at only one certain estimate (ratio) and plan their capital structure accordingly. The method used in this paper is based on the assumption that the firm changes its target ratio generically, then the ratio a firm could achieve is considered as if it was the target ratio. This point of view takes into account the generic aspects of planning for capital structure changes. According to the literature, floatation costs, firm's size, asset structure and the market conditions change over time which necessitate planning for capital structure generically, and the target ratios are changed accordingly. However, we experimented with the three methods plus our suggested one which utilizes the two ratios. The results showed slightly significant increase in our suggested measures.

[2] The expenses ratio is not assumed to measure all agency costs as discussed in the literature. Nevertheless, and according to the availability of data, this ratio can be considered a first-order estimate and easy-to-measure indicator of the presence of agency costs at the firm level.

## 4. Data and Methodology

### 4.1. *Data*

The data used in this paper is extracted from many sources. The data related to firms' income statement and balance sheet are from the firms' annual reports. The firms' market value, MB ratio, PE ratio, and industry averages are published by the stock market authorities in Egypt. The interest rate data is published by the IMF: International Financial Statistics 2000. The data covers seven years 1997–2003. The total number of firms included in the study is 99 firms. Firms were selected based on two criteria. First, the non-financial firms amongst the 100 actively trading firms in Egypt stock market. Second, the non-financial firms amongst the 100 firms with the highest market value. Table 2 reports the descriptive statistics of the variables examined in this study.

**Table 2.** Summary statistics of variables used for identifying predictors of the capital structure decision.

| Ratio/Proxy | Mean | SD | Min | Median | Max |
|---|---|---|---|---|---|
| $\Delta DR_t$ | −0.03 | 0.58 | −7.5 | −0.01 | 6.13 |
| $\Delta MV_t$ | 305307.7 | 508676.1 | 14 | 107000 | 3416770 |
| $\Delta DE$ | 2.62 | 2.74 | 0 | 1.6 | 17.14 |
| TGTDR | −0.01 | 0.38 | −6.13 | 0.001 | 4.5 |
| $\Delta ADRIND$ | −0.01 | 0.14 | −0.54 | −0.01 | 0.48 |
| $FATA_t$ | 0.24 | 0.3 | 0.002 | 0.18 | 5.33 |
| $\Delta NDTAX_t$ | −0.02 | 0.23 | −4.3 | 0 | 0.24 |
| $\Delta NDTA$ | −0.03 | 0.08 | −0.9 | 0 | 0.79 |
| $ECTR_t$ | 2 | 41.9 | 0 | 0 | 9.32 |
| $CETA_t$ | 5.48 | 12.14 | 0 | 1.01 | 12.32 |
| $GTA_t$ | 0.22 | 1.13 | −0.9 | 0.05 | 15.05 |
| $SG_t$ | 0.08 | 0.94 | −0.96 | 0.03 | 8.58 |
| MB | 2.62 | 0.58 | 1 | 3 | 3 |
| $BR_t$ | −6.1 | 21.1 | −36.9 | −14.8 | 18.5 |
| $DCR_t$ | 76.9 | 11.4 | −8.8 | 3.01 | 25.3 |
| $ER_t$ | 0.15 | 0.17 | −0.01 | 0.11 | 1.8 |
| $AUR_t$ | 0.74 | 0.85 | 0.01 | 0.56 | 13.52 |
| $SES_t$ | 0.08 | 0.13 | 0 | 0.05 | 1 |
| IC | 5.3 | 3.64 | 1 | 3 | 14 |
| Size | 2.05 | 0.81 | 1 | 2 | 3 |
| $\Delta OIS_t$ | −0.003 | 0.27 | −3.36 | 0.003 | 3.4 |
| $\Delta OIA_t$ | −0.02 | 0.8 | −12.2 | −0.01 | 12.2 |
| $\Delta EBITDA_t$ | −0.03 | 0.8 | −12.2 | −0.01 | 12.3 |
| $REA_{t+1}$ | 0.21 | 0.24 | 0 | 0.16 | 4.1 |
| $\Delta REA_t$ | −0.01 | 0.28 | −3.7 | 0.01 | 3.7 |
| $\Delta QR$ | −0.04 | 0.99 | −18.4 | 0.02 | 2.3 |
| $\Delta PM_t$ | 0.001 | 0.26 | −3.12 | 0.004 | 2.3 |
| $\Delta ROI_t$ | −0.01 | 0.8 | −12.4 | −0.002 | 12.4 |
| $\Delta CashR_t$ | −0.31 | 6.2 | −13.8 | −0.001 | 1.9 |
| $IR_t$ | 0.14 | 0.01 | 0.13 | 0.14 | 0.16 |
| $\Delta PE_t$ | 6.86 | 10.8 | −41.5 | 0.02 | 20.6 |
| $DPR_t$ | 0.94 | 11.3 | 0 | 0.35 | 25.1 |
| $\Delta CR_t$ | −0.01 | 0.99 | −18.1 | 0.02 | 6.1 |
| $\Delta WCR_t$ | 0.24 | 3.4 | −35.2 | 0.02 | 43.4 |
| $\Delta FCF_t$ | −2118.64 | 216753.48 | −1294370 | −7713 | 1702655 |

## 4.2. *Methodology*

The methodology applied in this study is divided into two related stages. The first stage is concerned with the identification of the relevant determinants of capital structure in a transitional market settings. This is a necessary stage since the literature on capital structure has been evolved in developed market settings which are different from those of transitional market settings. The second stage is concerned with the examination of the signaling effect of the relevant determinants of capital structure that are identified in the first stage. In both stages, the identification process employs the Bayesian technique which is described in the following section.

## 5. Stochastic Search Variable Selection

Stochastic Search Variable Selection (SSVS) was proposed by George and McCulloch (1993) for the regression model. The SSVS procedure can be outlined as follows. Consider the standard linear regression model

$$\mathbf{Y} = \mathbf{X}\beta + \varepsilon, \tag{1}$$

where $\mathbf{Y}$ is a $n \times 1$ observations vector of a dependent variable, $\beta = (\beta_1, \beta_2, \ldots, \beta_p)^{\mathrm{T}}$ is the vector of unknown regression coefficients, $\{\varepsilon_t\}$ is a sequence of independent normal variates with zero mean and variance $\sigma^2$ and $\mathbf{X} = (X_1, X_2, \ldots, X_p)$ is the design matrix which contains the observations of the predictors $(X_1, X_2, \ldots, X_p)$. The key idea of SSVS is to model each regression coefficient $\beta_i$ of $\beta$ as a realization from a scale mixture of two normal distributions:

$$\beta_i \mid \gamma_i \sim (1 - \gamma_i)N(0, \tau_i^2) + \gamma_i N(0, c_i^2 \tau_i^2), \tag{2}$$

and

$$P(\gamma_i = 1) = 1 - P(\gamma_i = 0) = p_i. \tag{3}$$

When $\gamma_i = 0$, $\beta_i \sim N(0, \tau_i^2)$ and $\beta_i \sim N(0, c_i^2 \tau_i^2)$ when $\gamma_i = 1$. Following George and McCulloch (1993), the parameters $\tau_i > 0$s are chosen small so that if $\gamma_i = 0$, then $\beta_i$ would probably be so small (i.e. tends to cluster around 0) and it could "safely" remove $X_i$ from the model. Then, the parameters $c_i's > 1$ are chosen large so that when $\gamma_i = 1$, then $\beta_i$ would probably estimated by nonzero and the variable $X_j$ should be included.

## 5.1. *Prior specification*

In accordance with Equation (2), a multivariate normal prior is a suitable choice for $\beta$. That is

$$\beta \mid \Gamma \sim N_p \left(0, D_\Gamma RD_\Gamma\right), \tag{4}$$

where, $N_r(0, \Delta)$ is the $r$-variate normal distribution with mean $0$ and variance $\Delta$, $\Gamma = (\gamma_1, \gamma_2, \ldots, \gamma_p)$, $R$ is the prior correlation matrix, $D = \mathrm{diag}\,(a_1\tau_1, \ldots, a_p\tau_p)$ with $a_i = 1$ if $\gamma_i = 0$ and $a_i = c_i$ if $\gamma_i = 1$.

George and McCulloch (1993) proposed a semiautomatic strategy for selecting $c_i$ and $\tau_i$ in linear regression model. Their strategy can be summarized as follows:

- Choose $c_i$ between 10 and 100. This range for $c_i$ seems to provide separation between $N(0, \tau_i^2)$ and $N(0, c_i^2\tau_i^2)$ which is large enough to yield a useful posterior and small enough to avoid Gibbs sampling convergence problems.
- Second they fit a linear regression model and save the standard errors of the coefficient estimates.
- Choose $\tau_i$ such that the ratio $\hat{\sigma}_{\beta_i}/\tau_i$ is constant—usually 1.

The above strategy is used in this study. For other strategies for prior formulation of SSVS, see George and McCulloch (1993, 1997).

The prior distribution on the error variance $\sigma^2$ is assumed to be an inverse Gamma

$$\sigma^2 \mid \Gamma \sim IG \left(\frac{\nu_\Gamma}{2}, \frac{\nu_\Gamma \lambda_\Gamma}{2}\right), \tag{5}$$

where $IG(\nu_\Gamma/2, \nu_\Gamma\lambda_\Gamma/2)$ is the inverse gamma distribution with parameters $\nu_\Gamma/2$ and $\nu_\Gamma\lambda_\Gamma/2$. The dependence between $\beta$ and $\sigma^2$ can be expressed via letting $\nu_\Gamma$ and $\lambda_\Gamma$ depend on $\Gamma$. For simplicity, we assume that $\nu_\Gamma = \nu$ and $\lambda_\Gamma = \lambda$.

A reasonable prior for $\Gamma$ assumes $\gamma_i'$s to be mutually independent with marginal distribution (3) so that

$$\zeta(\Gamma) = \prod p_i^{\gamma_i} (1 - p_i)^{1-\gamma_i}. \tag{6}$$

The uniform or indifference prior $\zeta(\Gamma) = 2^{-p}$ is a special case of (6) when $(p_i = 1/2)$, which means that each variable $X_i$ has an equal chance of being included.

Rather than calculating the posterior probabilities over all possible subsets, the SSVS uses the Gibbs sampling technique to simulate from the posterior distribution $\zeta(\mathbf{\Gamma} \mid \mathbf{y})$. This can be done by drawing sequentially from the conditional posteriors

$$\zeta(\beta, \sigma^2, \mathbf{\Gamma} \mid \mathbf{y}), \zeta(\sigma^2, \mid \mathbf{y}, \beta), \zeta(\gamma_i \mid \mathbf{y}, \beta, \sigma^2, \mathbf{\Gamma}_{-i}),$$

where $\mathbf{\Gamma}_{-i} = (\gamma_i, \ldots, \gamma_{i-1}, \gamma_{i+1}, \ldots, \gamma_p)$.

## 5.2. *Conditional posteriors*

The joint posterior density of $\beta, \sigma^2, \mathbf{\Gamma}$ given $\mathbf{Y}$ is given by

$$\zeta(\beta, \sigma^2, \mathbf{\Gamma} \mid \mathbf{Y}) \propto \frac{1}{(2\pi\sigma^2)^{\frac{n}{2}}} \exp\left\{-\frac{1}{2\sigma^2} (\mathbf{Y} - \mathbf{X}\beta)^{\mathrm{T}} (\mathbf{Y} - \mathbf{X}\beta)\right\}$$

$$\times \frac{1}{(2\pi)^{\frac{n}{2}} \mid \mathbf{D_\Gamma R D_\Gamma} \mid^{\frac{1}{2}}} \exp\left\{-\frac{1}{2}\beta^{\mathrm{T}} (\mathbf{D_\Gamma R D_\Gamma})^{-1} \beta\right\}$$

$$\times \frac{\left(\frac{v_\Gamma \lambda_\Gamma}{2}\right)^{\frac{\lambda_\Gamma}{2}}}{\Gamma\left(\frac{v_\Gamma}{2}\right)} \frac{1}{(\sigma^2)^{\frac{v_\Gamma}{2}+1}} \exp\left\{-\frac{v_\Gamma \lambda_\Gamma}{2\sigma^2}\right\}$$

$$\times \prod_{i=1}^{n} p_i^{\gamma_i} (1 - p_i)^{1-\gamma_i} \tag{7}$$

Using linear regression results and standard Bayesian techniques, the conditional posteriors for the model parameters are as follows.

The conditional posterior of $\beta$ is

$$\beta \sim \zeta(\beta \mid \mathbf{y}, \sigma^2, \mathbf{\Gamma}) = N(\mu_\beta^\star, \sigma^2 v_\beta^\star),$$

where,

$$\mu_\beta^\star = (X^{\mathrm{T}}X + (\mathbf{D_\Gamma})^{-1}\mathbf{R}^{-1}(\mathbf{D_\Gamma})^{-1})^{-1}(X^{\mathrm{T}}\mathbf{y}),$$
$$v_\beta^\star = (X^{\mathrm{T}}X + (\mathbf{D_\Gamma})^{-1}\mathbf{R}^{-1}(\mathbf{D_\Gamma})^{-1})^{-1}.$$

The conditional posterior of $\sigma^2$ is

$$\sigma^2 \sim \zeta(\sigma^2 \mid \mathbf{y}, \beta,) = IG\left(\frac{n + v_\Gamma}{2}, \frac{v_\Gamma \lambda_\Gamma + nS^2}{2}\right),$$

where $S^2 = n^{-1}(\mathbf{y} - X\beta)^{\mathrm{T}}(\mathbf{y} - X\beta)$. Thus, the parameter $\sigma^2$ can be sampled from Chi-square distribution using the transformation $(\lambda_\Gamma + nS^2/\sigma^2) \sim \chi^2_{v_\Gamma + n}$.

The conditional posterior probability function of $\gamma_i$ is a Bernoulli distribution. That is

$$\gamma_i \sim \zeta(\gamma_i \mid \mathbf{y}, \beta, \sigma^2, \mathbf{\Gamma}_{-i}) = \gamma_i \left(\frac{1}{\alpha + \delta}\right),$$

where

$$\alpha = \zeta(\beta \mid \Gamma_{-i}, \gamma_i = 1), \quad \zeta(\Gamma_{-i}, \gamma_i = 1) = \zeta(\beta \mid \Gamma_{-i}, \gamma_i = 1) \times p_i,$$
$$\delta = \zeta(\beta \mid \Gamma_{-i}, \gamma_i = 0), \quad \zeta(\Gamma_{-i}, \gamma_i = 1) = \zeta(\beta \mid \Gamma_{-i}, \gamma_i = 0) \times (1 - p_i).$$

### 5.3. *Implementation procedures*

The Gibbs sampling algorithm for the linear regression model can be implemented as follows:

(1) Specify starting values $(\beta)^0$, $(\sigma^2)^0$ and $(\Gamma)^0$ and set $j = 0$. A set of initial estimates of the model parameters can be obtained via fitting the full model to the data.
(2) Simulate

- $(\beta)^j \sim \zeta(\beta^j \mid \mathbf{y}, (\sigma^2)^{j-1}, (\Gamma)^{j-1})$,
- $(\sigma^2)^j \sim \zeta((\sigma^2)^j \mid \mathbf{y}, \beta^j, (\Gamma)^{j-1})$,
- $(\gamma_i)^{\mathbf{j}} \sim \zeta(\gamma_i)^{\mathbf{j}} \mid \mathbf{y}, \beta^{\mathbf{j}}, (\sigma^2)^{\mathbf{j}}, (\Gamma_{-\mathbf{i}})^{\mathbf{j}})$.

(3) Set $j = j + 1$ and go to 2.

This algorithm gives the next value of the Markov chain $\{\beta^{j+1}, (\sigma^2)^{j+1}, (\Gamma)^{j+1}\}$ by simulating each of the full conditionals where the conditioning elements are revised during a cycle. This iterative process is repeated for a large number of iterations and convergence is monitored. Later the chain attains convergence.

## 6. Results and Discussion

The SSVS procedure is applied with indifference prior $\Gamma = (1/2)^{33}$, $R = I$, $v = 0$, $(c_1 = c_2, \ldots, c_{33} = 10)$, and $(\tau_1 = \tau_2 = \cdots = \tau_{33} = 0.025)$ so that $\sigma'_{\beta_i}/\tau_i \approx 1$. Where $\sigma'_{\beta_i}$s are the standard errors of the least squares coefficient estimates. Analysis is implemented using Matlab and running under Pentium PC 1000 MHZ. The stating values for the parameters $\beta$ and $\sigma^2$ are chosen as the least squares estimates of the fitted full model and the resulting mean square error. The starting values for $\Gamma$ is assumed vector of ones. The implementation of the proposed Gibbs sampler is straightforward. The Gibbs sampler was run 100,000 iterations where every tenth value in the sequence was recorded and tabulated.

## 6.1. *The relevant determinants of capital structure in a transitional market*

The literature on theories of capital structure has evolved in a developed market settings mostly in the USA. Since then, studies in the determinants and theories of capital structure have been trying to examine the relevant effects of many factors of market imperfections on the issuance of debt and/or equity using mostly US data. As long as the market conditions and institutions in transitional economies are different from those in the developed markets, this requires an examination of the relevant determinants of capital structure in a transitional market settings. This is to be considered *a priori* step before the signaling effect is examined. A relatively large number of determinants of capital structure are pooled according to the results of previous studies in the literature to examine their relevancy to a transitional market settings. Then, the Bayesian methodology described above is carried out and the results are reported in Table 3.

Table 3 presents the five highest frequency subsets and their joint probability estimates and marginal probability estimates for the 33 predictors. The joint or marginal probabilities are estimated by the empirical relative joint or marginal frequencies. The joint probability estimates are displayed in Figure 1 while the top panel of Figure 2 displays marginal probability estimates.

It is clear from Table 3 that all the five promising subsets of determinants of capital structure include 11 variables, namely debt/equity ratio, target debt-ratio, average industry debt-ratio, fixed assets/total assets, non—debt tax shields/total assets, asset utilization ratio, size (measured by *ln* Assets), operating income/total assets, changes in retained earnings ratio and profit margin. It is interesting to notice that the elements of the first subset have highest marginal probability among all 33 predictors. This is a clear indication to the high association between these predictors of capital structure (independent variables) and the debt-ratio (the dependent variable). Therefore, the 11 variables can be considered as 'determinants of capital structure in Egypt' as an example of a transitional market.

To a large extent, these results are encouraging since they are very close to other research results in other developing countries (Booth *et al.*, 2001), where much similarities of the institutional structures are reported. For example, in their paper which is considered a contribution to the literature of capital structure, Booth *et al.* (2001) found that tangibility, profitability and size are quite significant predictors of capital structure in other developing

**Table 3.**   The five highest frequency subsets, or determinants, of capital structure.

| $\Delta Y_t = \Delta DR_t$ | Label | Subsets 1 | 2 | 3 | 4 | 5 | Marginal probability |
|---|---|---|---|---|---|---|---|
| $X_1$ | DE | ● | ● | ● | ● | ● | 1 |
| $X_2$ | TGTDR | ● | ● | ● | ● | ● | 0.8715 |
| $X_3$ | DRIND | ● | ● | ● | ● | ● | 0.997 |
| $X_4$ | FATA | ● | ● | ● | ● | ● | 1 |
| $X_5$ | NDTAX | | | | | | 0.0309 |
| $X_6$ | NDTA | ● | ● | ● | ● | ● | 1 |
| $X_7$ | ECTR | | | | | | 0.0097 |
| $X_8$ | CFIA | | ● | ● | | | 0.4682 |
| $X_9$ | GTA | | | | | | 0.0065 |
| $X_{10}$ | SG | | | | | | 0.0634 |
| $X_{11}$ | MB | | | | | | 0.0224 |
| $X_{12}$ | BR | | | | | | 0.0081 |
| $X_{13}$ | DCR | | | | | | 0.021 |
| $X_{14}$ | ER | | | | | ● | 0.3335 |
| $X_{15}$ | AUR | ● | ● | ● | ● | ● | 1 |
| $X_{16}$ | SES | | | | | | 0.018 |
| $X_{17}$ | IC | | | | | | 0.1165 |
| $X_{18}$ | SIZE | ● | ● | ● | ● | ● | 0.9404 |
| $X_{19}$ | OIS | | | | | ● | 0.3668 |
| $X_{20}$ | OIA | ● | ● | ● | ● | ● | 0.9524 |
| $X_{21}$ | EBITDA | | | | | | 0.3128 |
| $X_{22}$ | REA | ● | ● | | | | 0.485 |
| $X_{23}$ | DELREA | ● | ● | ● | ● | ● | 1 |
| $X_{24}$ | CR | | | | | | 0.1245 |
| $X_{25}$ | QR | | | | | | 0.0311 |
| $X_{26}$ | WCR | | | | | | 0.0107 |
| $X_{27}$ | CASHR | | | | | | 0.0672 |
| $X_{28}$ | IR | | | | | | 0.0058 |
| $X_{29}$ | PE | | | | | | 0.0072 |
| $X_{30}$ | DPR | | | | | | 0.0053 |
| $X_{31}$ | PM | ● | ● | ● | ● | ● | 0.9896 |
| $X_{32}$ | ROI | ● | ● | ● | ● | ● | 0.9997 |
| $X_{33}$ | FCF | | | | | | 0.0125 |
| Joint probability | | 0.0443 | 0.0415 | 0.0295 | 0.0259 | 0.0249 | |

countries. Especially, profitability was found in Booth *et al.*'s study as a striking predictor of capital structure in a sample of ten developing countries. In this study, four variables (fixed assets/total assets, size, operating income/total assets, and profit margin) are also found quite associated with capital structure.

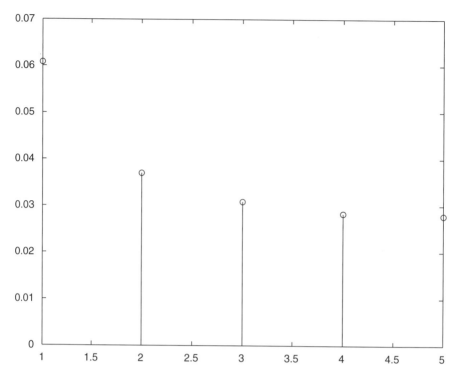

**Figure 1.**   The five highest frequency subsets of determinants of capital structure.

As a support to Booth *et al.*'s results, in this paper a firm's profitability is represented by two ratios which are operating income/total assets and profit margin. In addition, in Booth *et al.*'s study, tangibility and size were also found as good predictors of capital structure. In this study, asset tangibility (fixed assets/total assets) is found to have a high association (marginal probability = 1) with debt-ratio. Firms' size (*ln* Assets) is also found to have high association with (marginal probability = 0.9404) with debt-ratio. It is worth to note that in Booth *et al.*'s study, size is measured by the natural logarithm of sales and found among the good predictors of capital structure. Here, we note that the different measures of size and its significant results are to be considered as a support to the validity of size as a predictor of capital structure in developing countries.

As an investigation of the explanatory power of the identified predictors, 33 nested regressions were fitted where predictors were added one at a time in order of the decreasing marginal probability estimates. The descending ordered marginal probability estimates and the corresponding $R^2$ values are displayed

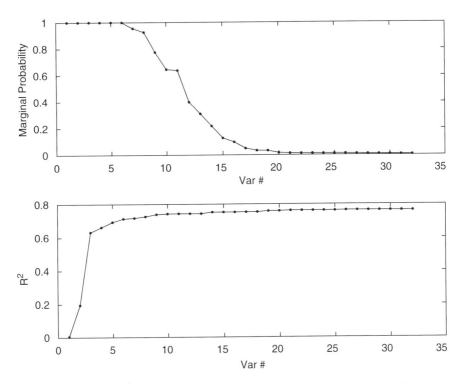

**Figure 2.** Top Panel, $R^2$ versus variable numbers. Bottom panel, marginal probability values.

in Figure 2. It is clear that $R^2$ values from the nested regressions increase most quickly for the variables with large marginal probability estimates. This suggests that the identified subset of determinants of capital structure using marginal probability estimates or the SSVS has a considerable explanatory power.

## 6.2. *Determinants of financial signaling in a transitional market*

As mentioned above in the methodology, the second stage is to examine the signaling effect of the relevant determinants of capital structure shown in Table 3. The same Bayesian procedures applied to the eleven relevant predictors of capital structure. Table 4 shows the five highest frequency subsets of the relevant determinants of capital structure that have a signaling effect on firms' market value. Table 4 shows that the first subset is associated with the highest joint probability (0.3248) indicating that it includes the most influential determinants

**Table 4.**    The five highest frequency subsets for the determinants of financial signaling.

| Independents | Label | 1 | 2 | 3 | 4 | 5 | Marginal probability |
|---|---|---|---|---|---|---|---|
| $X_1$ | DE | | | ● | ● | | 0.1379 |
| $X_2$ | TGTDR | | | | | | 0.0451 |
| $X_3$ | DRIND | | | | | | 0.0817 |
| $X_4$ | FATA | | | | | ● | 0.0753 |
| $X_6$ | NDTA | | | | | | 0.0383 |
| $X_{15}$ | AUR | | | | | | 0.0512 |
| $X_{18}$ | SIZE | ● | ● | ● | ● | ● | 1 |
| $X_{20}$ | OIA | | | | | | 0.0993 |
| $X_{23}$ | DELREA | ● | ● | ● | ● | ● | 1 |
| $X_{31}$ | PM | ● | | | ● | ● | 0.6241 |
| $X_{32}$ | ROI | | | | | | 0.0914 |
| Joint probability | | 0.3248 | 0.1678 | 0.0465 | 0.0461 | 0.0348 | |

*(Subsets span columns 1–5; Marginal probability is the final column.)*

of capital structure on firm's market value. The first subset includes three determinants: size (measured by the (*ln* Assets)), changes in retained earnings ratio, and profit margin ratio. The three determinants are associated with the highest marginal probability—1,1, and 0.6241 respectively, which are the highest marginal probability among the 11 relevant predictors of capital structure.

The joint or marginal probabilities are estimated by the empirical relative joint or marginal frequencies. The joint probability estimates are displayed in Figure 3.

## 6.3. *Examining the significance of the relevant determinants of financial signaling in a transitional market*

As shown in Table 4, the Bayesian methodology results in number of determinants of financial signaling that are most associated with firms' market value. Table 5 summarizes the group (or subset) of determinants of capital structure that helps signal firm's market value. This matches one of the conclusions drawn by Booth *et al.* (2001) for other developing countries.

The final results in Table 5 show that firm's capital structure *per se* is not one of the determinants of financial signaling. Rather, the determinants of capital structure (as examined in the literature) do have a signaling effect reflected by their association with firm's market value. According to the chosen subset, three determinants of capital structure have a signaling effect. These determinants

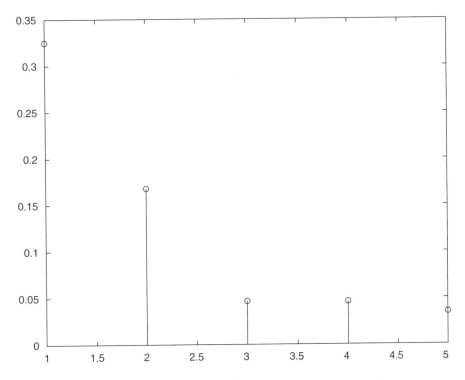

**Figure 3.**   The five highest frequency subsets of determinants of financial signaling.

are firm's size, financial flexibility and profitability. When combined together, the three determinants may lead to the conclusion that the signaling effect reflects the presence of the pecking order theory. That is, firms tend to use its profitability and financial flexibility as financing sources which affect its market value. This matches one of the conclusions drawn by Booth *et al.* (2001) for other developing countries.

It is noticeable that the results reported in Table 5 show the association between the relevant determinants of capital structure and the market value.

**Table 5.**   Determinants of financial signaling.

| Dimension of capital structure | Ratio and / or Proxy |
| --- | --- |
| Size | *ln* Assets |
| Financial flexibility | Changes in retained earnings/Total assets |
| Profitability | Profit margin ratio |

This association does not indicate the significance of the determinants of financial signaling. Consequently, a regression analysis is carried out to further show the significance of the determinants of financial signaling. The analysis hypothesizes a positive relationship between the three determinants of financial signaling and market value. The regression results are reported in Table 6.

The results in Table 6 show that firms' size and profitability are the only statistically significant determinants of financial signaling. The negative sign of size (*ln* Assets) indicates that market value is associated with small size firms. On the other hand, the positive sign of the profitability (profit margin ratio) indicates the positive contribution of the basic assumption of pecking order theory to the signaling effect. That is, the higher the firm's profitability, the higher its market value. These results match, to a large extent, with the result reported by Booth *et al.* (2001) that profitability is a striking predictor of capital structure in ten developing countries.

**Table 6.**   Significance of the determinants of financial signaling.

| Determinants of financial signaling | | |
|---|---|---|
| Dependent Variable Market Value | $MV_t$ | |
| Independents | Constant | 102621.8 |
| *ln* Assets$_t$ | Size | −29.49 (−3.63)*** |
| $\Delta REA_t$ | Changes in retained earnings/Total Assets | −34401.3 (−1.53) |
| $PM_t$ | Profit margin ratio | 86168.4 (2.82)*** |
| $N$ | | 411 |
| F statistics | | 5.17*** |
| $\overline{R}^2$ | | 0.03 |
| D–W test | | 1.83**** |

*Note*: Regression coefficients of the determinants of financial signaling. The dependent variable is firms' market value. The *t*-statistics are shown between brackets. The regression equation is free from multicollinearity (VIF < 5). The heteroskedastic effects are corrected using the White's HCSE, which improves the significance of the OLS estimates. ****D–W is significant at 2% two sided level of significance. ***Significant at the level 1%. **Significant at the level 5%. *Significant at the level 10%.

## 7. Conclusion

This paper presents an extension to the increasing literature on employing statistical modeling to financial studies. The Bayesian methodology employed in this paper provides an in-depth perspectives on the process of variable identification. As for the financial signaling hypothesis, the identification procedures provide well-established guidance to the practice of making signaling-oriented capital structure decisions. That is, the identified model in this study presents a good guidance to help managers take into account the capital structure-related determinants that help signal firm's market value. The final results, which are a good match with those of other developing countries, show that, among the significant relevant determinants of capital structure, firms' size and profitability are the two determinants that are significantly associated with a firm's market value, thus have a signaling effect. Recalling from the theories of capital structure, the basic premises of the pecking order theory are traceable in this study when taking firm's profitability as a proxy. In general, we would say that if Egypt has been included in other developing countries studies such as Booth *et al.*'s (2001), the results would have carried matchable implications. Therefore, the contribution element of this paper is that it provides validity to the determinants of capital structure in developing countries since this paper and Booth *et al.*'s (2001) paper follow two different analytical tools that imply different assumptions.

## References

Akaike, H., "Fitting Autoregressive Models for Control." *Annals of Mathematical Statistics* 21, 243–247 (1969).

Akaike, H., "Information Theory and an Extension of the Maximum Principle." *2nd International Symposium on information Theory*, Budapest: Akademia Kiado, pp. 267–281 (1969).

Ang, J. S., R. A. Cole, and J. W. Lin, "Agency Costs and Ownership Structure." *Journal of Finance* 55, 81–106 (2000).

Auerbach, A. J., "Real Determinants of Corporate Leverage." In B. M. Friedman (ed.), Corporate Capital Structure in the United States. Chicago: University of Chicago Press, pp. 301–322 (1985).

Baxter, N. D. and J. G. Cragg, "Corporate Choice Among Long-Term Financing Instruments." *Review of Economics and Statistics* 52, 225–235 (1970).

Bodenhammer, L., "The Effect of the Size of Public Offerings of Common Stocks upon Pre-offering Stock Prices." Unpublished Ph.D. dissertation, Harvard Business School (1968).

Boness, J., A. Chen and S. Jatusipitak, "Investigations of Nonstationary Prices." *Journal of Business* 47, 518–537 (1974).

Booth, L., V. Aivazian, A. Demirguc–Kunt and V. Maksimovic, "Capital Structure in Developing Countries." *The Journal of Finance* 56, 87–130 (2001).

Bosworth, B., "Patterns of Corporate External Financing." *Brookings Papers on Economic Activity* 2, 253–279 (1971).

Bowen, R. M., L. A. Daley and C. C. Huber, "Evidence on the Existence and Determinants of Inter-Industry Differences of Leverage." *Financial Management* 11, 10–20 (1982).

Bradley, M., A. Jarrell and E. H. Kim, "On the Existence of an Optimal Capital Structure: Theory and Evidence." *Journal of Finance* 39, 857–880 (1984).

Brown, P.J., M. Vannucci and T. Fearn, "Multivariate Bayesian Variable Selection and Prediction." *Journal of the Royal Statistical Society* Ser. B, 60, 627–642 (1998).

Carleton, W. T. and I. H. Silberman, "Joint Determination of Rate of Return and Capital Structure: An Econometric Analysis." *Journal of Finance* 32, 811–821 (1977).

Castanias, R., "Bankruptcy Risk and Optimal Capital Structure." *Journal of Finance* 38, 1617–1635 (1983).

Chen, A. H. and E. H. Kim, "Theories of Corporate Debt Policy: A Synthesis." *Journal of Finance* 34, 371–384 (1979).

Chib, S. and E. Greenberg, "Understanding the Metropolis-Hastings Algorithm." *The American Statistician* 49, 327–335 (1995).

Chipman, H., "Bayesian Variable Selection with Related Predictors." *The Canadian Journal of Statistics* 24, 17–36.

Clyde, M. A., "Bayesian model averaging and model search strategies (with discussion)." In J. M. Bernardo, J. O. Berger, A. P. Dawid and A. F. M. Smith (eds.), *"Bayesian Statistics"*, Vol. 6, Oxford University Press, pp. 157–185 (1999).

Clyde, M. A., H. DeSimone, and G. Parmigiani, "Prediction via Orthogonalized Model Mixing." *Journal of the American Statistical Association* 91, 1197–1208 (1996).

Clyde, M. and E. I. George, Empirical Bayes estimation in wavelet nonparametric regression. In P. Muller and B. Vidakovic (eds.), *"Bayesian Inference in Wavelet Based Models."* pp. 309–22 (1999). New York: Springer-Verlag.

Chung, K. H., "Asset Characteristics and Corporate Debt Policy: An Empirical Test." *Journal of Business Finance and Accounting* 20, 83–98 (1993).

Darrough, M. N. and N. M. Stoughton, "Moral Hazard and Adverse Selection: The Question of Capital Structure." *Journal of Finance* 41, 501–513 (1986).

DeAngelo, H. and R. Masulis, "Optimal Capital Structure Under Corporate and Personal Taxation." *Journal of Financial Economics* 8, 3–29 (1980).

Draper, N. and H. Smith, *"Applied Regression Analysis."* New York, John Wiley.

Fama, E. F. and M. H. Miller, *"The Theory of Finance."* NY: Holt, Rinehart, and Winston (1972).

Ferri, M. and W. Jones, "Determinants of Financial Structure: A New Methodological Approach." *Journal of Finance* 34, 631–644 (1979).

Fischer, E. O., R. Heinkel and J. Zechner, "Dynamic Capital Structure Choice: Theory and Tests." *Journal of Finance* 44, 19–40 (1989).

Foster, D. and E. George, "The Risk Inflation Criterion for Multiple Regression." *Ann. Statist.* 22, 1947–75 (1994).

Froot, K. A., D. S. Scharfstein and J. C. Stein, "Risk Management: Coordinating Corporate Investment and Financing Policies." *Journal of Finance* 48, 1629–1658 (1993).

Furnival, G. M. and R. W. Wilson, "Regression by Leaps and Bounds." *Technometrics* 16, 499–511 (1974).

George, E. and D. Foster, "Calibration and Empirical Bayes Variable Selection." *Biometrika* 87, 731–747 (2000).

Ghosh, A., F. Cai and W. Li, "The Determinants of Capital Structure." *American Business Review* 18, 129–132 (2000).

Gilson, S. C., "Transaction Costs and Capital Structure Choice: Evidence from Financially Distress Firms." *Journal of Finance* 52, 111–133 (1997).

Graham, J. R., "Debt and the Marginal Tax Rate." *Journal of Financial Economics* 41, 41–73 (1996).

―――. and C. R. Harvey, "The Theory and Practice of Corporate Finance: Evidence From the Field." *Journal of Financial Economics* 60, 187–243 (2001).

Grossman, S. and O. Hart, Corporate financial structure and managerial incentives. In McCall, J. (ed.), *"The Economics of Information and Uncertainty."* Chicago: University of Chicago Press (1982).

Gupta, M. C., "The Effect of Size, Growth and Industry on the Financial Structure of Manufacturing Companies." *Journal of Finance* 24, 517–529 (1969).

Hamada, R. S., "Portfolio Analysis, Market Equilibrium and Corporation Finance." *Journal of Finance* 24, 13–31 (1969).

Harris, M. and A. Raviv, "Capital Structure and the Informational Role of Debt." *Journal of Finance* 45, 321–349 (1990).

―――., "The Theory of Capital Structure." *Journal of Finance* 46, 297–355 (1991).

Homaifar, G., J. Zietz, and O. Benkato, "An Empirical Model of Capital Structure: Some New Evidence." *Journal of Business Finance and Accounting* 21, 1–14 (1994).

Hannan, E. J. and B. G. Quinn, "The Determination of the Order of an Autoregression." *Journal of the Royal Statistical Society B* 41, 190–195 (1979).

Heinkel, R., "A Theory of Capital Structure Relevance Under Imperfect Information." *Journal of Finance* 37, 1141–1150 (1982).

Hocking, R. R., "The Analysis and Selection of Variables in Linear Regression." *Biometrics* 32, 1–52 (1976).

Hovakimian, A., T. C. Opler, and S. Titman, "Debt-Equity Choice." *Journal of Financial and Quantitative Analysis* 36, 1–24 (2001).

Jensen, M. C. and W. H. Meckling, "Theory of the Firm: Managerial Behavior, Agency Costs and Ownership Structure." *Journal of Financial Economics* 3, 305–360 (1976).

Jensen, M. C., "Agency Costs of Free Cash Flow, Corporate Finance, and Takeovers." *American Economic Review* 76, 323–329 (1986).

John, K., "Risk-shifting Incentives and Signalling Through Corporate Capital Structure." *Journal of Finance* 42, 623–641 (1987).

Kim, H., J. McConnell, and P. Greenwood, "Capital Structure Rearrangements and the First Rules in an Efficient Capital Market." *Journal of Finance* 32, 789–810 (1977).

Keown, A. J., J. D. Martin, J. W. Petty and D. F. Scott, Jr., "Financial Mangement: Principles and Applications." 9th edition, Prentice Hall, (2002).

Kim, W. S. and E. H. Sorensen, "Evidence on the Impact of the Agency Costs of Debt on Corporate Debt Policy." *Journal of Financial and Quantitative Analysis* 21, 131–144 (1986).

Kjellman, A. and S. Hansen, "Determinants of Capital Structure: Theory versus Practice." *Scandinavian Journal of Management* 11, 91–102 (1995).

Lasfer, M. A., "Agency costs, Taxes and Debt." *European Financial Management* 1, 265–285 (1995).

Long, M. and I. Maltiz, "The Investment Financing Nexus: Some Empirical Evidence." *Midland Corporate Finance Journal* 3, 53–59 (1985).

Loughran, T. and J. R. Ritter, "The New Issues Puzzle." *Journal of Finance* 50, 23–52 (1995).

Lucas, D. J. and R. L. McDonald, "Equity Issues and Stock Price Dynamics." *Journal of Finance* 45, 1019–1043 (1990).

Mallows, C. L., "Some Comments on $C_p$." *Technometrics* 15, 661–676 (1973).

Marsh, P., An analysis of equity rights issues on the London Stock Exchange. Unpublished Ph.D. dissertation, London Graduate School of Business Studies, (1977).

——., "Equity Rights Issues and the Efficiency of the UK Stock Market." *Journal of Finance* 34, 839–862 (1979).

——., "The Choice Between Equity and Debt: An Empirical Study." *Journal of Finance* 37, 121–144 (1982).

Masulis, R. W., "The Effects of Capital Structure Change on Security Prices: A Study of Exchange Offers." *Journal of Financial Economics* 8, 139–178 (1980).

————., "The Impact of Capital Structure Change on Firm Value: Some Estimates." *Journal of Finance* 38, 107–126 (1983).

Martin, J. D. and D. F. Scott, Jr., "A Discriminant Analysis of the Corporate Debt-equity Decision." *Financial Management* 3, 71–79 (1974).

McConnell, J. and C. Muscarella, "Corporate Capital Expenditure Decisions and the Market Value of the Firm." *Journal of Financial Economics* 14, 399–422 (1985).

Miller, M. H., "The Modigliani-Miller Proposition after Thirty Years." *Journal of Economic Perspceties* 2, 99–120 (1988).

Miller, A. J., "*Subset Selection in Regression.*" Chapman and Hall, London, 1990.

Miller, M. H. and F. Modigliani, "Some Estimates of the Cost of Capital to the Electric Industry 1954–1957." *American Economic Review* 56, 333–341 (1966).

Modigliani, F. and M. H. Miller, "The Cost of Capital, Corporation Finance and the Theory of Investment." *American Economic Review* 48, 261–297 (1958).

Mossin, J., "Security Pricing and Investment Criteria in Competitive Markets." *American Economics Review* 59, 749–756 (1969).

Myers, S. C., "Determinants of Corporate Borrowing." *Journal of Financial Economics* 5, 147–175 (1977).

————., "The Capital Structure Puzzle." *Journal of Finance* 39, 575–592 (1984).

————. and N. S. Majluf, "Corporate Financing and Investment Decisions When Firms Have Information That Investors Do Not Have." *Journal of Financial Economics* 13, 187–221 (1984).

————., "Capital Structure." *Journal of Economics Perspectices* 15, 81–102 (2001).

Noe, T. H., "Capital Structure and Signaling Game Equilibria." *The Review of Financial Studies* 1, 331–355 (1988).

Opler, T., L. Pinkowitz, R. Stulz and R. Williamson, "The Determinants and Implications of Corporate Cash Holdings." *Journal of Financial Ecomomics* 52, 3–46 (1999).

Ozkan A., "Corporate Bankruptcies, Liquidation Costs and the Role of Banks." *The Manchester School* 64, 104–119 (1996).

————., "Determinants of Capital Structure and Adjustment to Long-run Target: Evidence from UK Company Panel Data." *Journal of Business Finance and Accounting* 28, 175–198 (2001).

Pinegar, J. M. and L. Wilbricht, "What Managers Think of Capital Structure Theory: A Survey." *Financial Management* 18, 82–91 (1989).

Rajan, R. G. and L. Zingales, "What Do We Know About Capital Structure? Some Evidence From International Data." *Journal of Finance* 50, 1421–1460 (1995).

Ross, S. A., "The Determination of Financial Structure: The Incentive-Signalling Approach." *Bell Journal of Economics* 8, 23–40 (1977).

————., "Some Notes on Financial Incentive-Signaling Models, Activity Choice and Risk Preferences." *Journal of Finance* 33, 777–794 (1978).

————., "Debt and Taxes and Uncertainty." *Journal of Finance* 40, 637–657 (1985).

Schwarz, E. and J. R. Aronson, "Some Surrogate Evidence in Support of the Concept of Optimal Capital Structure." *Journal of Finance* 22, 10–18 (1967).

Schwarz, G., "Estimating a Dimension of a Model." *Ann. Statist.* 6, 461–464 (1978).

Scott D. F. Jr., "Evidence on the Importance of Financial Structure." *Financial Management* 1, 45–50 (1972).

————. and J. D. Martin, "Industry Influence on Financial Structure." *Financial Management* 4, 67–73 (1975).

Schmidt, R. H., "Determinants of Corporate Debt Ratios in Germany." *European Finance Association Proceedings*, Amsterdam: North Holland (1976).

Shibata, R., "Asymptotically Efficient Selection of the Order of the Model for Estimating Parameters of a Linear Process." *Annals of Statistics* 8, 147–164 (1980).

Shyam-Sunder, L. and S. C. Myers, "Testing Static Tradeoff Against Pecking Order Models of Capital Structure." *Journal of Financial Economics* 51, 219–244 (1999).

Smith, A. F. M. and D. J. Spiegelhalter, "Bayes Factor and Choice Criteria for the Linear Models." *Journal of the Royal Statistical Society B* 42, 213–220 (1980).

Solnik, B. H. and J. Grall, "Eurobonds: Determining the Demand for Capital and the International Interest Rate Structure." *Journal of Bank Research* 5, 218–230 (1974/5).

Stiglitz, J., "A Reexamination of the Modigliani-Miller Theorem." *American Economic Review* 59, 784–793 (1969).

Stulz, R. M. and H. Johnson, "Managerial Discretion and Optimal Financing Policies." *Journal of Financial Economics* 26, 3–28 (1990).

Taggart R. A., Jr., "A Model of Corporate Financing Decisions." *Journal of Finance* 32, 1467–1484 (1977).

Titman, S. and R. Wessels, "The Determinants of Capital Structure Choice." *Journal of Finance* 43, 1–19 (1988).

Toy, N., A. Stonehill, L. Remmers, R. Wright and T. Beekhuisen, "A Comparative International Study of Growth, Profitability, and Risk as Determinants of Corporate Debt Ratios in the Manufacturing Sector." *Journal of Financial and Quantitative Analysis* 9, 875–886 (1974).

White, W. L., "Debt Management and the Form of Business Financing." *Journal of Finance* 29, 565–577 (1974).

Whited, T., "Debt, Liquidity Constraints, and Corporate Investment: Evidence from Panel Data." *Journal of Finance* 47, 1425–1460 (1992).

Williamson, O. E., "Corporate Finance and Corporate Governance." *The Journal of Finance* 43, 567–591 (1988).

Young, A. S., "The Bivar Criterion for Selecting Regressors." *Technometrics* 24, 151–156 (1982).

Ang, J. S., R. A. Cole and J. W. Lin, "Agency Costs and Ownership Structure." *Journal of Finance* 55, 81–106 (2000).

George, E. I. and R. E. McCulloch, "Variable Selection via Gibbs Sampling." *Journal of American Statistical Association* 88, 881–889 (1993).

George, E. I and R. E. McCulloch, "Approaches for Bayesian variable selection." Working Paper, University of Texas at Austin, 1996.

Auerbach, A. J., Real determinants of corporate leverage. In B. M. Friedman (ed.), "*Corporate Capital Structure in the United States.*" Chicago: University of Chicago Press, pp. 301–322 (1985).

Baxter, N. D. and J. G. Cragg, "Corporate Choice among Long-Term Financing Instruments." *Review of Economics and Statistics* 52, 225–235 (1970).

Bowen, R. M., L. A. Daley and C. C. Huber, "Evidence on the Existence and Determinants of Inter-Industry Differences of Leverage." *Financial Management* 11, 10–20 (1982).

Carleton, W. T. and I. H. Silberman, "Joint Determination of Rate of Return and Capital Structure: An Econometric Analysis." *Journal of Finance* 32, 811–821 (1977).

Castanias, R., "Bankruptcy Risk and Optimal Capital Structure." *Journal of Finance* 38, 1617–1635 (1983).

Chen, A. H. and E. H. Kim, "Theories of Corporate Debt Policy: A Synthesis." *Journal of Finance* 34, 371–384 (1979).

DeAngelo, H. and R. Masulis, "Optimal Capital Structure Under Corporate and Personal Taxation." *Journal of Financial Economics* 8, 3–29.

Dellaportas, P. and J. J. Foster, "Markov Chain Monte Carlo Model Determination for Hierrarchical and Graphical Log-Linear Models." *Biometrika* 86, 615–634 (1999).

Dellaportas, P., J. J. Forster and I. Ntzoufras, "On Bayesian Model and Variable Selection Using MCMC." *Statistics and Computing* (to appear), 2000.

Fischer, E. O., R. Heinkel and J. Zechner, "Dynamic Capital Structure Choice: Theory and Tests." *Journal of Finance* 44, 19–40 (1989).

Foster, D. and E. George, "The Risk Inflation Criterion for Multiple Regression." *Ann. Statist.* 22, 1947–75 (1994).

George, E. and D. Foster, "Calibration and Empirical Bayes Variable Selection." *Biometrika* 87, 731–747 (2000).

George, E. I. and D. P. Foster, "Calibration and Empirical Bayes Variable Selection." *Biometrika* 87, 731–748 (2000).

George, E. I. and R. E. McCulloch, "Variable Selection via Gibbs Sampling." *Journal of the American Statistical Society* 88, 881–889 (1993).

George, E. I. and R. E. McCulloch, Stochastic search variable selection, In *"Markov Chain Monte Carlo in Practice,"* W. R. Gilks, S. Richardson and D.J. Spiegelhalter, (eds.), pp. 203–214 London: Chapman & Hall.

George, E. I. and R. E. McCulloch, "Approaches for Bayesian Variable Selection." *Statist. Sinica* 7, 339–73 (1997).

George, E. I., R. E. McCulloch and R. Tsay, Two approaches to Bayesian Model selection with applications. In *"Bayesian Statistics and Econometrics: Essays in Honor of Arnold Zellner."* D. Berry, K. Chaloner and J. Geweke (eds.), 339–348 (1995) New York: Wiley.

George, E. I., Bayesian model selection, In *Encyclopedia of Statistical Sciences*, Update Vol. 3, S. Kotz, C. Read and D. Banks (eds.), pp. 39–46 (1998). New York: Wiley.

Geweke, J., Variable selection and model comparison in regression, In *Bayesian Statistics*, Vol. 5, J. M. Bernardo, J. O. Berger, A. P. Dawid and A. F. M. Smith (eds.), pp. 609–620 (1996). Oxford Press.

Ghosh, A., F. Cai and W. Li, "The Determinants of Capital Structure." *American Business Review* 18, 129–132 (2000).

Gilson, S. C., "Transaction Costs and Capital Structure Choice: Evidence from Financially Distress Firms." *Journal of Finance* 52, 111–133 (1997).

Graham, J. R. and C. R. Harvey, "The Theory and Practice of Corporate Finance: Evidence From the Field." *Journal of Financial Economics* 60, 187–243 (2001).

Grossman, S. and O. Hart, Corporate financial structure and managerial incentives. In J. McCall (ed.), *"The Economics of Information and Un-Certainty."* Chicago: University of Chicago Press.

Gupta, M. C., "The Effect of Size, Growth and Industry on the Financial Structure of Manufacturing Companies." *Journal of Finance* 24, 517–529 (1969).

Harris, M. and A. Raviv, "Capital Structure and the Informational Role of Debt." *Journal of Finance* 45, 321–349 (1990).

Harris, M. and A. Raviv, "The Theory of Capital Structure." *Journal of Finance* 46, 297–355 (1991).

Homaifar, G., J. Zietz and O. Benkato, "An Empirical Model of Capital Structure: Some New Evidence." *Journal of Business Finance and Accounting* 21, 1–14 (1994).

Hovakimian, A., T. C. Opler and S. Titman, "Debt-Equity Choice." *Journal of Financial and Quantitative Analysis* 36, 1–24 (2001).

Jensen, M. C. and W. H. Meckling, "Theory of the Firm: Managerial Behavior, Agency Costs and Ownership Structure." *Journal of Financial Economics* 3, 305–360 (1976).

Jensen, M. C., "Agency Costs of Free Cash Flow, Corporate Finance, and Takeovers." *American Economic Review* 76, 323–329 (1986).

Lasfer, M. A., "Agency costs, Taxes and Debt." *European Financial Management* 1, 265–285 (1995).

Lev, B., "Industry Average as Targets for Financial Ratios." *Journal of Accounting Research* 7, 290–299.

Long, M. and I. Maltiz, "The Investment Financing Nexus: Some Empirical Evidence." *Midland Corporate Finance Journal* 3, 53–59 (1985).

Lucas, D. J. and R. L. McDonald, "Equity Issues and Stock Price Dynamics." *Journal of Finance* 45, 1019–1043 (1990).

Mallows, C. L., "Some Comments on $C_p$." *Technometrics* 15, 661–76 (1973).

Marsh, P., "The Choice Between Equity and Debt: An Empirical Study." *Journal of Finance* 37, 121–144 (1982).

Martin, J. D. and D. F. Scott, Jr., "A Discriminant Analysis of the Corporate Debt-Equity Decision." *Financial Management* 3, 71–79 (1974).

Miller, M. H., "The Modigliani-Miller Proposition after Thirty Years." *Journal of Economic Perspectives* 2, 99–120 (1988).

Modigliani, F. and M. H. Miller, "Corporate Income Taxes and the Cost of Capital: A Correction." *American Economic Review* 53, 433–443 (1963).

Miller, A. J. *"Subset Selection in Regression."* Chapman and Hall, London, 1990.

Myers, S. C., "Determinants of Corporate Borrowing."*Journal of Financial Economics* 5, 147–175 (1977).

————., "The Capital Structure Puzzle." *Journal of Finance* 39, 575–592 (1984).

————. and N. S. Majluf, "Corporate Financing and Investment Decisions when Firms Have Information that Investors Do Not Have." *Journal of Financial Economics* 13, 187–221 (1984).

————., "Capital Structure." *Journal of Economics Perspectices* 15, 81–102 (2001).

Opler, T., L. Pinkowitz, R. Stulz and R. Williamson, "The Determinants and Implications of Corporate Cash Holdings." *Journal of Financial Ecomomics* 52, 3–46 (1999).

Ozkan, A., "Corporate Bankruptcies, Liquidation Costs and the Role of Banks." *The Manchester School* 64, 104–119 (1996).

————., "Determinants of Capital Structure and Adjustment to Long-run Target: Evidence From UK Company Panel Data." *Journal of Business Finance and Accounting* 28, 175–198 (2001).

Pinegar, J. M. and L. Wilbricht, "What Managers Think of Capital Structure Theory: A Survey." *Financial Management* 18, 82–91 (1989).

Prowse, S. D., "Institutional Investment Patterns and Corporate Financial Behavior in the U.S. and Japan." *Journal of Financial Economics* 27, 43–66 (1990).

Rajan, R. G. and L. Zingales, "What do we Know About Capital Structure? Some Evidence From International Data." *Journal of Finance* 50, 1421–1460 (1995).

Schwarz, G., "Estimating a Dimension of a Model." *Ann. Statist.* 6, 461–4 (1978).

Scott D. F., Jr., "Evidence on the Importance of Financial Structure." *Financial Management* 1, 45–50 (1972).

Shyam-Sunder, L. and S. C. Myers, "Testing Static Tradeoff Against Pecking Order Models of Capital Structure." *Journal of Financial Economics* 51, 219–244 (1999).

Schmidt, R. H., "Determinants of Corporate Debt Ratios in Germany." *European Finance Association Proceedings*, Amsterdam: North Holland (1976).

Schwarz, G., "Estimating the Dimension of a Model." *Ann. Statist.* 6, 461–4 (1978).

Shively, T. S., R. Kohn and S. Wood, "Variable Selection and Function Estimation in Additive Nonparametric Regression Using a Data-based Prior (with discussion)." *Journal of the American Statistical Association* 94, 777–806 (1999).

Schwarz, E. and J. R. Aronson, "Some Surrogate Evidence in Support of the Concept of Optimal Capital Structure." *Journal of Finance* 22, 10–18 (1967).

Shibata, R., "Asymptotically Efficient Selection of the Order of the Model for Estimating Parameters of a Linear Process." *Annals of Statistics* 8, 147–164 (1980).

Stulz, R., M. and H. Johnson, "Managerial Discretion and Optimal Financing Policies." *Journal of Financial Economics* 26, 3–28 (1990).

Taggart, R. A. Jr., "A Model of Corporate Financing Decisions." *Journal of Finance* 32, 1467–1484 (1977).

Titman, S. and R. Wessels, "The Determinants of Capital Structure Choice." *Journal of Finance* 43, 1–19 (1988).

Titman, S., "The Effect of Capital Structure on a Firm's Liquidation Decision." *Journal of Financial Economics* 13, 137–151 (1984).

Toy, N., A. Stonehill, L. Remmers, R. Wright and T. Beekhuisen, "A Comparative International Study of Growth, Profitability, and Risk as Determinants of Corporate Debt Ratios in the Manufacturing Sector." *Journal of Financial and Quantitative Analysis* 9, 875–886 (1974).

White, W. L., "Debt Management and the Form of Business Financing." *Journal of Finance* 29, 565–577 (1974).

White, R. W. and S. M. Turnbull, "The Probability of Bankruptcy For American Industrial Firms." Working paper IFA-4-74, London Graduate School of Business Studies, UK (1974).

Wakefield, J. C. and J. E. Bennett, "The Bayesian Modelling of Covariates for Population Pharmacokinetic Models." *Journal of the American Statistical Society* 91, 917–928 (1996).

Zellner, A., On assessing prior distributions and Bayesian regression analysis with g-prior distributions. In P. K. Goel and A. Zellner (eds.), *"Bayesian Inference and Decision Techniques: Essays in Honor of Bruno de Finietti,"* pp. 233–343 (1986). Amsterdam: North-Holland.

Chapter 9

# The Tendency of Firm Managers to Avoid Small Losses

Yi-Tsung Lee*
*National Chengchi University, Taiwan, R.O.C*

Ging-Ginq Pan
*National Pingtung University of Science and Technology, Taiwan, R.O.C*

We test the tendency of firm managers to report negative small earnings reluctantly, by analyzing earnings across firms listed on the Taiwan Stock Exchange. This paper provides evidence that corporate managers report small losses in earnings less often than small gains in earnings. To complement Burgstahler and Dichev (1997)'s study on cross-sectional evidence, we examine the managers' inclination to avoid small losses by comparing the reported earnings and the pre-managed earnings over time. By using pair-wise samples, our study demonstrates a strong preference of listed firms for reporting small gains rather than small losses. Since the motivation for the avoidance of losses is justified by prospect theory, we suggest that the regulators should improve earnings reporting quality by enhancing corporate governance.

**Keywords:** Earnings management; prospect theory; avoid small losses.

## 1. Introduction

This paper provides an examination of the prospect theory explanation on earnings management to avoid small losses. Previous studies document cross-sectional evidence of relatively higher frequencies of small positive earnings than those of small negative earnings. To complement past studies on cross-sectional evidence, we construct a statistical test, demonstrating that there is a strong inclination for managers to report small gains rather than small losses. To the best of our knowledge, there are few relevant papers that analyze the sample using a time-series data. Time-series data allow us to trace whether decision makers change their behaviors over time at reference point. Our empirical results provide evidence that the motivation for avoidance of losses can be justified by the prospect theory, even control for time periods, firm size and past performance.

---

*Corresponding author.

Managers try to maintain a pattern of positive earnings, and thus there are incentives to avoid small losses. The activities of earnings management are costly, and the costs increase with scale, and that is the reason why managers try to push earnings to a small scale. Prior investigations have well documented that firms exercise discretion to increase earnings when earnings are slightly below zero. Hayn (1995) and Barth, Elliot, and Finn (1995) report systematic evidence that there are incentives for earnings management to avoid reporting losses. Burgstahler and Dichev (1997) provide cross-sectional evidence that firms manage reported earnings to avoid losses.

Two explanations are often mentioned for firms that try to avoid small losses in earnings. Burgstahler and Dichev (1997) argue that transaction costs and prospect theory are the plausible reasons for avoidance of small losses in earnings. Regarding the transaction costs theory, they propose that firms which report earnings losses will bear high transaction costs with stakeholders. And thus, managers avoid reporting negative earnings in order to decrease the costs imposed in transactions with stakeholders.

As for the prospect theory, Kahneman and Tversky (1979) postulate that decision-makers derive value from gains and losses with respect to a reference point, and there is a kink in their value functions at the reference point (zero change); and the utility function is concave for gains and convex for losses. Burgstahler and Dichev (1997) drive more deeply in accounting issues on how managers move earnings from negative to positive ranges. They interpret prospect theory as the following: "Firms have incentives to manipulate earnings to affect the value perceived by stakeholders, and accordingly, earnings-increasing management around wealth reference points, in the vicinity of zero levels of earnings." In fact, both of the two arguments mentioned above are related to information-processing heuristics.

Following the spirit of prospect theory, Degeorge, Patel, and Zeckhauser (1999) propose psychology effects to explain for threshold-related compensation schedule, arguing that executives are likely to manage reported earnings in response, if the preferences of managers or the stakeholders are consistent with the prediction of prospect theory. They find that firms tend to report positive profits, sustain recent earnings, and meet analysts' expectations for earnings management. In the meantime, the positive profits threshold proves predominant. Burgstahler and Dichev (1997) and Degeorge *et al.* (1999) both follow the line of earnings management. Yet, the former dedicate on misreporting mechanisms (e.g., the manipulation of cash flow from operations, and changes in working capital), while the latter focus on both the direct earnings management (e.g., lowering prices to boost sales) and misreporting. As Burgstahler and Dichev (1997) suggest, a more direct and careful examination of the prospect theory explanation is needed and is left for future research.

Alternatively, Beatty, Ke and Petroni (2002) suggest that the avoidance to realize small losses is simply a reflection of the underlying distribution of earnings changes. Focusing on the public versus private distinction, they argue that shareholders of public banks are more likely to rely on simple earnings-based heuristics than those of private banks to evaluate bank performance, and therefore, public banks are more likely to use discretionary accounting procedures to avoid reporting small losses in earnings than private firms.

Our paper is relevant because we demonstrate the tendency of managers avoiding small losses, consistent with prospect theory. This study provides compelling empirical evidence based on the relationship between prospect theory and earnings management. First, before further examination, we would like to ascertain whether the inferences of past studies by Burgstahler and Dichev (1997) and Beatty *et al.* (2002) still hold in our samples. We follow their research to analyze small gains and losses. The results from cross-sectional perspective confirm that firms also report small gains more often than small losses during the sample period using a different sample out of the US firms.

Second, we examine the tendency of reporting small gains versus small losses for managers over the years by calculating the proportion of reporting small losses and the proportion of reporting small positive income for each sample firm over the years. And we construct statistic tests on reported small gains (losses) and pre-managed gains (losses). The results indicate that there is an unusually low probability of reporting small losses and unusually high probability of reporting small positive income, while the result does not exist in terms of the pre-managed earnings. We also show that no matter what time period, firm size and past earnings is, there is a tendency to avoid realizing small losses. Our results are consistent with prospect theory. To increase the quality of earning reporting, we suggest that the regulators should improve investors' rights and enhance corporate governance.

This paper is organized as follows. Section 2 describes the research design, including measurements, testing hypotheses and data. Section 3 presents the empirical results. After the discussion in Section 4, we conclude our paper in Section 5.

## 2. Empirical Design

### 2.1. *Reported earnings*

We focus on the threshold on absolute earnings. Reporting of small profits are often discussed in past studies, for zero is a fundamental psychological distinction of positive numbers and negative numbers. Zero earning is a natural reference point for firms which measure earnings. As Degeorge *et al.* (1999) state, zero earning is often used by banks as a threshold to initially screen business loan. A variety of approaches to scaling have been used in the accounting and finance literature by assets (e.g., Beatty *et al.*, 2002). Similar to their paper, we examine histograms of the reported net incomes on assets (ROA) to detect the existence of earnings management as follows:

$$\text{Reported ROA}_t = \frac{\text{Net incomes before tax}_t}{\text{Assets}_t}.$$

where

$\text{Assets}_t =$ The average of total assets at the end of fiscal year $t - 1$ and $t$.

Similar to Burgstahler and Dichev (1997), we sort the observations of reported earnings and plot the histograms of the distribution of reported earnings to see whether there are far too few earnings falling just below zero, and too many just above it. For comparison, we follow the procedure suggested by Degeorge *et al.* (1999) and Beatty *et al.* (2002), to construct our histograms. That is, we use a bin width of twice the interquartile range of the variable multiplied by the negative cube root of the sample size.

### 2.2. *Pre-managed earnings*

In addition to reported earnings, we calculate pre-managed earnings and show that the distribution of pre-managed earnings is different from that of reported earnings. This paper defines pre-managed earnings as follows:

$$\text{Pre-managed ROA}_t = \text{Reported ROA}_t - \text{Discretionary ROA}_t,$$

where

$$\text{Discretionary ROA}_t = \frac{\text{Discretionary incomes}_t}{\text{Assets}_t};$$

Since earnings management is often captured by discretionary incomes, including non-operating incomes and discretionary accruals (e.g., Jones (1991),

Dechow, Sloan and Sweenly (1995), and Rangan (1998)), we calculate the discretionary incomes to measure the pre-managed incomes. There are three kinds of estimates of the discretionary incomes.

### 2.2.1. Modified Jones model

The first one is measured by cross-sectional modified Jones model. Becker *et al.* (1998) use the Jones (1991) model to estimate discretionary accruals. To overcome the problem raised from limited sample size, Dechow and Jiambalvo (1994), DeFond and Subramanyam (1997), and Teoh, Welch and Wong (1998) adopt the modified Jones model. As to this model, we run the cross-sectional regression for each year, and then use the residuals as discretionary earnings.

$$\left(\frac{\text{Total accruals}_t}{\text{Assets}_t}\right) = \frac{\beta_0}{\text{Assets}_t} + \beta_1 \left[\frac{(\Delta\text{Revenue}_t - \Delta\text{Accounts receivable}_t)}{\text{Assets}_t}\right]$$
$$+ \beta_2 \left(\frac{\text{Depreciable fixed assets}_t}{\text{Assets}_t}\right) + \varepsilon_t$$

where

$\Delta$ = the change in variables at year $t$ and $t - 1$;

Total accruals$_t$ = $\Delta$ Current assets$_t$ $-$ $\Delta$ Current liabilities$_t$ $-$ $\Delta$ Cash$_t$
$+ \Delta$ (Current portion of long-term debt$_t$ $-$ Depletion expense$_t$).

### 2.2.2. Discretionary current accruals

The second is called discretionary current accruals. To precisely measure accruals, Teoh *et al.* (1998), Rangan (1998), and Hansen and Noe (1998) replace total accruals by current accruals. Accordingly, we adopt cross-sectional regression analysis for each year, and then use the residuals as the discretionary earnings. In the meantime, current accruals for a period are obtained by subtracting the change in current liabilities from the change in non-cash current assets for that period.

$$\frac{\text{Current accruals}_t}{\text{Assets}_t} = \frac{\beta_0}{\text{Assets}_t} + \beta_1 \left[\frac{(\Delta\text{Revenue}_t - \Delta\text{Accounts receivable}_t)}{\text{Assets}_t}\right] + \varepsilon_t$$

where

Current accruals$_t$ = $\Delta$Current assets$_t$ $-$ $\Delta$Cash and short-term investment$_t$
$- \Delta$Current liabilities$_t$ $+ \Delta$ Current potion of long-term debt$_t$.

### 2.2.3. *Non-operating incomes*

The third measure is estimated by non-operating incomes. As explained by Craig and Walsh (1989), extra-ordinary income adjustments are regarded as discretionary. Walsh, Craig and Clark (1991) proposed that discretionary activity may be affected by means of extra-ordinary item adjustment. Ryan, Heazlewood, and Andrew (1980) found that 77% of Australian companies disclosed extra-ordinary adjustment for the financial year 1978/79. However, in Taiwan, since extra-ordinary income seldom occurs, we adopt non-operating incomes. The measure of the variable is as follows:

$$\text{Discretionary ROA}_t = \left( \frac{\text{Net incomes before tax}_t - \text{Operating incomes}_t}{\text{Assets}_t} \right).$$

## 2.3. *Tendency of small earnings changes*

To measure the tendency of firms that avoid more small losses than small gains over time, we constructing the variables, PGa and PLa for each firm first. For each firm, PGa is the relative frequency of reported earnings falling just above zero based on the number of the available observations of reported earnings during the sample period for each firm. By the way, PLa presents the relative frequency of reported earnings falling just below zero based on the number of available observations of reported earnings during the sample period for each firm. To test the hypothesized avoidance of small negative earnings, we can first examine the difference between the probabilities of reported small gains and that of small losses, PGa − PLa.

**Hypothesis 1.** PGa − PLa > 0

The interval width for determining if the value falls into small losses or small gains is calculated by all of the available data; we use the same interval width for each firm and for each year. If there is a tendency for firms that are reluctant to realize small losses than small gains, PGa − PLa should be significantly greater than zero. On the contrary, we argue that the phenomenon of avoiding small losses should not exist in pre-managed earnings. To verify this argument, we construct two variables, PGb and PLb, for pre-managed earnings. PGb is defined as the frequency of pre-managed earnings falling just above zero divided by the available observations of pre-managed earnings. In the meantime, PLb is measured as the frequency of pre-managed earnings falling just below zero divided by the available observations of pre-managed earnings. If the actual firm performance is reflected in pre-managed earnings, we expect to see that:

**Hypothesis 2.** PGb − PLb ≤ 0,

That is, there is no small earnings management before the earnings are managed. It will be an important evidence that PGb is not greater than PLb when PGa is greater than PLa. Furthermore, when firms have preferences to avoid small losses, we expect that the difference for pre-managed earnings, PGb − PLb, is less than that for reported earnings, PGa − PLa. That is,

**Hypothesis 3.** (PGa − PLa) − (PGb − PLb) > 0

### 2.4. *Some robustness check*

#### 2.4.1. *Time period*

It is interesting to address whether the unusual pattern of small gains observed by past studies is due to earnings management instead of the underlying characteristics of the underlying distribution of earnings. First, we divide our sample period into the time periods of 1981–1990 and 1991–2001, and examine whether the results are robust for different time periods.

#### 2.4.2. *Assets*

Besides that, we also divide all sample firms into three groups based on assets, and detect whether the unusual pattern of the reluctance to report small losses could be different across various size groups. Becker *et al.* (1998) propose that firm size can proxy audit quality. Further, Ashari *et al.* (1994) point out that firm size is related to income smoothing. In Lang and Lundholm (1993), firm size has been shown to be positively related to disclosure quality. Schrand and Walther (2000) find that large firms are more likely to separately mention the nonrecurring item. Thus, we propose that large firms seem to be more transparent and to be less likely to manage earnings.

#### 2.4.3. *Past performance*

The recent performance is attributed by Degeorge *et al.* (1999) to be one of the thresholds for earnings management. Burgstahler and Dichev (1997) suggest that incentives to avoid earnings losses become stronger with the length of the preceding string of positive earnings. To verify the argument, we measure PGa,

PGb, PLa, and PLb using the frequency of reported earnings falling just above zero conditional on the past performance. The past performances of firms' reported earnings are measured by the average of the past three years reported earnings and that of the past five years respectively. Based on the prospect theory, this paper expects that if a firm experiences bad performance in the past, relative to good performance, it has a strong incentive to manage earnings once there is a chance to manipulate its earnings to be positive. Hence, we measure the variables PGa, PGb, PLa and PLb based on positive past earnings and negative earnings.

## 2.5. *Data*

Our data source is TEJ (Taiwan Economic Journal). We incorporate all listed firms except for firms that are regulated (financial institutions and banks).[1] The samples are excluded if one of the variables PGa, PLa, PGb, and PLb is missing for the sample period. Table 1 is a description of our sample firms. There are 157 and 178 sample firms, respectively, during the periods of 1981 to 1990 and 1991 to 2001. Since we focus on earnings, this study measures net incomes before tax. The mean of net incomes is NT$467 million and that of assets is NT$6, 737 million across firms from 1981 to 1990. The mean of net incomes is NT$624 millions and that of assets is NT$15,158 millions across firms from 1991 to 2001. For each firm the net incomes are scaled by the average total assets, return on assets (ROA), and the results are shown in the last column of Table 1. Though the net incomes are higher for the latter period, the assets also increase at the same period of time. Table 1 shows that the ROA is around 0.06 and 0.03, respectively, during the periods of 1981–1990 and 1991–2001, indicating that the ROA is higher during the former period.

We divide sample firms into three groups based on the average assets during the period 1981–2001. There are 59, 60 and 59 sample firms, respectively, in small-size group, median-size group and large-size group. The mean of net incomes is NT$45 millions, NT$197 millions and NT$1,446 millions, and the mean of assets is NT$2,653 millions, NT$6,207 millions and NT$27,649

---

[1]For a sample comparison of previous studies, Burgstahler and Dichev (1997) analyze observations, ranging from 3,000 to 4,000 on the COMPUSTAT databases for the years 1976–1994. They exclude banks, financial institutions and regulated firms. Beatty *et al.* (2002) use a sample of 707 public banks and 1,160 private banks during the period of 1988–1998 in the US market.

**Table 1.**   Descriptive statistics by time periods and assets.

| | Sample number | NI (in millions NT$) Mean STD | | Assets (in millions NT$) Mean STD | | ROA Mean | STD |
|---|---|---|---|---|---|---|---|
| *Time period* | | | | | | | |
| 1981–1990 | 157 | 467 | 1,267 | 6,737 | 13,817 | 0.0616 | 0.0965 |
| 1991–2001 | 178 | 624 | 2,285 | 15,158 | 26,399 | 0.0324 | 0.0804 |
| 1981–2001 | 178 | 571 | 2,002 | 12,317 | 23,280 | 0.0422 | 0.0860 |
| *Firm size* | | | | | | | |
| Small firm | 59 | 45 | 331 | 2,653 | 1,858 | 0.0272 | 0.0963 |
| Medium firm | 60 | 197 | 648 | 6,207 | 3,616 | 0.0409 | 0.0861 |
| Large firm | 59 | 1,446 | 3,178 | 27,649 | 34,825 | 0.0581 | 0.0713 |

*Notes*: In this paper, sample period starts from 1981 to 2001. The samples are divided into two categories according to the base year 1991, and into three categories according to firm size that is measured by the average book value of total assets across the sample period. NI is the net income before tax during the fiscal year. Assets are the book value of total assets at the end of the fiscal year. And ROA is the net income divided by the average book value of total assets during the fiscal year.

millions, respectively, for small-size group, median-size group and large-size group. The ROA is higher for large firms than small firms.

## 3. Empirical Results

### 3.1. *Earnings distributions*

Similar to Burgstahler and Dichev (1997), we first plot the cross-sectional distributions of reported earnings to investigate whether firms report small gains more than small losses. Reported earnings are annual net incomes before tax scaled by the average total assets for the fiscal year. There are 2,749 available observations of reported earnings. The samples are sorted by bin width equal to 0.01171 calculated by the formula $2(\text{IQR})N^{-1/3}$, where IQR is the sample interquartile range of reported earnings and $N$ is the number of available observations. The reported earnings before tax are shown in Figure 1.

In Figure 1, the number of frequency on the positive earnings (r.h.s) is greater than that of the negative earnings (l.h.s), and there is a jump right around zero earning firms. The first interval to the right of zero contains all observations in the interval (0, 0.01171). The frequency at the first interval is 270, which is the highest among all of the intervals. The frequency reduces gradually towards the firms with positive earnings. Within the interval of positive earnings from

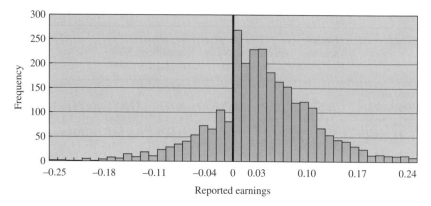

**Figure 1.**   The distribution of reported earnings. Reported earnings are annual net incomes before tax scaled by the average total assets for the fiscal year. The interval widths of the distributions are 0.01171 calculated by the formula $2(\mathrm{IQR})N^{-1/3}$, where IQR is the sample interquartile range of reported earnings and $N$ is the number of available observations. The location of zero on the horizontal axis is marked by the solid line. The first interval to the right of zero contains all observations in the interval (0, 0.01171) and the second interval contains (0.01171, 0.02341), and so on. 'Frequency' labeled in the vertical axis is the number of observations in a given interval.

0 to 0.11, the number of firms ranges from 270 to 110. Regarding the firms with negative earnings, the number of firms drop dramatically towards the negative earnings. Within the interval of negative earnings from 0 to −0.11, the number of firms ranges from 80 to 20.

As we expect, Figure 1 shows a single-peaked, bell-shaped distribution with an irregularity near zero. The distribution of reported earnings indicates that most firms tend to report positive earning, and in particular, firms tend to report small gains rather than small losses. These results are consistent with earnings management to avoid small losses. That is, reported earnings slightly less than zero occur much less frequently than would be expected given the smoothness of the remainder of the distribution, and earnings slightly greater than zero occur much more frequently than would be expected.

To provide some evidence on the comparison of *ex-ante* and *ex-post* results of earnings management, we also provide pre-managed earnings defined as scaled earnings minus discretionary earnings. The empirical distributions of pre-managed earnings help us detect whether the irregularity near zero exists or not. By adopting modified Jones model, discretionary current accruals, and non-operating incomes, respectively, we estimate pre-managed earnings in Figure 2. Panel A of Figure 2 is the distribution of pre-managed earnings measured by

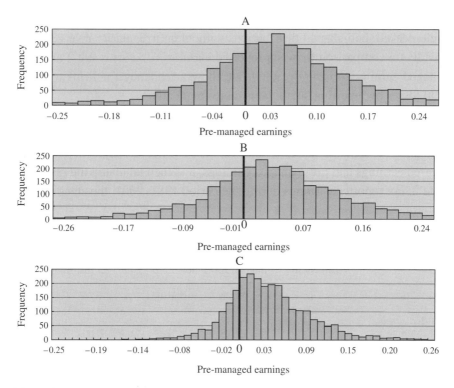

**Figure 2.** The distributions of pre-managed earnings. Pre-managed earnings are defined as scaled earnings minus discretionary earnings. We use three methods to calculate pre-managed earnings. Panel A is the distribution of pre-managed earnings measured by modified Jones model; Panel B is the distribution of pre-managed earnings measured by discretionary current accruals; and Panel C presents the distribution of pre-managed earnings measured by non-operating incomes. The distributions interval widths are 0.01747, 0.01647 and 0.0095 for Panel A, Panel B, and Panel C, respectively.

modified Jones model; Panel B is the distribution of pre-managed earnings measured by discretionary current accruals; and Panel C presents the distribution of pre-managed earnings measured by non-operating incomes.

Figure 2 shows there are more firms with positive earnings than negative earnings even before earnings managements. However, all of the pre-managed earnings distributions in Panels A, B and C are relatively smooth compared to that of Figure 1. For the first interval with positive earnings, the numbers of firms are around 200 no matter in Panels A, B, or C of Figure 2, while that of Figure 1 is around 270. Moreover, the highest frequency of firms are not located at the first interval, which induces that before earnings managements, earnings slightly greater than zero do not occur much more frequently than would be expected. Therefore, we find that pre-managed earnings are single-peaked, bell-shaped distributions without an irregularity near zero. By providing a comparison between reported earnings (*ex-post* results) and pre-managed earnings (*ex-ante* results), we show a tendency for firms to avoid small losses by reporting small gains more frequently.

Next, to test whether the distribution of earnings changes around zero is smooth, we follow the primary analysis in Burgstahler and Dichev (1997) by calculating the standardized difference for the two intervals adjacent to zero for reported earnings and pre-managed earnings, and then tabulated the results in Table 2. For reported earnings during the period 1981–2001, the standardized

**Table 2.**   Reported earnings and pre-managed earnings for interval just around zero.

| | Bin width | Interval Just Below Zero | | | Interval Just Above Zero | | |
|---|---|---|---|---|---|---|---|
| | | $n$ | $n/N$ | $z$-statistic | $n$ | $n/N$ | $z$-statistic |
| *Reported earnings* | | | | | | | |
| 1981–2001 | 0.01171 | 81 | 0.0295 | $-8.264^a$ | 269 | 0.098 | $7.283^a$ |
| *Pre-managed earnings* | | | | | | | |
| Modified Jones model | 0.01747 | 170 | 0.064 | $-0.097$ | 202 | 0.076 | 0.815 |
| Discretionary current accruals | 0.01647 | 185 | 0.069 | 0.470 | 205 | 0.076 | $-0.266$ |
| Non-operating incomes | 0.0095 | 176 | 0.064 | 0.000 | 221 | 0.080 | 0.927 |
| *Reported earnings classified by time period* | | | | | | | |
| 1981–1990 | 0.02128 | 44 | 0.0531 | $-3.801^a$ | 122 | 0.147 | $4.603^a$ |
| 1991–2001 | 0.01224 | 57 | 0.0323 | $-7.020^a$ | 185 | 0.105 | $5.760^a$ |
| *Reported earnings classified by firm size* | | | | | | | |
| Small firms | 0.01669 | 47 | 0.0509 | $-4.239^a$ | 126 | 0.137 | $4.178^a$ |
| Medium firms | 0.01713 | 42 | 0.0474 | $-3.198^a$ | 100 | 0.113 | $2.637^a$ |
| Large firms | 0.01773 | 46 | 0.0490 | $-4.347^a$ | 145 | 0.154 | $5.419^a$ |

*Notes*: This table counts the frequencies of reporting small gains (interval just above zero) and that of reporting small losses (interval just below zero). According to Burgstahler and Dichev (1997), $z$-statistic is used to test whether these two frequencies are statistically different from their own expected numbers. In the meantime, 'bin width' is calculated by $2(\text{IQR})N^{-1/3}$, where IQR is the sample interquartile range of the variable, $N$ is the number of available observations for each group. '$n$' is the frequency in the intervals near zero. In addition to reported earnings, pre-managed earnings are examined. There are three methods of estimates of the discretionary incomes: modified Jones model, discretionary current accruals and non-operating incomes. Samples are also classified into different time periods and firm sizes.
[a] represent statistical significance levels at the 1% levels.

difference for the interval immediately to the left of zero is $-8.264$ and that for the interval immediately to the right of zero is $7.283$. Both of the two values mentioned above are statistically significant. But the above phenomenon does not exist in pre-managed earnings. Under the methods measuring discretionary incomes, the standardized differences for the interval immediately to the left of zero are $-0.097, 0.470$, and $0$, respectively, and those for the interval immediately to the right of zero are $0.815, -0.266$, and $0.927$. The values all are statistically insignificant.

To examine whether firms behave differently in earnings management across time periods or across firm size, we also conduct the above test of reported earnings in different time periods and for different firm size groups. Table 2 reports the standardized differences for the interval immediately to the left of zero are statistically and significantly negative and that for the interval immediately to the right of zero are statistically and significantly positive, whatever kind of firm size is or whenever the sample period is. Hence, consistent with Burgstahler and Dichev (1997), it can be rejected that earnings are not managed to avoid losses. These results imply that firms tend to resist reporting small losses, in contrast to small gains. However, it is still unclear whether the tendency of avoiding realizing losses over time exists.

## 3.2. *The tendency of reporting small gains versus small losses*

In the previous section, we use cross-sectional data to uncover the phenomenon of earnings management. Now we examine the tendency for each firm by calculating the proportions of reported (pre-managed) small gains PGa (PGb) and reported (pre-managed) small losses PLa (PLb) over time. Then, we test the difference among these variables to investigate if firms tend to avoid more small losses than small gains over time. It will be an evidence for earnings management that PGa is greater than PLa, but PGb is not greater than PLb. In Table 3, PGa, PLa, PGb, and PLb are calculated and the difference of the variables are tabulated. In the table, pairwise *t*-test is adopted for the means and Wilcoxon test for the medians.

The difference of PGa with PLa is $6.55\%$ and $5\%$ in terms of mean and of median. As to Hypothesis 1, the *t*-statistic (*z*-statistic) of PGa $-$ PLa for mean (median) is $8.533$ ($7.460$). It means the proportion of reporting small gains is greater than that of reporting small losses with a high degree of

**Table 3.** The proportions of reported gains, reported losses, pre-managed gains and pre-managed losses.

|  | Number | Mean | Median | Stand. Dev. |
|---|---|---|---|---|
| *Reported earnings* | | | | |
| PGa | 178 | 0.0952 | 0.0833 | 0.0967 |
| PLa | 178 | 0.0298 | 0.0000 | 0.0506 |
| PGa − PLa | 178 | 0.0655 | 0.0500 | |
| (*t*-statistic or z-statistic) | | $(8.533)^a$ | $(7.460)^a$ | |
| *Pre-managed earnings modified Jones model* | | | | |
| PGb | 178 | 0.0738 | 0.0742 | 0.0702 |
| PLb | 178 | 0.0635 | 0.0572 | 0.0676 |
| PGb − PLb | 178 | 0.0103 | 0.0000 | |
| (*t*-statistic or z-statistic) | | (1.360) | (1.122) | |
| *Discretionary current accruals* | | | | |
| PGb | 178 | 0.0740 | 0.0625 | 0.0741 |
| PLb | 178 | 0.0689 | 0.0572 | 0.0711 |
| PGb − PLb | 178 | 0.0050 | 0.0000 | |
| (*t*-statistic or z-statistic) | | (0.657) | (0.769) | |
| *Non-operating incomes* | | | | |
| PGb | 178 | 0.0791 | 0.0690 | 0.0887 |
| PLb | 178 | 0.0611 | 0.0500 | 0.0833 |
| PGb − PLb | 178 | 0.0180 | 0.0000 | |
| (*t*-statistic z-statistic) | | $(2.110)^b$ | $(2.318)^b$ | |

*Notes*: This table examines whether PGa − PLa > 0 and PGb − PLb ≤ 0 in terms of mean and of median by using pairwise *t*-test and Wilcoxon test, respectively. PGa is the frequency of reported earnings falling just above zero divided by the available observations of reported earnings; PLa is the frequency of reported earnings falling just below zero divided by the available observations of reported earnings; PGb is the frequency of pre-managed earnings falling just above zero divided by the available observations of pre-managed earnings; and PLb is the frequency of pre-managed earnings falling just below zero divided by the available observations of pre-managed earnings. *t*-statistic is for pairwise *t*-test and z-statistic is for Wilcoxon test.
[a]represent statistical significance levels at the 1% levels.
[b]represent statistical significance levels at the 5% levels.

statistical significance. Furthermore, the second hypothesis, PGb − PLb ≤ 0, is also supported based on the results of *t*-statistics and z-statistics, except for the case of pre-managed earnings measured by non-operating incomes. For the modified Jones model (discretionary current accurals), the difference and

$t$-statistics of PGb − PLb are 1.03% and 1.360 (0.5% and 0.657) with a low degree of statistical significance. And the results of Wilcoxon test are consistent with those of pairwise $t$-test. In sum, the findings of Table 3 indicate that there exists the tendency of firms that avoid more small losses than small gains over time.

### 3.3. *Some robustness check*

Are the findings in the previous section changed by time period, firm size, or firm's past experience? In this section, we further discuss the difference of PGa − PLa and PGb − PLb under various circumstances.

Table 4 reports the empirical results divided by sub-periods. From 1981 to 1990, the values of PGa − PLa are significantly positive and those of PGb − PLb are not significantly different from zero under three methods of measuring discretionary incomes. That is, all hypotheses discussed in previous section can still be supported by empirical data, even if they are examined in different time period. Again, from 1991 to 2001, $t$-statistics are significantly positive for PGa − PLa but not for PGb − PLb. The results indicate that the tendency also holds in the latter period.

Particularly, when the difference of PGa − PLa with PGb − PLb is examined, Hypothesis 3 is also significantly supported whatever the method is and whenever the time period is. In columns 2 and 3 of Table 4, the differences are all significantly positive, especially for the latter period. The findings are consistent with those in previous section. However, when we compare the difference between PGa − PLa and PGa − PLa across time periods, the difference shown in the column 4 of Table 4 is not statistically significant. It demonstrates that the extent of avoidance reporting small losses holds persistently.

According to Ashari *et al.* (1994) and Becker *et al.* (1998), firm size is always mentioned as an important factor when the behavior of earnings management is discussed. Lang and Lundholm (1993) and Schrand and Walther (2000) provide evidence that firm size seems related to transparency. Here, in Table 5, samples are grouped into small, medium, and large based on the average total assets. Then, we examine PGa − PLa, PGb − PLb, and PGa − PLa, PGb − PLb by $t$-test for the large firms and the small firms. As a result, the values of PGa − PLa are all significantly positive. Except under the measure of non-operating incomes, the values of PGb − PLb are not significantly greater than zero. In the column 2 and 3 of Table 5, the $t$-statistics of the difference between PGa − PLa and

**Table 4.**   Small earnings management for different time periods.

| | 1981–1990 | 1991–2001 | Difference (t-statistic) |
|---|---|---|---|
| *Modified Jones Model* | | | |
| (PGa − PLa) | 0.0457 | 0.0263 | 0.0194 |
| (t-statistic) | (2.242)[b] | (2.249)[b] | (0.861) |
| (PGb − PLb) | −0.0231 | −0.0492 | 0.0261 |
| (t-statistic) | (−1.532) | (−5.971)[a] | (1.604) |
| (PGa − PLa) − (PGb − PLb) | 0.0688 | 0.0755 | −0.0067 |
| (t-statistic) | (2.267)[b] | (5.049)[a] | (−0.209) |
| *Discretionary current accruals* | | | |
| (PGa − PLa) | 0.0395 | 0.0236 | 0.0159 |
| (t-statistic) | (2.019)[c] | (1.862) | (0.759) |
| (PGb − PLb) | −0.0282 | −0.0484 | 0.0202 |
| (t-statistic) | (−1.796) | (−5.215)[a] | (1.109) |
| (PGa − PLa) − (PGb − PLb) | 0.0676 | 0.0719 | −0.0043 |
| (t-statistic) | (2.276)[b] | (4.198)[a] | (−0.133) |
| *Non-operating incomes* | | | |
| (PGa − PLa) | 0.0519 | 0.0071 | 0.0448 |
| (t-statistic) | (3.020)[a] | (0.580) | (2.145)[b] |
| (PGb − PLb) | −0.0170 | −0.0557 | 0.0386 |
| (t-statistic) | (−1.257) | (−5.307)[a] | (2.444)[b] |
| (PGa − PLa) − (PGb − PLb) | 0.0689 | 0.0627 | 0.0062 |
| (t-statistic) | (3.077)[a] | (3.738)[a] | (0.238) |

*Notes*: This table divides our sample into the time periods of 1981–1990 and 1991–2001, and check whether PGa − PLa > 0, PGb − PLb ≤ 0, and (PGa − PLa) − (PGb − PLb) > 0 in mean using *t*-test. PGa is the frequency of reported earnings falling just above zero divided by the available observations of reported earnings; PLa is the frequency of reported earnings falling just below zero divided by the available observations of reported earnings; PGb is the frequency of pre-managed earnings falling just above zero divided by the available observations of pre-managed earnings; and PLb is the frequency of pre-managed earnings falling just below zero divided by the available observations of pre-managed earnings.
[a]represent statistical significance levels at the 1% levels.
[b]represent statistical significance levels at the 2% levels.
[c]represent statistical significance levels at the 5% levels.

PGb − PLb for small firms and for large firms are significantly positive no matter how the discretionary incomes are measured. But, the differences of the related variables between large firms and small firms are not significant. That is, the results in Table 5 are consistent with the argument in Burgstahler and Dichev (1997) and Degeorge *et al.* (1999), which supports the prediction of prospect theory whatever the firm size is.

**Table 5.** The avoidance of small losses across firm sizes.

|  | Small firm | Large firm | Difference (t-statistic) |
|---|---|---|---|
| *Modified Jones Model* | | | |
| (PGa − PLa) | 0.0907 | 0.1038 | −0.0131 |
| (t-statistic) | (5.002)[a] | (4.859)[a] | (−0.467) |
| (PGb − PLb) | −0.0074 | 0.0078 | −0.0152 |
| (t-statistic) | (−0.431) | (0.483) | (−0.645) |
| (PGa − PLa) − (PGb − PLb) | 0.0981 | 0.0960 | 0.0021 |
| (t-statistic) | (3.604)[a] | (3.516)[a] | (0.063) |
| *Discretionary current accruals* | | | |
| (PGa − PLa) | 0.0884 | 0.1014 | −0.0131 |
| (t−statistic) | (4.764)[a] | (4.773)[a] | (−0.464) |
| (PGb − PLb) | 0.0362 | 0.0140 | 0.0221 |
| (t-statistic) | (1.979) | (0.946) | (0.940) |
| (PGa − PLa) − (PGb − PLb) | 0.0522 | 0.0874 | −0.0352 |
| (t-statistic) | (1.760)[c] | (3.352)[a] | (−1.042) |
| *Non-operating Incomes* | | | |
| (PGa − PLa) | 0.0862 | 0.0995 | −0.0133 |
| (t-statistic) | (4.746)[a] | (4.740)[a] | (−0.479) |
| (PGb − PLb) | 0.0407 | 0.0445 | −0.0038 |
| (t-statistic) | (2.250)[b] | (2.303)[b] | (−0.143) |
| (PGa − PLa) − (PGb − PLb) | 0.0455 | 0.0550 | −0.0095 |
| (t-statistic) | (1.737)[c] | (2.200)[b] | (−0.280) |

*Notes*: Samples are further classified into three groups based on the average book value of total assets. In this table, the smallest firms and largest firms are compared. The differences of PGa − PLa with PGb − PLb are tested by *t*-test. PGa is the frequency of reported earnings falling just above zero divided by the available observations of reported earnings; PLa is the frequency of reported earnings falling just below zero divided by the available observations of reported earnings; PGb is the frequency of pre-managed earnings falling just above zero divided by the available observations of pre-managed earnings; and PLb is the frequency of pre-managed earnings falling just below zero divided by the available observations of pre-managed earnings.
[a] represent statistical significance levels at the 1% levels.
[b] represent statistical significance levels at the 2% levels.
[c] represent statistical significance levels at the 5% levels.

Now, we would like to detect how the past performance of earnings influences the tendency of reporting small gains versus small losses. Table 6 (Table 7) reports the empirical results of the influence of past-three-year (past-five-year) earnings performance. As the previous section, we test Hypotheses 1, 2, and 3 for each category. Again, most of the results support all of hypotheses. We see that no matter how past performance is (positive earnings or negative

**Table 6.** The avoidance of small losses subsequent to positive/negative reported earnings for past three years.

|  | Positive earnings | Negative earnings | Difference (*t*-statistic) |
|---|---|---|---|
| *Modified Jones Model* | | | |
| (PGa − PLa) | 0.1006 | 0.0800 | 0.0206 |
| (*t*-statistic) | (4.630)[a] | (3.566)[a] | (1.324) |
| (PGb − PLb) | 0.0088 | 0.0034 | 0.0053 |
| (*t*-statistic) | (0.483) | (0.208) | (0.481) |
| (PGa − PLa) − (PGb − PLb) | 0.0918 | 0.0766 | 0.0152 |
| (*t*-statistic) | (3.021)[a] | (2.517)[a] | (0.848) |
| *Discretionary current accruals* | | | |
| (PGa − PLa) | 0.0898 | 0.0784 | 0.0114 |
| (*t*-statistic) | (4.094)[a] | (3.744)[a] | (0.652) |
| (PGb − PLb) | 0.0121 | 0.0357 | −0.0236 |
| (*t*-statistic) | (0.677) | (1.257) | (−1.088) |
| (PGa − PLa) − (PGb − PLb) | 0.0777 | 0.0428 | 0.0349 |
| (*t*-statistic) | (2.311)[b] | (1.063) | (1.246) |
| *Non-operating incomes* | | | |
| (PGa − PLa) | 0.1083 | 0.1009 | 0.0074 |
| (*t*-statistic) | (4.638)[a] | (4.343)[a] | (0.571) |
| (PGb − PLb) | 0.0162 | −0.0056 | 0.0218 |
| (*t*-statistic) | (0.644) | (−0.235) | (1.270) |
| (PGa − PLa) − (PGb − PLb) | 0.0922 | 0.1065 | −0.0144 |
| (*t*-statistic) | (2.941)[a] | (3.554)[a] | (−0.590) |

*Notes*: For each firm, PGa, PLa, PGb, and PLb are measured under positive past-three-years earnings and under negative past-three-years earnings, respectively. The differences of PGa − PLa with PGb − PLb are tested by pairwise *t*-test. PGa is the frequency of reported earnings falling just above zero divided by the available observations of reported earnings; PLa is the frequency of reported earnings falling just below zero divided by the available observations of reported earnings; PGb is the frequency of pre-managed earnings falling just above zero divided by the available observations of pre-managed earnings; and PLb is the frequency of pre-managed earnings falling just below zero divided by the available observations of pre-managed earnings. The past-three-years earnings is measured by the average of past three years reported earnings.
[a] represent statistical significance levels at the 1% levels.
[b] represent statistical significance levels at the 2% levels.

earnings), firms always have the preference to avoid small losses. In most cases, the extent of the avoidance does not differ between the firms experiencing positive earnings and those experiencing negative earnings. Based on the stakeholders' argument in Burgstahler and Dichev (1997), this evidence may be resulted from the consideration of the reaction in stock market. For

**Table 7.** The avoidance of small losses subsequent to positive/negative reported earnings for past five years.

| | Positive earnings | Negative earnings | Difference ($t$-statistic) |
|---|---|---|---|
| *Modified Jones Model* | | | |
| (PGa − PLa) | 0.1491 | 0.1685 | −0.0194 |
| ($t$-statistic) | $(3.614)^a$ | $(5.067)^a$ | (−0.883) |
| (PGb − PLb) | 0.0230 | −0.0157 | 0.0387 |
| ($t$-statistic) | (0.667) | (−0.697) | (1.672 ) |
| (PGa − PLa) − (PGb − PLb) | 0.1261 | 0.1842 | −0.0582 |
| ($t$-statistic) | $(2.128)^b$ | $(3.875)^a$ | $(−1.747)^b$ |
| *Discretionary current accruals* | | | |
| (PGa − PLa) | 0.1313 | 0.1536 | −0.0223 |
| ($t$-statistic) | $(4.124)^a$ | $(6.021)^a$ | (−0.999) |
| (PGb − PLb) | 0.0004 | 0.0008 | −0.0004 |
| ($t$-statistic) | (0.014) | (0.035) | (−0.023) |
| (PGa − PLa) − (PGb − PLb) | 0.1308 | 0.1527 | −0.0219 |
| ($t$-statistic) | $(2.865)^a$ | $(3.520)^a$ | (−0.729) |
| *Non-operating incomes* | | | |
| (PGa − PLa) | 0.1657 | 0.1712 | −0.0055 |
| ($t$-statistic) | $(3.399)^a$ | $(4.274)^a$ | (−0.188) |
| (PGb − PLb) | 0.0358 | −0.0114 | 0.0472 |
| ($t$-statistic) | (0.554) | (−0.336) | (0.958) |
| (PGa − PLa) − (PGb − PLb) | 0.1299 | 0.1826 | −0.0527 |
| ($t$-statistic) | (1.642) | $(3.854)^a$ | (−0.810) |

*Notes*: For each firm, PGa, PLa, PGb, and PLb are measured under positive past-five-years earnings and under negative past-five-years earnings, respectively. The differences of PGa − PLa with PGb − PLb are tested by pairwise $t$-test. PGa is the frequency of reported earnings falling just above zero divided by the available observations of reported earnings; PLa is the frequency of reported earnings falling just below zero divided by the available observations of reported earnings; PGb is the frequency of pre-managed earnings falling just above zero divided by the available observations of pre-managed earnings; and PLb is the frequency of pre-managed earnings falling just below zero divided by the available observations of pre-managed earnings. The past-five-years earnings is measured by the average of past five years reported earnings.
[a]represent statistical significance levels at the 1% levels.
[b]represent statistical significance levels at the 5% levels.

the firms whose past earnings are positive, their reporting losses will stock market price seriously, so they have strong incentives to keep their good records and to avoid losses. For the firms whose past earnings are negative, their reporting gains will encourage stock market price rise, so that they also have strong incentives to avoid losses.

## 4. Discussion

Managers try to maintain a pattern of positive earnings, and thus there are incentives to avoid small losses. It is consistent with the argument that managers try to push earnings to a small gain from a small loss under the consideration that the costs of earnings management increase with sale. This study provides a direct test on whether there is a tendency for managers to report negative small earnings reluctantly over time.

Past studies dedicate on the cross-sectional description of small earnings management (Hayn (1995), Barth *et al.* (1995), Burgstahler and Dichev (1997), Degeorge *et al.* (1999), and Beatty *et al.* (2002)). Following the spirit of prospect theory, Burgstahler and Dichev (1997) interpret that firms have incentives to manipulate earnings to affect the value perceived by stakeholders, and earnings-increasing management around wealth reference points, in the vicinity of zero levels of earnings. Degeorge *et al.* (1999) propose that executives are likely to manage reported earnings in response, if the preferences of managers or the stakeholders are consistent with the prediction of prospect theory.

Though they try to explore the motivations for firms avoiding small losses, a more direct and systematic examination of the motivations over time is still uncovered. Our paper is important because we exploit a powerful setting on analyzing prospect theory and earnings management. In particular, we focus on the tendency of managers that avoid small losses by comparing the reported earnings and the pre-managed earnings for each sample firm over time.

We find that there is a strong preference of firms reporting small gains rather than small losses, supporting the motivation for avoidance of losses justified by prospect theory. The tendency for managers to avoid small losses and report small gains over time may cause the reported earnings to lose the credibility from the public investors. During the past, the SEC in Taiwan implemented a very unique Guideline for Disclosure of Financial Forecasts by Public Companies to enhance the credibility of reported earning's quality. The merit of the regulation is to provide more information to the public from time to time. However, the earnings forecasts involved complicated issues in practice and therefore, may not be used as an informative tool for investors to evaluate stock performance. Recently, the mandatory forecast regulation has been cancelled due to a lot of debates.

Fan and Wong (2002) find that in some of the Asian economics, including Taiwan, there exist concentrated ownerships and cross-holding structures, and therefore, the earning credibility is weakened for such companies. Leuz, Nanda and Wysocki (2003) also address the relationship between corporate governance and the quality of reported earning. They document that earnings management is decreased for countries with strong investor protection and developed equity market. Our findings, together with their researches, provide an important implication for the regulators to improve earning reporting quality by strong investor rights and legal enforcements.

## 5. Conclusion

We examine the tendency of reporting small gains versus small losses for managers over the years by calculating the probability of reporting small losses and the probability of reporting small positive income for each sample firm over the years. Then, we construct statistical tests on reported small gains (losses) and pre-managed gains (losses). Our sample period is from 1981 to 2002, and the number of sample firms listed in Taiwan Stock Exchange is 178.

The results indicate that there is an unusually low probability of reporting small losses and unusually high probability of reporting small positive income; while, the result does not exist in terms of the pre-managed earnings. This implies that there is a strong preference of firms reporting small gains rather than small losses. We also find that managers tend to use accruals and non-operating incomes to achieve increases in earnings. The results still hold no matter what time period, firm size and past earnings are.

Is earnings management more severe in emerging markets (including Taiwan) compared to that in developed markets? By exploring the link between earning management and equity markets in emerging markets and developed markets, Bhattacharya, Daouk and Welker (2003) find that earnings management is more severe in emerging markets (including Taiwan) than in developed markets in all years. Leuz *et al.* (2003) also present country rankings for aggregate earnings management measures to study negative earnings avoidance and earnings smoothing in their cross-sectional analysis of earnings management across 31 countries. Among 31 countries, Taiwan is ranked as top 5 on the measure, implying that earnings management is severe in Taiwan. Though all countries exhibit the tendencies of loss avoidance, Taiwan is ranked 16th, and the value is about 2.765, which is still very high among 31 countries. Therefore, it seems that earnings management in Taiwan is severe.

Bhattacharya *et al.* (2003) find that an increase in earnings management in a country is linked to a decrease in trading in the stock market of that country because earnings management will result in an increase in information asymmetry and thereby affect the cost of equity. Since we find that the motivation for avoidance of losses is justified by the prospect theory, we suggest that the regulators should improve earnings reporting quality by enhancing corporate governance. Leuz *et al.* (2003) show that the quality of financial reports increases in investor protection. Warfield, Wild and Wild (1995) and Beasley, Carcello, Hermanson, and Lapides (2000) suggest that corporate governance mitigates the degree of earnings management and improves the quality of financial reporting. Therefore, we suggest the regulatory institutions to focus on enhancing the structure of corporate ownership, the incentives of preparers and auditors, and enforcement mechanisms to improve the quality of the financial reporting system.

## References

Ashari, N., H. C. Koh, S. L. Tan and W. H. Wong, "Factors Affecting Income Smoothing Among Listed Companies in Singapore." *Accounting and Business Research* 24, 291–301 (1994).

Barth, M., J. Elliot and M. Finn, "Market Rewards Associated with Increasing Earnings Patterns." Working paper, Cornell University (1995).

Beasley, M. S., J. V. Carcello, D. R. Hermanson and P. D. Lapides, "Fraudulent Financial Reporting: Consideration of Industry Traits and Corporate Governance Mechanisms." *Accounting Horizon* 14, 441–454 (2000).

Beatty, A., B. Ke and K. Petroni, "Earnings Management to Avoid Earnings Declines Across Publicly and Privately Held Banks." *The Accounting Review* 77, 547–570 (2002).

Becker, C. L., M. L. DeFond, J. Jiambalvo and K. R. Subramanyam, "The Effect of Audit Quality on Earnings Management." *Contemporary Accounting Research* 15, 1–24 (1998).

Bhattacharya, U., H. Daouk and M. Welker, "The World Price of Earnings Management." Working paper, Queen's University (2003).

Burgstahler, D. and I. Dichev, "Earnings Management to Avoid Earnings Decreases and Losses." *Journal of Accounting and Economics* 24, 99–126 (1997).

Craig, R. and P. Walsh, "Adjustments for 'Extraordinary Items' in Smoothing Reported Profits of Listed Australian Companies: Some Empirical Evidence." *Journal of Business Finance and Accounting* 16, 229–245 (1989).

Dechow, P. M. and J. Jiambalvo, "Debt Covenant Violation and Manipulation of Accruals, Accounting Choices in Troubled Companies." *Journal of Accounting and Economics* 17, 145–176 (1994).

Dechow, P. M., R. G. Sloan and A. P. Sweeney, "Detecting Earnings Management." *The Accounting Review*, 193–225 (1995).

DeFond, M. L. and K. R. Subramanyam, "Restrictions to Accounting Choices: Evidence From Auditor Realignment." Working paper, University of Southern California, 1997.

Degeorge, F., J. Patel and R. Zeckhauser, "Earnings Management to Excess Thresholds." *Journal of Business* 72, 1–33 (1999).

Fan, J. and T. Wong, "Corporate Ownership Structure and the Informativeness of Accounting Earnings in East Asia." *Journal of Accounting and Economics* 33, 401–426 (2002).

Hansen, G. A. and C. F. Noe, "Do Managers' Accrual Decision Speak Louder Than Words?" Working paper, Harvard University, 1998.

Hayn, C., "The Information Content of Losses." *Journal of Accounting and Economics* 20, 125–153 (1995).

Jones, J. J., "Earnings Management During Import Relief Investigations." *Journal of Accounting Research*, 193–228 (1991).

Kahneman, D. and A. Tversky, "Prospect Theory: An Analysis of Decision Under Risk." *Econometrica* 47, 263–291.

Lang, M. and R. Lundholm, "Cross-sectional Determinants of Analyst Rating of Corporate Disclosures." *Journal of Accounting Research*, 246–271 (1993).

Leuz, C., D. Nanda and P. D. Wysocki, "Earnings Management and Investor Protection: An International Comparison." *Journal of Financial Economics* 69, 505–527 (2003).

Leuz, C., D. Nanda and P. D. Wysocki, "Investor Protection and Earnings Management: An International Comparison." Working paper, The Wharton School of the University of Pennsylvania (2001).

Odean, T., "Are Investors Reluctant to Realize Their Losses." *The Journal of Finance* 53, 1775–1798 (1998).

Rangan, S., "Earning Management and the Performance of Seasoned Equity Offerings." *Journal of Financial Economics* 50, 101–122 (1998).

Ryan, J. B., C. T. Heazlewood and B. H. Andrew, "Australian company financial reporting: 1980." Australian Accounting Research Foundation, eds. (Accounting Research Study No. 9, 1980).

Schrand, C. and B. Walther, "Strategic Benchmarks in Earnings Announcements: The Selective Disclosure of Prior-Period Earnings Components." *The Accounting Review*, 151–176 (2000).

Teoh, S., I. Welch and T. Wong, "Earnings Management and the Under-Performance of Seasoned Equity Offerings." *Journal of Financial Economics* 50, 63–99 (1998).

Walsh, P., R. Craig and F. Clarke, "Big Bath Accounting Using Extraordinary Items Adjustments: Australian Empirical Evidence." *Journal of Business Finance and Accounting* 18, 173–189 (1991).

Warfield, T. D., J. J. Wild and K. L. Wild, "Managerial Ownership, Accounting Choices, and Informativeness of Earnings." *Journal of Accounting Economics* 20, 61–92 (1995).

Chapter 10

# Do Winners Perform Better Than Losers? A Stochastic Dominance Approach

Wing-Keung Wong
*National University of Singapore, Singapore*

Howard E. Thompson
*University of Wisconsin-Madison, USA*

Steven X. Wei*
*The Hong Kong Polytechnic University, Hong Kong*

Ying-Foon Chow
*Chinese University of Hong Kong, Hong Kong*

This paper offers an alternative view supporting the risk-based explanation of the momentum effect. Using stochastic dominance criteria, we find that the winners portfolio and the losers portfolio do not dominate each other. In general, the winners portfolio dominates at the right-hand side of the distribution of returns while the losers portfolio dominates at the left-hand side of the distribution. Our empirical results imply that the momentum profits provide neither an arbitrage opportunity nor a welfare improvement for rational investors *ex ante*. We interpret the evidence as follows: momentum profits are consistent with the notion of market rationality and market efficiency and are likely to be explained by omitted risk factors. Our findings also suggest that one possible reason why some investors prefer losers is because of less downside risk.

**JEL Classifications:** G12, G14.

**Keywords:** Momentum; stochastic dominance; market rationality; market efficiency.

## 1. Introduction

Among most, if not all, documented patterns in stock returns the momentum effect first documented for the period 1965–1989 by Jegadeesh and Titman (1993) seems to be the most puzzling. Since their original work, there have been many papers studying momentum in the stock market. A set of papers

---

*This paper was done when I was visiting the School of Banking and Finance, University of New South Wales, Australia.

has been devoted to substantiating the effect in other times and other markets.[1] Other studies have been devoted to explaining the result. These explanations have been attributed to behavioral factors;[2] misestimation in traditional efficient markets models;[3] and misspecification of the risks in efficient market models.[4] This paper examines the momentum effect over the period 1965–2000 focusing on possible misspecification of risks in efficient market models.

The traditional tests of market rationality compare observed returns to expected returns generated by some equilibrium model such as the CAPM. The presence of abnormal returns estimated from such models indicates market inefficiency on the one hand, or misestimated factors, omitted factors or model misspecification on the other. Once abnormal returns are found the next step is usually to try to explain them in terms of behavioral variables, misspecification of factors or in terms of omitted factors.[5]

Our approach differs from the traditional approach to studying momentum returns. We do not try to relate momentum returns to omitted factors. Nor do we try to specify an alternative asset pricing model. We do, however, adopt the expected utility model and study the return distribution directly. That is, we assume an asset or portfolio of assets is preferable to another asset or portfolio if it has a higher expected utility and the investor will maximize expected utility. We make no further assumptions about the utility function other than more is preferred to less[6] and we then focus our attention on the

---

[1] See, for example, Jegadeesh and Titman (2001), Rouwenhorst (1998) and Chan, Jegadeesh, and Lakonishok (1996).

[2] See Jegadeesh and Titman (1993, 1995), Grinblatt, Titman and Wermers (1995), Daniel, Hirshleifer, and Subrahmanyam (1998), Barberis, Schleifer, and Vishny (1998), Hong, Lim, and Stein (2000).

[3] For examples see Conrad and Kaul (1998), Berk, Green, and Naik (1999) and Lewellen (2002).

[4] See Harvey and Siddique (2000), Ang *et al.* (2001), Grundy and Martin (2001), Sagi and Seaholes (2001), Chordia and Shivakumar (2002), Dittmar (2002), Johnson (2002).

[5] For example Jegadeesh and Titman (1993) hypothesize under reaction to firm specific imformation; Chordia and Shivakumar (2002) use traditional macroeconomic factors to predict expected return for the succeeding month; Lee and Swaminathan (2000) study the impact of prior trading volume in explaining price momentum; Ang *et al.* (2001) relate a downside risk factor and hence a model specification to momentum returns.

[6] Our approach allows the utility function to change over time as long as more is preferred to less. We make no attempts to model a changing utility function such a specifying an asymmetric utility function with those properties as done by Bekaert and Harvey (1997) Bekaert, Hodrick and Marshall (1997) and Barberis, Huang and Santos (2001). These types of utility functions can allow for changing preferences over time but they must be specified in detail.

unconditional probability distribution of the top-decile winners and bottom-decile losers portfolios in the momentum investing strategy.

Each of the portfolios consists of a changing set of securities over time with the only characteristic that the individual stocks in the portfolio were recently either a top-decile winner or a bottom-decile loser. We form the unconditional empirical cumulative distribution functions (CDFs) for these portfolios and treat them as the distributions that investors base their portfolio decisions upon at each decision point in time. Given these distributions and individual investor's utility functions, the expected utility could be calculated by investors.[7] Such calculations would then allow investors to distinguish between alternative portfolios.

What we find in studying the momentum strategy over the period 1965–2000 and various sub-periods is that the average returns for the top-decile-winners portfolio exceeds that of the bottom-decile-losers portfolio over the succeeding 12 months. But we also find that the unconditional CDF of the top-decile-winners portfolio does not stochastically dominate the bottom-decile-losers portfolio. Thus we cannot say, using the maximization-of-expected-utility criterion that the one of the portfolios is preferred to the other. Given that investors have a variety of utility functions, it may be that some would prefer the bottom-decile-losers portfolio to its winners counterpart.

The results suggest that there are risk characteristics of a portfolio in addition to the first and second moments of the return distribution that bear upon investors' choices and search for these risk characteristics such as those made by Dittmat (2002), Harvey and Siddique (2000) and the downside risk variable by Ang, Chen, and Xing (2001) have promised.

Momentum returns, as we demonstrate from the data, are highly non-normal. The substantial deviation from normality and the relevance of higher order moments of asset returns to investors motivate the adoption of the stochastic dominance (SD) approach of this paper. Under the SD criteria, if one of two distinct existing assets or different portfolios stochastically dominates the other, then the notions of market rationality and market efficiency are rejected. Otherwise, the market rationality and market efficiency should not be

---

[7]Although the concept of investors maximizing their own utility functions is central to our analysis we emphasize that we, as researchers, need to make only minimal assumptions as to the characteristics of these utility functions.

rejected.[8] The momentum strategy seems to suggest that the returns to winners portfolio are too high (i.e., undervalued) while the returns to losers portfolio are too low (i.e., overvalued). We thus test the hypothesis that the winners portfolio dominates the losers portfolio for a considerable length of time under the SD rules.

Our empirical analyses reveal the following. First, there is no first order stochastic dominance (FSD) between the winners and the losers portfolios. As demonstrated by Bawa (1978) and Jarrow (1986), no FSD implies that it is impossible to create any arbitrage by using the momentum strategy. This may explain why the momentum profits have not been arbitraged away since discovery — there is indeed no arbitrage opportunity seen in the data. In other words, the momentum profits are by no means a free-lunch. Second, there is no higher order stochastic dominance between the winners and the losers portfolios.[9] This suggests that risk averse investors in the market are unlikely to be hedging against some systematic risk. Therefore, we interpret our findings as a strong evidence to support market rationality and the market efficiency hypotheses. In general, our findings show that the winners portfolio dominates at the right-hand side (or upside) of the distribution of returns while the losers portfolio dominates at the left-hand side (or downside) of the distribution. This leads to the conjecture that the distribution of the losers portfolio is skewed to the right relatively to that of the winners and this conjecture is confirmed by the skewness of the distribution. These suggest that one possible reason why some investors prefer the losers portfolio is because it has less downside risk. Jegadeesh and Titman (1993) pointed out that to the extent that high past returns may be partly due to high expected returns, the winner portfolios could potentially contain high-risk stocks that would continue to earn higher expected returns in the future. Our findings on the shape of the distribution would be consistent with this conjecture as the high-risk stocks could possibly make the distribution of the winners portfolios relatively skewed to the left. This further supports the notions of market rationality and the market efficiency hypotheses.

The intuition behind our results is straightforward. If investors hedge against various systematic risks in a general equilibrium framework, those hedges should be reflected in the whole distribution of asset returns and not likely to

---

[8]See Falk and Levy (1989) and Chow (2001).

[9]In this paper, we only consider SD criteria up to the first three orders.

be fully captured by the first two or three moments. The SD approach takes into account the whole distribution of returns with minimum assumptions on investors' preferences. Therefore, if we can show that all investors are likely to have preferences that conform to these minimum assumptions and we find no stochastic dominance, we can infer that any differences in return on the portfolios are not due to inefficiencies.[10] In other words, the momentum profits are not risk-free and the rational investors who are using the momentum strategy have to bear some risk. Specifically, since SD criteria do not depend on the typical risk-return trade-off imposed by conventional models, some previously offered explanations for the momentum effect, such as omitted risk factors or changes in investors' attitudes toward risk, are indeed reasonable. In the light of this evidence, potential explanations for the momentum effect such as macroeconomic factors appear to be more plausible.[11]

It is worth pointing out that although our results do not tell where to search for the omitted risk factors, they do imply that searching for risk factors or building up new rational asset pricing models is a useful direction for future research. In addition, our results do not eliminate the possibility of a behavioral interpretation. However, we emphasize that it is not necessary to explain the momentum effect by appealing to a behavioral approach.

The remainder of the paper is organized as follows. Section 2 briefly describes the stochastic dominance rules and the rationale behind our tests.[12] The data and sample characteristics arc discussed in Section 3. The empirical results of the paper are mainly provided in Section 4 while Section 5 conducts the robust analysis. We conclude the paper in Section 6.

## 2. Stochastic Dominance

### 2.1. *The stochastic dominance criteria*

Stochastic dominance provides a general set of rules for ranking risky assets, and has proved to be a powerful tool in both theory and applications. Over the last four decades, the stochastic dominance theory has been well

---

[10]For the returns to be arbitraged away there needs to be a set of investors who have both resources that are substantial and preferences that violate the minimum assumptions.

[11]See Chordia and Shivakumar (2002) for an analysis of macroeconomic factors.

[12]A short description of the algorithm used to implement the SD approach is provided in the Appendix.

developed[13] and many stochastic dominance comparisons have been carried out empirically.[14] While the MV criteria has been extended to larger sets of return distributions and utility functions since its birth, fewer restrictions on investor preference functions and asset return distributions are clearly desirable when ranking portfolios. The SD approach does just that without compromising its applicability. Empirical findings conclude SD rules to be effective in identifying a manageable subset of portfolios that can be considered efficient.

The basic principle underlying stochastic dominance is quite straightforward and grounded in the maximization of expected utility. As an example, suppose that investors attempt to choose between two risky assets, $X$ and $Y$, and suppose that the probability of exceeding any return in $X$ is always at least as high as that in $Y$. Regardless of the complexity of the distribution of returns to assets $X$ and $Y$, as long as investors are non-satiated, no one would buy asset $Y$ since the investor can always do better by holding asset $X$. Hence, an ordering of risky alternatives can be made without having to specify individuals' utility functions, the kinds of risk factors individuals would like to hedge against, or the specific return distributions to the risky assets.

In this example, $X$ might correspond to the return of the momentum portfolio with a distribution[15] $F$, and $Y$ might correspond to the return of another portfolio with a distribution $G$. Assuming that investors prefer more return to less, an investor wanting to maximize expected utility would prefer return distribution $F$, which lies to the right of distribution $G$. With distribution $F$, the chance of earning a higher return is always greater than with $G$, regardless of whether the investor likes or dislikes risk.

There are three major types of stochastic dominance: first order (FSD), second order (SSD), and third order (TSD). SD is generally described by considering two risky portfolios $X$ and $Y$. SD allows for the determination of an order of preference between $X$ and $Y$, if one exists. The SD rules are usually stated so that the first alternative, $X$, is preferred to the second, $Y$. The

---

[13] See for example Markowitz (1952), Tobin (1958), Fishburn (1964), Hadar and Russell (1971), Bawa (1978) and Wong and Li (1999).

[14] See Hanoch and Levy (1969), Baron (1977), Bookstaber and Clarke (1984), Booth, Tehranian and Trennepohl (1985), Seyhun (1993), Chow (2001) and Isakov and Morard (2001).

[15] That is the cumulative density function.

preferred set is the dominant set; the other is the dominated set. The dominant set is referred to as the efficient set. The three basic SD rules are:

(1) $X$ dominates $Y$ in the sense of FSD if and only if $F(x) \leq G(x)$ for all $x$ with strictly inequality for at least one value of $x$;

(2) $X$ dominates $Y$ in the sense of SSD if and only if $F_2(x) \leq G_2(x)$ for all $x$ with strictly inequality for at least one value of $x$; and

(3) $X$ dominates $Y$ in the sense of TSD if and only if mean of $X$ is at least as large as that of $Y$ and $F_3(x) \leq G_3(x)$ for all $x$ with strictly inequality for at least one value of $x$;

where $F$ and $G$ are cumulative density functions (CDF) of assets $X$ and $Y$ respectively; $F_2$ and $G_2$ are the areas under $F$ and $G$ respectively; and $F_3$ and $G_3$ are the areas under $F_2$ and $G_2$ respectively.

SD results imply hierarchy. FSD implies SSD, which in turn implies TSD. A finding that SSD exists does not imply that FSD exists and a finding that TSD exists in turn does not imply that SSD or FSD exist. When condition (1) is satisfied, the probability of realizing a return less than or equal to $x$ is greater for asset $Y$ than it is for asset $X$. Preference in the case where $F(x)$ lies entirely to the right of $G(x)$, condition (1), is readily apparent. It is extremely stringent, which limits its applicability to portfolio choice problems. When two CDFs cross, factors other than return (e.g., risk aversion) must be considered in order to establish dominance. If investors are risk averse, SSD can be applied. If $X$ dominates $Y$ under SSD, then all investors with utility functions having risk aversion will prefer $X$ to $Y$. If neither $X$ nor $Y$ dominates the other under SSD, then there may be investors who prefer $X$ and others who prefer $Y$. SSD allows CDFs to cross as long as the area under the CDF of $X$ is always less than the area under the CDF of $Y$. Analysis of TSD is similar except that it assumes that investors' absolute risk aversion decreases, which implies that investors prefer positive skewness.

We let $U(R)$ be the investor's utility function, with respect to return $R$, which is assumed to be differentiable to the third degree. The SD rules above are consistent with the principle of expected utility maximization,[16] such that:

(1) $X$ dominates $Y$ by FSD if and only if the utility of $X$ is greater than the utility of $Y$ for any utility function preferring more to less;

---

[16]See for example, Hanoch and Levy (1969), Hadar and Russell (1971), Meyer (1977) and Li and Wong (1999).

(2)  $X$ dominates $Y$ by SSD if and only if utility of $X$ is greater than utility of $Y$ for any risk averse utility function; and

(3)  $X$ dominates $Y$ by TSD if and only if the utility of $X$ is greater than the utility of $Y$ for any utility with decreasing absolute risk aversion.

This enables us to draw the following requirements on investors' utility functions. They must exhibit non-satiation ($U'(R) \geq 0$) under FSD; non-satiation and risk aversion ($U''(R) \leq 0$) under SSD; and non-satiation, risk aversion, and decreasing absolute risk aversion (DARA) ($U'''(R) \geq 0$) under TSD. If there is stochastic dominance, then the expected utility of the investor is always higher under the dominant asset than under the dominated asset. Consequently, the dominated asset would never be chosen.

## 2.2. *Stochastic dominance and market rationality*

Our focus here is how market rationality can be tested by using the SD rules without the need to identify a risk index or a specific model. In applying these rules, we look at the whole distribution of returns and not only at certain parameters, such as mean and variance. In examining market data, the criterion that SD employs is: Can some investors switch their portfolio choice and increase their expected utility given that others have no utility loss? If so, then independent of their specific preferences, the market data show that investors can benefit and market irrationality is implied.

Suppose that the winners portfolio $W$ represents the stocks for NYSE/AMEX/NASDAQ firms with the past six-month returns in the top decile, and the losers portfolio $L$ represents the stocks portfolio for NYSE/AMEX/NASDAQ firms whose past six-month returns are at the bottom decile. If $W$ dominates $L$ by FSD, there exists an arbitrage opportunity and all types of investors will increase their wealth and utility by switching from $L$ to $W$. Such a situation contradicts the notion of market rationality.[17]

Specifically, the SSD criterion assumes that all individuals have increasing utility with decreasing marginal utility functions. Given a market with these investors, if asset $W$ dominates asset $L$, then all investors would buy $W$ and (short) sell $L$. This will continue, driving up the price of asset $W$ relative to $L$, until the market price of $W$ relative to $L$ is high enough to make the marginal

---

[17]See Bawa (1978), Jarrow (1986), Bernard and Seyhun (1997) and Larsen and Resnick (1999) for more discussion of this condition.

investor indifferent between $W$ and $L$. But the higher price for $W$ (and lower price for $L$) implies lower expected return for $W$ (and higher expected return for $L$). This has the effect of altering the equilibrium distributions of returns until there is no SSD for the two assets. This means that in a rational market in which all individuals have increasing utility but decreasing marginal utility, we should not observe SSD between any two distinct assets, as well as any two different portfolios, continue to exist for a considerable length of time. We note that it should be possible in a rational market that two assets or portfolios where one SD dominates another for a short period of time. However, we claim that this phenomenon should not last for an extended period of time because market forces cause adjustment to a condition of no SSD if the market is rational.

A similar argument can be made for the TSD criterion which assumes that all investors' utility functions exhibit non-satiation, risk aversion, with decreasing absolute risk aversion. Given a market with these investors, we should not observe TSD between any two distinct assets continue to exist for a considerable length of time. However, if the market contains both investors with decreasing absolute risk aversion and investors with non-decreasing absolute risk aversion, then it is possible to have two different assets or portfolios, where one dominates another in the sense of TSD for a considerable length of time.[18] It should be noted that the SSD and TSD between any two distinct assets or different portfolios do not imply return arbitrage opportunities. Here we emphasize utility improvement or welfare gain for the higher order stochastic dominance, rather than risk-free profit opportunities. Essentially, we claim that there should be no opportunities for further welfare improvement or gain in a rational market so that we should not observe the SSD and TSD for any two different assets or portfolios for a considerable length of time.

Conceptually, market rationality within the SD framework is not different from the conventional understanding with some rational asset pricing models, such as the CAPM. The only difference is that the latter approach defines an abnormal return as excess return adjusted to some risk measure, while SD market rationality tests employ the whole distribution of returns. In particular, both SD and the asset pricing model based residual analyses are consistent with the concept of expected utility maximization. Given that no model is true, the

---

[18]Nevertheless, in our empirical study we found that $W$ and $L$ do not TSD dominate each other. This does not reject the hypothesis that all investors are non-satiated and risk averse with decreasing absolute risk aversion.

SD approach with less restrictions on both investors' preferences and return distributions seems to help us better understand the momentum effect.

## 2.3. *Stochastic dominance and market efficiency*

In the conventional theories of market efficiency if one is able to earn abnormal return for a considerable length of time, the market is considered to be inefficient. If new information is either quickly made public or is anticipated, the opportunity to use the new information to earn abnormal return is of limited value. This idea changes slightly when we move into a world where utility functions and return distributions are not as severely circumscribed. As Falk and Levy (1989) note, given that two investments $X$ and $Y$ exist, if by switching from $Y$ to $X$ (or by selling $Y$ short and holding $X$ long) an investor can increase his expected utility, then the market is inefficient.

The argument of market efficiency based on the findings of stochastic dominance is similar to that of market rationality. Since this paper deals with the momentum effect, let us elaborate on our example by using the winners portfolio $W$ and the losers portfolio $L$. First order SD of one portfolio over the other implies an arbitrage opportunity. If $W$ dominates $L$ by FSD, one will both increase profit and increase welfare by switching from $L$ to $W$ and hence we can conclude that the market is inefficient. Second-order SD does not imply any arbitrage opportunity, but implies the preference of one portfolio over another for risk-averse investors. If $W$ dominates $L$ by SSD, one may not make profit by switching from $L$ to $W$ but by switching risk averse investors will increase their expected utility. One can still claim that the market is inefficient if the market contains only risk averse investors. A similar argument can be made for the TSD criterion which assumes that all investors' utility functions exhibit non-satiation, risk aversion, with decreasing absolute risk aversion. If $W$ dominates $L$ by TSD, one may not make profit by switching from $L$ to $W$ but by doing that, the risk averse investors with decreasing absolute risk aversion will increase their expected utility and hence we can claim that the market is inefficient if the market contains only risk averse investors with decreasing absolute risk aversion.

Our empirical study shows that the market portfolio with the addition of the (zero-cost) momentum portfolio does not dominate the market portfolio in the sense of the FSD, SSD, and TSD and vice versa. This further confirms that the market efficiency hypothesis should not be rejected.

## 3. Data and Sample Characteristics

The stock return data to be investigated come from the daily and monthly tapes of the Center for Research on Securities Prices (CRSP) at the University of Chicago. Our sample is constructed from all stocks traded on the New York Stock Exchange (NYSE), American Stock Exchange (AMEX), and NASDAQ.[19] We use daily returns from CRSP for the period covering January 1, 1965, to December 31, 2000, including NASDAQ data which is only available post-1972. We use the CRSP's value-weighted returns of all stocks as the market portfolio.

Since we include all firms listed on the NYSE/AMEX and the NASDAQ, and use daily data to compute the relevant returns, the impact of small illiquid firms might be a concern. As in Jegadeesh and Titman (2001), we exclude all stocks priced below $5 at the beginning of the holding period to ensure that the results are not driven primarily by small and illiquid stocks or by bid-ask bounce.[20] The Jegadeesh and Titman (2001) sample differs from that of Jegadeesh and Titman (1993) since the latter includes NASDAQ stocks but excludes small and low priced stocks. The addition of NASDAQ stocks and the deletion of low priced stocks, however, have very little effect on average returns over the various horizons they consider, but they decrease standard errors and significantly lower the magnitude of the negative January returns.

To construct the momentum portfolios, we sort stocks into portfolios based on their returns over the past six months (month $-5$ to month $0$) and then group the stocks into ten equally weighted portfolios based on these ranks. We can consider holding periods of different months, but we will concentrate on portfolios held for six months (month 1 to month 6) following the ranking month as in Jegadeesh and Titman (2001). The momentum strategy designates winners and losers as the top ($W$) and the bottom ($L$) portfolios, and takes a long position in portfolio $W$ and a short position in portfolio $L$. We construct overlapping

---

[19]We eliminate in our sample the returns of ADRs, REITs, closed-end funds, etc. That is, we delete all of the stocks with a CRSP share code of 10 or 11.

[20]Unlike Jegadeesh and Titman (2001), we did not exclude firms that are smaller than the tenth NYSE percentile, i.e., those stocks with market capitalizations that would place them in the smallest NYSE decile. An alternative solution to this potential problem suggested in Ang *et al.* (2001) is to form all of our portfolios as value-weighted, which reduces the influence of smaller firms. It is worth noting that we repeat our tests with these alternative procedures and find that our conclusions remain qualitatively the same, and these checks show that our results are not biased by small firms.

portfolios following Jegadeesh and Titman (2001) to increase the power of our tests. In other words, a momentum decile portfolio in any particular month holds stocks ranked in that decile in any of the previous six ranking months.[21]

To examine the riskiness of the momentum strategy, we also construct the momentum portfolios and measure the returns on a daily basis. Similar to the portfolios formed on the monthly basis, we sort our stocks based upon the past six-month returns of all stocks in NYSE/AMEX and NASDAQ. Each month, an equal-weighted portfolio is formed based on six-month returns ending in the previous month. Similarly, equal-weighted portfolios are formed based on past returns that ended in the previous month, two months prior, and so on up to six months prior. We then take the simple average of six such portfolios on a daily basis. Hence, our first momentum portfolio consists of 1/6 of the returns of the best performers one month ago, plus 1/6 of the returns of the best performers two months ago, etc.

Table 1 provides the means and standard deviations of the monthly total return data separated by deciles and calendar months.[22] Similar to the results in Jegadeesh and Titman (1993, 2001), the difference between the $W$ and $L$ portfolio returns from 1965 to 1989 is 1.08% per month, which is reliably different from zero. The table reveals that this return pattern continues in the more recent 1990 to 2000 period. In this period, past winners outperformed past losers by 1.91% per month, which implied that the momentum profit seems to get larger rather than smaller even with two more years of data added since Jegadeesh and Titman (2001).[23]

---

[21] For example, a December winner portfolio comprises 10% of the stocks with the highest returns over the previous June–November period, the previous May–October and so on up to the previous January–June period. Each monthly cohort is assigned an equal weight in this portfolio.

[22] Stochastic dominance tests compare the distributions of total portfolio returns and, hence, implicitly take into account the differences in expected returns and risk. Compare, for instance, two portfolios, $W$ and $L$. Let portfolio $W$ have higher expected return than portfolio $L$. If the higher expected return to portfolio $W$ is due to its higher risk, then portfolio $W$ would also exhibit more extreme positive and negative returns and, therefore, would not stochastically dominate portfolio $L$. Consequently, the appropriate measure of returns is the total return.

[23] Following Jegadeesh and Titman (2001), Table 1 also presents the average value-weighted as well as equal-weighted returns for the stocks in the sample. It is observed that over the entire sample period of 1965–2000, the winners portfolio ($W$) outperform the value-weighted (equal-weighted) index by 0.71 (0.49)% per month while the losers portfolio ($L$) underperform the index by 0.62 (0.84)% per month. These results suggest that both winners and losers contribute about equally to momentum profits relative to the value-weighted index but not the equal-weighted index.

**Table 1.** Descriptive statistics (monthly).

| 1965–1989 | W | L | W − L | VWRD | EWRD |
|---|---|---|---|---|---|
| Mean | 1.64 | 0.56 | 1.08 | 0.92 | 1.27 |
| Std.dev. | 7.02 | 7.23 | 4.06 | 4.63 | 6.06 |
| Skewness | −0.81 | 0.3 | −1.09 | −0.37 | −0.16 |
| Kurtosis | 5.76 | 5.79 | 7.18 | 5.3 | 6.06 |
| Autocorrelation | 0.17 | 0.16 | 0.01 | 0.07 | 0.22 |
| $t$-statistic | 4.04 | 1.34 | 4.61 | 3.44 | 3.62 |
| Median | 2.01 | 0.42 | 1.42 | 0.89 | 1.41 |
| Maximum | 22.52 | 32.36 | 12.13 | 16.56 | 29.92 |
| Minimum | −33.73 | −29.05 | −19.31 | −22.49 | −27.08 |
| Jarque-Bera | 999 | 999 | 999 | 999 | 999 |
| $p$-value | 0 | 0 | 0 | 0 | 0 |
| 1990–2000 | W | L | W − L | VWRD | EWRD |
| Mean | 1.92 | 0 | 1.91 | 1.22 | 1.15 |
| Std.dev. | 8.69 | 6.3 | 6.13 | 4.1 | 4.88 |
| Skewness | 0.28 | −0.59 | 1.52 | −0.71 | −0.54 |
| Kurtosis | 6.1 | 4.75 | 13.67 | 4.41 | 5.02 |
| Autocorrelation | 0.06 | 0.31 | −0.08 | −0.05 | 0.29 |
| $t$-statistic | 2.53 | 0 | 3.59 | 3.42 | 2.72 |
| Median | 2.67 | 0.79 | 1.94 | 1.57 | 1.68 |
| Maximum | 35.99 | 16.5 | 33.64 | 10.7 | 14.95 |
| Minimum | −24.71 | −23.88 | −19.98 | −15.68 | −19.48 |
| Jarque-Bera | 999 | 999 | 999 | 999 | 999 |
| $p$-value | 0 | 0 | 0 | 0 | 0 |
| 1965–2000 | W | L | W − L | VWRD | EWRD |
| Mean | 1.72 | 0.39 | 1.34 | 1.01 | 1.23 |
| Std.dev. | 7.56 | 6.96 | 4.8 | 4.47 | 5.72 |
| Skewness | −0.31 | 0.12 | 0.6 | −0.46 | −0.23 |
| Kurtosis | 6.24 | 5.72 | 14.24 | 5.17 | 6.11 |
| Autocorrelation | 0.13 | 0.2 | −0.03 | 0.04 | 0.24 |
| $t$-statistic | 4.74 | 1.16 | 5.79 | 4.7 | 4.48 |
| Median | 2.31 | 0.54 | 1.57 | 1.24 | 1.53 |
| Maximum | 35.99 | 32.36 | 33.64 | 16.56 | 29.92 |
| Minimum | −33.73 | −29.05 | −19.98 | −22.49 | −27.08 |
| Jarque-Bera | 999 | 999 | 999 | 999 | 999 |
| $p$-value | 0 | 0 | 0 | 0 | 0 |
| 1990–1998 | W | L | W − L | VWRD | EWRD |
| Mean | 1.72 | 0.24 | 1.48 | 1.37 | 1.21 |
| Std.dev. | 6.44 | 6.08 | 3.02 | 3.91 | 4.62 |

(*Continued*)

**Table 1.**   (*Continued*)

| 1990–1998 | W | L | W − L | VWRD | EWRD |
|---|---|---|---|---|---|
| Skewness | −0.88 | −0.45 | −0.08 | −0.85 | −0.7 |
| Kurtosis | 4.51 | 4.72 | 3.07 | 5.49 | 6.34 |
| Autocorrelation | 0.19 | 0.27 | 0.04 | −0.02 | 0.3 |
| *t*-statistic | 2.78 | 0.41 | 5.1 | 3.63 | 2.72 |
| Median | 2.67 | 1.05 | 1.61 | 1.57 | 1.88 |
| Maximum | 13.29 | 16.5 | 10.1 | 10.7 | 14.95 |
| Minimum | −24.71 | −23.88 | −6.28 | −15.68 | −19.48 |
| Jarque-Bera | 999 | 16.9 | 0.15 | 999 | 999 |
| *p*-value | 0 | 0 | 0.93 | 0 | 0 |

| 1965–1998 | W | L | W − L | VWRD | EWRD |
|---|---|---|---|---|---|
| Mean | 1.66 | 0.47 | 1.19 | 1.04 | 1.25 |
| Std.dev. | 6.87 | 6.94 | 3.82 | 4.45 | 5.71 |
| Skewness | −0.83 | 0.18 | −1.01 | −0.47 | −0.24 |
| Kurtosis | 5.56 | 5.78 | 7.22 | 5.42 | 6.37 |
| Autocorrelation | 0.18 | 0.18 | 0.01 | 0.05 | 0.24 |
| *t*-statistic | 4.89 | 1.38 | 6.29 | 4.71 | 4.43 |
| Median | 2.31 | 0.59 | 1.51 | 1.24 | 1.55 |
| Maximum | 22.52 | 32.36 | 12.13 | 16.56 | 29.92 |
| Minimum | −33.73 | −29.05 | −19.31 | −22.49 | −27.08 |
| Jarque-Bera | 999 | 999 | 999 | 999 | 999 |
| *p*-value | 0 | 0 | 0 | 0 | 0 |

*Notes*: This table reports the summary statistics on the monthly returns of various portfolios expressed as monthly percentages. *W* is the equal-weighted portfolio of 10% of the stocks with the highest returns over the previous six months, *L* is the equal-weighted portfolio of 10% of the stocks with the lowest returns over the previous six months, so *W* − *L* is the momentum portfolio formed based on past six-month returns and held for six months. In addition, VWRD is the CRSP value-weighted returns with dividends, and EWRD is the CRSP equal-weighted returns with dividends. Autocorrelation refers to first-order autocorrelation. Jarque-Bera refers to the Jarque and Bera (1987) normality test statistic, with "999" indicating a value of greater than 30. The full sample period is from 1965 to 2000 for a total of 432 observations, while the sub-sample periods are from 1965 to 1989 (300 observations) and from 1990 to 2000 (132 observations). As a check, we also include the Jegadeesh and Titman (2001) sample periods from 1990 to 1998 (108 observations) and from 1965 to 1998 (408 observations).

Descriptive statistics of the daily total return data separated by deciles and calendar months are reported in Table 2. It can be seen that on the daily basis, the difference between the *W* and *L* portfolio returns from 1965 and 1989 is 0.05% per day, which is reliably different from zero. The table also reveals that this return pattern continues in the more recent 1990–2000 period. In this period, past winners outperformed past losers by 0.08% per day, despite the

**Table 2.** Descriptive statistics (daily).

| 1965–1989 | W | L | W − L | VWRD | EWRD |
|---|---|---|---|---|---|
| Mean | 0.08 | 0.03 | 0.05 | 0.04 | 0.07 |
| Std.dev. | 1.06 | 0.93 | 0.56 | 0.85 | 0.73 |
| Skewness | −1.17 | −0.13 | −1.03 | −1.37 | −1.02 |
| Kurtosis | 23.17 | 16.01 | 13.18 | 35.61 | 20.56 |
| Autocorrelation | 0.3 | 0.38 | 0.32 | 0.21 | 0.4 |
| $t$-statistic | 5.91 | 2.79 | 6.54 | 3.95 | 7.34 |
| Median | 0.15 | 0.07 | 0.07 | 0.06 | 0.12 |
| Maximum | 11.77 | 9.59 | 4.96 | 8.67 | 6.95 |
| Minimum | −15.39 | −11.07 | −5.5 | −17.17 | −10.48 |
| Jarque-Bera | 999 | 999 | 999 | 999 | 999 |
| $p$-value | 0 | 0 | 0 | 0 | 0 |
| 1990–2000 | W | L | W − L | VWRD | EWRD |
| Mean | 0.1 | 0.03 | 0.08 | 0.06 | 0.11 |
| Std.dev. | 1.38 | 0.91 | 0.86 | 0.91 | 0.68 |
| Skewness | −0.62 | −0.54 | −0.62 | −0.34 | −1.17 |
| Kurtosis | 17.76 | 10.83 | 35.62 | 8.25 | 12.48 |
| Autocorrelation | 0.24 | 0.29 | 0.3 | 0.07 | 0.28 |
| $t$-statistic | 4.01 | 1.62 | 4.72 | 3.37 | 8.91 |
| Median | 0.21 | 0.09 | 0.1 | 0.08 | 0.18 |
| Maximum | 14.98 | 5.76 | 12.11 | 4.83 | 4.71 |
| Minimum | −14.48 | −6.83 | −9.21 | −6.59 | −6.22 |
| Jarque-Bera | 999 | 999 | 999 | 999 | 999 |
| $p$-value | 0 | 0 | 0 | 0 | 0 |
| 1965–2000 | W | L | W − L | VWRD | EWRD |
| Mean | 0.09 | 0.03 | 0.06 | 0.05 | 0.08 |
| Std.dev. | 1.17 | 0.93 | 0.67 | 0.87 | 0.71 |
| Skewness | −0.91 | −0.25 | −0.8 | −1.01 | −1.07 |
| Kurtosis | 21.56 | 14.51 | 34.85 | 25.64 | 18.63 |
| Autocorrelation | 0.27 | 0.35 | 0.31 | 0.16 | 0.36 |
| $t$-statistic | 7.09 | 3.23 | 7.95 | 5.17 | 10.92 |
| Median | 0.17 | 0.07 | 0.08 | 0.07 | 0.14 |
| Maximum | 14.98 | 9.59 | 12.11 | 8.67 | 6.95 |
| Minimum | −15.39 | −11.07 | −9.21 | −17.17 | −10.48 |
| Jarque-Bera | 999 | 999 | 999 | 999 | 999 |
| $p$-value | 0 | 0 | 0 | 0 | 0 |
| 1990–1998 | W | L | W − L | VWRD | EWRD |
| Mean | 0.1 | 0.04 | 0.06 | 0.06 | 0.12 |
| Std.dev. | 1.04 | 0.81 | 0.51 | 0.79 | 0.6 |

(*Continued*)

**Table 2.**   (*Continued*)

| 1990–1998 | W | L | W − L | VWRD | EWRD |
|---|---|---|---|---|---|
| Skewness | −1.17 | −0.83 | −0.49 | −0.59 | −1.53 |
| Kurtosis | 10.92 | 11.12 | 6.11 | 10.13 | 13.37 |
| Autocorrelation | 0.25 | 0.32 | 0.29 | 0.09 | 0.29 |
| *t*-statistic | 4.53 | 2.45 | 5.32 | 3.89 | 9.67 |
| Median | 0.21 | 0.1 | 0.08 | 0.08 | 0.18 |
| Maximum | 5.55 | 4.11 | 2.61 | 4.83 | 2.77 |
| Minimum | −8.66 | −6.83 | −3.3 | −6.59 | −5.45 |
| Jarque-Bera | 999 | 999 | 999 | 999 | 999 |
| *p*-value | 0 | 0 | 0 | 0 | 0 |
| **1965–1998** | **W** | **L** | **W − L** | **VWRD** | **EWRD** |
| Mean | 0.08 | 0.04 | 0.05 | 0.05 | 0.08 |
| Std.dev. | 1.05 | 0.9 | 0.55 | 0.83 | 0.7 |
| Skewness | −1.17 | −0.27 | −0.92 | −1.2 | −1.13 |
| Kurtosis | 20.13 | 15.39 | 11.84 | 30.35 | 19.98 |
| Autocorrelation | 0.28 | 0.37 | 0.31 | 0.18 | 0.38 |
| *t*-statistic | 7.39 | 3.61 | 8.3 | 5.35 | 10.87 |
| Median | 0.16 | 0.08 | 0.08 | 0.07 | 0.14 |
| Maximum | 11.77 | 9.59 | 4.96 | 8.67 | 6.95 |
| Minimum | −15.39 | −11.07 | −5.5 | −17.17 | −10.48 |
| Jarque-Bera | 999 | 999 | 999 | 999 | 999 |
| *p*-value | 0 | 0 | 0 | 0 | 0 |

*Notes*: This table reports the summary statistics on the daily returns of various portfolios expressed as daily percentages. $W$ is the equal-weighted portfolio of 10% of the stocks with the highest returns over the previous six months, $L$ is the equal-weighted portfolio of 10% of the stocks with the lowest returns over the previous six months, so $W - L$ is the momentum portfolio formed based on past six-month returns and held for six months. In addition, VWRD is the CRSP value-weighted returns with dividends, and EWRD is the CRSP equal-weighted returns with dividends. Autocorrelation refers to first-order autocorrelation. Jarque-Bera refers to the Jarque and Bera (1987) normality test statistic, with "999" indicating a value of greater than 30. The full sample period is from 1965 to 2000 for a total of 9,065 observations, while the sub-sample periods are from 1965 to 1989 (6,285 observations) and from 1990 to 2000 (2,780 observations). As a check, we also include the Jegadeesh and Titman (2001) sample periods from 1990 to 1998 (2,276 observations) and from 1965 to 1998 (8,561 observations).

fact that there seems to be a significant increase in the variability of returns (measured by standard deviation and kurtosis). On the whole, the results are similar to those found on the monthly basis.

Jegadeesh and Titman (1993) find a striking seasonality in momentum profits. They document that the winners outperform losers in all months except January but the losers significantly outperform the winners in January. In

**Table 3.** Momentum portfolio returns in January and outside January (monthly).

|  |  | $N$ | $W$ | $L$ | $W - L$ | $t$-statistic | % Positive |
|---|---|---|---|---|---|---|---|
| | Jan | 25 | 5.47 | 7.73 | −2.27 | −1.86 | 44 |
| 1965–1989 | Feb–Dec | 275 | 1.29 | −0.09 | 1.39 | 6.22 | 71.27 |
| | All | 300 | 1.64 | 0.56 | 1.08 | 4.61 | 69 |
| | Jan | 11 | 3.45 | 3.17 | 0.28 | 0.32 | 27.27 |
| 1990–2000 | Feb–Dec | 121 | 1.78 | −0.29 | 2.06 | 3.58 | 71.9 |
| | All | 132 | 1.92 | 0 | 1.91 | 3.59 | 68.18 |
| | Jan | 36 | 4.85 | 6.34 | −1.49 | −1.65 | 38.89 |
| 1965–2000 | Feb–Dec | 396 | 1.44 | −0.15 | 1.59 | 6.8 | 71.46 |
| | All | 432 | 1.72 | 0.39 | 1.34 | 5.79 | 68.75 |
| | Jan | 9 | 2.83 | 3.42 | −0.59 | −0.78 | 11.11 |
| 1990–1998 | Feb–Dec | 99 | 1.62 | −0.05 | 1.67 | 5.51 | 71.72 |
| | All | 108 | 1.72 | 0.24 | 1.48 | 5.1 | 66.67 |
| | Jan | 34 | 4.77 | 6.59 | −1.82 | −1.98 | 35.29 |
| 1965–1998 | Feb–Dec | 374 | 1.38 | −0.08 | 1.46 | 8.01 | 71.39 |
| | All | 408 | 1.66 | 0.47 | 1.19 | 6.29 | 68.38 |

*Notes*: This table reports the average monthly momentum portfolio returns, the associated $t$-statistics to test whether the returns are reliably different than zero, and the percentages of monthly momentum returns are positive. The table reports returns for January as well as non-January months, and returns in the 1965–1989, Jegadeesh and Titman (1993) sample period, the 1990–2000 subsequent period, as well as the entire 1965–2000 period. $W$ is the equal-weighted portfolio of 10% of the stocks with the highest past six-month returns, and $L$ is the equal-weighted portfolio of 10% of the stocks with the lowest past six-month returns, so $W - L$ is momentum portfolio formed based on past six-month returns and held for six months.

Jegadeesh and Titman (2001), unreported analysis that replicates the momentum strategies using the sample selection criteria in Jegadeesh and Titman (1993) found results very similar to theirs for the 1990s, suggesting that the earlier finding was not a statistical fluke. We performed similar analysis and Table 3 reports the momentum profits in January and non-January months for our monthly sample. The momentum profits in January for this sample are also negative in most periods but they are only marginally significant. The January momentum profits, however, are significantly smaller than the momentum profits in other calendar months in all sample periods. This seasonality could potentially be a statistical fluke; January is one of the 12 calendar months and it is possible that in any one of the calendar month momentum profits are negative. Specifically, one can examine the out-of-sample performance of the strategy in January to examine whether this seasonality is real or whether it was the result of looking too closely at the data.

**Table 4.**   Momentum portfolio returns in January and outside January (daily).

|           |         | $N$   | $W$  | $L$  | $W - L$ | $t$-statistic | % Positive |
|-----------|---------|-------|------|------|---------|---------------|------------|
|           | Jan     | 529   | 0.25 | 0.35 | −0.1    | −3.65         | 48.96      |
| 1965–1989 | Feb–Dec | 5,756 | 0.06 | 0    | 0.06    | 8.25          | 59.29      |
|           | All     | 6,285 | 0.08 | 0.03 | 0.05    | 6.54          | 58.42      |
|           | Jan     | 231   | 0.18 | 0.18 | 0       | 0.04          | 55.41      |
| 1990–2000 | Feb–Dec | 2,549 | 0.1  | 0.01 | 0.08    | 4.86          | 59.55      |
|           | All     | 2,780 | 0.1  | 0.03 | 0.08    | 4.72          | 59.21      |
|           | Jan     | 760   | 0.23 | 0.3  | −0.07   | −2.87         | 50.92      |
| 1965–2000 | Feb–Dec | 8,305 | 0.07 | 0.01 | 0.07    | 9.21          | 59.37      |
|           | All     | 9,065 | 0.09 | 0.03 | 0.06    | 7.95          | 58.67      |
|           | Jan     | 192   | 0.15 | 0.19 | −0.04   | −0.94         | 55.73      |
| 1990–1998 | Feb–Dec | 2,084 | 0.09 | 0.03 | 0.07    | 6.01          | 59.31      |
|           | All     | 2,276 | 0.1  | 0.04 | 0.06    | 5.32          | 59.01      |
|           | Jan     | 721   | 0.22 | 0.31 | −0.09   | −3.64         | 50.76      |
| 1965–1998 | Feb–Dec | 7,840 | 0.07 | 0.01 | 0.06    | 10.13         | 59.3       |
|           | All     | 8,561 | 0.08 | 0.04 | 0.05    | 8.3           | 58.58      |

*Notes*: This table reports the average daily momentum portfolio returns, the associated $t$-statistics to test whether the returns are reliably different than zero, and the percentages of daily momentum returns are positive. The table reports returns for January as well as non-January months, and returns in the 1965–1989, Jegadeesh and Titman (1993) sample period, the 1990–2000 subsequent period, as well as the entire 1965–2000 period. $W$ is the equal-weighted portfolio of 10% of the stocks with the highest past six-month returns, and $L$ is the equal-weighted portfolio of 10% of the stocks with the lowest past six-month returns, so $W - L$ is the momentum portfolio formed based on past six-month returns and held for six months.

When daily returns are examined, the results are similar as shown in Table 4, except we now find that the daily returns of the momentum portfolio are significantly negative during January for the period 1965–1989 and the period 1965–2000. Interestingly enough, while the daily returns of the momentum portfolio are significant in all other months for all sample periods, the returns are insignificant for the post-1990 periods. Another point to note is that in terms of the percentages of daily momentum returns that are positive, the month of January (49%–56%) is similar to the other months (58%–60%) in all sample periods. Could this be the result of small firms?

## 4. Empirical Evidence on Stochastic Dominance

We shall first examine whether the winners portfolio ($W$) dominates the losers portfolio ($L$) in the sense of stochastic dominance (SD) using the Davidson

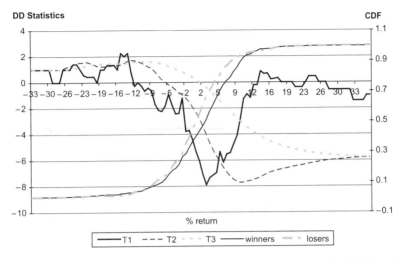

**Figure 1.** Plot of the CDF of the monthly returns of winners and losers and their DD statistics from 1965 to 2000.

and Duclos (2000) test.[24] Using the entire sample from 1965 to 2000, we partition the range of both monthly and daily returns for $W$ and $L$ into 100 equal-distanced intervals.[25] The results of the Davidson–Duclos $t$-statistics (DD statistics) for monthly returns are shown in Figure 1.[26]

For the period January 1965 to December 2000, we find that the empirical cumulative density function (CDF) of $W$ is greater than that of $L$ in the first 30 intervals (return from $-33.73\%$ to $-12.81\%$). This means that the probability of $W$ is greater than that of $L$ in any of the first 30 percentiles, and hence $L$ is preferred to $W$ for any investor in the sense of FSD in this region. From the 31st interval to the 67th interval (returns from $-12.11\%$ to $12.98\%$), the empirical CDF of $L$ is greater than that of $W$. This means that the probability of $L$ in any of these intervals is greater than that of $W$ and hence $W$ is preferred to $L$ in the sense of FSD in this region. For the remaining intervals (returns from $13.68\%$ to $35.99\%$), the DD statistics are very small. This finding is interesting in the

---

[24]There are several SD tests; we choose the test from Davidson and Duclos, described in the Appendix.

[25]We can use more intervals but our results remain qualitatively the same after trying various alternatives.

[26]In all the figures, we will report the T1–T3 of the DD tests as defined in Equation (1) with the numerators to be $\hat{D}_W^s - \hat{D}_L^s$. In order to make the comparison easy, we will report CDF of Winners and Losers. We use the returns instead of the percentiles in the $x$-axis.

sense that, when FSD is used as the decision criteria, $L$ is preferred to $W$ for the bottom one-third of the range, while $W$ is preferred to $L$ in the middle one-third region, and no portfolio dominates each other for the top one-third range. On the whole, $W$ does not dominate $L$ in the sense of FSD over the entire sample period, even though the sample mean return on $W$ is significantly higher than that of $L$.

To investigate whether $W$ dominates $L$ in the sense of higher order stochastic dominance, it is useful to recall that $W$ is preferable to $L$ in the sense of SSD if and only if the utility of $W$ will be higher than the utility of $L$ for any risk averse investor, and $W$ is preferable to $L$ in the sense of TSD if and only if the utility of $W$ will be higher than the utility of $L$ for any risk averse investor exhibiting decreasing absolute risk aversion (DARA). The results of the region of dominance between $W$ and $L$ in the sense of SSD and TSD are clear as there is only one change in sign. From Figure 1, we find that $L$ is preferred to $W$ in the first 40 percentiles (returns from $-33.73\%$ to $5.84\%$) of the SSD test and in the first 50 percentiles (return from $-33.73\%$ to $-0.05\%$) of the TSD test, while $W$ is preferred to $L$ in the rest of the distribution.[27] This means that any risk averse investor will prefer $L$ to $W$ in the lower range of returns while they will prefer $W$ to $L$ in the upper range of returns. Again, on the whole, $W$ does not dominate $L$ in the sense of SSD or TSD over the entire sample period, even though the sample standard deviation and skewness of returns on $W$ and $L$ may not differ significantly.

Though the above results do not provide strong support that $W$ dominates $L$, one may still argue that $W$ could be preferable to $L$ as most DD statistics favoring $W$ are significantly different from zero while all DD statistics favoring $L$ are not significant. Nevertheless, the total number of monthly returns is only 432 for the entire sample period, which is too small to obtain completely convincing results. The simulation study in Chow (2001) shows that the power of the test can be as low as 0.319 for sample size of 600, 0.634 for sample size of 1000. Tse and Zhang (2004) and Lean, Wong and Zhang (2004) further study the power of the DD statistics and find that the power of DD statistics is reasonably good for sample size of 2000.[28] In order to increase the power of our test, and as a further investigation into the momentum strategy, we examine the daily returns for the portfolios $W$ and $L$ and the results are shown in Figure 2.

---

[27]The detailed analyses for monthly returns and daily returns are available on request.

[28]See Tse and Zhang (2004) and Lean *et al.* (2004) for an analysis of the power of the SD tests.

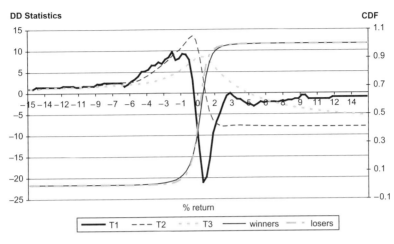

**Figure 2.** Plot of the CDF of the daily returns of winners and losers and their DD statistics from 1965 to 2000.

As in the case of monthly returns, we partition the range of the return for $W$ and $L$ into $100^{29}$ equal intervals. The results for the daily returns are similar to those for monthly returns. $W$ does not dominate $L$ in the sense of FSD, SSD, or TSD over the bottom range of returns except now the range that favors $L$ is longer (i.e., the range that favors $W$ is shorter) and more DD statistics favoring $L$ are significantly different from zero even at 1% level. Specifically, the findings are as follows:

(1) In the first 49 percentiles (returns from $-15.08\%$ to $-0.51\%$), the empirical CDF of $W$ is greater than that of $L$ and hence in this region $L$ is preferred to $W$ for any investor in the sense of FSD. For instance, the DD statistic is as large as 9.76 (in the 43rd percentile) and is significant at 1% level. In the remaining range (from the 50th interval to the end and returns

---

[29]Finer partitions will be useful to investigate the behavior of the distribution in detail but the DD statistics and all other SD statistics, which rely on the comparison of the distributions at a finite number of grid points, have to choose independent grid points. Too fine partitions will results in dependent grid points. Tse and Zhang (2004) and Lean *et al.* (2004) recommend to use the critical value based on 10 grid to ensure the grids are close to independent. In this paper, we follow the suggestion from Lean *et al.* (2004) to make ten major partitions and make further nine minor partitions between any consecutive major partitions (totally 100 partitions) to check the consistency of the magnitudes and the signs of the DD statistics between any two major consecutive partitions. However, the critical values are used based on the ten major grid points, they are 3.691, 3.25 and 3.043 for 1%, 5%, and 10% level of significance.

from $-0.20\%$ to $14.98\%$), $W$ is preferred to $L$ for any risk averse investor with the DD statistics as large as (in negative value) $-21.06$ which is significant at 1% level.

(2) For the SSD test, we find that in the first 52 percentiles (returns from $-15.08\%$ to $-0.40\%$), $L$ is in fact preferred to $W$ for any risk averse investor and the DD statistics are as large as 13.48 (in the 49th interval) which is significant at 1% level. In the remaining range (from the 52nd interval to the end, returns from $0.71\%$ to $14.98\%$), $W$ is preferred to $L$ for any risk averse investor with the DD statistics remain around $-7.90$ which is significant at 1% level.

(3) As for the TSD test, we find that in the first 65 percentiles (returns from $-15.08\%$ to $4.35\%$), $L$ is preferred to $W$ for any DARA investor in this region and the DD statistics are as large as 8.54 (in the 52nd percentile) which is significant at 0.01 level. On the other hand, $W$ is preferred to $L$ for any DARA investor in the remaining range (returns from $4.65\%$ to $14.98\%$) with the DD statistics declined to as low as $-5.33$ (in the 100th interval) which is significant at 1% level.

In summary, $W$ does not significantly dominate $L$ in the sense of FSD, SSD, and TSD over the entire sample period and vice versa. As $L$ is preferred to $W$ in the lower range while $W$ is preferred to $L$ in the upper range in the sense of FSD, SSD, and TSD, an implication is that some investors may in fact prefer the losers portfolio $L$ in equilibrium depending on their utility functions. Our findings suggest that one possible reason why some investors prefer losers is because of less downside risk.

## 5. Additional Robustness Checks

### 5.1. *Pre- and post-1990 experience*

A potential criticism of the stochastic dominance results shown so far is that the overall sample includes data from pre-1990 when the momentum effect was first discovered. If the momentum effect is not due to some statistical artifact, then it should be present in an independent data sample. Moreover, the momentum effect received increased publicity during the 1990s in the financial press and academic studies. Consequently, if a sufficient number of investors have attempted to exploit the momentum effect, then the pricing anomaly would be expected to be smoothed throughout the year and thereby disappear. To test

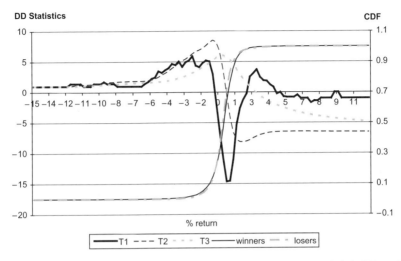

**Figure 3.** Plot of the CDF of the daily returns of winners and losers and their DD statistics from 1965 to 1989.

these possibilities, pre-1990 and post-1990 data[30] are analyzed separately in the following. We test for SD between $W$ and $L$, using daily returns and monthly returns from 1965 to 1989 and 1990 to 2000. As the results for monthly returns are similar to that for daily returns but have less power in obtaining a reliable result due to the smaller sample sizes, for simplicity we only report the results of daily returns in Figures 3 and 4.[31]

In comparing $W$ and $L$, we find that neither portfolio dominates the other in the sense of FSD, SSD, and TSD in both sub-periods for both daily returns and for monthly returns. As the results from these two sub-periods exhibit remarkably similar stochastic dominance characteristics as the overall sample for both daily returns and monthly returns, the momentum effect has not disappeared with the increased publicity. We find that the momentum portfolio characteristics remain similar in the two periods.

---

[30]The pre-1990 period used in our paper is the same as that used in Jegadeesh and Titman (2001) while our post-1990 period (1990–2000) is different from and that used in Jegadeesh and Titman (2001). We obtained all the results for the period from 1990 to 1998 as to compare the results from Jegadeesh and Titman (2001). As our findings show that the results from 1990 to 1998 draw the same conclusion as that of 1990–2000. We skip the results for the period 1990–1998 but the results are available on request.

[31]The results of monthly returns are available on request.

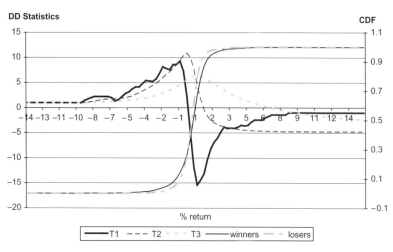

**Figure 4.**    Plot of the CDF of the daily returns of winners and losers and their DD statistics from 1990 to 2000.

## 5.2. *Seasonality*

Momentum profits in January are often negative (except the period 1990–2000), as shown in Tables 3 and  4. Does this seasonality affect our result? In this section, we repeat our previous tests with the samples deleting all of January returns. Clearly this would be an unimplementable investment strategy. However, it will help us to see how the January effect impacts the results from our studies. Eliminating January may also create substantial biases against our conclusion that no market inefficiency is revealed by the momentum profits that have been observed for more than two decades. Nonetheless, as a robust check, we want to consider whether our claim still holds under this biased scenario. Due to the restrictions in the sample size, it is infeasible for us to investigate this issue using monthly returns. We therefore investigate the stochastic dominance between $W$ and $L$ in January as well as non-January months for the whole sample period and the two sub-periods. The results are summarized in Figures 5–8.[32]

While the results of non-January returns for the whole period as well as for the two sub-periods confirm what we have found before, the results for

---

[32]For simplicity, we skip the figures of the non-January returns in the sub-periods as they are similar to the figure of the non-January returns in the whole period but they are available on request.

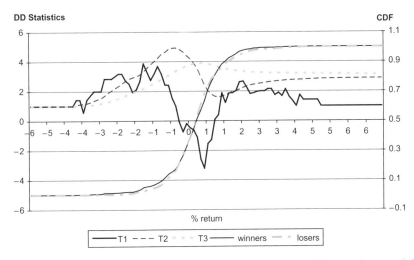

**Figure 5.** Plot of the CDF of the daily returns of January winners and January losers and their DD statistics from 1965 to 2000.

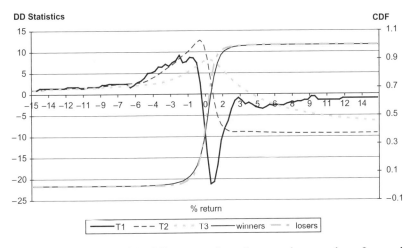

**Figure 6.** Plot of the CDF of the daily returns of non-January winners and non-January losers and their DD statistics from 1965 to 2000.

January returns shown in Figures 5, 7 and 8 are quite interesting. We know from Tables 3 and 4 that January $W$ has a smaller mean return than $L$ for the whole sample period and the first sub-period (1965–1989), the period from 1990 to 1998 and the average January return for $W$ is only marginally higher than that of the $L$ from 1990 to 2000. From Figures 5 and 7, we observe that the range where $L$ dominates $W$ is significantly more than that when we do not consider January returns separately. In addition, from Figure 5, we find

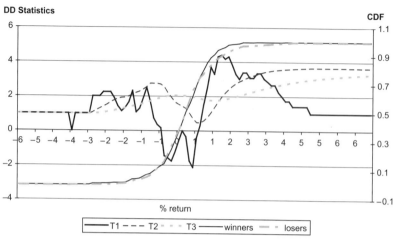

**Figure 7.**    Plot of the CDF of the daily returns of January winners and January losers and their DD statistics from 1965 to 1989.

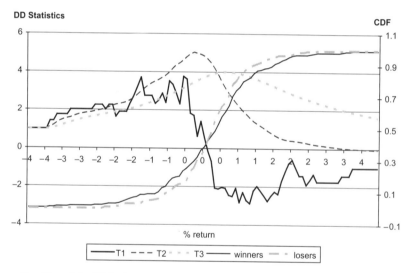

**Figure 8.**    Plot of the CDF of the daily returns of January winners and January losers and their DD statistics from 1990 to 2000.

that the first order DD statistics ($T1$) are all positive (with some statistically significant at the 1% level) except the range from the 45th percentile to 52nd percentile in which the $T1$ are negative (but none of them are significant at the 10% level. Similar results can be drawn from Figure 7. In other words, $L$ can be seen to dominate $W$ in the sense of FSD for the month of January for the entire sample period and before 1990. In this regard, it should be of no surprise that our results indicate that $L$ also dominates $W$ in the sense of SSD and TSD for the same periods, since it is known that FSD implies SSD which in turn implies TSD. We note that the second and the third order DD statistics ($T2$ and $T3$) are all positive for the entire range with some statistically significant at the 1% level in both Figures 5 and 7. The evidence of such dominance, however, is much weaker since 1990 as shown in Figure 8. To this end, we would conjecture that the significant January effect of the momentum profits has indeed been reduced through the (potential) arbitrage or hedging activities from the rational investors since 1990.

## 5.3. *Other considerations*

Our findings that the winners portfolio dominates at the right-hand side of the distribution of returns while the losers portfolio dominates at the left-hand side of the distribution are consistent with the conjecture that the distribution of the losers portfolio is skewed to the right relatively to the winners. We confirm this conjecture from Tables 1 and 2. Table 1 shows that except the period 1990–2000, the skewness of $L$ is greater than that of $W$ for any period for monthly data while Table 2 shows that the skewness of $L$ is greater than that of $W$ for any period without exception for daily data. The results from Table 2 are more reliable and the conjecture that the losers portfolio is skewed to the right relatively to the winners is confirmed.

One may worry whether the stochastic dominance conditions may be sensitive to outliers and may not be stationary for different sub-periods. For the monthly data from 1965 to 2000, the minimum return in $L$ was $-29\%$ and $-34\%$ for $W$, while the maximum returns for $W$ and $L$ are respectively 36% and 32%. Stationarity of the stochastic dominance results is examined by splitting the sample period 1965–2000 into two almost equal sub-periods of 1965–1981 and 1981–2000 as in Jegadeesh and Titman (2001). With these two sub-periods, each sub-period contains more than 200 observations to estimate the cumulative density functions. While not shown,[33] the sub-period analysis indicates that all the results continue to hold for each sub-period. Similar results were obtained when daily returns are examined using the same methodology. Hence, even though there are some year-to-year variations in the realizations of the returns, the cumulative probabilities for different portfolios are approximately

---

[33]The results are available on request.

stationary relative to each other. Outliers will only affect the results at the ends of the distribution. In our findings, there is only one change of sign for the DD statistics in most cases and the values of the DD statistics are changing smoothly. These results show that our findings are not subject to the influence of outliers.

Grundy and Martin (2001) have pointed out the potential impact of transaction costs on momentum profits. To determine whether such an adjustment is necessary in this study, we analyze month-to-month turnover with the momentum portfolios. Our examination shows that the average turnover of winner portfolios is no greater than that of loser portfolios. Although transaction costs would lower the actual returns to a trader employing the momentum strategies, the rebalancing costs would be similar across portfolios so that relative portfolio performance would be unchanged. Thus, transaction costs do not need to be explicitly included in our analysis since they would not affect the stochastic dominance results.

## 6. Concluding Remarks

This paper examines the momentum effect using a stochastic dominance (SD) approach. Our empirical results demonstrate that the momentum profits are consistent with market rationality and market efficiency associated with the SD rules. In particular, we find that the winners portfolio and the losers portfolio do not dominate each other in terms of the FSD, SSD and TSD, which implies that the winners portfolio is not undervalued while the losers portfolio is not overvalued based on an unknown and possibly complicated risk-based asset pricing model.[34] The tests are designed based on the following two arguments.

---

[34]As mentioned in Jegadeesh and Titman (2001), although the documented momentum profits have been well accepted, the source of the profits and the interpretation of the evidence are still widely debated. Some have argued that the results provide strong evidence of market inefficiency, others have argued that the returns from these strategies are either compensation for risk, or alternatively, the product of data mining. To investigate this issue further, we examine the stochastic dominance properties between a well diversified portfolio and the well-diversified portfolio plus the momentum portfolio ($W - L$). Specifically, we will consider the market portfolio $M$ and the portfolio $M + (W - L)$. If the momentum portfolio is indeed a free lunch then $M + (W - L)$ should dominate $M$ in the sense of stochastic dominance. Otherwise, the returns from the momentum strategy could well be a compensation for risk. As the findings of the stochastic dominance between $M$ and $M + (W - L)$ is similar to that between $W$ and $L$, our claim is confirmed by our further test on the SD between the market portfolio and the addition of the (zero-cost) momentum portfolio.

First, in a rational market, there should be no SD between any two distinct assets or different portfolios for a reasonable lengthy of time. Otherwise, we should reject market rationality and market efficiency. Second, any SD efficient portfolio should not be dominated by any other portfolios in the sense of SD. As pointed out in the previous sections, the two tests are not equivalent and they complement each other. Notably, we emphasize that the tests conducted in this paper offer the same conclusion: The momentum profits are consistent with market rationality and market efficiency.

How robust are our empirical findings? First, we find that our results are consistent no matter whether monthly or daily samples are examined. Second, we investigate our findings by dividing the sample into two sub-periods, namely 1965–1989 and 1990–2000. These two sample periods are chosen similarly to those in Jegadeesh and Titman (2001). The results are qualitatively the same as those for the whole period. Third, we consider the effect of seasonality since the momentum profits are often negative in January. Apparently, deleting the January returns would bias the tests against our conclusion. While deleting the January returns might not be implementable in practice, we still find that our conclusion passes the tests under the extreme scenario. Overall, we can conclude that our empirical findings are robust.

The principal disadvantage of the SD approach is that it may be sensitive to outliers. A single negative return in portfolio can undermine the dominance results. However, in spite of such sensitivity, historical returns for the last 35 years exhibit no strong SD characteristics for the momentum portfolios. We also note from our findings that $W$ and $L$ dominate each other in varied but very long intervals in the distribution; while outliers affect only towards the endpoints and/or occur in very short intervals. This confirms that our results are not affected by the outliers.

It might be worth noting that some other evidence in the literature is consistent with our conclusion. For example, momentum profits have continued to exist since their discovery. It is difficult to believe that the momentum profits would still exist if they were not associated with some risk factors. Recent work such as Harvey and Siddique (2000), Ang *et al.* (2001) and Dittmar (2002) have pointed out higher order moments of return distributions should matter in pricing assets and portfolios. In this regard, our results are consistent with their claims.

The feature that we consistently find is that the losers portfolio dominates the winners portfolio for over a substantial portion of the range of return. In all cases[35] — daily returns, monthly returns, and various time periods — the losers portfolio dominates over the lower portion of the return distribution while the winners portfolio dominates the losers portfolio at high returns. This result may be related to the hypothesis that economic variables are significant in explaining momentum put forward by Chordia and Shivakumar (2002).

Periods of low returns may be periods of poor general stock market performance. In these periods, investors may choose portfolios that attempt to avoid downside risk which the losers portfolio may very well have an advantage over the winners portfolio. In a period of high returns the winners portfolio dominates. Both the winners and losers portfolios have positive returns but the expected return on the winners portfolio is higher.[36] This feature of the conditional distribution may weigh more heavily on the investor's decision than avoiding downside risk. However, it is unlikely that the distributions that result from conditioning on return being in a certain range would coincide with distributions conditioned on "poor", "indifferent" and "great" economic periods.

In summary, the results documented in this study provide strong support for the hypothesis that the high momentum returns can be attributed to omitted risk factors. Regardless of investors' attitudes toward risk, degree of risk aversion, or seasonal variations in risk or risk premia, the non-SD results for the period 1965–2000 indicate that momentum returns were not too high to be equilibrium returns. These findings imply that the potential explanations of the momentum effect are more likely to be associated with various forms of the risk factor-based hypothesis, which are consistent with market rationality. One important implication of our empirical results is that searching for risk factors or building up new risk-based asset pricing models is the right direction of the further research on the momentum effects.

At last, we discuss the power of the SD test over the $t$-test. The $t$-test is commonly used to compare the difference of two means but it requires the assumption of normality for the distribution. As such, many academicians prefer to use the median test to the $t$-test as the median test does not require any assumption on the distribution and it can be used to compare the difference between two medians. It is obvious that the SD test is much more

---

[35]Except the case for the returns in January in which the losers portfolio dominates the winners portfolio for the entire range.

[36]Except the case for returns in January in which the losers portfolio has a higher mean.

powerful than the median test as in our study, we use the estimate of the $0, 1, 2, \ldots, 49, 50, 51, \ldots, 99, 100$ pencentiles of the distribution while the median (50 pencentile) is only one of the estimate in the SD test. Hence, we are not surprise SD test enables us to draw conclusion for the whole distribution with very minimum assumptions, much more conclusion than drawn from median test or $t$-test.

## Appendix A. Implementation of Stochastic Dominance Tests

The early work of Beach and Davidson (1983) examined dominance at the first order. Recently, several methods have been proposed for testing for stochastic dominance. These tests can be divided into two groups. The first group relies on the comparison of the distributions at a finite number of grid points, for example, see Anderson (1996), Xu (1997) and Davidson and Duclos (2000). The second group propose the use of the infermum or supermum statistics over the support of the distributions, for example, see Whitmore (1978), Levy and Kroll (1979), McFadden (1989) and Kaur, Rao and Singh (1994). Tse and Zhang (2004) and Lean *et al.* (2004) found that, in general, the tests in the first group perform better than those in the second group and in the first group, the test recommended by Davidson and Duclos (2000) is one of the best choice. Hence we are using DD statistics in this paper.

Consider a random sample of $N_w$ observation $w_i, i = 1, 2, \ldots, N_w$ from a population of Winners portfolio with distribution function $F_w$. Define $D_W^1(x) = F_W(x)$ and let $D_W^s(x) = \int_{-\infty}^{x} D_W^{s-1}(u)du$, for any integer $s \geq 2$. Suppose $l_i, i = 1, 2, \ldots, N_L$ is a random sample from the population of losers portfolio with distribution function $F_L$. $D_L^s(x)$ is defined similarly. $W$ is said to dominate $L$ stochastically at order $s$ if $D_L^s(x) \geq D_W^s(x)$ for all $x$, with strict inequality for some $x$. If this is true, we write $W_{-s}L$. As $W$ and $L$ are correlated, $N_w = N_L = N$ and we let $(y_i, z_i)$ be a paired observation. Davidson and Duclos (2000) considered the following sample statistics:

$$\hat{D}_W^s(x) = \frac{1}{N(s-1)!} \sum_{i=1}^{N} (x - y_i)_+^{s-1},$$

$$\hat{D}_L^s(x) = \frac{1}{N(s-1)!} \sum_{i=1}^{N} (x - z_i)_+^{s-1},$$

$$\hat{V}_W^s(x) = \frac{1}{N} \left[ \frac{1}{N((s-1)!)^2} \sum_{i=1}^{N} (x - y_i)_+^{2(s-1)} - \hat{D}_W^s(x)^2 \right],$$

$$\hat{V}_L^s(x) = \frac{1}{N}\left[\frac{1}{N((s-1)!)^2}\sum_{i=1}^N (x-z_i)_+^{2(s-1)} - \hat{D}_L^s(x)^2\right],$$

$$\hat{V}_{W,L}^s(x) = \frac{1}{N}\left[\frac{1}{N((s-1)!)^2}\sum_{i=1}^N (x-y_i)_+^{s-1}(x-z_i)_+^{s-1} - \hat{D}_W^s(x)\hat{D}_L^s(x)\right],$$

and proposed the following normalized statistic:

$$T^s(x) = \frac{\hat{D}_W^s(x) - \hat{D}_L^s(x)}{\sqrt{\hat{V}^s(x)}}, \tag{1}$$

where $\hat{V}^s(x) = \hat{V}_W^s(x) + \hat{V}_L^s(x) - 2\hat{V}_{W,L}^s(x)$ for testing the equality of $D_L^s(x)$ and $D_W^s(x)$. They show that, under $H_0$: $D_L^s(x) = D_W^s(x)$, $T^s(x)$ is asymptotically distributed as a standard normal variate.

To test for stochastic dominance, $H_0$ has to be examined for the full support; which is empirically impossible. A compromise is to test $H_0$ for a pre-designed finite number of value of $x$. As multiple hypotheses are involved, test based on multiple comparison with procedure proposed by Bishop, Formby and Thistle (1992) has to be adopted. Following Bishop *et al.*, we consider fixed values $x_1, x_2, \ldots, x_k$ and use their corresponding statistics $T^s(x_i)$ for $i = 1, 2, \ldots, k$ to test the following hypotheses:

$$\begin{aligned}
&H_0 : D_W^s(x_i) = D_L^s(x_i) \quad \text{for all } x_i; \\
&H_A : D_W^s(x_i) \neq D_L^s(x_i) \quad \text{for some } x_i; \\
&H_{A1} : W \succ_s L; \quad \text{and} \\
&H_{A2} : L \succ_s W.
\end{aligned}$$

The overall null hypothesis $H_0$ is the logical intersection of several hypotheses (one for each $x_i$) while the overall alternative hypothesis $H_A$ is the logical union of these hypotheses. To control for the probability of rejecting the overall null hypothesis, Bishop *et al.* (1992) suggested using the studentized maximum modulus distribution with $k$ and infinite degrees of freedom, denoted by $M_{\infty,\alpha}^k$.

We denote the $1-\alpha$ percentile of $M_\infty^k$ by $M_{\infty,\alpha}^k$, which was tabulated by Stoline and Ury (1979) and adopt the following decision rules:

1. If $|T^s(x_i)| < M_{\infty,\alpha}^k$ for $i = 1, \ldots, k$ accept $H_0$;
2. If $-T^s(x_i) > M_{\infty,\alpha}^k$ for all $i$ and $T^s(x_i) > M_{\infty,\alpha}^k$ for some $i$ accept $H_{A1}$;
3. If $T^s(x_i) > M_{\infty,\alpha}^k$ for all $i$ and $-T^s(x_i) < M_{\infty,\alpha}^k$ for some $i$ accept $H_{A2}$;
4. If $T^s(x_i) > M_{\infty,\alpha}^k$ for some $i$ and $-T^s(x_i) > M_{\infty,\alpha}^k$ for some $i$ accept $H_A$.

In this paper, we also apply rule 1 to test the stochastic dominance between the market portfolio $M$ and the portfolio $M + (W - L)$. In this case, we simply replace $L$ by the market portfolio $M$ and replace $W$ by $M + (W - L)$ in rule 1.

The first problem of appointing the DD statistics is the power of the statistics. Tse and Zhang (2004) and Lean *et al.* (2004) studied the power of the DD statistics and find that the power of DD statistics is reasonably good for sample size of 2000 and basically DD statistic for any order fails to be normally distributed for any sample size smaller than 2000. In this connection, we will recommend to use the DD statistics with sample size greater than 2000.

Another problem of adopting DD statistics is the choice of the grid points. In practice, choosing more the grid points will be better in the comparison of the stochastic dominance between two distributions. However, the critical value $M_{\infty,\alpha}^k$ relies on a choice of k independent grid points. Too many grid points will be dependent. In this connection, Lean *et al.* (2004) recommended to choose 10 major grid points so that the grid points are far enough to be reasonably independent, while we can choose finer partitions between any two consecutive grid points, to make sure that there are no dramatical changes in the sign and the magnitudes of the DD statistics between any two major consecutive grid points. The critical values based on the 10 major grid points and very large sample size are 3.691, 3.25 and 3.043 for 1%, 5%, and 10% levels of significance respectively.

## Acknowledgment

The first author would also like to thank Professor Robert B. Miller and Professor Howard E. Thompson for their continuous guidance and encouragement. Special thanks also to Professor Cheng-Few Lee and the anonymous referees for their valuable comments that have significantly improved this manuscript. Our deepest thanks to Hooi Hooi Lean for her assistance. The research was partially supported by the Research Grant from the National University of Singapore.

## References

Ang, A., J. Chen and Y. H. Xing, "Downside Risk and the Momentum Effect." NBER Working Paper No. 8643 (2001).

Anderson, C., "Nonparametric Tests of Stochastic Dominance in Income Distributions." *Econometrica* 64, 1183–1193 (1996).

Barberis, N., A. Shleifer and R. W. Vishny, "A Model of Investor Sentiment." *Journal of Financial Economics* 49, 307–343 (1998).

Barberis, N., M. Huang and T. Sartos, "Prospect Theory and Asset Prices." *Quarterly Journal of Economics* 116, 1–53 (2001).

Baron, D. P., "On the Utility Theoretic Foundations of Mean-Variance Analysis." *Journal of Finance*, 32(5), 1683–1697 (1977).

Bawa, V. S., "Safety-First, Stochastic Dominance, and Optimal Portfolio Choice." *Journal of Financial and Quantitative Analysis* 13, 255–271 (1978).

Beach, C. M. and R. Davidson, "Distribution-Free Statistical Inference with Lorenz Curves and Income Shares." *Review of Economic Studies* 50, 723–735 (1983).

Bekaert, G. and C. R. Harvey, "Emerging Equity Market Volatility." *Journal of Financial Economics* 43(1), 29–77 (1977).

Bekaert, G., R. J. Hodrik and D. A. Marshall, "The Implications of First Order Risk Aversion for Asset Market Risk Premiums." *Journal of Monetary Economics* 40, 3–39 (1997).

Berk, J. B., R. C. Green and V. Naik, "Optimal Investment, Growth Options, and Security Returns." *Journal of Finance* 54, 1553–1607 (1999).

Bernard, V. L. and H. N. Seyhun, "Does Post-Earnings-Announcement Drift in Stock Prices Reflect a Market Inefficiency? A Stochastic Dominance Approach." *Review of Quantitative Finance and Accounting* 9, 17–34 (1997).

Bishop, J. A., J. P. Formly and P. D. Thistle, "Convergence of the South and Non-South Income Distributions." *American Economic Review* 82, 262–272 (1992).

Bookstaber, R. and R. Clarke, "Option Portfolio Strategies: Measurement and Strategies." *Journal of Business* 57, 469–492 (1984).

Booth, J. R., H. Tehranian and G. L. Trennepohl, "Efficiency Analysis and Option Portfolio Selection." *Journal of Financial and Quantitative Analysis* 20, 435–450 (1985).

Chan, L. K. C., N. Jegadeesh and J. Lakonishok, "Momentum Strategies." *Journal of Finance* 51, 1681–1713 (1996).

Chordia, T. and L. Shivakumar, "Momentum, Business Cycle and Time-Varying Expected Returns." *Journal of Finance* 57, 985–1019 (2002).

Conrad, J. and G. Kaul, "An Anatomy of Trading Strategies." *Review of Financial Studies* 11, 489–519 (1998).

Chow, K. V., "Marginal Conditional Stochastic Dominance, Statistical Inference, and Measuring Portfolio Performance." *Journal of Financial Research* 24, 289–307 (2001).

Daniel, K., D. Hirshleifer and A. Subrahmanyam, "Investor Psychology and Security Market Under- and Over-reactions." *Journal of Finance* 53, 1839–1886 (1998).

Davidson, R. and J. Y. Duclos, "Statistical Inference For Stochastic Dominance and For the Measurement of Poverty and Inequality." *Econometrica* 68, 1435–1464 (2000).

Dittmar, R. F., "Nonlinear Pricing Kernels, Kurtosis Preference, and Evidence from the Cross Section of Equity Returns." *Journal of Finance* 57, 369–403 (2002).

Falk, H. and H. Levy, "Market Reaction to Quarterly Earnings' Announcements: A Stochastic Dominance Based Test of Market Efficiency." *Management Science* 35, 425–446 (1989).

Fishburn, P. C., *Decision and Value Theory*. New York: Wiley (1964).

Grinblatt, M., S. Titman and R. Wermers, "Momentum Strategies, Portfolio Performance and Herding: A Study of Mutual Fund Behavior." *American Economic Review* 85, 1088–1105 (1995).

Grundy, B. D. and J. S. Martin, "Understanding the Nature of Risks and the Sources of Rewards to Momentum Investing." *Review of Financial Studies* 14, 29–78 (2001).

Hadar, J. and W. R. Russell, "Stochastic Dominance and Diversification." *Journal of Economic Theory* 3, 288–305 (1971).

Hanoch, G. and H. Levy, "Efficiency Analysis of Choices Involving Risk." *Review of Economic Studies* 36, 335–346 (1969).

Harvey, C. R. and A. Siddique, "Conditional Skewness in Asset Pricing Tests." *Journal of Finance* 55, 1263–1295 (2000).

Hong, H., T. Lim and J. C. Stein, "Bad News Travels Slowly: Size, Analyst Coverage and the Profitability of Momentum Strategies." *Journal of Finance* 55, 265–295 (2000).

Isakov, D. and B. Morard, "Improving Portfolio Performance with Option Strategies: Evidence from Switzerland." *European Financial Management* 7, 73–91 (2001).

Jarque, C. M. and A. K. Bera, "A Test for Normality of Observations and Regression Residuals." *International Statistical Review* 55, 163–172 (1987).

Jarrow, R., "The Relationship between Arbitrage and First Order Stochastic Dominance." *Journal of Finance* 41, 915–921 (1986).

Jegadeesh, N. and S. Titman, "Returns to Buying Winners and Selling Losers: Implications for Stock Market Efficiency." *Journal of Finance* 48, 65–91 (1993).

Jegadeesh N. and S. Titman, "Overreaction, Delayed Reaction and Contrarian Profits." *Review of Financial Studies* 8, 973–993 (1995).

Jegadeesh N. and S. Titman, "Profitability of Momentum Strategies: An Evaluation of Alternative Explanations." *Journal of Finance* 56, 699–720 (2001).

Johnson, T. C., "Rational Momentum Effects." *Journal of Finance* 57, 585–608 (2002).

Kaur, A. B. L., S. P. Rao and H. Singh, "Testing for Second Order Stochastic Dominance of Two Distributions." *Econometric Theory* 10, 849–866 (1994).

Larsen, G. A. Jr. and B. G. Resnick, "A Performance Comparison between Cross-Sectional Stochastic Dominance and Traditional Event Study Methodologies." *Review of Quantitative Finance and Accounting* 12, 103–112 (1999).

Lean, H. H., W. K. Wong and X. B. Zhang, "A Study of the Power of the Stochastic Dominance Tests." Working Paper, National University of Singapore (2004).

Lee, C. M. and B. Swaminathan, "Price Momentum and Trading Volume." *Journal of Finance* 55, 2017–2069 (2000).

Levy, H and Y. Kroll, "Efficiency Analysis with Borrowing and Lending Criteria and their Effectiveness." *Review of Economics and Statistics* 2, 13–37 (1979).

Lewellen, J. "Momentum and Autocorrelation in Stock Returns." *Review of Financial Studies* 15, 533–563 (2002).

Li, C. K. and W. K. Wong, "A Note on Stochastic Dominance for Risk Averters and Risk Takers." *RAIRO Recherche Operationnelle* 33, 509–524 (1999).

Markowitz, H., "Portfolio Selection." *Journal of Finance* 7, 77–91 (1952).

McFadden, D., "Testing for stochastic dominance," in *Studies in the Economics of Uncertainty*, T. B. Fomby and T. K. Seo, (eds.), Springer Verlag: New York (1989).

Meyer, J., "Second Degree Stochastic Dominance with Respect to a Function." *International Economic Review* 18, 476–487 (1977).

Rouwenhorst, K. G., "International momentum strategies." *Journal of Finance* 53, 267–284 (1998).

Sagi, J. S. and M. S. Seaholes, "Firm-Level Momentum: Theory and Evidence." Working Paper, University of California at Berkeley (2001).

Seyhun, H. N., "Can Omitted Risk Factors Explain the January Effect? A Stochastic Dominance Approach." *Journal of Financial and Quantitative Analysis* 28, 195–212 (1993).

Stoline, M. R. and H. K. Ury, "Tables of the Studentized Maximum Modulus Distribution and an Application to Multiple Comparison among Means." *Technometrics* 21, 87–93 (1979).

Tobin, J., "Liquidity Preference as Behavior towards Risk." *Review of Economics Studies* 25, 65–86 (1958).

Whitmore, G. A., "Statistical tests for stochastic dominance," In *Stochastic Dominance: An Approach to Decision Making under Risk*, G. A. Whitmore and M. C. Findlay, (eds.), Lexington Book, Lexington: MA (1978).

Tse, Y. K. and X. Zhang, "A Monte Carlo Investigation of Some Tests for Stochastic Dominance." *Journal of Statistical Computation and Simulation* 74, 361–378 (2004).

Wong, W. K. and C. K. Li, "A Note on Convex Stochastic Dominance Theory." *Economics Letters* 62, 293–300 (1999).

Xu, K., "Asymptotically Distribution-Free Statistical Test for Generalized Lorenz Curves: An Alternative Approach." *Journal of Income Distribution* 7, 45–62 (1997).

## Chapter 11

# The Shift Function for the Extended Vasicek Model

Shyan Yuan Lee
*National Taiwan University, Taiwan, R.O.C*

Cheng Hsi Hsieh
*National Taipei College of Business, Taiwan, R.O.C*

This study has two main purposes. The paper first derives the shift function and bond price formulas for the Hull–White extended Vasicek model, which simultaneously fits current yield curve and volatility curve. The result of Kijima and Nagayama (1994) is extended by allowing the instantaneous standard deviation of the short rate to be time-dependent, which permits the closed-form formulas for the shift function and bond price to be derived. By applying these formulas, the shift function and the bond price at each node can be obtained without calculation on a tree. Some numerical examples are given to demonstrate the effectiveness of these formulas. The second purpose of this study is to discuss how to estimate the "unobservable" time-dependent standard deviation of the short rate from the "observable" spot rate volatility curve. The theoretical relation between the time-dependent standard deviation of the short rate and the volatility curve of the spot rate is derived. This paper demonstrates this relation for two different functional forms of the time-dependent standard deviation of the short rate, and also shows how to estimate the time-dependent standard deviation via this relation.

**Keywords:** Shift function; yield curve; volatility curve; extended Vasicek model; trinomial tree.

## 1. Introduction

Financial economists have long been interested in modeling the term structure of interest rates. There are two methods of constructing the term structure model—the equilibrium model and the arbitrage-free model. Equilibrium models (e.g. Cox, Ingersoll, and Ross, 1985) usually start with assumptions about economic variables and derive a process for the short rate. They then explore what the process implies for bond prices and option prices. In general, bond prices and option prices must satisfy a partial differential equation (PDE), in which case the closed-form solution for the PDE does not exist. For some specific processes of short rates, however, (e.g. the Ornstein–Uhlenbeck process and the square-root process) the equilibrium models do have closed-form solutions. Though the closed-form solution has the advantage of computing prices of interest rate assets, such equilibrium models have a serious drawback in that they are not consistent with the current term structure. Because of this drawback, financial economists prefer to construct the arbitrage-free model, which is consistent with the current term structure.

Three main approaches to construct arbitrage-free models have previously been proposed that involve modeling the discount bond prices (e.g. Ho and Lee, 1986), the instantaneous forward rates (e.g. Heath, Jarrow, and Morton, 1990, 1992), and the short rate (e.g. Black, Derman, and Toy, 1990; Black and Karasinski, 1991; Hull and White, 1990). Since these arbitrage-free models generally do not have closed-form solutions for bond or option prices, the tree valuation approach is used to price interest rate derivatives. Moreover, if arbitrage-free models begin by modeling the discount bond prices or the instantaneous forward rates, both processes usually result in non-Markovian models that cannot be analyzed by a tree with the recombining property. In this circumstance, the Monte-Carlo simulation approach is often used. In contrast, when the short rate is modeled, the resulting model is generally of the Markov type, to which the tree approach can easily be applied. In order to avoid the problems associated with a non-recombining tree or Monte Carlo simulation, modeling the short rate has become more popular in recent years. The ideas presented in this paper follow this trend and investigate the Hull–White model.

Hull and White (1990) provided the extended Vasicek model as follows:

$$dr(t) = (\phi(t) - a(t)r(t))dt + \sigma(t)dz_t, \tag{1}$$

where $a(t)$ is the mean-reversion rate of the short rate and dz is a Wiener process. If $\phi(t)$ and $\sigma(t)$ are allowed to be time-dependent, the extended Vasicek model fits both the current term structure and the current volatilities of all interest rates. However, although this model is suitable for the initial market environment, the pricing formulas for bonds and options cannot be readily utilized. Hull and White (1994) then proposed a robust two-stage procedure to construct a trinomial tree for the short rate which follows the process as:

$$dr(t) = (\phi(t) - ar(t))dt + \sigma dz_t, \tag{2}$$

where $a$ and $\sigma$ are positive constants.

Kijima and Nagayama (1994) proposed a similar numerical procedure. Within the Hull–White model, Kijima and Nagayama obtained the shift function, $\theta(t)$, directly from the current term structure without any calculation on a trinomial tree. They also proposed a new procedure to construct a trinomial tree for the short rate by focusing on symmetric movements of Wiener processes, and provided numerical evidence to support the effectiveness of their approach. Moreover, to apply the tree approach to the model Equation (1), Hull and White (1996) and Kijima and Nagayama (1996) extended their tree approaches to account for the situation where $a$ and $\sigma$ are time-dependent, or, more generally, where they are both time- and state-dependent.

Although the numerical procedures of Hull and White (1994) and Kijima and Nagayama (1994) are different, the theoretical model for both approaches is the same. In particular, the theoretical model is a special case of the extended Vasicek model, with a constant mean-reversion rate of the short rate, $a$, and a constant standard deviation of the short rate. In this study, the theoretical model is further extended to include time-dependent standard deviation, $\sigma(t)$. The rationale for this extension is that interest rates have become more volatile since macro policy changed in October 1979, and hence it is desirable to build a model which simultaneously reflects the time-varying volatility of interest rates and incorporates more market information. Thus, setting the standard deviation of the short rate to be time-dependent may be more appropriate than to be constant. This provides the incentive to explore the model simultaneously fitting the current yield curve and volatility curve.

Given the current term structure and the current volatilities of all interest rates, the closed-form formulas for the shift function and the bond price are derived in this study. These formulas are particularly useful when a trinomial tree for the short rate is constructed to price interest rate derivatives. For the yield curve which is differentiable with time, and the volatility curve which can be integrated with time, the value of the shift function can first be calculated using the formula without any calculation on a tree. This value can then be applied to the tree-building procedures proposed by either Hull and White (1996) or Kijima and Nagayama (1996) to build a trinomial tree. According to Kijima and Nagayama's (1994) study, constructing the tree in this way is more efficient than constructing the tree directly by calculating shift function on the tree. Analogously, the derived bond price formula can be used to calculate the bond price at each node without any calculation on the tree. To demonstrate the effectiveness of this procedure, these formulas are applied to numerical examples where the yield curve and the volatility curve are exponential functions. When the exact function of the volatility curve is difficult to identify, the volatility curve can be set to a step function. The similar closed-form formulas for this case are also derived, and numerical examples are provided to verify the effectiveness of the formulas.

The rest of this paper is organized as follows. Section 2 briefly describes the two different tree-building procedures proposed by Hull and White (1994) and Kijima and Nagayama (1994), and also introduces the extended version of both tree-building procedures, Hull and White (1996), and Kijima and Nagayama (1996). In Section 3, the shift function and the bond price formulas for the model of Equation (2) are derived with time-dependent $\sigma(t)$. Some numerical examples are given to demonstrate the effectiveness of pricing interest rate derivatives with the formulas. In Section 4, formula related $\sigma(t)$ to the volatility curve of the spot rate is derived. The estimation of $\sigma(t)$ from the volatility curve of the spot rate is also discussed. Section 5 concludes this paper.

## 2. Numerical Procedures for the One-Factor Interest Rate Model

The formulas derived in this paper provide an efficient way of constructing a trinomial tree for the short rate, and of calculating the bond price at each node. These formulas can be applied to the two tree approaches mentioned above. In this section, Hull and White (1994) and Kijima and Nagayama (1994) tree-building procedures are briefly introduced. Then the extended version of both procedures discussed in Hull and White (1996) and Kijima and Nagayama (1996) are summarized for the situation where $\sigma$ is time-dependent, or, more generally, $\sigma$ is both time- and state-dependent.

### 2.1. *Hull and white interest rate tree*

Hull and White (1994) considered the one-factor term structure model that follows the process as Equation (2). In this model, $\phi(t)$ is determined so as to make the model consistent with the initial yield curve, but the volatility parameters $a$ and $\sigma$ are held constant. The valuation formula of a European option on a pure discount bond can easily be derived from this model. However, a valuation formula for American-type options does not exist because this option's value is conditional on future movements of the short rate $r$. Hull and White (1994) proposed a robust two-stage procedure to construct a trinomial tree to represent movements in $r$.

In the first stage, Hull and White decomposed $r(t)$ as $r(t) = x(t) + \theta(t)$ (where $\theta(t)$ is the shift function) and constructed a trinomial tree for $x(t)$ which follows the process as:

$$dx(t) = -axdt + \sigma dz_t, \quad x(0) = 0. \tag{3}$$

They provided some criteria to determine the shape of the trinomial tree. Probabilities at each node are computed by matching the mean and variance of $dx(t)$ over the next time interval $\Delta t$. The vertical distance between the nodes was set as $\Delta x = \sqrt{3V}$, where $V$ is the variance of $dx(t)$ over the next time interval $\Delta t$. Based on these settings, a trinomial tree for $x(t)$, which is initially zero and follows the process in Equation (3), can be constructed.

The second stage in the tree construction is to convert the tree for $x(t)$ into a tree for $r(t)$, which involves forward induction. Based on the current term structure, $\theta(t)$ is computed at each time period, and the tree for $x(t)$ is converted to a tree for $r(t)$ period-by-period. Advancing from time zero to the end of the tree, the location of the nodes at each time step was adjusted so as to match the initial term structure. This produces a tree for $r(t)$ that is consistent with the initial term structure.

When $\sigma$ in Equation (2) is a function of time, the above tree-building procedure requires modification to additionally provide an identical match to the initial volatility environment. If $\sigma$ is time-dependent, the variance of $dx(t)$ and the vertical distance between the nodes vary with time. The tree for $dx(t)$ will, then, not be recombining and quickly explode. Hull and White (1996) discussed how to overcome this difficulty by extending the Hull and White (1994) tree-building procedure to construct a tree for $x(t)$ with $\sigma(t)$. Analogous to the constant $a$ and $\sigma$ case, Hull and White (1996) first built a tree for $x(t)$, where

$$dx(t) = -a(t)x(t)dt - \sigma(t)dz_t.$$

They defined $(i, j)$ as the node which represents $t = i\Delta t$ and $x = j\Delta x$, and denoted $x_{i,j}$ as the value of $x$ at node $(i, j)$. The vertical space between adjacent nodes at time $t_{i+1}$ is set equal to $\sqrt{3V_i}$, where $V_i = \sigma(t_i)^2(1-e^{-2a(t_i)\Delta t})/2a(t_i)$. If the value of $x$ at the $j$th node at time $i\Delta t$ is $x_{i,j}$, the mean and standard deviation of $x$ at time $(i + 1)\Delta t$ conditional on $x = x_{i,j}$ at time $i\Delta t$ are approximately $x_{i,j} + M_i x_{i,j}$ and $\sqrt{V_i}$ respectively, where $M_i = (e^{-a(t_i)\Delta t} - 1)$. These are matched by branching from $x_{i,j}$ to either $x_{i+1,k-1}$, $x_{i+1,k}$, or $x_{i+1,k+1}$, where $k$ is chosen so that $x_{i+1,k}$ is as close as possible to $x_{i,j} + M_i x_{i,j}$. The displacements, $\theta(t)$, are then calculated so that the tree can match the initial term structure. This produces a tree for $r(t)$ consistent with the initial term structure and initial volatility.

## 2.2. *Kijima and Nagayama interest rate tree*

Kijima and Nagayama (1994) provided an alternative trinomial tree for Equation (3). They constructed the trinomial tree based on symmetric movements of the

Wiener process rather than asymmetric movements of $x(t)$. They discretized the time parameter $t$ and approximate Equation (3) by

$$\Delta x_i = -a x_i \Delta t + \sigma \Delta z_i \tag{4}$$

where $x_i = x(i \Delta t)$, $z_i = z(i \Delta t)$, and $\Delta x_i = x_{i+1} - x_i$, $\Delta z_i = z_{i+1} - z_i$ for $i = 0, 1, 2, \ldots, N - 1$. Since $z_i$ is normally distributed with mean zero and variance $t$, which requires the recombining property of the tree, they assumed that movements of the discretized Wiener process follow:

$$\sigma \Delta z_i = \begin{cases} \beta (1 - a \Delta t)^i & \text{with probability } p_i, \\ 0 & \text{with probability } 1 - 2 p_i, \\ -\beta (1 - a \Delta t)^i & \text{with probability } p_i, \end{cases} \tag{5}$$

where $\beta$ and $p_i$ are determined so as to satisfy the variance condition of $z_i$. Based on Equations (4) and (5), they obtained a tree with the recombining property to represent movements of $x(t)$. The value of $x$ at time $i \Delta t$ is:

$$j\beta(1 - a \Delta t)^{i-1}, \quad -i \leq j \leq i.$$

Increments in $x$ at time $i \Delta t$ decrease with respect to $i$, which characterizes the mean reverting property.[1]

Similar to Hull and White (1996), Kijima and Nagayama (1996) extended the above numerical procedure to be applicable to the model that follows the process as:

$$dr(t) = a(t)[\phi(t) - r(t)]dt + \sigma(r, t)dz_i$$

They decomposed $r(t)$ as $r(t) = x(t) + \theta(t)$ and defined

$$dx(t) = -a(t)x(t)dt + \delta(x, t)dz_t, \quad 0 \leq t \leq T; x(0) = 0. \tag{6}$$

To construct a tree for $dx(t)$, Kijima and Nagayama (1996) used the following equation to approximate Equation (6):

$$\Delta x_i = -a_i x_i \Delta t + \sigma(x_i + \theta_i, i \Delta t) \Delta z_i.$$

---

[1] However, this feature may cause the geometry of the tree to shrink as time advances. Kijima and Nagayama provided a sufficient condition to ensure the tree's completion. See Kijima and Nagayama (1994).

Since $\sigma(x_i + \theta_t, i\Delta t)\Delta z_i$ is a normal distribution with mean zero and variance, they assumed the following discretized Wiener process with the recombining property:

$$\sigma(x_i + \theta_i, i\Delta t)\Delta z_i = \begin{cases} \beta_i & \text{with probability } p(i, x_i), \\ 0 & \text{with probability } 1 - 2p(i, x_i), \\ -\beta_i & \text{with probability } p(i, x_i), \end{cases}$$

where $\beta_i = \beta_0 \prod_{k=1}^{i}(1 - a_k \Delta t)$ for $i = 1, 2, \ldots, N-1$. Kijima and Nagayama (1996) derived the formulas for $\beta_i$ and $p(i, x_i)$ so as to satisfy the variance condition of $\sigma(x_i + \theta_i, i\Delta t)\Delta z_i$ and then obtained the discretized stochastic process $\{x_i\}$ as:

$$x_{i+1} = \begin{cases} x_i(1 - a_i\Delta t) + \beta_i & \text{with probability } p(i, x_i), \\ x_i(1 - a_i\Delta t) & \text{with probability } 1 - 2p(i, x_i), \\ x_i(1 - a_i\Delta t) - \beta & \text{with probability } p(i, x_i), \end{cases}$$

for $i = 1, 2, \ldots, N-1$ and $x_0 = 0$. Since, $x_i(1 - a_i\Delta t) = j\beta_i$ the value of $x$ at time $i\Delta t$ is $\{j\beta_{i-1}, -i \leq j \leq i\}$ for $i = 1, 2, \ldots, N$ and $x_0 = 0$.[2]

In the second stage, $\theta(t)$ is computed at each time period by using forward induction, and the tree for $x(t)$ is converted to a tree for $r(t)$ period by period in order to match the initial term structure.

## 3. Formulas for the Shift Function and the Bond Price

The Hull and White (1996) and Kijima and Nagayama (1996) tree approaches are applicable to the extended Vasicek model following Equation (1). Neither approach uses a formula to compute the value of the shift function. If there were a formula for the shift function, however, the tree-building efficiency in the second stage would be improved, as suggested by Kijima and Nagayama (1994). Analogously, if the formula for the bond price existed, the bond price at each node could easily be calculated, particularly when $t$ approaches zero. In this section, the closed-form solutions of the shift function and the bond price for the extended Vasicek model with constant $a$ and time-dependent $\sigma(t)$ are derived.

---

[2]The tree-building procedure mentioned above has two main drawbacks. First, it is difficult to determine a sequence $\{\beta_i\}$ to satisfy the variance condition of $\sigma\Delta z$. Second, if $i\beta_{i-1} \geq (i+1)\beta_i$ for some $i \leq N$, the tree is non-increasing, i.e. the geometry of the tree shrinks as time proceeds. For detailed discussion on how to overcome these two difficulties, please refer to Kijima and Nagayama (1996).

Assume $a(t) = a$ is a constant. Let $r(t) = x(t) + \theta(t)$ where $x(t)$ and $\theta(t)$ follow the processes as:

$$\begin{cases} dx(t) = -ax(t)dt - \sigma(t)dz, & x(0) = 0, \\ d\theta(t) = (\phi(t) - a\theta(t))dt, & \theta(0) = r(0) \end{cases} \tag{7}$$

Proposition 1 shows the formula of $\theta(t)$, which can be calculated directly from the initial term structure of the spot rate without any calculation on a tree. The Proof of Proposition 1 can be found in Appendix.

**Proposition 1**

*Let $Y(t)$ for $t \geq 0$ be the current yield curve, then*

$$\theta(t) = [tY(t)]' + \int_0^t \frac{\sigma^2(S)}{a}\left(e^{-a(t-s)} - e^{-2a(t-s)}\right)ds.$$

It is easy to verify that the formula for $\theta(t)$ is equivalent to the one in Kijima and Nagayama (1994) when $\sigma(t) = \sigma$. Proposition 2 below, explicitly shows the formula for the pure discount bond price. This proposition is useful when the bond option formula in Merton (1973) is used to evaluate a European call option that has exercise price $X$ and expires at time $s$ on a discount bond expiring at time $T (T \geq s \geq t)$. The bond option formula in Merton (1973) is

$$c(t, s, T) = P(t, T)N(h) - XP(t, s)N(h - \sigma_p), \tag{8}$$

where

$$h = \frac{1}{\sigma_p}\ln\frac{P(t, T)}{P(t, s)X} + \frac{\sigma_p}{2},$$

$$\sigma_p^2 = \int_t^s \sigma^2(\tau)[B(\tau, T) - B(\tau, s)]^2 ds,$$

$$B(t, T) = \frac{1 - e^{-a(\tau - t)}}{a}.$$

Note that if $\sigma(t)$ is time-independent (i.e. $\sigma$ is a constant), the bond option formula in Equation (8) is the result in Jamshidian (1989).

**Proposition 2**

*Let $P(t, T)$ be the price at time $t$ of a pure discount bond that pays $1 at time $T$, then*

$$p(t, T) = \frac{p(0, T)}{p(0, t)}\exp\left\{B(t, T)[(tY(t))' - r(t)]\right.$$

$$\left. -\frac{1}{2}\int_0^t [b(u, T) - b(u, t)]^2 du\right\}.$$

where $b(t, T) = \int_t^T \sigma(t)e^{-a(s-t)}ds$. The proof can also be found in Appendix.

Since it can be complicated to identify the function form of $\sigma^2(t)$, a step function can be used to approximate the function of $\sigma^2(t)$. Propositions 1 and 2 where $\sigma^2(t)$ is a step function are re-derived. First, the time period $[0, T]$ is divided into sub-periods $[t_0, t_1], [t_1, t_2], \ldots, [t_{N-1}, t_N]$, with $t_0 = 0, t_N = T$. Second, the function form of $\sigma^2(t)$ is assumed to be $\sigma^2(t) = \sigma_1^2$ for $t_0 \le t \le t_1$ and $\sigma_n^2$ for $t_{n-1} < t \le t_n$ with $n = 2, 3, \ldots, N$. Through the end of this paper, let $\sum_{i=\gamma}^{\delta} f(i) = 0$ if $\delta < \gamma$, where $f(i)$ is the function of $i$. By substituting this functional form of $\sigma^2(t)$ into the formulas in Propositions 1 and 2, the following results can be obtained.

**Proposition 3**

*Let $Y(t)$ for $t \ge 0$ be the current yield curve, then formulas for the shift function and the bond price are provided respectively by:*

$$\theta(t) = [t\,Y(t)'] + \sum_{i=1}^{n-1} \frac{\sigma_i^2}{2a^2} \left[2e^{-a(t-t_i)} - 2e^{-a(t-t_{i-1})} - e^{-2a(t-t_i)} + e^{-2a(t-t_{i-1})}\right]$$

$$+ \frac{\sigma_n^2}{2a^2} \left[1 - e^{-a(t-t_{n-1})}\right]^2$$

*and*

$$P(t, T) = \frac{P(0, T)}{P(0, t)} \exp\{B(t, T)[(t\,Y(t))' - r(t)]$$

$$- \frac{1}{4a^3} \left[\sum_{i=1}^{n-1} \sigma_i^2 (e^{-aT} - e^{-at})^2 (e^{-2at_i} - e^{-2at_{i-1}})\right.$$

$$\left. + \sigma_n^2 (e^{-aT} - e^{-at})^2 (e^{-2at} - e^{-2at_{n-1}})\right]$$

*for $t_0 \le t \le t_1$ with $n = 1$ and $t_{n-1} < t \le t_n$ with $n = 2, 3, \ldots, N$.*

Following are two examples to illustrate the effectiveness of the formulas presented above.

**Example 1**

Let $Y(t) = 0.08 - 0.05e^{-0.18t}$ (which corresponds approximately to the term structure in the US at the beginning of 1994) and $\sigma^2(t) = \sigma^2 e^{-mt}$. Suppose that $a = 0.1, m = 0.09, \sigma = 0.02$, and $T = 5$. From Propositions 1 and 2, $\theta(0) = 0.03$, $\theta(1) = 0.0459$, $\theta(2) = 0.0583$, $\theta(3) = 0.0678$, $\theta(4) = 0.0751$, $\theta(5) = 0.0806$, and $P(0, 5) = 0.7420$, $P(1, 5) = 0.8948\ \exp(-3.2968r(1))$, $P(2, 5) = 0.9412\ \exp(-2.5918r(2))$, $P(3, 5) = 0.9740\ \exp(-1.8127r(3))$,

$P(4, 5) = 0.9936 \exp(-0.9516r(4))$, where $r(t)$ is the short rate at $t$. After the tree for $r(t)$ has been constructed, the bond price at each node can be calculated by applying the bond price formula to the corresponding $r(t)$ at each node. Moreover, supposing that $X = 0.8$, from Equation (8) the current values $(t = 0)$ of the European call options which expire at $s = 1, 2, 3, 4$ on a pure discount bond expiring at $T = 5$ can be calculated as $c(0, 1, 5) = 0.0078$, $c(0, 2, 5) = 0.0247$, $c(0, 3, 5) = 0.0562$ and $c(0, 4, 5) = 0.1017$.

## Example 2

Let $Y(t) = 0.08 - 0.05e^{-0.18t}$ and $\sigma^2(t) = \sigma_n^2 = \sigma^2 e^{-mt_n}$ for $t_0 \le t \le t_1$ with $n = 1$, and $t_{n-1} < t \le t_n$ with $n = 2, 3, \ldots, N$. From Proposition 3 and based on the same parameter values as those in Example 1, it can be verified that $\theta(0) = 0.03$, $\theta(1) = 0.0459$, $\theta(2) = 0.0583$, $\theta(3) = 0.0678$, $\theta(4) = 0.0750$, $\theta(5) = 0.0805$, and $P(1, 5) = 0.8949 \exp(-3.2968r(1))$, $P(2, 5) = 0.9412 \exp(-2.5918r(2))$, $P(3, 5) = 0.9741 \exp(-1.8127r(3))$, $P(4, 5) = 0.9936 \exp(-0.9516r(4))$. Similar to Example 1 by setting $X = 0.8$, the current values $(t = 0)$ of the European call options that expire at $s = 1, 2, 3, 4$ on a pure discount bond expiring at $T = 5$ can be calculated as $c(0, 1, 5) = 0.0075$, $c(0, 2, 5) = 0.0243$, $c(0, 3, 5) = 0.0562$ and $c(0, 4, 5) = 0.1017$.

## 4. Estimation of the Time-Dependent Standard Deviation of the Short Rate

The rationale for extending the standard deviation of the short rate to be time-dependent, $\sigma(t)$, is to simultaneously take into account the facts that interest rates have become more volatile, and the theoretical model has to incorporate market information as much as possible. Although setting the standard deviation of the short rate to be time-dependent may be more appropriate than to be constant, the standard deviation of the short rate is not observable. One can estimate the standard deviation of the short rate from the forward rate volatilities by calibrating the market price of instruments, such as cap, floor, and swaption. However, some countries may not have liquid markets for these products mentioned above. In this case, estimating the standard deviation of the short rate from spot rate volatilities seems to be appropriate. This section, then, explores how to estimate $\sigma(t)$ via the theoretical relation between $\sigma(t)$ and the spot rate volatility curve.

Based on Equation (7),

$$dr(t) = (\phi(t) - ar(t))dt - \sigma(t)dz_t.$$

By Arnold (1974), this stochastic linear equation has the following solution:

$$r(s) = e^{-a(s-t)}r(t) + e^{-as}\left(\int_t^s e^{ax}\phi(x)dx + \int_t^s e^{ax}\sigma(x)dz_x\right), \quad t \le s.$$

Moreover, recall that $R(t, T) = \int_t^T r(s)ds$, where $R(t, T)$ is the non-annualized spot rate ranges from $t$ to $T$. Therefore, $\mathrm{Var}_t[R(t, T)]$ can be obtained as the following:

$$\mathrm{Var}_t[R(t, T)] = \int_t^T \left[\int_x^T e^{-a(s-x)}\sigma(x)ds\right]^2 dx. \tag{9}$$

Equation (9) states the relation between $\mathrm{Var}_t[R(t, T)]$ and $\sigma(t)$. Since $\mathrm{Var}_t[R(t, T)]$ can be calculated from historical data, $\sigma(t)$ can be estimated through this relation. This section discusses how to estimate two functional forms of $\sigma(t)$, e.g. the exponential form and the step-function form.

Let, $\sigma^2(t) = \sigma^2 e^{-mt}$, $t = 0$, and $T = t$. The spot rate volatility can be expressed as:

$$\mathrm{Var}_0[R(0, t)] = \frac{\sigma^2}{a^2}\left[\frac{1}{m} + \frac{2a^2}{m(2s-m)(m-a)}e^{-mt}\right.$$
$$\left. - \frac{2}{m-a}e^{-at} + \frac{1}{2a-m}e^{-2at}\right]. \tag{10}$$

$\sigma(t)$ can then be estimated by choosing $a, \sigma^2, m$ to minimize the following function:

$$\min_{a,\sigma^2,m} \sum_t \left(\hat{\mathrm{V}}\mathrm{ar}_0[R(0, t)] - \mathrm{Var}_0[R(0, t)]\right)^2 \quad \text{for } t > 0,$$

where $\hat{\mathrm{V}}\mathrm{ar}_0[R(0, t)]$ is the variance of the spot rate $R(0, t)$, and $\mathrm{Var}_0[R(0, t)]$ is the theoretical variance given by Equation (10).

Besides of $\sigma^2(t) = \sigma^2 e^{-mt}$, $\sigma^2(t)$ can be set to be a step function defined as $\sigma^2(t) = \sigma_1^2$ for $t_0 \le t \le t_1$ and $\sigma_n^2$ for $t_{n-1} < t \le t_n$ with $n = 2, 3, \ldots, N$. The theoretical relation between this functional form of $\sigma^2(t)$ and $\mathrm{Var}_0[R(0, t)]$ can be derived as follow:

$$\mathrm{Var}_0[R(0, t)] = \sum_{i=1}^{n-1}\frac{\sigma_i^2}{a^2}\left[(t_i - t_{i-1}) - \frac{2}{a}\left(e^{-a(t-t_i)} - e^{-a(t-t_{i-1})}\right)\right.$$
$$\left. + \frac{1}{2a}\left(e^{-2a(t-t_i)} - e^{-2a(t-t_{i-1})}\right)\right] + \frac{\sigma_n^2}{a^2}\left[(t - t_{n-1})\right.$$

$$-\frac{2}{a}\left(1-\mathrm{e}^{-a(t-t_{n-1})}\right)+\frac{1}{2a}\left(1-\mathrm{e}^{-2a(t-t_{n-1})}\right)\Bigg] \qquad (11)$$

for $t_0 \leq t \leq t_1$ with $n = 1$ or $t_{n-1} < t \leq t_n$ with $[t_0, t_1]$.

Equation (11) seems very complicated, however, it has the following intuitive properties: First, for $t_{n-1} < t \leq t_n$ where $n = 1, 2, \ldots, N$, $\mathrm{Var}_0[R(0, t)]$ is a function of $a$ and $\sigma_i^2$ with $i = 1, 2, \ldots, n$. Second, Equation (11) is a strict increasing function of $t$. This is one of the properties of Wiener process that variance of $dz$ is proportional to the length of the time interval considered. Finally, if $\sigma^2(t)$ degenerates to a constant, Equation (11) degenerates to the following commonly-known equation:

$$\mathrm{Var}_0[R(0, t)] = \frac{\sigma^2}{a^2}\left[t - \frac{\mathrm{e}^{-2at}}{2a} + 2\frac{\mathrm{e}^{-at}}{a} - \frac{3}{2a}\right].$$

The theoretical relation between $\sigma^2(t)$ in the form of a step function and $\mathrm{Var}_0[R(0, t)]$ is expressed in Equation (11). The step function of $\sigma^2(t)$ can be estimated from the historical variance of spot rates via this relation. On estimating $a$ and $\sigma_i^2$ with $i = 1, 2, \ldots, N$, however, since there are $N + 1$ parameters to be estimated, the number of the variance of spot rates cannot be less than $N + 1$ in order to provide enough degrees of freedom to estimate $a$ and $\sigma_i^2$ for $i = 1, 2, \ldots, N$. There are some suggestions to estimate these $N + 1$ parameters:

1. Compute variances for $N + 1$ spot rates and then substitute these $N + 1$ variances into Equation (11) to form $N + 1$ equations. The $N + 1$ parameters can then be obtained by solving these $N + 1$ equations. Usually, it is not easy to solve non-linear simultaneous equations; however, the following suggestion will shorten the time to solve these $N + 1$ nonlinear simultaneous equations. First, compute only one variance for a spot rate in each sub-period except the sub-period $[t_0, t_1]$, where two variances of spot rates must be computed. Second, use the first two non-linear equations, which is formed by the two variances in the sub-period $[t_0, t_1]$, to solve two parameters, $a$ and $\sigma_i^2$. Once $a$ and $\sigma_i^2$ have been solved, other parameters, $\sigma_i^2$ with $i = 2, 3, \ldots, N$, can be solved sequentially and linearly.

2. Compute $M > N - 1$ variances of spot rates and then apply the nonlinear optimization method to estimate $a$ and $\sigma_i^2$ for $i = 1, 2, \ldots, N$. For example,

minimize the following nonlinear optimization equation by controlling $a$ and $\sigma_i^2$ for $i = 1, 2, \ldots, N$:

$$\underset{a, \sigma_i^2}{\text{Min}} \sum_{j=1}^{M} \left(\hat{\text{Var}}_0[R(0, t_j)] - \text{Var}_0[R(0, t_j)]\right)^2 \quad \text{for } t > 0 \text{ and } i = 1, 2, \ldots, N$$

where $M > N - 1$ is the number of variances of spot rates.

3. Equation (11) indicates that if the value of $a$ is known in advance, the relations of $\sigma_i^2$ for $i = 1, 2, \ldots, N$ are linear. Therefore, $\sigma_i^2$ can be easily calculated from the following equation by applying the grid search method:

$$\underset{\sigma_i^2}{\text{Min}} \sum_{j=1}^{M} \left(\hat{\text{Var}}_0[R(0, t_j)] - \text{Var}_0[R(0, t_j)]\right)^2 \quad \text{for } t > 0 \text{ and } i = 1, 2, \ldots, N.$$

$$(12)$$

To search the best estimates of $a$ and $\sigma_i^2$, $a$ is set between some reasonable interval in arbitrary increments and then $\sigma_i^2$ are computed for each $a$, respectively. After all possible $a$ and $\sigma_i^2$ are calculated, the best estimates of $a$ and $\sigma_i^2$ are those leading to the minimum of Equation (12).

The above three methods can be used to estimate $a$ and $\sigma_i^2$. After $\sigma^2(t)$ is estimated from the volatility curve of current spot rate, Proposition 3 can be utilized to build the Hull–White (1996) or the Kijima–Nagayama tree (1996), and hence any interest rate derivatives can be priced.

## 5. Conclusion

By setting the mean-reversion rate of the short rate at a constant and allowing the instantaneous standard deviation of the short rate to be time-dependent within the Hull and White extended Vasicek model, this study obtains closed-form formulas for the shift function and the bond price that are consistent with both the initial yield curve and the initial volatility curve. Moreover, the theoretical relation between time-dependent $\sigma^2(t)$ and the current volatility curve of spot rates is derived. When either Hull and White (1996) or Kijima and Nagayama (1996) tree-building procedures are used to construct a trinomial tree for the short rate, $\sigma^2(t)$ can be estimated from initial volatility curve first; and then the shift function is computed according to the derived formula rather than being calculated on a tree. After the tree is built, the derived bond price formula can be used to compute the bond price at each node. This shortens the computation time, particularly when the time interval of the tree is very small.

## Appendix

### *Proof of Proposition 1*

Although it can be proven with the Hull–White (1990) framework, Proposition 1 will be proven in the Heath–Jarrow–Morton (1992, hereafter HJM) framework with an exponential dampened volatility structure of the forward rate for two reasons: 1) the HJM model will degenerate to Hull–White (1990) model by setting the volatility of the instantaneous forward rate to be an exponential dampened form, and 2) the derivation of the shift function would be simpler in the HJM model.

With the HJM framework and the risk-neutral measure, the stochastic process of the instantaneous forward rate would be

$$\mathrm{d}f(t, T) = -b(t, T)\sigma(t, T)\mathrm{d}t - \sigma(t, T)\mathrm{d}\tilde{z}_t, \tag{A.1}$$

where $f(t, T)$ is the instantaneous forward rate, $\sigma(t, T)$ is the volatility structure of $f(t, T)$, and $\mathrm{d}\tilde{z}_t$ is a Wiener process. By setting $\sigma(t, T)$ to be $\sigma(t)e^{-a(T-t)}$, which is an exponential dampened form, the HJM model degenerate to Hull–White model (1990). Integrating both sides of Equation (A.1) with $t$ and realizing that $f(t, t) = r(t)$, the process of the short rate can be obtained as:

$$r(t) = f(0, t) - \int_0^t b(s, t)\sigma(s)e^{-a(t-s)}\mathrm{d}s + \int_0^t \sigma(s)e^{-a(t-s)}\mathrm{d}\tilde{z}_s \tag{A.2}$$

where $b(t, T) = -\int_t^T \sigma(t)e^{-a(u-t)}\mathrm{d}u$. Comparing Equation (A.2) with Equation (7) and noting that $r(t) = \theta(t) + x(t)$, it is easy to prove that the first two parts and the last part of the r.h.s of Equation (A.2) correspond to $\theta(t)$ and $x(t)$, respectively. Therefore, the shift function can be expressed as:

$$\theta(t) = f(0, t) + \int_0^t \left[ \int_s^t \sigma(s)e^{-a(u-s)}\mathrm{d}u \right] \sigma(s)e^{-a(t-s)}\mathrm{d}s$$

$$= [tY(t)]' + \int_0^t \frac{\sigma^2(S)}{a} \left( e^{-a(t-s)} - e^{-2a(t-s)} \right) \mathrm{d}s. \tag{A.3}$$

If $\sigma(t)$ is a constant, Equation (A.3) can be proven to degenerate to the result in Kijima and Nagayama (1994).

## Proof of Proposition 2

Under the risk-neutral measure, the price of a discount bond, $P(t, T)$, follows the process as:

$$\frac{\mathrm{d}P(t, T)}{P(t, T)} = r(t)\mathrm{d}t + b(t, T)\mathrm{d}\tilde{z}_i, \tag{A.4}$$

where $b(t, T) = -\int_t^T \sigma(t)e^{-a(u-t)}du$. Integrating both sides of Equation (A.4) gets

$$P(t, T) = \frac{P(0, T)}{P(0, t)}\exp\left\{ -\frac{1}{2}\int_0^t \left[b^2(s, T) - b^2(s, t)\right]\mathrm{d}s \right.$$
$$\left. + \int_0^t [b(s, T) - b(s, t)]\widetilde{d}z_s \right\}. \tag{A.5}$$

After substituting Equation (A.2) into Equation (A.5) to eliminate the $\mathrm{d}\tilde{z}_s$ term, Proposition 2 can then be proven. Analogously, if $\sigma(t)$ is a constant, the result in Proposition 2 can also degenerate to the result in Kijima and Nagayama (1994).

## References

Arnold, L., *Stochastic Differential Equations: Theory and Applications*. A Wiley Interscience Publication, John Wiley & Sons, 1974.

Black, F., E. Derman and W. Toy, "A One-Factor Model of Interest Rates and Its Application to Treasury Bond Options." *Financial Analysts Journal* 46, 33–39 (1990).

Black, F. and P. Karasinski, "Bond and Option Pricing when Short Rates are Lognormal." *Financial Analysts Journal* 47, 52–59 (1991).

Cox, J. C., J. E. Ingersoll and S. A. Ross, "A Theory of the Term Structure of Interest Rates." *Econometrica* 53, 385–407 (1985).

Heath, D., R. Jarrow and A. Morton, "Bond Pricing and the Term Structure of Interest Rates: A Discrete Time Approximation." *Journal of Financial and Quantitative Analysis* 25, 419–440 (1990).

Heath, D., R. Jarrow and A. Morton, "Bond Pricing and the Term Structure of Interest Rates: A New Methodology for Contingent Claims Valuation." *Econometrica* 60, 77–105 (1992).

Ho, T. S. and S. Lee, "Term Structure Movements and Pricing Interest Rate Contingent Claim." *Journal of Finance* 41, 1011–1028 (1986).

Hull, J. and A. White, "Pricing Interest-Rate-Derivative Securities." *The Review of Financial Studies* 3, 573–592 (1990).

Hull, J. and A. White, "Numerical Procedures for Implementing Term Structure Models I: Single-Factor Models." *Journal of Derivatives* 2, 7–16 (1994).

Hull, J. and A. White, "Using Hull–White Interest Rate Trees." *Journal of Derivatives* 4, 26–36 (1996).

Jamshidian, F., "An Exact Bond Option Formula." *Journal of Finance* 44, 205–209 (1989).

Kijima, M. and I. Nagayama, "Efficient Numerical Procedures for the Hull–White Extended Vasicek Model." *The Journal of Financial Engineering* 3, 275–292 (1994).

Kijima, M. and I. Nagayama, "A Numerical Procedure for the General One-Factor Interest Rate Model." *The Journal of Financial Engineering* 5, 317–337 (1996).

Merton, R. C., "Theory of Rational Option Pricing." *Bell Journal of Econometric and Management Science* 4, 141–183 (1973).

Chapter 12

# Beating or Meeting Earnings-Based Target Performance in CEOs' Annual Cash Bonuses*

Simon S. M. Yang
*Adelphi University, USA*

Prior studies show that the compensation committee often uses pre-specified target performance in CEOs' cash bonus plans to evaluate executives' ability to achieve the expected performance. Executives may face different incentive outcomes when they fall short of, meet, or beat the target performance. This paper examines whether the compensation committee places more weight on beating target performance than meeting target performance in contracting CEOs' cash bonuses. Specifically, three alternative measures are used, namely, permanent earnings, consensus of analysts' forecasts and average earnings growth as a proxy for target performance. It is found that the compensation committee seems to place more contract value on above-target than on-target performance. Result also shows that permanent earnings seem to be the strongest proxy that can be used to approximate target performance.

**JEL Classifications:** J33, M41.

**Keywords:** Cash bonus compensation; accounting earnings.

## 1. Introduction

The compensation packages granted to chief executive officers (CEOs) typically consist of some types of incentive plans — stock-based and cash bonuses. While stock-based compensation is often used to reward the manager's ability in a firm's future profitability and long-term growth opportunities (Narayanan, 1996; Paul, 1992), cash bonus plans are more frequently used to compensate executives' short-term performance. Firms often use cash bonus plans to motivate executives to be more productive and beat some target benchmarks in a short run. The cash bonus has been adopted primarily to provide short-term incentives to mitigate problems such as risk aversion (Smith and Watts, 1992; Holmstrom, 1979) and tenure horizon problems (Narayanan, 1985; Jensen and Meckling, 1979). When awarded with cash bonus plans,

---

* This paper has benefited from the reviews and comments from 12th Global Conference on the Theories and Practices of Security and Financial Market.

managers are found to have a higher incentive to choose projects that yield quicker results at the expense of higher net present value projects that yield cash flows later in time (Narayanan, 1985). Also, when executives approach the retirement horizon and their tenure with the firm is shorter than the firm's optimal investment horizon, executives tend to prefer cash bonuses over stock-based incentives because cash bonuses provide a fast and immediate reward.

A typical executive bonus plan consists of two parts: the *performance threshold* and *target performance.* The performance threshold features a pre-specified *minimum* desired performance standard that must be achieved before any bonuses can be paid out; the target performance reflects the shareholders' *expected* growth in accounting-based performance in the year ahead.[1] However, little has been understood about target performance because firms seldom disclose proprietary compensation details. The proxy statement of General Electric Corp. for the year of 2003, for example, states some general bases of target cash bonuses for executives including (1) financial performance (e.g., financial results, investor expectations, profitable growth, capital structure), (2) integrity of management (e.g., transparency management and corporate governance) and (3) non-financial evaluations (e.g., technology use, digitization initiatives, and customer relationships). The determinants of target performance are found to relate to firms' expectations on future investment and the extent of executives' positions and decision-making authority (Indjejikian and Nanda, 2002). Therefore, the targeted performance in executive compensation contracts reflects important information regarding shareholders' expectations of desired performance in both financial and non-financial areas. Through a formal contracting design in the cash bonus plan, target performance is used to convey the firm's expectations of desirable growth to its executives.

Since target performance is a goal-expected assessment measure, an executive can fall short of, meet, or beat the target expectation when a pre-specified benchmark is used to assess his ability in achieving the desired expectation in any given year. Beating (missing) the benchmark allows the firm's compensation committee to justify higher (lower) compensation

---

[1] For example, Michael Eisner, Disney's CEO, has an accounting-based performance cash bonus agreement, in which the cash bonus is measured as the excess of actual earnings per share (EPS) over target EPS multiplied by the number of shares outstanding. The target EPS reflects expected growth and is calculated from the average of EPS in past years (i.e., base EPS) multiplied by 1.075 (Crawford, Franze, and Smith, 1998).

levels for executives (Matsunaga and Park, 2001). In this paper, it is proposed that when CEOs beat the target benchmark and have above-target (or unexpectedly good) performance, it signals different information for executives' outstanding performance from when they just meet the target benchmark. I expect CEOs to receive incrementally more cash bonus rewards for achieving unexpectedly good performance than for meeting the expected standard. In other words, the unexpected above-target performance is projected to be viewed more importantly by the compensation committee than expected on-target performance because the unexpected performance indicates that CEOs have a better ability to manage the firm and are likely to make profitable returns in a short horizon.

Because details of CEOs' compensation contracts are not publicly available, this paper uses three alternative measures, namely, permanent earnings, consensus of analysts' forecasts, and average earnings growth, to approximate the expectations of a firm on target performance. These three measures have been used as an evaluation benchmark in the assessment of a manager's performance for different purposes; no studies, however, seem to examine them as a target expectation and compare their differences in cash bonuses. Permanent earnings are a measure used to illustrate a firm's value of revisions in expected future earnings (Koremendi and Lipe, 1987). The consensus of analysts' forecasts is a benchmark used to represent a broad estimate on financial and non-financial targets (Burgstahler and Eames, 2003). Earnings growth is often used to assess the expected growth of earnings and the sustainability and persistence of earnings patterns. These three performance benchmarks are all frequently used to approximate some types of expectations for a firm. In this paper, we test whether the executives' expected/unexpected performance (i.e., meeting/beating the benchmark of these three measures) has different impacts on their cash bonus plans.

With a total of 2,230 firm-year observations drawn from the intersection of data from ExecuComp and data sets containing accounting and financial information for firms in the US, we find that unexpected above-target performance has more contract value than expected on-target performance in an executive's cash bonus. When an executive beats the expected target benchmark, he enjoys more incremental compensation in the form of bonuses than when he meets the target. In three alternative measures, we find that using permanent earnings as a proxy for the expected benchmark is the strongest link between expected target performance and bonus rewards.

This paper is motivated by prior studies examining the executive cash bonus and pay–performance relation. Many studies show that executive bonus plans are associated with accounting decisions that generate higher accounting income. When bonuses are near upper or lower boundaries, executives tend to manipulate earnings accordingly (Healy, 1985; Chen and Lee, 1995; Holthausen, Larcker, and Sloan, 1995). From a perspective of missing an expected benchmark, Matsunaga and Park (2001) show that a significant adverse penalty is imposed on CEO annual cash bonuses when the firm's quarterly earnings fall short of the consensus of analysts' forecasts. Arora and Alam (1999) predict that firms adopting bonus plans are more likely to have lower expected earnings because it is then easier for managers to achieve this lower benchmark. In addition to those findings, this paper contributes to the compensation literature by providing evidence that the compensation committee views beating the expected target performance as more important than meeting the expected one. In the context of agency theory, this paper corroborates the link between performance evaluation and managerial incentive because an accounting-based measure is one of the most prevalently used performance measures. Accounting earnings have served multiple informational roles (e.g., valuation, future profitability) and contain multiple-period information (e.g., earnings persistence, sustainable earnings and accruals revisions) in executives' compensation contracts.[2] This paper suggests that unexpected earnings resulting from beating expected target performance may have different information roles from expected earnings in cash bonus plans.

In the next section, we describe components in executive bonuses and develop a testable hypothesis. Section 3 discusses using alternative measures as the proxy for target performance. Section 4 presents the research design and Section 5 describes the empirical models and sample selection. Section 6 concludes the study.

---

[2]The key link between agency theory and managerial compensation relies on (1) controllability — a performance measure should be adopted only when manager can control or has a significant influence; (2) quality of performance measure — how well the performance measure is aligned with executives' actions and shareholders' values (Indjejikian, 1999). The unexpected growth components imbedded in accounting earnings reflect executives' controllable efforts on beating a pre-specified target performance, which is stated in a bonus plan designed to align executives' incentives with shareholder values.

## 2. Pay–Performance Relation in Bonus Plans and Hypothesis Development

### 2.1. *Pay–performance relation*

Prior studies examine how shareholders use cash bonuses to align firm interest with executive benefits and how accounting information can be used to evaluate executives' performance in designing bonus plans. As shown in Figure 1, a typical executive bonus plan generally includes three components: performance measures, performance standards, and pay-performance relations (Indjejikian and Nanda, 2002). Figure 1 depicts an executive bonus plan often specifying a minimum bonus (corresponding to a threshold performance level) and a maximum bonus (corresponding to a performance maximum). Performance threshold (or base earnings) is a minimum expected performance standard that has to be achieved before any basic bonus can be paid out. Once executives achieve the base earnings, they are considered as meeting the minimum desired expectation on firm performance.

The pay–performance relation in incentive zones usually can be divided into two parts: expected performance and unexpected performance. The range between target performance and the performance threshold indicates

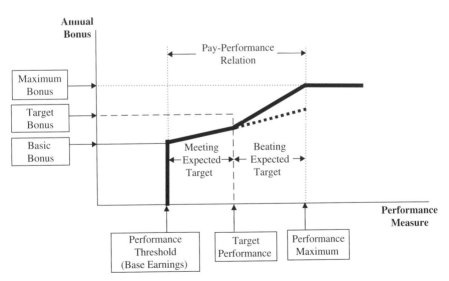

**Figure 1.** Executive annual bonus plan. This graph is partially adapted and modified from Murphy (2001, 251).

an expected performance range, to the extent that it reflects a firm's implicitly desired goal and expected performance in a compensation contract. If an executive's performance falls in the range of the expected benchmark, he then *meets* a firm's expectations and earns the corresponding proportion of the maximum *target bonus*. The target bonus, by definition, reflects important information about a firm's pre-determined incentive design decisions to motivate executives and conveys a firm's expected, and often unobservable, goal in its management control system. The upper half range of the pay–performance relation is an unexpected performance range, which indicates an executive's performance that exceeds a firm's normal expectation. In this range, an executive then *beats* the expected benchmark and proves to the compensation committee that his ability to create firm value is better than originally expected. The cash bonuses that an executive can earn by beating the target bonus are dependent on how close his performance is to the performance maximum.

## 2.2. *Target performance*

In terms of target performance, prior research has documented that executives adjust earnings in order to meet a given earnings benchmark (e.g., Burgstahler and Dichev, 1997; Burgstahler and Eames, 2003). When executives fall short of the target performance, Matstunaga and Park (2001) find that the compensation committee views this as a signal of poor performance and places significant incremental adverse penalties on CEO cash bonuses. Holthausen *et al.* (1995) and Healy (1985) examine the effects of the upper bound (or performance maximum) and lower bound (or performance threshold) in cash bonuses on executives' operational decisions. Others studies (e.g., Lambert and Larcker, 1987; Sloan, 1993) investigate how different performance measures such as accounting earnings and stock prices are used in the area of pay–performance of executive contracts. However, little evidence is available on bonuses granted to CEOs when they beat such target benchmarks.[3] Also, most studies implicitly assume that the pay–performance relation is a liner function between performance measure and annual bonus. As such, it implies

---

[3]One notable exception may include a recent article by Boschen *et al.* (2003), whose paper focuses on the long-run effects of unexpected firm performance on CEO compensation. This paper is distinctly different from theirs because it examines short-run cash bonuses and uses different proxies for expected (or target) performance.

that the compensation committee views meeting or beating target performance equally. In this paper, we propose that pay–performance is not a liner relation between performance measure and annual bonus; instead, the above-target performance should be viewed as more important than on-target performance because it differentiates a great executive's performance from a good one. A non-linear pay–performance bonus contract is used by the compensation committee to encourage executives to take more risks and to align their interests and responsibilities with those of shareholders.

## 2.3. *Non-linear pay–performance relations and hypothesis development*

The non-linear pay–performance relation in incentive zones has been examined by many empirical and theoretical studies. Using a comprehensive survey of annual incentive plans, Murphy (2001) finds that firms, which use internally determined performance standards such as year-to-year earnings growth, annual budget goals, or pre-specified targets set subjectively by the board of directors, tend to adopt a convex pay–performance relation in bonus plans.[4] Studies also investigate the consequences of adopting non-linear pay–performance relations in bonus plan contracts. One avenue of studies focuses on the adoption of non-linearities in bonus plans inducing certain degree of reporting manipulation. For example, Degeorge, Patel and Zeckahuser (1999) and Healy (1985) examine executives' motivation and managerial actions to manipulate the performance measures used in determining their bonus payoffs. In contrast, the other avenue shows that the executive's risk-taking behavior is significantly influenced by the shape of the bonus contract. Jensen and Murphy (1990) find the pay–performance sensitivity is smaller in the convex case than in the liner case. They suggest that executives facing a linear incentive contract will avoid taking any risk beyond meeting the target performance, while executives facing a contract with the convex incentive zone will optimally select a higher level of risk. Adding a non-linear incentive into an executive's

---

[4]The internal performance standards categorized by Murphy (2001) are performances that executives can take actions to affect the standard setting process and are thus held responsible for their controllable outcomes. Murphy (2001) shows that most of firms (76%) in his proprietary sample use multiple internal performance standards, of which 48% adopt non-linear pay–performance relations in the incentive bonus zone.

contract package also causes a change in the executive's attitude toward risk-taking and optimal bonus contract (Ross, 1999; Martellini and Urosevic, 2003). A non-linear pay-performance contract is found to increase the likelihood for executives to take projects with higher levels of risks; it also improves their perception on viewing the bonus contract as an optimal one. In this paper, we propose that more weight is expected to be placed on beating target performance than on meeting target performance in contracting CEOs' cash bonuses because the compensation committee utilizes a non-linear incentive zone to encourage CEOs' risk-taking behavior. As such, an executive with above-target performance is expected to be viewed as more valuable, taking more risks, and thus is rewarded with more bonuses than the one with on-target performance. The hypothesis is formally stated below.

**Hypothesis.** The compensation committee will place more weight on beating target performance than on meeting the expected target performance in determining a CEO's cash bonus.

## 2.4. *Test of hypothesis*

The pay–performance relation can be addressed in the following function between bonuses and performance measures.

$$
\begin{aligned}
\text{Annual bonus} &= \text{Actual performance} \times \text{Bonus adjustment factor}^5 \\
&= [\omega_1(\text{Actual earnings} - \text{Target earnings}) + \omega_2 \\
&\quad (\text{Target earnings})] \times \text{Bonus adjustment factor} \\
&= [\omega_1(\text{Unexpected component}) + \omega_2(\text{Expected component})] \\
&\quad \times \text{Bonus adjustment factor} \quad\quad\quad\quad (1)
\end{aligned}
$$

To examine meeting/beating target performance, accounting-based performance are decomposed into expected (or meeting target performance) and unexpected (or beating target performance) components and predict that each component has different weights on executives' cash bonuses. We predict that the weight on unexpected performance, $\omega_1$, will be greater than expected performance, $\omega_2$, because a cash bonus is usually used to provide incentive for managers to take greater risks and undertake higher return projects in the short

---

[5]The bonus adjustment factor is often used by firms to adjust past performance such as firm size, prior investments, and past growth. Examples may include numbers of shares outstanding and/or the bonus percentage used to offset the compounded growth in earnings.

term. To test the hypothesis, we first use different proxies to separate expected components from unexpected components of earnings. We then regress executives' cash bonuses with these two components to compare their difference in slope coefficients.

## 3. Proxies for Target Benchmark

This paper examines the association of executive bonus plans with various measures for target performance and attempts to find whether an executive can gain incrementally more from his unexpectedly good performance. In an incentive contract, the target performance conveys unobservable information about expected earnings. However, firms rarely publicly disclose detailed information about bonus plan components, so that there is little theoretical guidance about how the target performance is formulated in managerial incentive contracts. This paper uses three alterative measures as a proxy for a firm's expectation on executives' target performance.

### 3.1. *Permanent earnings*

The first proxy for target performance used in the paper is permanent earnings because permanent earnings are one of the commonly used estimates for the expectation on the current period of earnings. Permanent earnings show a firm's anticipated value by calibrating the effects of time-serial parameters on the revisions in expected future earnings. Pecuniary rewards are empirically found to vary directly with the extent that reported earnings are expected to persist (Nwaeze, Yang and Yin, 2004; Baber, Kang, and Kumar, 1998). This paper uses permanent earnings as one of the proxies for target performance also because prior studies have shown that the compensation committee considers both the magnitude of current-period earnings innovations and the likelihood of those innovations persisting into the future. In a cash bonus plan, transitory innovations on performance not only exist, but also are of great concern because they are frequently found to be used as an opportunistic tool for executives to earn an unsupported reward (e.g., Chen and Lee, 1995).[6]

---

[6]Because of the existence of transitory innovations, other common ways to estimate earnings expectations such as using past-period earnings in the random walk model, may not be appropriate or feasible.

This paper follows prior studies using an IMA(1,1) model to estimate permanent earnings (e.g., Beaver, Lamber and Morse, 1980; Collins and Kothari, 1989; among others). Time-serial permanent earnings have been well-characterized as the effect of earnings innovations on expected future earnings (Kormendi and Lipe, 1987). Changes in permanent earnings reflect the revisions in expectations of current and future earnings; that is, the unexpected growth (or change) on earnings adds new information to the direction of a long-term earnings trend.[7] The change in permanent earnings is equal to $(1 - \theta)e_t$, where $e_t$ is earnings innovation at the time $t$, and $\theta$ is a moving average parameter. This measure indicates that only the portion of $(1 - \theta)$ on earnings innovation is the new unexpected and sustainable performance, which is expected to persist in the future. The remaining portion on reported earnings thus is treated as expected performance, which includes transitory earnings and past-period permanent earnings, because both components of earnings have already been anticipated in the previous period.[8]

## 3.2. *Consensus of analysts' forecasts*

Analyst forecast is another common form used to evaluate executives' performance. Meeting or beating contemporaneous analysts' expectations seems to increase management's credibility for being able to meet the expectations of a firm's constituents (e.g., creditors and boards) and allows managers to enjoy a market premium of lower cost of capital and more capital investments (Kasznik and McNichols, 2002; Bartov, Givoly and Hayn, 2002). On the other hand, executive annual cash bonuses are adversely penalized when a firm's performance falls short of the consensus of analysts' forecasts (Mastunaga and Park, 2001). Executives who are consistently monitored by investors and shareholders have

---

[7]Please refer to Collins and Kothari (1989) and Cheng, Lee and Yang (2004) for detailed model derivation in an IMA(1,1) earnings model: $\Delta X_t = e_t - \theta e_{t-1}$.

[8]Mathematically, it may be viewed as follows: $X_t = X_t^P + X_t^T = \Delta X_t^P + (X_{t-1}^P + X_t^T)$, where $X_t^P$, $\Delta X_t^P$, and $X_t^T$ are permanent components, changes in permanent components and transitory components of earnings at time $t$, respectively. The past permanent earnings (i.e., $X_{t-1}^P$) and transitory earnings (i.e., $X_t^T$), are treated as current-period expected performance. It is because a firm's earnings expectation usually includes past performance and some noises. The best expectation available on earnings at time $t$ is the past permanent components of earnings. The noises are also expected and are reflected in transitory earnings because they are not sustainable and will reverse in the future. It is only the changes in permanent components of earnings, $\Delta X_t^P$, representing the sustainable new information regarding the unexpected growth of a firm.

strong incentives to meet or beat the threshold of analysts' expectations because the executives' rewards — both employment decisions and compensation benefits — greatly depend on the expected earnings achieved on the analysts' watch (Degeorge, Patel, and Zeckahuser, 1999).

The consensus of analysts' forecasts are used to approximate target performance because prior studies suggest this estimate relates to future earnings expectations and growth opportunity. For example, Bradshaw (2004) finds that analysts use different valuation models to forecast earnings and to project long-term growth. Recent studies suggest that analysts often consider growth as a primary determinate of stock recommendations (Bradshaw, 2002; Block, 1999). In designing a bonus contract, it is prevalent for the compensation committee to use analysts' forecasts as one of their expectation benchmarks to assess managers' performance. This measure is adopted into bonus plans also because the consensus of analysts' forecasts contains other non-financial and non-tangible information such as manager's reputation, competitive advantage, product quality or market share etc., which present a firm's potential to grow in a broader sense.

## 3.3. *Average earnings growth*

The last measure used to approximate target performance is the moving-average earnings growth. This measure is a performance indicator that reflects the current-period expected growth on earnings, estimated from an average of earnings growth rates of the prior five years. The expected average earnings growth is important because it reflects executives' performance in investment activities such as research and development (R&D) and capital expenditures. Earnings growth is a crucial measure in incentive contracts because prior studies find that a CEO's target bonus is significantly associated with the firm's growth opportunity (Indjejikian and Nanda, 2002). The satisfaction of shareholders on managers' performance is found to relate directly to their strategic implementation of a firm's growth opportunity (Bushman, Indjejikian and Smith, 1996). In addition, short-term executive compensation plans are consistently shown to be associated with changes in corporate decision-making to increase capital expenditures (Waegelein, 1988) and R&D investment (Cheng, 2004; Dechow and Sloan, 1991). The adjustment on R&D budgets, as reflected in earnings growth, is also found to strongly relate to corporate earnings targets (Bange and De Bondt, 1998).

## 4. Research Design

### 4.1. *Sample selection*

The sample of this paper is based on the intersection of ExecuComp, I/B/E/S, Compustat and CRSP databases. CEO compensation data are first obtained from ExecuComp from 1992 to 1998. Firms not paying cash bonuses to their executives are deleted. Compustat and CRSP provide firm-specific financial and stock return information for control variables. In addition, observations with changes in CEOs are deleted because full-year compensation data may not be available. We then merge the sample with I/B/E/S to obtain the mean forecast of financial analysts and other control variables related to analyst forecasts. Similar to prior compensation studies (e.g., Matsunaga and Park, 2001), we delete the top and bottom 1% of the distributions of the dependent variable to reduce the influence of extreme observations. After deleting firms with missing information, the selection procedure yields a total of 2,230 firm-year observations in my final sample. All the firms in my sample are US-based and have paid cash bonuses to their executives.

### 4.2. *Empirical model*

We first regress executives' cash bonuses with reported aggregate accounting earnings to show that accounting earnings is an important determinant to evaluate executives' performance.

$$\text{Bonus}_{i,t} = a + b \, (\text{Earnings}_{i,t}), \tag{2}$$

where Bonus is executives' cash bonus compensation for firm $i$ at the time $t$ and earnings are reported as earnings per share excluding extraordinary items. The subscription $i$ is omitted for simplicity. Coefficient $b$ in Equation (2) measures the direct association between reported accounting earnings and cash bonuses. However, Equation (2) may be misspecified and incomplete because it implicitly constrains various earnings components embedded in reported earnings to be equal. By using different proxies for target performance as discussed in the previous section, reported accounting earnings are further decomposed into expected and unexpected components to investigate the associations of cash bonus with various performances conveyed by earnings components. All the definitions and measures of earnings components are specifically listed in Table 1.

**Table 1.** A summary of the determinants of executive cash bonus and definitions of measures.

| Symbol | Predictor variable and measures | Predicted sign with cash bonus |
|---|---|---|
| *Measure of permanent earnings* | | |
| $X^P$ | Changes in permanent earnings estimated from multiplying earnings persistence ($= 1 - \theta$) with earnings residuals | + |
| $X^T$ | Expected past permanent earnings and current transitory components of earnings. $X^T$ is estimated from the difference between actual earnings and $X^P$ | +<br>$X^P > X^T$ |
| *Measure of consensus of analysts' forecasts* | | |
| $X^E$ | Expected earnings, the mean forecast on earnings from financial analysts | + |
| $X^{UE}$ | Unexpected earnings, the difference between actual earnings and expected earnings | +<br>$X^{UE} > X^E$ |
| *Measure of Average Earnings Growth* | | |
| $X^G$ | Expected earnings growth, estimated from multiplying prior-year earnings with a prior five-year moving average of earnings growth rates | + |
| $X^{UG}$ | Unexpected earnings growth, the difference between actual earnings and expected earnings | +<br>$X^{UG} > X^G$ |
| Other control variables | | |
| SIZE | Book value at the beginning of year | + |
| BSAL | Previous base salary | + |

(*Continued*)

**Table 1.**   (*Continued*)

| Symbol | Predictor variable and measures | Predicted sign with cash bonus |
|--------|--------------------------------|:------------------------------:|
| RISK | Company's beta estimated from the market model | + |
| NOEST | Numbers of financial analysts following | + |
| UP | Numbers of upward forecasts from financial analysts | + |
| DOWN | Numbers of downward forecasts from financial analysts | − |
| RET | Abnormal stock returns | + |

*Notes:*

Earnings per share, $X$ = reported earnings per share excluding extraordinary items (EPSPX, #58);

Permanent earnings, $X^P$ = earnings persistence, $(1 - \theta)$, multiplying earnings residuals, where moving average; parameter, $\theta$, and earnings residuals are derived from the IMA(1,1) model;

Transitory earnings, $X^T$ = the difference between reported earnings and permanent earnings;

Expected earnings, $X^E$ = the mean of financial analysts' annual forecasts on earnings at the time $t - 1$;

Unexpected earnings, $X^{UE}$ = the difference between reported earnings and expected earnings;

Expected earnings growth, $X^G$ = earnings at the prior year earnings multiplying $(1 + g)$, where expected earnings growth rates, $g$, are estimated from a prior five-year moving average of earnings growth rates;

Unexpected earnings growth, $X^{UG}$ = the difference between reported earnings and expected earnings growth.

Control variables are defined as follows:

Size = book value of equity (#60) at the beginning of year $t$;

Bsal = base salary at the beginning of year $t$;

Risk = firm-specific $\beta$ estimated from the market model;

Noest = numbers of financial analysts following the firm at the time $t$;

Up = numbers of financial analysts revised upward at the time $t$;

Down = numbers of financial analysts revised downward at the time $t$;

Ret = abnormal stock returns estimated from the market model.

As in Equation (1), the weighting factors, $\omega_1$ and $\omega_2$, represent the different incentive weights placed on earnings components. We anticipate that the more incentive value the earnings component has, the higher the weight on the regression slope coefficient. The decomposed earnings components are combined in regression models to test whether the slope coefficients on unexpectedly good performance (or beating the target) is larger than that of expected performance (or meeting the target). If the slope coefficient on the unexpected component of earnings is significantly larger than that on the expected component of earnings (i.e., $\omega_1 > \omega_2$), then the compensation committee placing more weight on unexpected performance than on expected performance is supported.

In multivariate regression analyses, other variables are included to control for risk, firm size, numbers of analysts followed, and previous base salary. Abnormal stock return is also included as an alternative performance measure because stock prices have been consistently used in managers' performance evaluations in addition to accounting earnings (Halthausen *et al.*, 1995). These variables are used to control for some omitted factors not directly examined in the study. As shown in the later sections, the major inferences are not statistically and quantitatively altered when variables like firm size, alternative performance and risk are added.

## 5. Results

Table 2 presents descriptive statistics for the compensation and explanatory variables used in the paper. Panel A of Table 2 shows that the mean and median cash bonuses for CEOs average $423,410 and $258,490, respectively. These bonuses used in this study seem reasonably comparable to $412,000 and $344,300 reported in Indjejikian and Nanda (2002). Like conventional compensation packages, the sample shows that a sizable portion (around 80%) of executives' compensation plans is rewarded with cash bonuses.

Panel B shows that reported accounting earnings seem to correlate more with expected earnings components (0.906, 0.687 and 0.430 for transitory, expected earnings from analysts, and expected earnings growth, respectively) than with unexpected counterparts (0.327, 0.520 and 0.304). As shown in Panel B, the three different proxies for unexpected performance are all highly correlated. Permanent earnings, for example, are highly correlated with unexpected earnings estimated from a consensus of analysts' forecasts (0.521 and 0.599 for the Pearson and Spearman correlations, respectively). This high

**Table 2.**   Sample descriptive statistics and correlation coefficients.

| Variable | Mean | Standard deviation | 75% | Median | 25% |
|---|---|---|---|---|---|
| *Panel A: Descriptive statistics* | | | | | |
| Compensation measures (in 000$) | | | | | |
| Cash bonus, BONUS | 423.41 | 539.32 | 550.00 | 258.49 | 75.00 |
| Salary | 529.10 | 285.96 | 675.00 | 476.50 | 332.50 |
| | | | | | |
| Performance measure and proxies for target performance | | | | | |
| Earnings, $X$ | 1.028 | 1.191 | 1.650 | 0.951 | 0.400 |
| Permanent earnings, $X^P$ | 0.082 | 0.487 | 0.228 | 0.056 | −0.053 |
| Financial analyst expectations, $X^E$ | 1.286 | 0.947 | 1.760 | 1.120 | 0.610 |
| Expected growth rate | 0.085 | 1.469 | 0.351 | 0.129 | −0.136 |
| | | | | | |
| Control variables | | | | | |
| SIZE (own equity, in 000$) | 1,033.77 | 2,188.98 | 932.90 | 308.45 | 124.10 |
| RISK | 1.174 | 0.982 | 1.502 | 1.088 | 0.730 |
| NOEST | 10.929 | 8.112 | 15 | 9 | 5 |
| UP | 1.011 | 1.859 | 1 | 0 | 0 |
| DOWN | 1.341 | 2.428 | 2 | 0 | 0 |
| Abnormal stock returns, RET | −0.019 | 0.412 | 0.177 | −0.013 | −0.213 |

*Panel B: Pearson (above) and Spearman correlation coefficients between different earnings components and proxies for target performance*

| | Earnings $X$ | Permanent earnings $X^P$ | Transitory earnings $X^T$ | Expected earnings $X^E$ | Unexp. earnings $X^{UE}$ | Expected earnings growth $X^G$ | Unexpected earnings growth $X^{UG}$ |
|---|---|---|---|---|---|---|---|
| $X$ | | 0.327* | 0.906* | 0.687* | 0.520* | 0.430* | 0.304* |
| $X^P$ | 0.314* | | −0.103 | −0.031 | 0.521* | −0.088 | 0.421* |
| $X^T$ | 0.905* | −0.017 | | 0.790* | 0.264* | 0.548* | 0.103 |
| $X^E$ | 0.744* | −0.019 | 0.826* | | −0.148* | 0.535* | −0.052* |
| $X^{UE}$ | 0.416* | 0.599* | 0.182* | −0.114* | | −0.011 | 0.402* |
| $X^G$ | 0.530* | −0.117 | 0.662* | 0.613* | −0.001 | | −0.695* |
| $X^{UG}$ | 0.221* | 0.552* | 0.016 | −0.085* | 0.437* | −0.576* | |

*Notes*: Executives' cash bonuses are obtained from EXECUCOMP data set and a total number of observations with all the variables available is 2,230. Variable definitions are described in the Table 1.
*$P < 0.01$.

correlation is also consistent with prior findings that these three proxies are common to some, but not all, extents to indicate a firm's expectations of desired earnings and other financial or non-financial performances.

Tables 3–5 reveal whether the compensation committee places more incentive weight on beating a target performance than on meeting one. Different

**Table 3.**  Associations of accounting earnings and permanent/transitory earnings with executives' cash bonuses.

| | Univariate test | | Multivariate test | |
| --- | --- | --- | --- | --- |
| | Earnings | Permanent/Transitory earnings | Earnings | Permanent/Transitory earnings |
| Intercept | 340.36 (31.27)* | 346.62 (31.63)* | −282.62 (−8.65)* | −271.46 (−8.28)* |
| Earnings variables | | | | |
| $X$ | 108.01 (16.76)* | | 67.756 (7.81)* | |
| $X^P$ | | 168.70 (11.09)* | | 127.28 (6.31)* |
| $X^T$ | | 98.20 (14.42)* | | 57.156 (6.18)* |
| Control variables | | | | |
| SIZE | | | 0.035 (6.69)* | 0.036 (6.83)* |
| BSAL | | | 0.775 (16.31)* | 0.783 (16.49)* |
| RISK | | | 168.98 (8.81)* | 162.26 (8.43)* |
| NOEST | | | 3.850 (2.39)* | 3.732 (2.32)* |
| UP | | | 0.875 (0.15) | 0.055 (0.01) |
| DOWN | | | −11.123 (−2.70)* | −11.051 (−2.69)* |
| RET | | | 197.77 (6.12)* | 173.61 (5.25)* |
| Adjusted $R^2$(%) | 4.97 | 5.30 | 30.15 | 30.43 |
| $N$ | 5,346 | | 2,456 | |
| F-value for $X^P > X^T$ | | 19.38* | | 10.69* |

*Notes*: Variable definitions are listed in Table 1. Permanent earnings are changes in current-year permanent components of earnings, which indicate unexpected performance on persistent earnings innovations; transitory earnings, include prior-year permanent components of earnings and current transitory components of earnings. Numbers in parentheses are $t$-values. Observations lying above 99% or below 1% of the distribution of each variable are deleted as outliers.

*$P < 0.01$.

**Table 4.**   Associations of accounting earnings and consensus of analysts' forecasts with executives' cash bonuses.

| | Univariate test | | Mulivariate test | |
|---|---|---|---|---|
| | Earnings | Meeting/Beating analysts' consensus | Earnings | Meeting/Beating analysts' consensus |
| Intercept | 258.29 (28.79)* | 247.71 (22.73)* | −174.73 (−8.47)* | −141.53 (−6.54)* |
| Earnings variables | | | | |
| $X$ | 139.76 (23.16)* | | 76.869 (11.48)* | |
| $X^E$ | | 146.04 (20.67)* | | 52.381 (6.29)* |
| $X^{UE}$ | | 127.40 (13.52)* | | 114.92 (11.25)* |
| Control variables | | | | |
| SIZE | | | 0.040 (8.90)* | 0.044 (9.51)* |
| BSAL | | | 0.726 (20.50)* | 0.758 (21.10)* |
| RISK | | | 62.461 (7.85)* | 56.802 (7.08)* |
| NOEST | | | 3.681 (2.91)* | 3.220 (2.55)* |
| UP | | | 16.153 (3.82)* | 14.091 (3.32)* |
| DOWN | | | −5.078 (−1.65) | −3.608 (−1.17) |
| RET | | | 131.64 (29.69)* | 104.56 (5.68)* |
| Adjusted $R^2$ (%) | 8.26 | 8.29 | 29.69 | 30.07 |
| $N$ | 5,946 | | 4,315 | |
| $F$-value for $X^{UE} > X^E$ | 2.92 | | 24.19* | |

*Notes*: Variable definitions are listed in Table 1. The expected earnings, $X^E$, are the consensus of financial analysts' forecasts on current-period earnings and unexpected earnings, $X^{UE}$, are the difference between reported earnings and expected earnings. Observations lying above 99% or below 1% of the distribution of each variable are deleted as outliers.
*$P$ < 0.01.

**Table 5.** Associations of accounting earnings and expected earnings growth with executives' cash bonuses.

| | Univariate test | | Multivariate test | |
|---|---|---|---|---|
| | Earnings | Expected/Unexpected earnings growth | Earnings | Expected/Unexpected earnings growth |
| Intercept | 309.16 (35.29)* | 308.24 (33.90)* | −181.57 (−8.45)* | −177.69 (−8.18)* |
| Earnings variables | | | | |
| $X$ | 124.66 (22.47)* | | 77.612 (12.30)* | |
| $X^G$ | | 125.32 (21.59)* | | 75.214 (11.58)* |
| $X^{UG}$ | | 123.53 (19.60)* | | 81.414 (11.57)* |
| Control variables | | | | |
| SIZE | | | 0.037 (7.93)* | 0.038 (8.01)* |
| BSAL | | | 0.714 (19.89)* | 0.715 (19.91)* |
| RISK | | | 69.531 (7.70)* | 68.869 (7.62)* |
| NOEST | | | 3.590 (2.82)* | 3.542 (2.79)* |
| UP | | | 17.450 (4.13)* | 17.262 (4.98)* |
| DOWN | | | −2.454 (−0.78) | −2.348 (−0.75) |
| RET | | | 135.51 (7.66)* | 132.08 (7.39)* |
| Adjusted $R^2$(%) | 6.63 | 6.85 | 29.44 | 29.45 |
| $N$ | 6,856 | | 4,253 | |
| $F$-value for $X^{UG} > X^G$ | 0.14 | | 1.48 | |

Notes: Observations lying above 99% or below 1% of the distribution of each variable are deleted as outliers. Numbers in parentheses are $t$-values. Variable definitions are listed in Table 1.
*$P < 0.01$.

measures are used to approximate target performance in incentive plans. Permanent earnings reflect earnings expectations estimated from the time-serial and firm-specific changes in a sustainable earnings trend; the consensus of analysts' forecasts reflects a rich and broad expectation from professional and institutional investors. Expected growth indicates an expectation made from the past growth patterns of earnings.

Table 3 shows that when time-serial parameters are used to approximate the permanence of earnings growth, the executive cash bonus is more (less) related to permanent (transitory) earnings. Permanent earnings in Table 3 indicate changes in permanent components of earnings, which reflect that the new information for unexpected performance has been added to a moving time-serial earnings trend and such changes are expected to persist into the future. Transitory earnings consist of two parts: (1) transitory components of earnings at the current period (i.e., noises) and (2) current-year earnings expectations (i.e., best estimated from prior-year permanent components of earnings). Note that using permanent earnings to proxy for target performance indicates a firm's time-serial earnings expectation. In the univariate analysis, the decomposition of reported accounting earnings into these two components increases the explanatory power about 6.6% (an increase in adjusted $R^2$ from 4.97% to 5.30%). Both slope coefficients on the expected growth component (i.e., transitory earnings) and unexpected growth component (i.e., permanent earnings) are positive and significant. The regression coefficient on permanent earnings, 168.70, is significantly larger than transitory earnings ($F$-value $= 19.38$ with $p$-value $< 0.01$). This result supports my predication that a compensation committee seems to place more weight on beating target performance than on meeting the expected target performance in a CEO's cash bonus.

Also note that after adding control variables, the coefficient on permanent earnings remains significantly larger than that on transitory earnings ($F$-value $= 10.69$ with $p$-value $< 0.01$). The signs on slope coefficients of control variables in regression models are all as expected. For example, the larger the firm is (e.g., SIZE estimated from book value of a firm, or NOEST estimated from numbers of analysts following the firm), the larger cash bonuses granted to executives. Also, firms tend to reward more cash compensations for executives taking more risk (RISK, 162.26 with $t$-value $= 8.43$).

Table 4 presents evidence that beating the consensus of analysts' forecasts has a higher contractual value than meeting the consensus in incentive bonus plans after controlling for numbers of upward and downward forecasts.

In the univariate test, the slope coefficients on expected earnings and unexpected earnings estimated from the consensus of analysts' forecasts seem not significantly different ($F$-value $= 2.92$). This insignificant result may be partly attributable to the fact that some firms in the sample fall into the lower portion of expected consensus.[9] Also, some analysts may revise previous forecasts up or down because the information becomes more feasible and clearer when the time is closer to the announcement of financial statements. Even if executives beat the consensus of analysts' forecasts, it is still possible that the new consensus may have already been revised down from early forecasts.

Table 4 shows the slope coefficient on unexpected earnings performance for beating analysts' forecasts, 114.92, with $t$-value of 11.25, which is significantly larger than that on expected performance, 52.38, with $t$-value of 6.29, after controlling for the size and numbers of downward and upward forecast revisions. This result supports my prediction that the compensation committee places more weight on beating target performance than on meeting the expected target performance in a CEO's cash bonus.

Many studies have used the prior-year's earnings level, $X_{t-1}$, as an earnings expectation at the current period. When earnings follow a random walk process, all earnings innovations are expected to persist into the future; therefore, prior-year's level of earnings becomes a natural approximation for the current earnings expectation. However, using level of earnings at prior year as the current earnings expectation is often subject to the influence of extreme performance in a single year. As far as cash bonuses are concerned, using prior-year earnings as the current earnings expectation does not take into consideration the impact of transitory and opportunistic performance, which is often reported in prior studies. It may also fail to incorporate the operating results of executives' investment decisions, which usually take five years or longer to implement. In Table 5, an average of earnings growth rates is used at prior five years as an earnings expectation to avoid any extreme earnings innovation in a single year. This measure reflects a firm's average growth opportunity and investment strategies impounded in accounting earnings in the

---

[9]In the sample, there are about 44.17% beating consensus of analyst's forecasts, 1.41% just meeting the number, and 54.41% of observations passing basic performance threshold but staying in the low part of expected consensus. Even the mean bonus ($504,180) for executives beating analyst consensus is substantially larger than those missing analyst consensus ($388,508), some adverse penalties may exist for the latter group who achieve the basic expectations but still miss the consensus of analysts' forecasts.

past five years. Expected earnings growth also reflects a change in corporate capital and R&D expenditures (Waegelein, 1998; Dechow and Sloan, 1991). In addition, this measure is consistent with prior findings that executives' target bonuses are positively associated with a firm's growth opportunities (Indjeikian and Nanda, 2002).

Table 5 presents that average earnings growth is a weak proxy for target performance to differentiate unexpected performance from what is expected. Even after controlling for variables on risk, size and stock prices, the slope coefficients on these two performance components are still not significantly different (75.214 and 81.414). This result suggests that even though short-term accounting earnings provide important information on the firm's capital and investment expenditures, past earning growth may have a limited role used as a benchmark for setting target performance in incentive plans.

Table 6 includes three different proxies together in regression models to compare their usefulness as target performance in cash bonus plans on a pair-wise basis. After controlling for size, risk and base salary, we find that the pair-wise comparisons of three proxies indicate that the strongest proxy for unexpected performance (or beating target performance) in incentive plans in a high to low order is: permanent component, unexpected analysts' expectations and unexpected earnings growth. In a full model that contains all three proxies, permanent earnings (71.77 with $t$-value $= 2.66$) seem to be the strongest form that can be used to approximate target performance. The financial analysts' consensus is a marginally better proxy for target performance than that for average earnings growth. This result reflects that while three proxies all carry important but different information about executives' performances, permanent earnings seem to be more favorably used to set the target performance in cash bonus plans.

Because details of target performance in executives' compensation contracts are not publicly available, three different earnings-based measures are used to approximate the expected target performance in this paper. As such, the regression results on the association of annual bonus with expected target performance may be attributable, in part, to the effect of expected earnings and earnings surprise. In order to control for the possible effects from earnings surprise, Table 7 uses an indicator variable as a robustness test to represent executives' performance beating earnings-based target performance. Beat($X^P$) is used to indicate that executives beat the permanent earnings-based target performance; it takes the value of one when current permanent earnings

**Table 6.** Permanent earnings, consensus of financial analysts' forecasts, average earnings growth in executives' cash bonuses.

| Models | Int. | Earn. | Permanent earnings $X^P$ | Beating analyst's earnings $X^{UE}$ | Unexp. earnings growth $X^{UG}$ | Control variables | | | | | | | Adj. $R^2$ (%) |
| | | | | | | SIZE | BSAL | RISK | NOEST | UP | DOWN | RET | |
|---|---|---|---|---|---|---|---|---|---|---|---|---|---|
| X−X−X | −282.45 | 72.39 | | | | 0.04 | 0.78 | 165.23 | 2.88 | 2.88 | −11.26 | 194.86 | 30.79 |
| | (−8.33)* | (7.36)* | | | | (6.97)* | (15.67)* | (8.38)* | (1.72) | (0.47) | (−2.63)* | (5.81)* | |
| P-UE-X | −250.48 | 49.37 | 73.04 | 34.44 | | 0.04 | 0.80 | 153.84 | 2.51 | 0.86 | −10.45 | 150.08 | 31.25 |
| | (−7.08)* | (4.21)* | (2.79)* | (1.71)* | | (7.33)* | (16.00)* | (7.75)* | (1.50) | (0.14) | (−2.44)* | (4.24)* | |
| P-X-UG | −265.66 | 57.86 | 87.34 | | 3.53 | 0.04 | 0.79 | 156.78 | 2.73 | 1.58 | −11.19 | 163.48 | 31.17 |
| | (−7.77)* | (5.49)* | (3.45)* | | (0.44) | (7.16)* | (15.89)* | (7.92)* | (1.64) | (0.26) | (−2.62)* | (4.75)* | |
| X-UE-UG | −249.44 | 52.53 | | 52.74 | 6.68 | 0.04 | 0.80 | 157.98 | 2.44 | 1.17 | −9.87 | 160.77 | 31.04 |
| | (−7.04)* | (4.49)* | | (2.75)* | (0.85) | (7.40)* | (15.92)* | (7.96)* | (1.46) | (0.19) | (−2.30)* | (4.57)* | |
| P-UE-UG | −250.24 | 49.31 | 71.77 | 33.86 | 1.59 | 0.04 | 0.80 | 153.95 | 2.51 | 0.85 | −10.43 | 150.04 | 31.22 |
| | (−7.07)* | (4.20)* | (2.66)* | (1.66) | (0.20) | (7.31)* | (15.97)* | (7.75)* | (1.50) | (0.14) | (−2.43)* | (4.24)* | |

*Notes:* A total number of observations is equal to 2,230. Observations lying above 99% or below 1% of the distribution of each variable are deleted as outliers. Numbers in parentheses are *t*-values. Notations for X, P, UE, and UG in the first column indicate not available, changes in permanent earnings, unexpected analyst's earnings and unexpected earnings growth, respectively. Variable definitions are listed in Table 1.
*$P < 0.01$.

**Table 7.** Robustness test: Using an indicator variable to represent executives' performance beating earnings-based target performance.

| | Target performance measures | | | |
| | Permanent earnings | Analysts' consensus | Earnings growth | Full model |
| --- | --- | --- | --- | --- |
| Intercept | $-282.70\ (-10.91)^*$ | $-273.76\ (-10.56)^*$ | $-277.27\ (-10.67)^*$ | $-279.49\ (-10.78)^*$ |
| Earnings variable and Interaction variable | | | | |
| $X$ | $40.172\ (3.40)^*$ | $59.649\ (6.40)^*$ | $76.889\ (8.71)^*$ | $35.492\ (2.95)^*$ |
| Beat($X^P$)*$X$ | $55.059\ (4.66)^*$ | | | $46.898\ (3.48)^*$ |
| Beat($X^{UE}$)*$X$ | | $37.952\ (4.11)^*$ | | $27.264\ (2.65)^*$ |
| Beat($X^{UG}$)*$X$ | | | $12.066\ (1.34)$ | $-11.019\ (-1.10)$ |
| Control variables | | | | |
| SIZE | $0.021\ (4.63)^*$ | $0.022\ (4.78)^*$ | $0.022\ (4.75)^*$ | $0.021\ (4.62)^*$ |
| BSAL | $0.723\ (18.59)$ | $0.720\ (18.51)^*$ | $0.718\ (18.38)^*$ | $0.724\ (18.63)^*$ |
| RISK | $136.72\ (9.14)^*$ | $133.58\ (8.90)^*$ | $136.67\ (9.09)^*$ | $134.65\ (9.00)^*$ |
| NOEST | $4.448\ (3.43)^*$ | $4.657\ (3.59)^*$ | $4.663\ (3.58)^*$ | $4.458\ (3.44)^*$ |
| UP | $1.528\ (0.33)$ | $0.494\ (0.11)$ | $1.558\ (0.34)$ | $0.883\ (0.19)$ |
| DOWN | $-6.441\ (-1.96)^*$ | $-6.708\ (-2.04)^*$ | $-7.808\ (-2.37)^*$ | $-5.882\ (-1.79)^*$ |
| RET | $187.80\ (7.37)^*$ | $182.15\ (7.10)^*$ | $191.95\ (7.49)^*$ | $182.36\ (7.12)^*$ |
| Adjusted $R^2$ (%) | 38.00 | 37.86 | 37.45 | 38.14 |

*Notes:* All variable definitions are the same as listed in Table 1.

Beat($X^P$)  =  an indicator of beating permanent earnings; the value is set equal to 1 if current permanent earnings are greater than prior-year permanent earnings and 0 otherwise.

Beat($X^{UE}$)  =  an indicator of beating the consensus of financial analysts' forecasts; the value is set equal to 1 if current realized earnings are greater than analysts' consensus and 0 otherwise.

Beat($X^{UG}$)  =  an indicator of beating the expected average earnings growth; the value is set equal to 1 if current realized earnings are greater than expected earnings growth and 0 otherwise.

Observations lying above 99% or below 1% of the distribution of each variable and cause extreme influential regression results are deleted as outliers. Numbers in parentheses are *t*-values.

* $P < 0.01$.

are greater than prior-year permanent earnings and zero otherwise. Beat($X^{UE}$) and Beat($X^{UG}$) are an indicator variable set to the value of one when realized earnings are greater than consensus of financial analysts' forecasts or expected earnings growth, respectively and zero otherwise. If the hypothesis is true that the compensation committee places more weight on beating target performance, a positive interaction coefficient between the indicator variable and realized earnings is expected in executives' bonus regressions. The result for individual and full models in Table 7 confirms the hypothesis. The interaction slope coefficients on beating prior-year permanent earnings (Beat($X^{P}$) = 55.059 with $t$-value = 4.66) and analysts' consensus (Beat($X^{UE}$) = 37.952 with $t$-value = 4.11) are both positive and significant. Similar to the result in Table 5, the slope coefficient on the interaction between realized earnings and the indicator of beating expected earnings growth is only moderate (12.066 with $t$-value = 1.34). The result remains the same in the full model when including all three target performances together. In sum, Table 7 supports the prediction that more weight is placed on beating target performance than meeting target performance in contracting CEOs' cash bonuses.

## 6. Summary

Target performance in CEOs' bonus plans is an implicit and unobservable earnings expectation on a CEO's performance. In a review of studies on executive incentive, Ittner and Larcker (1998) propose that the use and choice of appropriate economic value measures for internal decision-making and compensation purposes is a key element to corporate governance. This paper examines whether an executive gains incrementally from his unexpectedly good performance by beating the target benchmark stated in cash bonus plans. In the financial market, meeting earnings expectations is often highly rewarded by a notable increase in prices on the market (Bartov *et al.*, 2002; McNighols and Kasznik, 2002). In the mechanism of corporate governance, missing earnings benchmarks has a severely adverse effect on an executive's annual bonus (Matsunaga and Park, 2001). By examining compensation patterns in the long run, Boschen, Duru, Gordon, and Smith (2003) find that an unexpected good stock price performance is associated with an increase in CEO pay for several years. This paper predicts and tests whether CEOs beating the target benchmark signals different information from meeting the target performance in a short-term incentive contract such as a cash bonus plan. We find that the compensation committee seems to place more contract value on above-target than on-target performance. This result thus suggests that the pay-for-performance relation in an executive cash bonus plan is a non-linear function — more incentives are offered to reward executives' unexpectedly great performance than expected good one. This paper also suggests that the compensation committee uses more information from permanent earnings to design target performance in bonus plans, as compared to a consensus of analysts' forecasts and average earnings growth.

## References

Arora, A. and P. Alam, "The Effect of Adopting Accounting-Based Bonus and Performance Incentive Plans on the Earnings Response Coefficient." *Journal of Accounting, Auditing and Finance* 14, 1–28 (1999).

Baber, W. R., S. Kang and K. R. Kumar, "Accounting Earnings and Executive Compensation: The Role of Earnings Persistence." *Journal of Accounting and Economics* 25, 169–193 (1998).

Bange, M. and W. De Bondt, "R&D Budgets and Corporate Earnings Targets." *Journal of Corporate Finance* 4, 153–184 (1998).

Bartov, E., D. Givoly and C. Hayn, "The Rewards to Meeting or Beating Earnings Expectations." *Journal of Accounting Economics* 33, 173–204 (2002).

Beaver, W., R. Lambert and D. Morse, "The Information Content of Security Prices." *Journal of Accounting and Economics* 2, 3–28 (1980).

Block, S, "A Study of Financial Analysts: Practice and Theory." *Financial Analysts Journal* 55, 86–95 (1999).

Boschen, J., A. Duru, L. Gordon and K. Smith, "Accounting and Stock Price Performance in Dynamic CEO Compensation Arrangements." *The Accounting Review* 78(1), 143–168 (2003).

Bradshaw, M., "How do Analysts Use their Earnings Forecasts in Generating Stock Recommendations?" *The Accounting Review* 79(1), 25–50 (2004).

———, "The Use of Target Prices to Justify Sell-Side Analysts' Stock Recommendations." *Accounting Horizons* 27–41 (March, 2002).

Burgstahler, D. C. and M. Eames, "Earnings Management to Avoid Losses and Earnings Decreases: Are Analysts Fooled?" *Contemporary Accounting Research* (20), 253–294 (2003).

Burgstahler, D. and C. Dichev, "Earnings Management to Avoid Earnings Decreases and Losses." *Journal of Accounting & Economics* 24(1), 99–126 (1997).

Bushman, R., R. Indjejikian and A. Smith, "CEO Compensation: The Role of Individual Performance Evaluation." *Journal of Accounting and Economics* 21, 161–193 (1996).

Cheng, S, "R&D Expenditures and CEO Compensation." *The Accounting Review* 79(2), 305–328 (2004).

Crawford, D., D. Franz and R. Smith, "Miachel Eisner's Compensation Agreement with Disney." *Issues in Accounting Education* 13(4), 957–973 (1998).

Chen, K. C. W. and C. J. Lee, "Executive Bonus Plans and Accounting Trade-offs: The Case of Oil and Gas Industry, 1985–86." *The Accounting Review* 70(1), 91–111 (1995).

Cheng, A., B. Lee and S. Yang, "The Information Content of Permanent and Transitory Components in Earnings Changes and Earnings Levels." Working Paper, University of Houston, USA (2004).

Collins, D.W. and S. P. Kothari, "An Analysis of Intertemporal and Cross-sectional Determinants of Earnings Response Coefficients." *Journal of Accounting and Economics* 11, 143–182 (1989).

Dechow, P. and R. Sloan, "Executive Incentive and the Horizon Problems: An Empirical Investigation." *Journal of Accounting Economics* 14(1), 51–89 (1991).

Degeorge, R., J. Patel and R. Zeckhauser, "Earnings Management to Exceed Thresholds." *Journal of Business* 72(1), 1–33 (1999).

Healy, P, "The Effect of Bonus Schemes on Accounting Decisions." *Journal of Accounting and Economics* 7, 85–107 (1985).

Holmstrom, B, "Moral Hazard and Observability." *The Bell Journal of Economics* 10(1), 74–91 (1979).

Holthausen, R., D. Larcker and R. Sloan, "Annual Bonus Schemes and the Manipulation of Earnings." *Journal of Accounting and Economics* 19, 29–74 (1995).

Indjejikian, R, "Performance Evaluation and Compensation Research: An Agency Perspective." *Accounting Horizons*, 13(2), 147–157 (1999).

———. and D. Nanda, "Executive Target Bonuses and What They Imply About Performance Standards." *The Accounting Review* 77(4), 793–819 (2002).

Ittner, C. and D. Larcker, "Innovations in Performance Measurement: Trends and Research Implications." *Journal of Management Accounting Research* 10, 206–238 (1998).

Jensen, M. C. and W. H. Meckling, "Rights and Production Functions: An Application to Labor-Managed firms and Codetermination." *Journal of Business* 52(4), 469–506 (1979).

Jensen, M. C. and K. Murphy, "Performance Pay and Top-Management Incentives." *Journal of Political Economy* 98, 225–264 (1990).

Kasznik, R. and M. McNichols, "Does Meeting Earnings Expectations Matter? Evidence from Analyst Forecast Revisions and Share Prices." *Journal of Accounting Research* 40(3), 727–759 (2002).

Kormendi, R. and R. Lipe, "Earnings Innovations, Earnings Persistence and Stock Returns." *Journal of Business* 60, 323–346 (1987).

Lambert, R. and D. Larcker, "An Analysis of The Use of Accounting and Market Measures of Performance in Executive Compensation Contracts." *Journal of Accounting Research* 25, 85–129 (1987).

Matsunaga, S. R. and C. Park, "The Effect of Missing a Quarterly Earnings Benchmark on the CEO's Annual Bonus." *The Accounting Review* 76(3), 313–332 (2001).

Murphy, K., "Performance Standards in Incentive Contracts." *Journal of Accounting and Economics* 30, 245–278 (2001).

Martellini, L. and B. Urosevic, "On the Valuation and Incentive Effects of Executive Cash Bonus Contract." Working Paper (2003).

Narayanan, M. P., "Form of Compensation and Managerial Decision Horizon." *Journal of Financial and Quantitative Analysis* 31(4), 467–491 (1996).

———, "Managerial Incentives for Short-term Results." *Journal of Finance* 40(5), 1469–1484 (1985).

Nwaeze, E., S. Yang and Q. Yin, "The Role of Cash Flow in CEO Cash Compensation." Working Paper, Rutgers University, USA (2004).

Paul, J., "On the Efficiency of Stock-based Compensation." *The Review of Financial Studies* 5(3), 471–502 (1992).

Ross, S., "Some Notes on Compensation, Agency Theory, and the Duality of Risk Aversion and Riskiness." Working Paper, MIT Sloan School (1999).

Sloan, R., "Accounting Earning and Top Executive Compensation." *Journal of Accounting and Economics* 16, 55–100 (1993).

Smith, C. and R. Watts, "The Investment Opportunity Set and Corporate Financing, Dividend, and Compensation Policies." *Journal of Financial Economics* 32, 263–292 (1992).

Waegelein, J. F., "The Association Between the Adoption of Short-term Bonus Plans and Corporate Expenditures." *Journal of Accounting Public Policy* 7(1), 43–63 (1988).

Chapter 13

# ‾Corporate Diversification and the Price-Earnings Association

Ben-Hsien Bao
*Hong Kong Polytechnic University, Hong Kong*

Da-Hsien Bao
*Rowan University, USA*

This study investigates the effect of diversification on the association between firm value and earnings using both the levels and the changes analyses. Results show that: (1) the association between stock price and earnings for diversified firms is higher than that for focused firms, (2) the association is stronger when degree of diversification is higher, and (3) the association is improved significantly when quality of earnings is also considered.

**Keywords:** Corporate diversification; firm valuation; quality of earnings; levels analysis; changes analysis.

## 1. Introduction

Prior studies have examined the effect of corporate diversification from three different perspectives. The valuation studies focus on the effect on firm value, the event studies examine the effect on stock return, and the profit performance studies evaluate the effect on firm profit. Results, however, are inconclusive and usually contradictory.

The valuation studies generally have followed the excess value approach or the Tobin's $q$ approach. The excess value studies focus solely on the diversified firms that have multiple business segments. The excess value of a diversified firm is defined as the difference between its imputed value and actual value, where the imputed value is the total value of all business segments that operate as separate and independent companies.[1] Positive excess value indicates that diversification enhances value while negative excess value indicates that

---

[1]The excess value approach studies (1) calculate the imputed value of each business segment of a diversified firm by multiplying the median ratio, determined by focused firms in the same industry, of capital to assets (or sales, or earnings) by the segment's assets (or sales, or earnings), (2) sum the imputed values of all segments, and (3) subtract the sum from the firm's actual value to derive the excess value. Positive excess value indicates that diversification enhances value while negative excess value indicates that diversification diminishes value.

diversification diminishes value. The Tobin's $q$ studies compare the $q$ values of diversified firms with those of focused firms, where focused firms are firms with a single business segment. [2] If the segments of a diversified firm do not respond adequately to investment opportunities, in comparison with a focused firm, then Tobin's $q$ for the diversified firm should be smaller than that for the focused firm. Some studies have shown that diversified firms have a negative excess value, i.e., they trade at a discount relative to focused firms, a phenomenon called diversification discount (e.g., Berger and Ofek, 1995; Lins and Servaes, 2002). Other studies have not found such a discount (e.g., Hyland and Diltz, 2002). Lins and Servaes (1999) have shown a significant diversification discount in Japan and UK, but not in Germany. Some studies have shown that Tobin's $q$ and firm diversification are negatively related, i.e., diversified firms' $q$ is lower than focused firms' $q$ (e.g., Lang and Stulz, 1994). Some studies have found that diversified firms' $q$ is higher than focused firms' $q$ (e.g., Hyland and Diltz, 2002). Other studies have not found evidence of inefficient response to investment opportunities by diversified firms (e.g., Whited, 2001).

The event studies examine the cumulative abnormal returns surrounding the diversification/refocusing announcements. Market reacts positively to the announcements if cumulative abnormal returns are positive and significant. Some studies have shown market's positive reaction to refocusing announcements (e.g., Berger and Ofek, 1999; Desai and Jain, 1999). Some studies have shown market's positive reaction to diversification announcements (e.g., Billett and Mauer, 2000; Graham, Hemmon, and Wolf, 2002). Other studies have shown market's positive reaction to both acquisition and divestiture announcements (e.g., Mulherin and Boone, 2000).

Performance studies generally compare the performance in terms of profit between diversified firms and focused firms. Profit performance is measured by operating margin (e.g., Berger and Ofek, 1995; Lins and Servaes, 2002), return on assets (e.g., Berger and Ofek, 1995; Singh, Mathur, Gleason, and Etebari, 2001), return on sales (e.g., Palepu, 1985), or return on equity (e.g., Singh *et al.*,

---

[2]Tobin's $q$ is the ratio of market value of a firm to replacement cost of all assets of that firm. The Tobin's $q$ approach studies assume that Tobin's $q$ is (1) a proxy for investment/growth opportunities, and (2) an indication of a firm's value given by the financial markets. If the segments of a diversified firm do not respond adequately to investment opportunities, in comparison to a focused firm, then Tobin's $q$ for the diversified firm should be smaller than that for the focused firm. If the financial markets value a firm more highly as a total going concern than just as a collection of its assets, then Tobin's $q$ for that firm should be higher than 1.

2001). Some studies have shown that diversified firms have a smaller operating margin (e.g., Berger and Ofek, 1995; Lins and Servaes, 2002), and a smaller return on assets (e.g., Berger and Ofek, 1995). Some studies have found that diversified firms have a larger return on equity (e.g., Singh *et al.*, 2001). Other studies have found that return on sales and return on assets are not significantly different between diversified firms and focused firms (e.g., Palepu, 1985; Singh *et al.*, 2001).

Thus, numerous empirical studies have examined the effect of diversification on firm value, stock return, and profit performance with mixed results. Martin and Sayrak (2003), however, have claimed that research on corporate diversification in the last decade has evolved in three successive rounds with more definitive results in the third round. Evidence from the first round has shown that diversification destroys firm value while evidence from the second round has shown that diversification does not destroy firm value. Evidence from the most recent round has shown that diversification actually creates firm value. The major reason for value creation by diversified firms, provided by Hadlock, Ryngaert, and Thomas (2001), is that diversification alleviates asymmetric information problems between managers and shareholders. Diversified firms, therefore, have better access to capital markets (Martin and Sayrak, 2003) and have higher values.

Prior empirical studies in accounting have shown that there is a positive and significant association between firm value and earnings. If the problem of managers' holding private information is less severe for diversified firms, then earnings information is more reliable and verifiable with less noise for diversified firms. It, therefore, can be argued that the price-earnings association for diversified firms is higher than that for focused firms, i.e., earnings response coefficient for diversified firms is higher and the coefficient of determination for diversified firms is also higher. Diversified firms have different degrees of diversification. It, therefore, can also be argued that the price-earnings association is higher for diversified firms with higher degrees of diversification. Prior accounting research has also claimed that quality of earnings is positively associated with firm value. Thus, diversification and quality of earnings should jointly and positively affect the association between price and earnings.

The major purpose of this study is to investigate whether price-earnings association for diversified firms is indeed higher than that for focused firms. In addition, this study investigates the association when quality of earnings is also considered. Results should determine whether diversification information could shed additional light on the price-earnings association. Results should also determine whether additional information on quality of earnings is useful. Investors and analysts can rely more heavily on the price-earnings association when analyzing diversified firms if results show that the association between price and earnings is higher for diversified firms.

This study is different from prior diversification studies in many respects. Methodologically, it uses the levels approach and the changes approach (not the excess value approach, the event studies approach, or the Tobin's $q$ approach). It studies the price-earnings association (not firm value or firm performance). It should provide additional evidence on the usefulness of diversification information.

Results of this study show that the association between stock prices and earnings for diversified firms is higher than that for focused firms. The association is higher if the degree of diversification is higher. The explanatory power of the association is improved significantly by also incorporating quality of earnings information.

Sections 2 and 3 briefly review the approaches used in prior accounting valuation studies, and the control variables. They are followed by description of data, analyses and results of analyses. Conclusions are given in the last section.

## 2. The Association between Firm Value and Earnings

Two approaches have been adopted by prior accounting research studies to examine the association between stock prices and earnings: the levels approach and the changes approach (e.g., Kothari, 1992). The levels approach can be represented by the following equation:

$$\frac{P_t}{P_{t-1}} = \alpha + \beta \frac{E_t}{P_{t-1}} + \varepsilon, \tag{1}$$

where $P$ is the price per share, and $E$ is the earnings per share.

Both the dependent variable and the independent variable are normalized by beginning price per share. $\beta$ in Equation (1) is expected to be positive and significant, i.e., earnings levels are positively and significantly associated with stock price levels.

The changes approach can be represented by the following equation:

$$\frac{P_t}{P_{t-1}} = \alpha + \beta \frac{E_t}{P_{t-1}} + \varepsilon. \tag{2}$$

Both the dependent variable and the independent variable are normalized by beginning price per share. $\beta$ in Equation (2) is expected to be positive and significant, i.e., earnings changes are positively and significantly associated with stock price changes.

Regressions based on Equations (1) and (2) can be performed separately on diversified firms and focused firms. The association between firm value and earnings for diversified firms is expected to be higher than that for focused firms because diversified firms have less severe information asymmetry problems and their earnings are less noisy (Hadlock *et al.*, 2001). Comparisons of the regression results can determine the impact of incorporating diversification information, e.g., if all regression coefficients are positive and significant, and $R^2$ values for regressions performed on diversified firms are higher than those for regressions performed on focused firms, then the association between firm value and earnings is higher for diversified firms.

Regressions can also be performed on all sample firms using indicator variables (Barth, Elliott, and Finn, 1999). The levels analysis with an indicator variable can be shown as:

$$\frac{P_t}{P_{t-1}} = \alpha + \beta_1 \frac{E_t}{P_{t-1}} + \beta_2 \left( \text{GROUP} \times \frac{E_t}{P_{t-1}} \right) + \varepsilon. \qquad (3)$$

where GROUP is an indicator variable; it equals 1 for diversified firms, and 0 for focused firms.

The difference between diversified firms and focused firms is represented by $\beta_2$.[3] If diversified firms have a higher price levels-earnings levels multiple, then $\beta_2$ in Equation (3) should be positive and statistically significant. If diversified firms have a lower price levels-earnings levels multiple, then $\beta_2$ in Equation (3) should be negative and statistically significant.

The changes analysis with an indicator variable can be represented by the following equation:

$$\frac{(P_t - P_{t-1})}{P_{t-1}} = \alpha + \beta_1 \frac{(E_t - E_{t-1})}{P_{t-1}}$$
$$+ \beta_2 \left( \text{GROUP} \times \frac{(E_t - E_{t-1})}{P_{t-1}} \right) + \varepsilon. \qquad (4)$$

The difference between diversified firms and focused firms is determined by $\beta_2$. If diversified firms have a higher price changes-earnings changes multiple, then $\beta_2$ in Equation (4) should be positive and statistically significant.

---

[3]For diversified firms: $E[P_t/P_{t-1}] = \alpha + (\beta_1 + \beta_2)E_t/P_{t-1}$, where $E$ is the expectation operator. For focused firms: $E[P_t/P_{t-1}] = \alpha + \beta_1 E_t/P_{t-1}$. The difference, therefore, is determined by $\beta_2$.

If diversified firms have a lower price changes-earnings changes multiple, then $\beta_2$ in Equation (4) should be negative and statistically significant.

## 3. Control Variables

Numerous control variables are proposed by prior studies to control for variables, other than earnings, that may affect the price–earnings relation. This study includes those variables that have been identified in prior studies as statistically significant. They are cash flow to total assets ratio (e.g., Hyland and Diltz, 2002), assets turnover (e.g., Singh *et al.*, 2001), total liabilities to total assets ratio (e.g., Hyland and Diltz, 2002; Singh *et al.*, 2001), the logarithm of sales (e.g., Singh *et al.*, 2001), and Tobin's $q$ (e.g., Hyland and Diltz, 2002).

Cash flow from operations to total assets ratio measures a firm's operating performance. Assets turnover measures the efficiency of using assets to generate sales. Total liabilities to total assets ratio measures the effect of monitor, since debts can serve as monitoring devices. The logarithm of sales is used primarily as a scale variable. Tobin's $q$ measures investment/growth opportunities. It is approximated by the following equation (Hyland and Diltz, 2002):

$$q = \frac{(\text{MVE} + \text{TA} - \text{EQ})}{\text{TA}}, \tag{5}$$

where MVE is the market value of the firm's equity, TA is the firm's total assets, and EQ is the firm's book equity.

Results (presented later) based on univariate comparisons between the diversified firms and the focused firms also confirm the significance of these control variables in this study.[4] In addition, dummy variables representing different fiscal years can also be incorporated to control for the year-to-year variations.[5]

---

[4]Univariate comparisons reported in Table 1 show that the means of cash flow from operations to total assets ratio, assets turnover, total liabilities to total assets ratio, the logarithm of sales, and Tobin's $q$ between the diversified firms and the focused firms are significantly different.

[5]Theoretically, firm performance is positively associated with firm value. It, therefore, can conjecture that cash flow from operations to total assets ratio and assets turnover are also positively associated with firm value, i.e., their regression coefficients are positive. Barth *et al.* (1999) have claimed that the price-earnings multiple is an increasing function of growth and a decreasing function of risk. Tobin's $q$, an investment/growth opportunity measure, therefore should be positively associated with firm value, i.e., its regression coefficient is positive. Total liabilities to total assets ratio, a risk measure, should be negatively associated with firm value, i.e., its regression coefficient is negative. The signs of the logarithm of sales and the year dummies are not pre-determined.

Thus, all the control variables can be included in Equations (1)–(4) to perform regression analyses:

$$\frac{P_t}{P_{t-1}} = \alpha + \frac{\beta_1 E_t}{P_{t-1}} + \beta_2 \text{ CASHTA} + \beta_3 \text{ ATURN}$$
$$+ \beta_4 \text{ TLTA} + \beta_5 \text{ LOGSA} + \beta_6 \ Q + \beta_7 \text{ YR}_1 + \beta_8 \text{ YR}_2$$
$$+ \beta_9 \text{ YR}_3 + \beta_{10} \text{ YR}_4 + \beta_{11} \text{ YR}_5 + \varepsilon, \tag{6}$$

$$\frac{(P_t - P_{t-1})}{P_{t-1}} = \alpha + \frac{\beta_1 (E_t - E_{t-1})}{P_{t-1}} + \beta_2 \text{ CASHTA}$$
$$+ \beta_3 \text{ ATURN} + \beta_4 \text{ TLTA} + \beta_5 \text{ LOGSA}$$
$$+ \beta_6 \ Q + \beta_7 \text{ YR}_1 + \beta_8 \text{ YR}_2 + \beta_9 \text{ YR}_3$$
$$+ \beta_{10} \text{ YR}_4 + \beta_{11} \text{ YR}_5 + \varepsilon, \tag{7}$$

$$\frac{P_t}{P_{t-1}} = \alpha + \frac{\beta_1 E_t}{P_{t-1}} + \beta_2 \left( \text{GROUP} \times \frac{E_t}{P_{t-1}} \right)$$
$$+ \beta_3 \text{ CASHTA} + \beta_4 \text{ ATURN} + \beta_5 \text{ TLTA}$$
$$+ \beta_6 \text{ LOGSA} + \beta_7 \ Q + \beta_8 \text{ YR}_1 + \beta_9 \text{ YR}_2$$
$$+ \beta_{10} \text{ YR}_3 + \beta_{11} \text{ YR}_4 + \beta_{12} \text{ YR}_5 + \varepsilon, \tag{8}$$

$$\frac{(P_t - P_{t-1})}{P_{t-1}} = \alpha + \frac{\beta_1 (E_t - E_{t-1})}{P_{t-1}} + \beta_2 (\text{GROUP} \times \left( \frac{(E_t - E_{t-1})}{P_{t-1}} \right)$$
$$+ \beta_3 \text{ CASHTA} + \beta_4 \text{ ATURN} + \beta_5 \text{ TLTA}$$
$$+ \beta_6 \text{ LOGSA} + \beta_7 \ Q + \beta_8 \text{ YR}_1 + \beta_9 \text{ YR}_2$$
$$+ \beta_{10} \text{ YR}_3 + \beta_{11} \text{ YR}_4 + \beta_{12} \text{ YR}_5 + \varepsilon, \tag{9}$$

where CASHTA is the cash flow from operations to total assets ratio; ATURN the assets turnover ratio; TLTA the total liabilities to total assets ratio; LOGSA the logarithm of sales; $Q$ is the Tobin's $q$, and YRs are the year dummies; there are five year dummy variables for this study, i.e., one less than the number of years of observations.[6]

## 4. Data

Firms meeting the following criteria are selected for this study:

1. They are non-financial firms.
2. They are non-utilities firms.

---

[6]Data are collected from 1996 to 2001, i.e., six years.

3. Their segment sales data from 1996 to 2001 are available in the Research Insight database.[7]

Following Hyland and Diltz (2002), financial firms (SIC 6000–6999) and utilities firms (SIC 4900–4999) are excluded. Financial firms are eliminated because their financial ratios are difficult to be compared with non-financial firms' financial ratios. Utilities firms are excluded because of their regulated nature. 4,029 firms with six years of observations are selected. Fourteen firm-year outliers are deleted using the Cook's distance criterion.[8] The final sample consists of 24,160 firm-year observations.

Selected descriptive statistics of the firm-year observations are presented in Table 1. There are more focused firms than diversified firms. Diversified firms in general are larger than focused firms in cash, total assets, total liabilities, common equity, sales, number of common shares, cash flow from operations, capital expenditure, and research and development expense. They have a higher assets turnover ratio, and have a lower total liabilities to total assets ratio, cash flow from operations to total assets ratio, research and development expense to total assets ratio, capital expenditure to total sales ratio, and Tobin's $q$. Earnings per share, price per share, and three-year sales growth rate between the diversified firms and the focused firms are not significantly different. Price-earnings ratio for diversified firms is significantly higher than that for focused firms, i.e., this result seems to suggest that earnings have a higher impact on price for diversified firms.

## 5. Levels and Changes Analyses

### 5.1. *Levels analyses*

Levels regressions, represented by Equation (1), are performed on the full sample, the diversified firms, and the focused firms, respectively. Levels regressions are also performed by adding the year dummies to control for potential yearly effect. Results are presented in Table 2.

All regression coefficients for earnings level are positive and statistically significant, i.e., there is a positive and significant association between price

---

[7]Research insight provides seven years of segment data (from 1996 to 2002). 2002 has too many missing segment sales values, and therefore is not included in this study.

[8]There are several outlier identification methods (Belsley, Kuh, and Welsch, 1980). Following Barth *et al.* (1999), the Cook's distance criterion is used.

**Table 1.**   Descriptive statistics.

| | Focused | | | Diversified | | | |
|---|---|---|---|---|---|---|---|
| | N | Mean | Std.Dev. | N | Mean | Std.Dev. | *t*-value |
| CASH | 15701 | 70.35 | 366.78 | 8440 | 280.70 | 1,321.73 | 18.65*** |
| TA | 15707 | 728.68 | 3,394.48 | 8442 | 4,179.72 | 18,426.80 | 22.76*** |
| TL | 15678 | 462.65 | 2,485.00 | 8420 | 2,828.25 | 15,019.10 | 19.24*** |
| CE | 15693 | 258.60 | 1,171.39 | 8434 | 1,298.84 | 4,737.69 | 26.06*** |
| SALE | 15656 | 632.93 | 2,778.91 | 8442 | 3,286.26 | 11,957.92 | 26.47*** |
| EPS | 15261 | −5.30 | 703.48 | 8313 | −0.43 | 60.93 | 0.63 |
| SHARE | 15266 | 50.56 | 247.42 | 8313 | 146.37 | 524.83 | 19.01*** |
| OPCASH | 15514 | 70.18 | 404.80 | 8375 | 390.20 | 1,682.08 | 22.52*** |
| CAPEX | 15404 | 59.13 | 300.64 | 8280 | 270.09 | 1,333.68 | 18.77*** |
| SAL3G | 14552 | 77.27 | 3,510.35 | 8379 | 19.06 | 54.42 | −1.52 |
| PRICE | 14516 | 30.84 | 1,316.02 | 8122 | 20.51 | 50.88 | −0.71 |
| R_D | 9372 | 26.84 | 179.23 | 4800 | 163.25 | 645.48 | 19.07*** |
| ATURN | 15347 | 1.14 | 1.11 | 8408 | 1.18 | 0.91 | 2.89*** |
| TLTA | 15658 | 1.93 | 34.54 | 8420 | 0.60 | 0.59 | −3.52*** |
| LOGSA | 14952 | 1.72 | 1.11 | 8442 | 2.53 | 1.01 | 55.26*** |
| CASHTA | 15681 | 0.23 | 0.26 | 8440 | 0.11 | 0.15 | −38.69*** |
| LOGTA | 15689 | 1.80 | 1.50 | 8442 | 2.57 | 1.01 | 41.97*** |
| R_DTA | 9364 | 0.17 | 0.48 | 4800 | 0.06 | 0.11 | −16.50*** |
| CAPESA | 14709 | 1.36 | 48.44 | 8280 | 0.11 | 0.37 | −2.35** |
| Q | 14436 | 5.24 | 67.25 | 8110 | 1.91 | 2.59 | −4.45*** |
| PE | 14295 | 10.44 | 135.97 | 8084 | 15.58 | 140.64 | 2.68*** |

*Notes*: CASH is the cash balance (million dollars); TA the total assets (million dollars); TL the total liabilities (million dollars); CE the common equity (million dollars); SALE the sales (million dollars); EPS the basic earnings per share excluding extraordinary items (dollars); SHARE the outstanding common shares (million shares); OPCASH is operating activity −net cash flow (million dollars); CAPEX the capital expenditure (million dollars); SAL3G the three-year sales growth; PRICE the close price per share (dollars); R_D the research and development expense (million dollars); ATURN the asset turnover; TLTA the total liabilities to total assets; LOGSA the logarithm of sales; CASHTA the cash to total assets; LOGTA the logarithm of total assets; R_DTA the research and development expense to total assets; CAPESA the capital expenditure to sales; *Q* the Tobin's *q*; and PE the price-earnings ratio.
There are 24,160 firm-year observations (15,718 focused and 8,442 diversified).
*t*-values are for testing differences in means.
***Significant at $\alpha = 0.01$ level.

level and earnings level for the entire sample, for the diversified firms, and for the focused firms. The earnings response coefficient for the diversified firms is much higher than that for the focused firms. The coefficients of determination ($R^2$) for the diversified firms are much higher than those for the focused firms (0.31 versus 0.01), i.e., the association between price level and earnings

**Table 2.**   Levels analyses.

|  | All | All | Focused | Focused | Diversified | Diversified |
|---|---|---|---|---|---|---|
| $N$ | 21,629 | 21,629 | 13,651 | 13,651 | 7,978 | 7,978 |
| Intercept | 1.39 | 1.37 | 1.37 | 1.42 | 1.38 | 1.21 |
|  | (24.62)*** | (8.98)*** | (29.81)*** | (12.45)*** | (10.79)*** | (2.92)*** |
| $E$ | 0.41 | 0.41 | 0.10 | 0.10 | 0.49 | 0.49 |
|  | (78.32)*** | (78.37)*** | (13.61)*** | (13.62)*** | (60.55)*** | (60.61)*** |
| YR97 |  | −0.15 |  | −0.23 |  | 0.03 |
|  |  | (−0.72) |  | (−1.49) |  | (0.06) |
| YR98 |  | −0.13 |  | −0.08 |  | −0.30 |
|  |  | (−0.66) |  | (−0.50) |  | (−0.57) |
| YR99 |  | 0.37 |  | 0.50 |  | 0.26 |
|  |  | (1.82)* |  | (3.11)*** |  | (0.52) |
| YR00 |  | −0.32 |  | −0.39 |  | −0.15 |
|  |  | (−1.60) |  | (−2.38)* |  | (−0.31) |
| YR01 |  | 0.34 |  | −0.07 |  | 0.90 |
|  |  | (1.68)* |  | (−0.43) |  | (1.81)* |
| Adjusted $R^2$ | 0.2209 | 0.2215 | 0.0133 | 0.0133 | 0.3149 | 0.3154 |

*Notes*: The dependent variable is year-end price per share normalized by beginning price per share. $E$ is the earnings per share normalized by beginning price per share; YR97 is a dummy variable (= 1 if the year = 1997; = 0 otherwise); YR98 is a dummy variable (= 1 if the year = 1998; = 0 otherwise); YR99 is a dummy variable (= 1 if the year = 1999; = 0 otherwise); YR00 is a dummy variable (= 1 if the year = 2000; = 0 otherwise); YR01 is a dummy variable (= 1 if the year = 2001; = 0 otherwise).
The numbers of firm-year observations with missing values for the six regressions are 2,531, 2,531, 2,067, 2,067, 464, and 464, respectively.
*t*-values are in parentheses.
***, *Significant at $\alpha = 0.01$ level, 0.10 level, respectively.

level for the diversified firms is higher than that for the focused firms. Adding year dummies does not significantly improve the regression results, i.e., the coefficients of determination basically remain the same.

## 5.2. *Changes analyses*

Changes regressions, represented by Equation (2), are performed on the full sample, the diversified firms, and the focused firms, respectively. Changes regressions are also performed by adding the year dummies to control for potential yearly effect. Results are presented in Table 3.

All regression coefficients for earnings change are positive and statistically significant, i.e., there is a positive and significant association between price change and earnings change for the entire sample, for the diversified firms, and

**Table 3.** Changes analyses.

| | All | All | Focused | Focused | Diversified | Diversified |
|---|---|---|---|---|---|---|
| $N$ | 21,555 | 21,555 | 13,592 | 13,592 | 7,963 | 7,963 |
| Intercept | 0.27 | 0.31 | 0.35 | 0.39 | 0.24 | 0.21 |
| | (4.69)*** | (1.98)** | (7.47)*** | (3.40)*** | (1.76)* | (0.48) |
| EC | 0.24 | 0.24 | 0.05 | 0.05 | 0.29 | 0.29 |
| | (64.90)*** | (64.89)*** | (9.68)*** | (9.61)*** | (49.49)*** | (49.49)*** |
| YR97 | | −0.12 | | −0.21 | | 0.04 |
| | | (−0.54) | | (−1.32) | | (0.06) |
| YR98 | | −0.10 | | −0.07 | | −0.18 |
| | | (−0.45) | | (−0.43) | | (−0.34) |
| YR99 | | 0.32 | | 0.50 | | 0.22 |
| | | (1.53) | | (3.07)*** | | (0.42) |
| YR00 | | −0.40 | | −0.37 | | −0.44 |
| | | (−1.91)* | | (−2.24)** | | (−0.83) |
| YR01 | | 0.06 | | −0.11 | | 0.47 |
| | | (0.26) | | (−0.68) | | (0.89) |
| Adjusted $R^2$ | 0.1634 | 0.1638 | 0.0068 | 0.0088 | 0.2352 | 0.2352 |

*Notes*: The dependent variable is change in price per share normalized by beginning price per share. EC is change in earnings per share normalized by beginning price per share. YR97 is a dummy variable (= 1 if the year = 1997; = 0 otherwise); YR98 is a dummy variable (= 1 if the year = 1998; = 0 otherwise); YR99 is a dummy variable (= 1 if the year = 1999; = 0 otherwise). YR00 is a dummy variable (= 1 if the year = 2000; = 0 otherwise). YR01 is a dummy variable (= 1 if the year = 2001; = 0 otherwise).
The numbers of firm-year observations with missing values for the six regressions are 2,605, 2,605, 2,126, 2,126, 479, and 479, respectively.
*t*-values are in parentheses.
***, **, *Significant at $\alpha = 0.01$ level, 0.05 level, 0.10 level, respectively.

for the focused firms. The earnings response coefficient for the diversified firms is much higher than that for the focused firms. The coefficients of determination for the diversified firms are much higher than those for the focused firms (0.23 versus 0.01), i.e., the association between price change and earnings change for the diversified firms is higher than that for the focused firms. Adding year dummies does not significantly improve the regression results, i.e., the coefficients of determination basically remain the same.

## 5.3. *Levels analyses with an indicator variable*

Results of levels analyses presented in Table 2 show that the coefficients of determination for the diversified firms are higher than those for the focused firms. They imply that the association between price level and earnings level

**Table 4.**   Levels analyses with an indicator variable.

| | | | | | |
|---|---|---|---|---|---|
| N | 21,629 | 21,605 | 21,567 | 20,981 | 20,978 |
| Intercept | 1.37 | 1.28 | 1.15 | 1.07 | 0.97 |
| | (24.86)*** | (18.04)*** | (10.94)*** | (8.71)*** | (5.82)*** |
| E | 0.10 | 0.10 | 0.10 | 0.06 | 0.06 |
| | (9.01)*** | (9.01)*** | (9.02)*** | (4.77)*** | (4.76)*** |
| GROUP*E | 0.38 | 0.38 | 0.38 | 0.43 | 0.43 |
| | (29.78)*** | (29.75)*** | (29.72)*** | (33.48)*** | (33.48)*** |
| CASHTA | | 0.51 | 0.61 | | 0.46 |
| | | (2.13)** | (2.47)* | | (1.64) |
| ATURN | | | 0.10 | 0.12 | 0.13 |
| | | | (1.69)* | (2.13)** | (2.36)** |
| TLTA | | | | −0.05 | −0.05 |
| | | | | (−4.77)*** | (−4.55)*** |
| LOGSA | | | | 0.02 | 0.05 |
| | | | | (0.40) | (0.97) |
| Q | | | | 0.05 | 0.04 |
| | | | | (5.77)*** | (5.54)*** |
| Adjusted $R^2$ | 0.2516 | 0.2517 | 0.2519 | 0.2718 | 0.2719 |

*Notes*: The dependent variable is year-end price per share normalized by beginning price per share. $E$ is the earnings per share normalized by beginning price per share; GROUP is an indicator variable (=1 if diversified; = 0 if focused); CASHTA is cash to total assets; ATURN is asset turnover; TLTA is total liabilities to total assets; LOGSA is the logarithm of sales; and $Q$ is Tobin's $q$.

The numbers of firm-year observations with missing values for the five regressions are 2,531, 2,555, 2,593, 3,179, and 3,182, respectively.

$t$-values are in parentheses.

***, **, *Significant at $\alpha = 0.01$ level, 0.05 level, 0.10 level, respectively.

is higher for the diversified firms. Conclusions, however, are generated from regressions performed separately on the diversified firms and the focused firms, but not on the entire sample. Levels regressions using an indicator variable, represented by Equation (3), can provide stronger tests.[9] Additional regressions are also performed by including some of the control variables.[10] Results of the levels regressions with an indicator variable are presented in Table 4.

---

[9]Prior studies have used two different approaches to test the association. One approach is to compare the coefficients of determination. The higher the coefficient is, the higher the association is. The major drawback of this approach is that there is no statistical test for the significance of the difference. The other approach is to use the indicator variable. There is significance test for the difference of the two sample groups.

[10]Year dummies do not improve the regression results.

All regression coefficients for earnings level are positive and statistically significant, i.e., there is a positive and significant association between price level and earnings level for the entire sample. All regression coefficients for the indicator variable term are also positive and statistically significant. This result is important since it shows the diversified firms have a higher price-earnings multiple, i.e., statistically the association between price level and earnings level for the diversified firms is significantly higher than that for the focused firm. Coefficients for cash flow from operations to total assets ratio, assets turnover ratio, and Tobin's $q$ generally are positive and significant while coefficient for total liabilities to total assets ratio is negative and significant. Adding control variables does not change the conclusions, i.e., (1) price level is positively and significantly associated with earnings level, and (2) the association between price level and earnings level is higher for the diversified firms. Adding control variables does not significantly improve the regression results, i.e., the coefficients of determination basically remain the same.

## 5.4. *Changes analyses with an indicator variable*

Results of changes analyses presented in Table 3 show that the coefficients of determination for the diversified firms are higher than those for the focused firms. They imply that the association between price change and earnings change is higher for the diversified firms. Conclusions, however, are generated from regressions performed on either the diversified firms or the focused firms, but not on the entire sample. Changes regressions using an indicator variable, represented by Equation (4), can provide stronger tests. Additional regressions are also performed by including some of the control variables.[11] Results of the changes regressions with an indicator variable are presented in Table 5.

All regression coefficients for earnings change are positive and statistically significant, i.e., there is a positive and significant association between price change and earnings change for the entire sample. All regression coefficients for the indicator variable term are also positive and statistically significant. This is an important result in that it shows that the diversified firms have a higher price change-earnings change multiple, i.e., statistically the association between price change and earnings change for the diversified firms is significantly higher than that for the focused firm. Coefficients for cash flow from

---

[11]Year dummies do not improve the regression results.

**Table 5.**   Changes analyses with an indicator variable.

| N | 21,555 | 21,532 | 21,528 | 20,944 | 20,941 |
|---|---|---|---|---|---|
| Intercept | 0.31 | 0.20 | 0.06 | 0.00 | −0.20 |
|  | (5.30)*** | (2.65)*** | (0.56) | (−0.03) | (−1.24) |
| EC | 0.05 | 0.05 | 0.05 | 0.06 | 0.06 |
|  | (6.19)*** | (6.19)*** | (6.17)*** | (6.54)*** | (6.56)*** |
| GROUP*EC | 0.24 | 0.24 | 0.24 | 0.23 | 0.23 |
|  | (25.15)*** | (25.13)*** | (25.15)*** | (24.80)*** | (24.79)*** |
| CASHTA |  | 0.60 | 0.71 |  | 0.57 |
|  |  | (2.38)** | (2.73)*** |  | (1.97)** |
| ATURN |  |  | 0.10 | 0.11 | 0.13 |
|  |  |  | (1.66)* | (1.94)* | (2.22)** |
| TLTA |  |  |  | −0.05 | −0.05 |
|  |  |  |  | (−4.88)*** | (−4.62)*** |
| LOGSA |  |  |  | 0.02 | 0.06 |
|  |  |  |  | (0.45) | (1.14) |
| Q |  |  |  | 0.05 | 0.05 |
|  |  |  |  | (5.76)*** | (5.49)*** |
| Adjusted $R^2$ | 0.1873 | 0.1874 | 0.1875 | 0.2044 | 0.2045 |

*Notes*: The dependent variable is change in price per share normalized by beginning price per share. EC is the change in earnings per share normalized by beginning price per share; GROUP is an indicator variable (=1 if diversified; = 0 if focused); CASHTA is cash to total assets; ATURN is asset turnover; TLTA is total liabilities to total assets; LOGSA is the logarithm of sales; and Q is Tobin's q.

The numbers of firm-year observations with missing values for the five regressions are 2,605, 2,628, 2,632, 3,216, and 3,219, respectively.

*t*-values are in parentheses.

***, **, *Significant at $\alpha = 0.01$ level, 0.05 level, 0.10 level, respectively.

operations to total assets ratio, assets turnover ratio, and Tobin's *q* are positive and significant while coefficient for total liabilities to total assets ratio is negative and significant. Adding control variables does not change the conclusions, i.e., (1) price change is positively and significantly associated with earnings change, and (2) the association between price change and earnings change is higher for the diversified firms. Adding control variables does not significantly improve the regression results, i.e., the coefficients of determination basically remain the same.

## 6. Total Diversification

Analyses in the previous section classify firms into one of the two groups: the diversified firms and the focused firms. They have not considered diversified firms' degree of diversification. Total diversification index, a measure of degree of diversification, is proposed by Jacquemin and Berry (1979) and used by Palpepu (1985). It is defined as:

$$TD = \sum P_i \ln \left( \frac{1}{P_i} \right),$$  (10)

where TD is the total diversification index, $P_i$ is the percentage of the $i$th segment's sales as the total sales of the firm.

The total diversification index measures the degree of diversification since a focused firm has a TD of zero while a diversified firm has a positive TD. In addition, diversified firms with different degrees of diversification have different TD values.

Levels analysis can be performed by incorporating the total diversification index to test the usefulness of the degree of diversification information. It is represented as follows:

$$\frac{P_t}{P_{t-1}} = \alpha + \beta_1 \frac{E_t}{P_{t-1}} + \beta_2 \left( TD \times \frac{E_t}{P_{t-1}} \right) + \varepsilon$$  (11)

Equation (11) is similar to Equation (3). The only difference is that TD in Equation (11) replaces GROUP in Equation (3). Control variables can also be incorporated into the regressions.[12] Results are reported in Table 6.

All regression coefficients for earnings level are positive and statistically significant, i.e., there is a positive and significant association between price level and earnings level for the entire sample. All regression coefficients for the TD term are also positive and statistically significant. This result is significant since it shows that the higher the degree of diversification is, the higher the price-earnings multiple is, i.e., statistically the association between price level and earnings level is higher if the degree of diversification is higher. Coefficients for cash flow from operations to total assets ratio, assets turnover ratio, and Tobin's $q$ generally are positive and significant while coefficient for total liabilities to total assets ratio is negative and significant. Adding control variables does not change the conclusions, i.e., (1) price level is positively and significantly associated with earnings level, and (2) the association between price level and earnings level is higher for a higher degree of diversification. Adding control variables does not significantly improve the regression results, i.e., the coefficients of determination basically remain the same. Comparisons

---

[12] Year dummies do not improve the regression results.

**Table 6.**  Levels analyses with total diversification index.

| N | 21,629 | 21,605 | 21,567 | 20,981 | 20,978 |
|---|---|---|---|---|---|
| Intercept | 1.37 | 1.28 | 1.15 | 1.07 | 0.91 |
| | (24.64)*** | (17.87)*** | (10.85)*** | (8.68)*** | (5.80)*** |
| E | 0.18 | 0.18 | 0.18 | 0.14 | 0.14 |
| | (15.57)*** | (15.57)*** | (15.57)*** | (11.97)*** | (11.95)*** |
| TD*E | 0.29 | 0.29 | 0.29 | 0.34 | 0.34 |
| | (22.34)*** | (22.31)*** | (22.29)*** | (25.34)*** | (25.35)*** |
| CASHTA | | 0.52 | 0.62 | | 0.46 |
| | | (2.14)** | (2.46)** | | (1.63) |
| ATURN | | | 0.10 | 0.12 | 0.13 |
| | | | (1.65)* | (2.07)** | (2.30)** |
| TLTA | | | | −0.05 | −0.05 |
| | | | | (−4.71)*** | (−4.49)*** |
| LOGSA | | | | 0.02 | 0.05 |
| | | | | (0.34) | (0.91) |
| Q | | | | 0.05 | 0.04 |
| | | | | (5.73)*** | (5.49)*** |
| Adjusted $R^2$ | 0.2385 | 0.2386 | 0.2388 | 0.2557 | 0.2557 |

*Notes*: The dependent variable is year-end price per share normalized by beginning price per share. $E$ is the earnings per share normalized by beginning price per share; TD the total diversification index; CASHTA is cash to total assets; ATURN is asset turnover; TLTA is total liabilities to total assets; LOGSA the logarithm of sales; and $Q$ is Tobin's $q$.

The numbers of firm-year observations with missing values for the five regressions are 2,531, 2,555, 2,593, 3,179, and 3,182, respectively.

*t*-values are in parentheses.

***, **, *Significant at $\alpha = 0.01$ level, 0.05 level, 0.10 level, respectively.

of the coefficients of determination in Tables 4 and 6, however, indicate that $R^2$s are not improved by considering the degree of diversification.

Changes analysis can be performed by incorporating the total diversification index to test the usefulness of knowing degree of diversification. It is represented as follows:

$$\frac{(P_t - P_{t-1})}{P_{t-1}} = \alpha + \beta_1 \frac{(E_t - E_{t-1})}{P_{t-1}} + \beta_2 \left( TD \times \frac{(E_t - E_{t-1})}{P_{t-1}} \right) + \varepsilon. \quad (12)$$

Equation (12) is similar to Equation (4). The only difference is that TD in Equation (12) replaces GROUP in Equation (4). Control variables can also be incorporated into the regressions.[13] Results are reported in Table 7.

---

[13]Year dummies do not improve the regression results.

**Table 7.** Changes analyses with total diversification index.

| | | | | | |
|---|---|---|---|---|---|
| N | 21,555 | 21,532 | 21,528 | 20,944 | 20,941 |
| Intercept | 0.31 | 0.20 | 0.06 | −0.01 | −0.21 |
| | (5.29)*** | (2.65)*** | (0.56) | (−0.08) | (−1.30) |
| EC | 0.07 | 0.07 | 0.07 | 0.07 | 0.07 |
| | (8.18)*** | (8.18)*** | (8.16)*** | (8.69)*** | (8.70)*** |
| TD*EC | 0.23 | 0.23 | 0.23 | 0.22 | 0.22 |
| | (23.56)*** | (23.54)*** | (23.56)*** | (23.10)*** | (23.09)*** |
| CASHTA | | 0.59 | 0.71 | | 0.58 |
| | | (2.36)** | (2.71)** | | (1.98)** |
| ATURN | | | 0.10 | 0.11 | 0.13 |
| | | | (1.67)* | (1.92)* | (2.21)** |
| TLTA | | | | −0.05 | −0.05 |
| | | | | (−4.87)*** | (−4.61)*** |
| LOGSA | | | | 0.03 | 0.07 |
| | | | | (0.52) | (1.21) |
| Q | | | | 0.05 | 0.05 |
| | | | | (5.74)*** | (5.47)*** |
| Adjusted $R^2$ | 0.1844 | 0.1846 | 0.1847 | 0.2014 | 0.2015 |

*Notes*: The dependent variable is change in price per share normalized by beginning price per share. EC is the change in earnings per share normalized by beginning price per share; TD the total diversification index; CASHTA is cash to total assets; ATURN is asset turnover; TLTA is total liabilities to total assets. LOGSA the logarithm of sales; and Q is Tobin's $q$. The numbers of firm-year observations with missing values for the five regressions are 2,605, 2,628, 2,632, 3,216, and 3,219, respectively.
*t*-values are in parentheses.
***, **, *Significant at $\alpha = 0.01$ level, 0.05 level, 0.10 level, respectively.

All regression coefficients for earnings change are positive and statistically significant, i.e., there is a positive and significant association between price change and earnings change for the entire sample. All regression coefficients for the TD term are also positive and statistically significant. This result is significant since it shows that the higher the degree of diversification is, the higher the price change-earnings change multiple is, i.e., statistically the association between price change and earnings change is higher if the degree of diversification is higher. Coefficients for cash flow from operations to total assets ratio, assets turnover ratio, and Tobin's $q$ are positive and significant while coefficient for total liabilities to total assets ratio is negative and significant. Adding control variables does not change the conclusions, i.e., (1) price change is positively and significantly associated with earnings change, and (2) the association between price change and earnings change is higher for a higher degree of diversification. Adding control variables does not significantly improve the regression results, i.e., the coefficients of determination basically remain the same. Comparisons of the coefficients of determination in Tables 5 and 7, however, indicate that $R^2$s are not improved by considering the degree of diversification.

## 7. Analyses by Incorporating Quality of Earnings Information

Results presented in previous sections show that the association between firm value and earnings for diversified firms is higher than that for the focused firms. Comparisons of the coefficients of determination, however, indicate that regression results are not significantly improved by also considering degree of diversification. Prior research suggests that quality of earnings may also be incorporated into the regressions. One widely used measure of earnings' quality is proposed by Sloan (1996). He has suggested that quality of earnings can be measured by the extent of net cash flows from operations component of earnings versus accruals component of earnings; the higher the former is, the better the quality is. Using Sloan's (1996) approach, sample firms can be classified into two groups: those with quality earnings and those with non-quality earnings. In this study, a firm is classified as a quality earnings firm if (1) its cash component of earnings is higher than the total sample mean cash component, (2) cash flow per share from operations is positive, and (3) earnings per share is positive.[14]

Levels analysis by considering both diversification and quality of earnings is represented as follows:

$$\frac{P_t}{P_{t-1}} = \alpha + \frac{\beta_1 E_t}{P_{t-1}} + \beta_2 \left( \text{GROUP} \times \frac{E_t}{P_{t-1}} \right)$$
$$+ \beta_3 \left( \text{QUAL} \times \frac{E_t}{P_{t-1}} \right) + \varepsilon, \tag{13}$$

where QUAL is an indicator variable for quality of earnings; it equals 1 for quality earnings firms and 0 for non-quality earnings firms.

The association between price level and earnings levels for quality earnings firms should be higher than that for non-quality earnings firms, i.e., $\beta_3$ in Equation (13) is expected to be positive and significant. Control variables can also be incorporated into the regressions. Results are reported in Table 8.

---

[14]Cash component is measured by cash flow from operations divided by earnings. Firms with negative cash flows from operations and/or negative earnings are non-quality firms.

**Table 8.** Level analyses with diversification and quality of earnings.

| N | 21,292 | 21,292 | 20,688 | 20,688 |
|---|---|---|---|---|
| Intercept | 1.09 | 1.12 | 1.03 | 0.98 |
| | (32.65)*** | (12.42)*** | (12.32)*** | (8.82)*** |
| E | 0.10 | 0.10 | 0.05 | 0.05 |
| | (14.46)*** | (14.47)*** | (8.71)*** | (8.74)*** |
| GROUP*E | 0.33 | 0.33 | 0.37 | 0.37 |
| | (42.70)*** | (42.74)*** | (54.70)*** | (54.75)*** |
| QUAL*E | 7.89 | 7.89 | 7.90 | 7.90 |
| | (198.16)*** | (198.31)*** | (231.50)*** | (231.67)*** |
| ATURN | | | 0.08 | 0.08 |
| | | | (2.71)*** | (2.81)*** |
| TLTA | | | −0.05 | −0.05 |
| | | | (−8.56)*** | (−8.34)*** |
| LOGSA | | | −0.11 | −0.11 |
| | | | (−3.98)*** | (−3.99)*** |
| CASHTA | | | 0.34 | 0.36 |
| | | | (2.31)** | (2.40)** |
| Q | | | 0.04 | 0.04 |
| | | | (10.28)*** | (9.99)*** |
| YR97 | | −0.14 | | −0.03 |
| | | (−1.17) | | (−0.27) |
| YR98 | | −0.10 | | −0.00 |
| | | (−0.84) | | (−0.04) |
| YR99 | | 0.35 | | 0.39 |
| | | (2.97)*** | | (3.75)*** |
| YR00 | | −0.38 | | −0.23 |
| | | (−3.15)*** | | (−2.17)** |
| YR01 | | 0.06 | | 0.16 |
| | | (0.54) | | (1.56) |
| Adjusted $R^2$ | 0.7371 | 0.7377 | 0.7973 | 0.7977 |

*Notes*: The dependent variable is year-end price per share normalized by beginning price per share. $E$ is the earnings per share normalized by beginning price per share; GROUP is an indicator variable (=1 if diversified; = 0 if focused); QUAL is an indicator variable (=1 if quality earnings; = 0 if non-quality earnings); ATURN is asset turnover; TLTA the total liabilities to total assets; LOGSA the logarithm of sales; CASHTA is cash to total assets; $Q$ is Tobin's $q$; YR97 is a dummy variable (= 1 if the year = 1997; = 0 otherwise); YR98 is a dummy variable (= 1 if the year = 1998; = 0 otherwise); YR99 is a dummy variable (= 1 if the year = 1999; = 0 otherwise); YR00 is a dummy variable (= 1 if the year = 2000; = 0 otherwise); YR01 is a dummy variable (= 1 if the year = 2001; = 0 otherwise).

The numbers of firm-year observations with missing values for the four regressions are 2,868, 2,868, 3,472, and 3,472, respectively.

*t*-values are in parentheses.

***, **Significant at $\alpha = 0.01$ level, 0.05 level, respectively.

All regression coefficients for earnings level are positive and statistically significant, i.e., there is a positive and significant association between price level and earnings level for the entire sample. All regression coefficients for the GROUP term are positive and statistically significant, i.e., the diversified firms have a higher price-earnings multiple than the focused firms. All regression coefficients for the QUAL term are also positive and statistically significant, i.e., the quality earnings firms have a higher price-earnings multiple than the non-quality earnings firms. Coefficients for cash flow from operations to total assets ratio, assets turnover ratio, and Tobin's $q$ are positive and significant while coefficients for total liabilities to total assets ratio and the logarithm of sales are negative and significant. Adding control variables does not change the conclusions, i.e., (1) price level is positively and significantly associated with earnings level, (2) the association between price level and earnings level is higher for diversified firms, and (3) the association between price level and earnings level is higher for quality earnings firms. Adding control variables does not significantly improve the regression results, i.e., the coefficients of determination basically remain the same. Comparisons of the coefficients of determination in Tables 4 and 8, however, indicate that $R^2$s are improved by also considering quality of earnings.

Changes analysis by considering both diversification and quality of earnings is represented as follows:

$$
\frac{(P_t - P_{t-1})}{P_{t-1}} = \alpha + \beta_1 \frac{(E_t - E_{t-1})}{P_{t-1}} + \beta_2 \left( \text{GROUP} \times \frac{(E_t - E_{t-1})}{P_{t-1}} \right)
$$
$$
+ \beta_3 \left( \text{QUAL} \times \frac{(E_t - E_{t-1})}{P_{t-1}} \right) + \varepsilon. \tag{14}
$$

The association between price change and earnings change for quality earnings firms should be higher than that for non-quality earnings firms, i.e., $\beta_3$ in Equation (14) is expected to be positive and significant. Control variables can also be incorporated into the regressions. Results are reported in Table 9.

All regression coefficients for earnings change are positive and statistically significant, i.e., there is a positive and significant association between price change and earnings change for the entire sample. All regression coefficients for the GROUP term are positive and statistically significant, i.e., the diversified firms have a higher price change-earnings change multiple than the focused firms. All regression coefficients for the QUAL term are also positive and statistically significant, i.e., the quality earnings firms have a higher

**Table 9.** Changes analyses with diversification and quality of earnings.

| $N$ | 21,221 | 21,221 | 20,652 | 20,652 |
|---|---|---|---|---|
| Intercept | 0.13 | 0.19 | −0.27 | −0.28 |
| | (3.02)*** | (1.59) | (−2.30)** | (−1.82)* |
| EC | 0.02 | 0.02 | 0.01 | 0.01 |
| | (2.39)** | (2.37)** | (2.00)** | (1.99)** |
| GROUP * EC | 0.25 | 0.25 | 0.25 | 0.25 |
| | (35.25)*** | (35.29)*** | (37.54)*** | (37.56)*** |
| QUAL * EC | 5.14 | 5.14 | 5.14 | 5.14 |
| | (131.39)*** | (131.42)*** | (142.49)*** | (142.51)*** |
| ATURN | | | 0.06 | 0.05 |
| | | | (1.33) | (1.29) |
| TLTA | | | −0.05 | −0.05 |
| | | | (−6.75)*** | (−6.56)*** |
| LOGSA | | | 0.05 | 0.05 |
| | | | (1.22) | (1.31) |
| CASHTA | | | 0.61 | 0.62 |
| | | | (2.90)*** | (2.96)*** |
| $Q$ | | | 0.05 | 0.05 |
| | | | (7.99)*** | (7.78)*** |
| YR97 | | −0.08 | | 0.03 |
| | | (−0.47) | | (0.18) |
| YR98 | | −0.02 | | 0.07 |
| | | (−0.11) | | (0.46) |
| YR99 | | 0.30 | | 0.31 |
| | | (1.93)* | | (2.11)** |
| YR00 | | −0.41 | | −0.29 |
| | | (−2.59)*** | | (−1.96)* |
| YR01 | | −0.13 | | −0.07 |
| | | (−0.86) | | (−0.47) |
| Adjusted $R^2$ | 0.5522 | 0.5526 | 0.5989 | 0.5992 |

*Notes*: The dependent variable is change in price per share normalized by beginning price per share. EC is the change in earnings per share normalized by beginning price per share; GROUP is an indicator variable (=1 if diversified; = 0 if focused); QUAL is an indicator variable (=1 if quality earnings; = 0 if non-quality earnings); ATURN is asset turnover; TLTA is total liabilities to total assets; LOGSA is the logarithm of sales; CASHTA is cash( to total assets; $Q$ is Tobin's $q$; YR97 is a dummy variable (= 1 if the year = 1997; = 0 otherwise); YR98 is a dummy variable (= 1 if the year = 1998; = 0 otherwise); YR99 is a dummy variable (= 1 if the year = 1999; = 0 otherwise); YR00 is a dummy variable (= 1 if the year = 2000; = 0 otherwise); YR01 is a dummy variable (= 1 if the year = 2001; = 0 otherwise).

The numbers of firm-year observations with missing values for the four regressions are 2,939, 2,939, 3,508, and 3,508, respectively.

*t*-values are in parentheses.

***, **, *Significant at $\alpha = 0.01$ level, 0.05 level, 0.10 level, respectively.

price change-earnings change multiple than the non-quality earnings firms. Coefficients for cash flow from operations to total assets ratio, and Tobin's $q$ are positive and significant while coefficient for total liabilities to total assets ratio is negative and significant. Adding control variables does not change the conclusions, i.e., (1) price change is positively and significantly associated with earnings change, (2) the association between price change and earnings change is higher for diversified firms, and (3) the association between price change and earnings change is higher for quality earnings firms. Adding control variables does not significantly improve the regression results, i.e., the coefficients of determination basically remain the same. Comparisons of the coefficients of determination in Tables 5 and 9, however, indicate that $R^2$s are improved by also considering quality of earnings.

The following levels regression can also be performed to compare the price-earnings multiples among four sample groups: quality earnings diversified firms, quality earnings focused firms, non-quality earnings diversified firms, and non-quality earnings focused firms:

$$\frac{P_t}{P_{t-1}} = \alpha + \beta_1 \frac{E_t}{P_{t-1}} + \beta_2 \left( G1 \times \frac{E_t}{P_{t-1}} \right) + \beta_3 \left( G2 \times \frac{E_t}{P_{t-1}} \right)$$
$$+ \beta_4 \left( G3 \times \frac{E_t}{P_{t-1}} \right) + \varepsilon, \tag{15}$$

where G1 is an indicator variable; it equals 1 for quality earnings diversified firms and 0 otherwise; G2 an indicator variable; it equals 1 for quality earnings focused firms and 0 otherwise; and G3 is an indicator variable; it equals 1 for non-quality earnings diversified firms and 0 otherwise.

This regression uses the non-quality earnings focused firms as the base group. Quality earnings diversified firms/quality earnings focused firms/non-quality earnings diversified firms have a higher price-earnings multiple than non-quality earnings focused firms if $\beta_2/\beta_3/\beta_4$ is positive and significant. Quality earnings diversified firms/quality earnings focused firms/non-quality earnings diversified firms have a lower price-earnings multiple than non-quality earnings focused firms if $\beta_2/\beta_3/\beta_4$ is negative and significant. In addition, the values of $\beta_2$, $\beta_3$, and $\beta_4$ determine the relative magnitude of the price-earnings multiple among the three sample groups. Control variables can also be incorporated into the regressions. Results are reported in Table 10.

The regression coefficient for earnings level is positive and statistically significant, i.e., there is a positive and significant association between price level and earnings level. All regression coefficients for the indicator terms are positive and statistically significant, i.e., all three sample groups have a higher price-earnings multiple than the base group. The ranking of the magnitude of price-earnings multiple is: quality earnings diversified firms, quality earnings focused firms, non-quality earnings diversified firms, and then non-quality earnings focused firms. Coefficients for cash flow from operations to total assets

**Table 10.** Comparison among four sample groups.

|  | Levels | Changes |
|---|---|---|
| $N$ | 20,688 | 20,652 |
| Intercept | 1.02 | −0.03 |
|  | (9.21)*** | (−0.27) |
| $E$ | 0.06 | |
|  | (8.92)*** | |
| EC | | 0.05 |
|  | | (10.56)*** |
| G1 * E | 8.29 | |
|  | (240.31)*** | |
| G1 * EC | | 7.26 |
|  | | (212.06)*** |
| G2 * E | 3.66 | |
|  | (8.75)*** | |
| G2 * EC | | 0.11 |
|  | | (2.06)** |
| G3 * E | 0.37 | |
|  | (54.70)*** | |
| G3 * EC | | 0.21 |
|  | | (37.80)*** |
| ATURN | 0.09 | 0.28 |
|  | (3.06)*** | (2.28)** |
| TLTA | −0.05 | −0.05 |
|  | (−8.34)*** | (−7.83)*** |
| LOGSA | −0.10 | 0.00 |
|  | (−3.34)*** | (0.09) |
| CASHTA | 0.34 | 0.40 |
|  | (2.30)** | (2.37)** |
| $Q$ | 0.04 | 0.04 |
|  | (9.99)*** | (9.25)*** |
| YR97 | −0.03 | −0.06 |
|  | (−0.29) | (−0.46) |
| YR98 | −0.03 | −0.03 |
|  | (−0.32) | (−0.26) |

*(Continued)*

**Table 10.**   *(Continued)*

|  | Levels | Changes |
|---|---|---|
| YR99 | 0.37 | 0.32 |
|  | (3.54)*** | (2.73)*** |
| YR00 | −0.24 | −0.35 |
|  | (−2.27)** | (−2.97)*** |
| YR01 | 0.15 | −0.13 |
|  | (1.41) | (−1.07) |
| Adjusted $R^2$ | 0.7987 | 0.7428 |

*Notes*: The dependent variable for the levels regression is in price per share normalized by beginning price per share. The independent variable for the changes regression is change in price per share normalized by beginning price per share. $E$ is the earnings per share normalized by beginning price per share; EC is change in earnings per share normalized by beginning price per share; G1 $= 1$ for quality earnings diversified firms; $= 0$ otherwise; G2 $= 1$ for quality earnings focused firms; $= 0$ otherwise; G3 $= 1$ for non-quality earnings diversified firms; $= 0$ otherwise; ATURN is asset turnover; TLTA is total liabilities to total assets; LOGSA is the logarithm of sales; CASHTA is cash to total assets; $Q$ is Tobin's $q$; YR97 is a dummy variable ($= 1$ if the year $= 1997$; $= 0$ otherwise); YR98 is a dummy variable ($= 1$ if the year $= 1998$; $= 0$ otherwise); YR99 is a dummy variable ($= 1$ if the year $= 1999$; $= 0$ otherwise); YR00 is a dummy variable ($= 1$ if the year $= 2000$; $= 0$ otherwise); YR01 is a dummy variable ($= 1$ if the year $= 2001$; $= 0$ otherwise).
*t*-values are in parentheses.
***, **Significant at $\alpha = 0.01$ level, 0.05 level, respectively.

ratio, assets turnover ratio, and Tobin's $q$ are positive and significant while coefficient for total liabilities to total assets ratio is negative and significant.

The following changes regression can also be performed to compare the price change-earnings change multiples among the four sample groups: quality earnings diversified firms, quality earnings focused firms, non-quality earnings diversified firms, and non-quality earnings focused firms:

$$\frac{(P_t - P_{t-1})}{P_{t-1}} = \alpha + \frac{\beta_1(E_t - E_{t-1})}{P_{t-1}} + \beta_2 \left( G1 \times \frac{(E_t - E_{t-1})}{P_{t-1}} \right)$$
$$+ \beta_3 \left( G2 \times \frac{(E_t - E_{t-1})}{P_{t-1}} \right)$$
$$+ \beta_4 \left( G3 \times \frac{(E_t - E_{t-1})}{P_{t-1}} \right) + \varepsilon. \qquad (16)$$

This regression uses the non-quality earnings focused firms as the base group. Quality earnings diversified firms/quality earnings focused firms/non-quality earnings diversified firms have a higher price change-earnings change multiple than non-quality earnings focused firms if $\beta_2/\beta_3/\beta_4$ is positive and significant. Quality earnings diversified firms/quality earnings focused firms/non-quality earnings diversified firms have a lower price change-earnings change multiple than non-quality earnings focused firms if $\beta_2/\beta_3/\beta_4$ is negative and significant. In addition, the values of $\beta_2$, $\beta_3$, and $\beta_4$ determine the relative magnitude of the price change-earnings change multiple among the three sample groups. Control variables can be incorporated into the regressions. Results are also reported in Table 10.

The regression coefficient for earnings change is positive and statistically significant, i.e., there is a positive and significant association between price change and earnings change. All regression coefficients for the indicator terms are positive and statistically significant, i.e., all three sample groups have a higher price change-earnings change multiple than the base group. The ranking of the magnitude of price-earnings multiple is: quality earnings diversified firms, non-quality earnings diversified firms, quality earnings focused firms, and then non-quality earnings focused firms. Coefficients for cash flow from operations to total assets ratio, assets turnover ratio, and Tobin's $q$ are positive and significant while coefficient for total liabilities to total assets ratio is negative and significant.

## 8. Conclusions

The major purpose of this study is to examine the effect of diversification on the association between price and earnings using both the levels and the changes analyses. Results show that the association for diversified firms is higher than that for focused firms. The association is higher if the degree of diversification is higher. The association is stronger if quality of earnings is also included in the analyses. Thus, information about diversification and degree of diversification is useful for firm valuation. Investors and analysts, therefore, can rely more heavily on the price-earnings association when analyzing diversified firms.

Three issues deserve additional attention. The first is the sample selection procedure. Numerous prior studies have included only sample firms having data for all variables that are required for all the statistical analyses, i.e., a firm is deleted even if it has only one missing value for one variable. The sample size would have been significantly smaller if this stringent sample selection procedure had been adopted by this study.

The second issue is the measure of degree of diversification. This study only considers the total diversification index. Results show that the association between price and earnings are higher for a higher degree of diversification. Using the total diversification index in regressions, however, does not improve the coefficient of determination. Other measures such as the relative diversification index (Palepu, 1985) and Herfindahl's index (Jacquemin and Berry, 1979) can be tested in future studies.

The third issue is the cause of diversification. It has been discussed by prior diversification studies without definitive conclusions (e.g., Denis, Denis, and Sarin, 1997; Hyland and Diltz, 2002). This study relies on the information asymmetry argument proposed by Hadlock *et al.* (2001). Prior non-diversification studies may also be used to conjecture the cause for future studies. For example, diversified firms tend to be larger in size than focused firms (as shown in Table 1). Larger firms tend to have more analysts following and therefore their earnings should have a higher association with stock prices (Bhushan, 1989). Diversified firms tend to have smaller earnings variability and therefore their earnings should have a higher association with stock prices (Kim, Kim, and Pantzalis, 2001).[15]

## References

Albrecht, W. D. and F. M. Richardson, "Income Smoothing by Economy Sector." *Journal of Business Finance and Accounting* 17, 713–730 (1990).

Badrinath, S. G., G. D. Day and J. R. Kale, "Patterns of Institutional Investment, Prudence, and the Managerial 'Safety-Net' Hypothesis'." *Journal of Risk and Insurance* 56, 605–629 (1989).

Barth, M. E., J. A. Elliott and M. W. Finn, "Market Rewards Associated With Patterns of Increasing Earnings." *Journal of Accounting Research* 37, 387–413 (1999).

---

[15]The conjecture definitely is tentative. For example, Moses (1987) argues that larger firms tend to smooth their earnings since large earnings increases are perceived as signals of monopolistic practices and large earnings decreases are perceived as crisis. Smoothing, therefore, leads to a smaller variability of earnings. Albrecht and Richardson (1990), on the other hand, argue that larger firms tend not to smooth their earnings because they are followed more closely by the public. A smaller variability of earnings may lead to a lower firm value since there is an inverse relation between risk (measured by variability of earnings) and value, and may lead to a higher firm value since institutional investors and individual investors tend to avoid firms with fluctuating earnings (Badrinath, Day and Kale, 1989). Thus, there are no definitive conclusions from prior non-diversification studies.

Belsley, D. A., E. Kuh and R. E. Welsch, *Regression Diagnostics*, New York, Wiley (1980).

Berger, P. G. and E. Ofek, "Diversification's Effect on Firm Value." *Journal of Financial Economics* 37, 39–65 (1995).

Berger, P. G. and E. Ofek, "Causes and Effects of Corporate Refocusing Programs." *Review of Financial Studies* 12, 311–345 (1999).

Billett, M. T. and D. C. Mauer, "Diversification and the Value of Internal Capital Markets: The Case of Tracking Stock." *Journal of Banking & Finance* 24, 1457–1490 (2000).

Bhushan, R., "Firm Characteristics and Analyst Following." *Journal of Accounting and Economics* 11, 255–274 (1989).

Denis, D. J., D. K. Denis and A. Sarin, "Agency Problems, Equity Ownership, and Corporate Diversification." *Journal of Finance* 52, 135–160 (1997).

Desai, H. and P. C. Jain, "Firm Performance and Focus: Long-run Stock Market Performance Following Spinoffs." *Journal of Financial Economics* 54, 75–101 (1999).

Graham, J. R., M. L. Hemmon and J. G. Wolf, "Does Corporate Diversification Destroy Value?" *Journal of Finance* 57, 695–720 (2002).

Hadlock, C. J., M. Ryngaert and S. Thomas, "Corporate Structure and Equity Offerings: Are There Benefits to Diversification?" *Journal of Business* 74, 613–3 (2001).

Hyland, D. C. and J. D. Diltz, "Why Firms Diversify: An Empirical Examination." *Financial Management* 31, 51–81 (2002).

Jacquemin, A. P. and C. H. Berry, "Entropy Measure of Diversification and Corporate Growth." *Journal of Industrial Economics* 27, 359–369 (1979).

Kim, C. F., S. Kim and C. Pantzalis, "Firm Diversification and Earnings Volatility: An Empirical Analysis of U.S.-Based MNC's." *American Business Reviews* 19, 26–38 (2001).

Kothari, S. P., "Price-earnings Regressions in the Presence of Prices Leading Earnings: Earnings Levels Versus Changes Specifications and Alternative Deflators." *Journal of Accounting and Economics* 15, 173–202 (1992).

Lang, L. H. P. and R. M. Stulz, "Tobin's $q$, Corporate Diversification, and Firm Performance." *Journal of Political Economy* 102, 1248–1280 (1994).

Lins, K. V. and H. Servaes, "International Evidence on the Value of Corporate Diversification." *Journal of Finance* 54, 2215–2239 (1999).

Lins, K. V. and H. Servaes, "Is Corporate Diversification Beneficial in Emerging Markets?" *Financial Management* 31, 5–31 (2002).

Martin, J. D. and A. Sayrak, "Corporate Diversification and Shareholder Value: A Survey of Recent Literature." *Journal of Corporate Finance* 9, 37–57 (2003).

Moses, O. D., "Income Smoothing and Incentives: Empirical Tests Using Accounting Changes." *The Accounting Review* 62, 358–377 (1987).

Mullherin, J. H. and A. L. Boone, "Comparing Acquisitions and Divestitures." Working Paper, Pennsylvania State University (2002).

Palepu, K., "Diversification Strategy, Profit Performance and the Entropy Measure." *Strategic Management Journal* 6, 239–255 (1985).

Singh, M., I. Mathur, K. C. Gleason and A. Etebari, "An Empirical Examination of the Trend and Performance Implications of Business Diversification." *Journal of Business & Economic Studies* 7, 25–51 (2001).

Sloan, R. G., "Do Stock Prices Fully Reflect Information in Accruals and Cash Flows About Future Earnings?" *The Accounting Review* 71, 289–315 (1996).

Whited, T. M., "Is It Inefficient Investment that Causes the Diversification Discount?" *Journal of Finance* 56, 1667–1691 (2001).

# Chapter 14

## ————Taking Positive Interest Rates Seriously ————

Enlin Pan
*Chicago Partners, LLC, USA*

Liuren Wu*
*Baruch College, City University of New York, USA*

We present a dynamic term structure model in which interest rates of all maturities are bounded from below at zero. Positivity and continuity, combined with no arbitrage, result in only one functional form for the term structure with three sources of risk. We cast the model into a state-space form and extract the three sources of systematic risk from both the US Treasury yields and the US dollar swap rates. We analyze the different dynamic behaviors of the two markets during credit crises and liquidity squeezes.

**JEL Classification:** E43, E47, C51, C53, G12.

**Keywords:** Term structure; positivity; quadratic forms; forecasting; state-space estimation.

## 1. Introduction

Many term structure models have been proposed during the last two decades, yet most of these models imply positive probabilities of negative interest rates. Other models guarantee interest rate positivity, but very often imply that interest rates at certain maturities cannot go below a certain positive number. Asserting that an interest rate can be negative or cannot be lower than, say, 3%, is equally counterintuitive for academics and troublesome for practitioners. In this paper, we propose a dynamic term structure model where interest rates of all maturities are bounded below at exactly zero.

Such a reasonable and seemingly innocuous contention, together with the assumption of continuity and no arbitrage, generates several striking results. First, the term structure of interest rates collapses to one functional form, determined by the solution to a scalar Riccati equation. Second, the term structure is governed by exactly three sources of risk, only one of which is dynamic. This dynamic risk factor follows a special two-parameter square-root process under the risk-neutral measure, and the two parameters of the process determine the

---

*Corresponding author.

other two sources of risk. The model has no extra parameters in addition to these three risk factors.

The most surprising result is the collapse of dimensionality. We obtain the three sources of risk without any *a priori* assumption on the exact dimensionality of the state-space. The dynamic factor controls the level of the interest rate curve. The two parameters control the slope and curvature of the yield curve. Although the two parameters can be time varying, their dynamics do not affect the pricing of the interest rates. Therefore, we regard them as static factors.

Despite its simplicity, our model captures the observed yield curve very well. In particular, the model captures nicely the well-documented hump shape in the term structure of forward rates. By a simple transformation, we can represent the whole term structure by the maximum forward rate, the maturity of the maximum forward rate, and the curvature of the forward rate curve at the maximum. We can also use the instantaneous interest rate (level), the slope, and the curvature of the forward-rate curve at the short end as the three factors. Such transformations not only comply with the empirical findings and intuition, but also simplify the daily fitting of the forward-rate curve.

To investigate the empirical performance of the model in fitting the term structure of interest rates, we calibrate the model to the weekly data of both US Treasury yields and US dollar swap rates over the eight years from December 14, 1994 to December 28, 2000. The model fits both markets well. The pricing errors are mostly within a few basis points. The estimation also generates a time series of the three factors from both markets. The intuitive explanation of the three factors further enhances our understanding of the two interest rate markets. We find that although the average level spread between the swap rates and the Treasury yields are small, the spread can become exceptionally large during credit events such as the late 1998 hedge fund crisis and during the Treasury liquidity squeeze in 2000.

The paper is organized as follows. Section 2 describes the relevant literature that forms the background of our study. Section 3 elaborates on how the contention of interest rate positivity and continuity collapses the dimensionality of the state-space to three. In Section 4, we analyze the properties and different representations of the three sources of risk. In Section 5, we fit the model to both the US Treasury yields and the US dollar swap rates. In Section 6, we explore the possibility of adding jumps to such a model while maintaining positive interest rates. Section 7 concludes.

## 2. Background

Many term structure models allow positive probabilities of negative interest rates. The inconsistency in terms of negative interest rates in these models is often excused on the grounds of "good" empirical performance and "small probability" of negative interest rates. Although this is true in many cases, the values of some derivatives are extremely sensitive to the possibility of negative rates (Rogers, 1996). For such derivatives, the prices inferred from these "negative" interest rate models can be absurd.

The literature has taken three approaches in generating positive interest rates. The first approach specifies the instantaneous interest rate as a general quadratic function of some Gaussian state variable. Examples of quadratic term structure models include Ahn, Dittmar, and Gallant (2002), Beaglehole and Tenney (1991, 1992), Brandt and Chapman (2002), Brandt and Yaron (2001), Constantinides (1992), El Karoui, Myneni, and Viswanathan (1992), Jamshidian (1996), Leippold and Wu (2002, 2003), Longstaff (1989), and Rogers (1997). This approach can guarantee the positivity of the instantaneous interest rate by one parametric restriction. However, the underlying dynamics very often imply that interest rates at some other maturities can either become negative or cannot go below a certain positive number. Asserting that an interest rate can be negative or cannot be lower than, say, 3%, is equally absurd. For example, no rational traders are willing to offer free floors at any strictly positive level of interest rates. Our model is mostly related to this approach. Instead of assuming a quadratic form for only the instantaneous interest rate, we require that interest rates at all maturities are quadratic functions of a finite-dimensional state vector. We further constrain the functions to have no linear or constant terms so that all interest rates are bounded from below at exactly zero.

The second approach derives positive interest rates based on the specifications of the pricing kernel. For example, Flesaker and Hughston (1996) derive a condition on the discount bond price that guarantees positive interest rates. However, the rational log-normal model they come up with from this condition has several issues: The short rate implied from the model is bounded from both above and below, and the model remains arbitrage-free only up to a certain point (Babbs, 1997). Jin and Glasserman (2001) show how the framework of Heath, Jarrow, and Morton (1992) is related to the positive rate framework of Flesaker and Hughston (1996).

The third approach treats nominal interest rates as options and hence guarantee positive interest rates. Examples include Black (1995), Gorovoi and Linetsky (2003), and Rogers (1995). In addition, Goldstein and Keirstead (1997) generate positive interest rates by modeling them as processes with reflecting or absorbing boundaries at zero. However, these models are rarely analytically tractable.

The collapse of dimensionality to three under our model is consistent with the empirical findings of factor analysis in, among others, Litterman and Scheinkman (1991), Knez, Litterman, and Scheinkman (1994), and Heidari and Wu (2003). The dimension of three has also become the consensus choice in recent empirical works on model designs, e.g., Backus, Foresi, Mozumdar, and Wu (2001), Balduzzi, Das, Foresi, and Sundaram (1996), Chen and Scott (1993), Dai and Singleton (2000, 2002, 2003), and Duffee (2002). However, these three-factor models have 10 to 20 free parameters. The estimates of many of these parameters show large standard errors. Therefore, in applying these models, we not only need to control and price the risk of the three state variables (factors), but we must also be concerned with the uncertainty and risk associated with the many parameter estimates. Recently, Longstaff, Santa-Clara, and Schwartz (2001) address the issue of overfitting in pricing American swaptions. In contrast, under our model, the three factors capture all that is uncertain. We have no other parameters to estimate and hence no other risks to bear. Furthermore, we find that the empirical performance of our model in fitting the term structure of US swap rates and Treasury yields is comparable to the much more complicated models.

The collapse of dimensionality is also observed in the geometric analysis of Pan (1998). In this paper, we link the collapse of dimensionality to the risk-neutral dynamics of the interest rates. To guarantee that all interest rates are bounded below from zero, we start with the assumption that all continuously compounded spot rates are quadratic forms of a finite-dimensional state vector. This setup belongs to the quadratic class of Leippold and Wu (2002). Nevertheless, the resulting term structure behaves as if all spot rates are proportional to one dynamic factor, which follows a special two-parameter square root process. Thus, the final model falls within the affine class of Duffie and Kan (1996) and is very close to the model of Cox, Ingersoll, and Ross (1985). In a way, our model illustrates the inherent link between the affine class and the quadratic class of term structure models.

With some transformation, we can define the three interest rate factors in terms of the level, the maturity, and the curvature of the maximum forward rate. Thus, the model can naturally generate a hump-shaped term structure. Recent evidence supports such a hump shape. For example, Brown and Schaefer (2000) find that, in nearly ten years of daily data on US Treasury STRIPS from 1985 to 1994, the implied two-year forward rate spanning years 24–26 is lower than the forward rate for years 14 and 16 on 98.4% of occasions. The average difference in these rates is 138 basis points. A similar downward tilt also appears in estimates of forward rates derived from the prices of coupon bonds in the US Treasury market and in the UK market for both real and nominal government bonds. Given the initial upward-sloping term structure in most observations, the downward slopes in the very long term imply a hump-shaped term structure for the forward rates.

## 3. The Model

We fix a filtered complete probability space $\{\Omega, \mathcal{F}, \mathbb{P}, (\mathcal{F}_t)_{0 \leq t \leq T}\}$ that satisfies the usual technical conditions[1] with $T$ being some finite, fixed time. We assume that the uncertainty of the economy is governed by a finite-dimensional state vector $\mathbf{u}$.

**Assumption 1** (Diffusive State Vector). *Under the probability space $\{\Omega, \mathcal{F}, \mathbb{P}, (\mathcal{F}_t)_{0 \leq t \leq T}\}$, the state vector $\mathbf{u}$ is a $d$-dimensional Markov process in some state space $\mathcal{D} \subset \mathbb{R}^d$, solving the stochastic differential equation:*

$$d\mathbf{u}_t = \mu(\mathbf{u}_t)dt + \Sigma(\mathbf{u}_t)d\mathbf{z}_t, \tag{1}$$

*where $\mathbf{z}_t$ is a vector Wiener process in $\mathbb{R}^d$, $\mu(\mathbf{u}_t)$ is an $d \times 1$ vector defining the drift, and $\sigma(\mathbf{u}_t)$ is an $n \times n$ matrix defining the diffusion of the process. We further assume that $\mu(\mathbf{u}_t)$ and $\Sigma(\mathbf{u}_t)$ satisfy the usual regularity conditions such that the above stochastic differential equation allows a strong solution.*

For ease of notation, we assume for now that the process is time homogeneous. For any time $t \in [0, T]$ and time-of-maturity $T \in [t, T]$, we assume that the market value at time $t$ of a zero–coupon bond with maturity $\tau = T - t$

---

[1] For technical details, see, for example, Jacod and Shiryaev (1987).

is fully characterized by $P(\mathbf{u}_t, \tau)$ and that the instantaneous interest rate, or the short rate, $r$, is defined by continuity:

$$r_t \equiv \lim_{\tau \downarrow 0} \frac{-\ln P(\mathbf{u}_t, \tau)}{\tau}. \tag{2}$$

We further assume that there exists a risk-neutral measure, or a martingale measure, $\mathbb{P}^*$, under which the bond price can be written as

$$P(\mathbf{u}_t, \tau) = \mathbb{E}_t^* \left[ \exp \left( -\int_t^T r_s ds \right) \right], \tag{3}$$

where $\mathbb{E}_t^*[\cdot]$ denotes expectation under measure $\mathbb{P}^*$ conditional on the filtration $\mathcal{F}_t$. Under certain regularity conditions, the existence of such a measure is guaranteed by no-arbitrage. The measure is unique when the market is complete.[2]

Let $\mu^*(\mathbf{u}_t)$ denote the drift function of $\mathbf{u}_t$ under measure $\mathbb{P}^*$. The diffusion function $\Sigma(\mathbf{u}_t)$ remains the same under the two measures by virtue of the Girsanov's theorem.

The spot rate of maturity $\tau$ is defined as

$$y(\mathbf{u}_t, \tau) \equiv -\frac{1}{\tau} \ln P(\mathbf{u}_t, \tau). \tag{4}$$

The instantaneous forward rate is defined as

$$f(\mathbf{u}_t, \tau) \equiv -\frac{\partial \ln P(\mathbf{u}_t, \tau)}{\partial \tau}. \tag{5}$$

**Assumption 2** (Positive interest rates). *The spot rates, $y$, take the following quadratic form of the state vector $\mathbf{u}$,*

$$y(\mathbf{u}_t, \tau) = \frac{1}{\tau} \mathbf{u}_t^\top A(\tau) \mathbf{u}_t, \tag{6}$$

*where $A(\tau)$ is a positive definite matrix so that all spot rates are bounded from below at zero.*

As the asymmetric part of $A$ has zero contribution to the spot rate, we also assume that $A$ is symmetric with no loss of generality.

In principle, the positivity of interest rates can be guaranteed either through a quadratic form or through an exponential function. However, the exponential family is not consistent with any diffusion dynamics for the state vector (see Björk and Christensen, 1999; Filipović, 1999, 2000). Furthermore, the history of interest rates across the world (witness Switzerland and, in recent times,

---

[2]Refer to Duffie (1992) for details.

Japan) shows that we must allow an interest rate of zero to be reachable. Zero is not reachable if interest rates are specified as exponential functions of the state variable, but can be reached under our quadratic specification by letting the state vector **u** approach the vector of zeros. The fact that **u** can be small argues against the inclusion of linear terms, since the linear term would dominate when the state vector is small, thus potentially allowing negative interest rates.

**Proposition 1** (Bond Pricing). *Under the assumptions of diffusion state dynamics in (1) and positive interest rates in (6), the term structure of zero–coupon bonds is given by*

$$P(r_t, \tau) = \exp\left(-c(\tau) r_t\right), \tag{7}$$

*where $r_t$ is the instantaneous interest rate and follows a square-root process under the risk-neutral measure $\mathbb{P}^*$,*

$$dr_t = -\kappa r_t dt + \sigma \sqrt{r_t}\, dw_t, \tag{8}$$

*with $\kappa \in \mathbb{R}$, $\sigma \in \mathbb{R}^+$ being constant parameters and $w_t$ being a newly defined scaler Wiener process. The maturity coefficient $c(\tau)$ is determined by the following Riccati equation:*

$$c'(\tau) = 1 - \kappa c(\tau) - \frac{1}{2}\sigma^2 c(\tau)^2, \tag{9}$$

*with the boundary condition $c(0) = 0$.*

Although we start with a $d$-dimensional state vector, the dimension of the term structure collapses to one. The proof of the bond pricing formula follows standard argument. We solve for the coefficients $c(\tau)$ by applying the Feynman–Kac formula and the principle of matching.

**Proof.** Applying the Feynman–Kac formula to the zero price function in (3) yields:

$$r(\mathbf{u}) P(\mathbf{u}, \tau) = \frac{\partial P(\mathbf{u}, \tau)}{\partial t} + \mathcal{L}^* P(\mathbf{u}, \tau), \tag{10}$$

where $\mathcal{L}^*$ denotes the infinitesimal generator under the risk-neutral measure $\mathbb{P}^*$ and is given by

$$\mathcal{L}^* P(\mathbf{u}, \tau) = \left[\frac{\partial P}{\partial \mathbf{u}}\right]^\top \mu^*(\mathbf{u}) + \frac{1}{2}\mathrm{tr}\left[\left(\frac{\partial^2 P}{\partial \mathbf{u} \partial \mathbf{u}^\top}\right)\left(\Sigma(\mathbf{u})\, \Sigma(\mathbf{u})^\top\right)\right].$$

The quadratic specification for the spot rate in (6) implies that the instantaneous interest rate also has a quadratic form:

$$r(\mathbf{u}) = \mathbf{u}^\top A'(0)\,\mathbf{u}. \tag{11}$$

Plugging the quadratic specifications for the spot rate in (6) and for the short rate in (11) into Equation (10), we have

$$
\begin{aligned}
\mathbf{u}^\top A'(0)\mathbf{u} = \mathbf{u}^\top A'(\tau)\,\mathbf{u} &- 2\mathbf{u}^\top A(\tau)\,\mu^*(\mathbf{u}) - \mathrm{tr}\left[A(\tau)\left(\Sigma(\mathbf{u})\,\Sigma(\mathbf{u})^\top\right)\right] \\
&+ 2\left[\mathbf{u}^\top A(\tau)\,\Sigma(\mathbf{u})\Sigma(\mathbf{u})^\top A(\tau)\,\mathbf{u}\right],
\end{aligned} \tag{12}
$$

which should hold for all maturity $\tau$ and states $\mathbf{u}$.

To maintain the quadratic nature of the equation in (12), we need the diffusion term $\Sigma(\mathbf{u})$ to be independent of the state vector $\mathbf{u}$. Let $V \equiv \Sigma\Sigma^\top$ denote a positive definite symmetric constant matrix. Indeed, via a rotation of indices, we can set $V = I$ with no loss of generality.

Equation (12) becomes

$$
\begin{aligned}
\mathbf{u}^\top A'(0)\mathbf{u} = \mathbf{u}^\top A'(\tau)\,\mathbf{u} &- 2\mathbf{u}^\top A(\tau)\,\mu^*(\mathbf{u}) - \mathrm{tr}\,(A(\tau)\,V) \\
&+ 2\mathbf{u}^\top A(\tau)^2\,V\mathbf{u}.
\end{aligned} \tag{13}
$$

Furthermore, to balance the power of the equation, we decompose the drift function $\mu^*$ into two parts, $\mu^*(\mathbf{u}) = \mu_1(\mathbf{u}) - B\mathbf{u}$, where $B$ denotes a constant matrix and is assumed to be symmetric with no loss of generality. The first part $\mu_1(\mathbf{u}, t)$ satisfies the equality:

$$-2\mathbf{u}^\top A(\tau)\,\mu_1(\mathbf{u}) - \mathrm{tr}(A(\tau)\,V) = 0. \tag{14}$$

That is, the role of $\mu_1(\mathbf{u})$ is to cancel out the constant term on the r.h.s. of Equation (13). However, since the drift term $\mu_1(\mathbf{u})$ cannot depend on maturity $\tau$, for equality (14) to hold, we must be able to factor out the maturity dependence

$$A(\tau) = a(\tau)\,D, \tag{15}$$

where $a(\tau)$ is a scalar and $D$ is a positive definite symmetric matrix independent of $\tau$. This maturity separation determines the most important result of this article: the collapse of dimensionality.

Given the maturity separation, Equation (14) becomes

$$-2\mathbf{u}^\top D\mu_1(\mathbf{u}) - \mathrm{tr}\,(DV) = 0. \tag{16}$$

Equation (13) becomes

$$a'(0)\,\mathbf{u}^\top D\mathbf{u} = a'(\tau)\,\mathbf{u}^\top D\mathbf{u} + a(\tau)\,2\mathbf{u}^\top DB\mathbf{u} + a(\tau)^2\,2\mathbf{u}^\top D^2 V\mathbf{u}. \tag{17}$$

For this equation to hold for all states $\mathbf{u} \in \mathbb{R}^d$, we need

$$a'(0)\,D = a'(\tau)\,D + 2a(\tau)\,DB + 2a(\tau)^2\,D^2 V. \tag{18}$$

After rearrangement, we have

$$a'(\tau)\,I = a'(0)\,I - 2a(\tau)\,B - 2a(\tau)^2\,DV. \tag{19}$$

Since the equation needs to hold for all elements of the matrix, we must have

$$2B = \kappa I; \quad DV = \frac{1}{4}vI. \tag{20}$$

We hence obtain the ordinary differential equation,

$$a'(\tau) = a'(0) - \kappa a(\tau) - \frac{1}{2}va(\tau)^2. \tag{21}$$

Furthermore, let $x = \mathbf{u}^\top D\mathbf{u}$, the zero price can then be written as

$$-\ln P = \mathbf{u}^\top A(\tau)\,\mathbf{u} = a(\tau)\,\mathbf{u}^\top D\mathbf{u} = a(\tau)\,x. \tag{22}$$

Next, given the state vector process

$$d\mathbf{u} = (\mu_1(\mathbf{u}) - B\mathbf{u})\,dt + \sqrt{V}\,d\mathbf{z},$$

by Itô's Lemma, we obtain the process for $x$ under $\mathbb{P}^*$,

$$\begin{aligned} dx &= 2\mathbf{u}^\top D(d\mathbf{u}) + \mathrm{tr}\,(DV)\,dt \\ &= \left(2\mathbf{u}^\top D\mu_1(\mathbf{u}) + \mathrm{tr}\,(DV) - 2\mathbf{u}^\top DB\mathbf{u}\right)dt + 2\mathbf{u}^\top D\sqrt{V}\,d\mathbf{z} \\ &= -\kappa x\,dt + \sqrt{vx}\,dw. \end{aligned}$$

We obtain the last equality by applying (16) and by defining a new Wiener process $w$:

$$dw = \frac{2\mathbf{u}^\top D\sqrt{V}\,d\mathbf{z}}{\sqrt{4\mathbf{u}^\top DV D\mathbf{u}}} = \frac{2\mathbf{u}^\top D\sqrt{V}\,d\mathbf{z}}{\sqrt{v\mathbf{u}^\top D\mathbf{u}}} = \frac{2\mathbf{u}^\top D\sqrt{V}\,d\mathbf{z}}{\sqrt{vx}}.$$

The instantaneous interest rate is $r_t = a'(0) x_t$. A rescaling of index

$$c(\tau) = a(\tau)/a'(0), \quad \sigma = \sqrt{va'(0)}, \tag{23}$$

gives us

$$-\ln P = c(\tau) r_t, \tag{24}$$

with

$$c'(\tau) = 1 - \kappa c(\tau) - \frac{1}{2}\sigma^2 c(\tau)^2 \tag{25}$$

$$dr_t = -\kappa r_t dt + \sigma\sqrt{r_t}\, dw. \tag{26}$$

The initial condition $c(0) = 0$ is determined by the fact that $P(r_t, 0) = 1$.

■

Under our model, due to the maturity separability, the dimension of the state-space collapses to one. Bonds are priced as if there is only one dynamic factor. This one dynamic factor follows a two-parameter square-root process under the risk-neutral measure $\mathbb{P}^*$. We leave the dynamics of this factor under the physical measure $\mathbb{P}$ unspecified. The specification of the physical dynamics can be separately determined to match the time-series properties of interest rates while satisfying the constraints implied by the Girsanov theorem.

The two parameters of the square-root process determine both the risk-neutral dynamics of the single dynamic factor, and the shape of the yield curve via the ordinary differential equation in (25). In our empirical application, we relax the time-homogeneity assumption and allow the two parameters to vary over time so that we can fit the yield curve at each day. Nevertheless, the bonds are priced as if the two parameters are constant. We hence label them as static factors. Therefore, we obtain a three-factor term structure model. However, this three-factor structure is not a result of exogenous specification, but of a collapse of dimensionality due to the seemingly innocuous contention that all rates are bounded below from zero.

Our three-factor model contrasts sharply with traditional three-factor models in that the three factors in our model summarize everything that is uncertain about the shape of the term structure. Traditional three-factor models often contain many parameters in addition to the three factors. The estimates of these parameters often exhibit large standard errors. Therefore, such models are subject to parameter risk. Under our specification, there are no other risk-neutral parameters to be estimated and hence no other risks to be concerned with — except, of course, the risk of the model itself.

Treating $\kappa$ and $\sigma$ as constants, we can solve the term structure coefficients $c(\tau)$ analytically:

$$c(\tau) = \frac{2\left(1 - e^{-2\lambda\tau}\right)}{4\lambda - (2\lambda - \kappa)\left(1 - e^{-2\lambda\tau}\right)}, \tag{27}$$

with $\lambda = \frac{1}{2}\sqrt{\kappa^2 + 2\sigma^2}$. We can see immediately that $c(\tau) > 0$ for all $\tau > 0$. Furthermore, since the short rate follows a square-root process, it is bounded below from zero. Therefore, all spot rates are bounded below from zero. Indeed, in our model, all spot rates follow a square-root process.

Although we start with a quadratic specification for the spot rates, the final bond pricing formula says that spot rates are proportional to one dynamic factor. The square-root dynamics of the short rate brings our model very close to the traditional term structure model of Cox *et al.* (1985). The key difference lies in the absence of a constant term in the drift of the risk-neutral dynamics and the absence of a constant term in the affine structure of the bond yields. A constant term in the affine structure drives the boundary away from zero and hence violates our assumption that all rates are bounded from zero.

We solve the coefficients $c(\tau)$ treating $\kappa$ and $\sigma$ as constants. Yet, in our application, we allow the two parameters to vary every day to fit the current yield curve. Thus, there seems to be inconsistency between the two practices. However, the inconsistency is only an illusion since we treat $\kappa$ and $\sigma$ not as time-inhomogeneous parameters, but as static factors. We explicitly recognize the risk associated with the time variation of these factors and hedge the risk away by forming portfolios that are first-order neutral to their variation. Due to the low dimensionality of the factor structure, neutrality can be achieved with a maximum of only four instruments. In contrast, in a traditional three-factor model with more than ten parameters, making a portfolio first-order neutral to all parameters and state variables is impractical due to transaction costs.

Our practice is also decisively different from traditional time-inhomo-geneous specifications as often applied under the framework of Heath *et al.* (1992). In these specifications, the model parameters are allowed to vary over time in such a way that we can always fit the current observed term structure perfectly. Thus, these models have little to say about the fair pricing of the yield curve. Furthermore, accommodating the whole yield curve often necessitates accepting an infinite dimensional state space, which create difficulties for hedging practices.

## 4. The Hump-Shaped Forward Rate Curve

The term structure of the long forward rates has been persistently downward sloping (Brown and Schaefer, 2000). Given the initial upward sloping term structure in most observations, the downward slopes in the very long term imply a hump-shaped term structure for the forward rates. Our model captures very nicely the hump shape of the forward rate curve.

We can rotate the system and redefine the three factors explicitly on the hump shape of the forward rate curve. Formally, we let $F$ denote the maximum of the instantaneous forward rate (the peak of the hump), $M$ the maturity at which the forward rate reaches its maximum, and $\lambda$ some measure of the curvature of the forward rate curve at the maximum. Then, the instantaneous forward rate at maturity $\tau$ is given by[3]

$$f(\tau) = F \operatorname{sech}^2 [\lambda(\tau - M)]. \tag{28}$$

The parameter $\lambda$ is related to the curvature of the forward rate curve at the maximum by:

$$\delta(M) \equiv \frac{f''(M)}{f(M)} = -2\lambda^2. \tag{29}$$

The new triplet $[F, M, \lambda]$ defines the same term structure as the original triplet $[r, \kappa, \sigma]$. They are linked by,

$$F = r\left(1 + \frac{\kappa^2}{2\sigma^2}\right), \quad M = -\frac{1}{\lambda}\operatorname{arctanh}\left(\frac{\kappa}{2\lambda}\right), \quad \lambda = \frac{1}{2}\sqrt{\kappa^2 + 2\sigma^2}.$$

$$r = F \operatorname{sech}^2(\lambda M), \quad \kappa = -2\lambda \tanh(\lambda M), \quad \sigma^2 = 2\lambda^2 \operatorname{sech}^2(\lambda M). \tag{30}$$

The new formulation defines the forward rate curve by controlling the exact shape of the curve at the hump. Thus, if we observe a forward rate curve, we can determine the value of the three factors very easily. In our estimation, we model $T \equiv 1/\lambda$ instead of $\lambda$, because it has a natural interpretation of time scale.

---

[3]Refer to Appendix A for a derivation.

In contrast, the original triplet of factors $[r, \kappa, \sigma]$ define the risk-neutral dynamics of the short rate. They also define the level, the slope, and the curvature of the forward rate curve at the short end ($\tau = 0$):

$$f'(0) = r, \quad \frac{f'(0)}{f(0)} = -\kappa, \quad \delta(0) = \frac{f''(0)}{f(0)} = \kappa^2 - \sigma^2.$$

Thus, we see clearly how the risk-neutral dynamics of the short rate interacts with the shape of the forward rate curve. The drift parameter $\kappa$ controls the initial slope of the forward rate curve. The initial curve is upward sloping when $\kappa$ is negative. On the other hand, the instantaneous volatility term $\sigma$ contributes to the curvature of the forward rate curve. The larger the variance, the more concave the forward rate curve.

Furthermore, the two points of the forward rate curve at $t = 0$ and $t = M$ are linked by a unit-free quantity $\gamma = \tanh(\lambda M)$:

$$\frac{f(0) - f(M)}{f(M)} = \gamma^2, \quad \frac{\delta(M) - \delta(0)}{\delta(M)} = 3\gamma^2.$$

Based on these observations, the calibration of the forward rate curve is fairly simple. The factors can be directly mapped to the level and shape of the forward rate curve.

Empirical studies (Litterman and Scheinkman, 1991; Heidari and Wu, 2003) have identified three common factors from the US Treasuries and the swap rates. The three common factors represent the level, the slope, and the curvature of the term structure. In our model, we map the level, the slope, and the curvature of the forward rate curve into a consistent dynamic term structure model. We also map them into the risk-neutral dynamics of the underlying dynamic factor.

## 5. Fitting the US Treasury Yields and US Dollar Swap Rates

To investigate the model's performance, we calibrate the model to two sets of data. One is US Treasury constant maturity par yields and the other is US dollar swap rates of the same maturities. We investigate the goodness of fit of the model on the two sets of data. We also extract the three factors from the two markets for each day and analyze the time series dynamics of these factors.

### 5.1. *Data and estimation*

We obtain both the swap rate data and the constant maturity Treasury yields from Lehman Brothers. The maturities include 2, 3, 5, 7, 10, 15, and 30 years.

The data are weekly (Wednesday) closing mid quotes from December 14, 1994 to December 28, 2000 (316 observations).

Table 1 reports the summary statistics of the swap rates and Treasury par yields. We observe an upward-sloping mean term structure for both swaps and US Treasuries. The standard deviation for both the levels and the first differences exhibit a hump-shaped term structure with the plateau coming at three-year to five-year maturities. Interest rates are highly persistent. The excess skewness and kurtosis estimates are small for both levels and first differences.

We are interested not only in the empirical fit of the model on the yield curves of different markets, but also in the time series properties of the three factors $X \equiv [F, M, T]$ at each date. (The choice of $[F, M, T]$ over $[r, \kappa, \sigma]$ in the estimation is only for numerical stability reasons.) If we can forecast the three factors, we will be able to forecast the yield curve. A natural way to capture both the daily fitting of the cross-section of the term structure and the forecasting of the time series of interest rates is to formulate the framework into a state-space system and estimate the system using Kalman (1960) filter.

For the estimation, we assume that the three factors can be forecasted via a simple VAR(1) system:

$$X_t = A + \Phi X_{t-1} + \varepsilon_t, \tag{31}$$

where $\varepsilon$ denotes the forecasting residuals. We use this forecasting equation as the state propagation equation, with $\varepsilon$ as the state propagation error with covariance matrix $Q$. We then construct the measurement equations based on the valuation of the par yields on the Treasury and swap market, respectively,

$$S_t(\tau) = h(X_t, \tau) + e_t, \tag{32}$$

where $h(X_t, \tau)$ denotes the model-implied value of the par yield of maturity $\tau$ as a function of the factors $X_t$ and $e_t$ denotes the measurement error, which we assume has a covariance matrix of $R$. Since the US Treasury par bond and the US dollar swap contract both have semi-annual payment intervals, the model-implied par yield is given by

$$h(X_t, \tau) = 200 \frac{1 - P(\tau)}{\sum_{i=1}^{2\tau} P(i/2)}, \tag{33}$$

where $P(\tau)$ denotes the model-implied value of the zero coupon bond (discount factor) and is given in Equation (7). Since the measurement equation is non-linear in the state vectors, we apply the extended Kalman Filter, under which the conditional variance update is based on a first-order Taylor expansion.

**Table 1.**  Summery statistics of US dollar swap rates and US treasury par yields.

| Mat | Swap | | | | | Treasury | | | | |
|---|---|---|---|---|---|---|---|---|---|---|
| | Mean | Std | Skew | Kurt | Auto | Mean | Std | Skew | Kurt | Auto |
| *Levels* | | | | | | | | | | |
| 2 | 6.190 | 0.656 | 0.343 | 0.293 | 0.971 | 5.799 | 0.631 | -0.050 | 0.858 | 0.969 |
| 3 | 6.303 | 0.657 | 0.266 | 0.224 | 0.971 | 5.857 | 0.654 | -0.071 | 0.798 | 0.969 |
| 5 | 6.454 | 0.642 | 0.133 | 0.004 | 0.971 | 5.947 | 0.681 | -0.143 | 0.672 | 0.969 |
| 7 | 6.560 | 0.629 | 0.061 | -0.147 | 0.971 | 5.994 | 0.672 | -0.081 | 0.522 | 0.970 |
| 10 | 6.681 | 0.615 | -0.022 | -0.300 | 0.971 | 6.059 | 0.669 | -0.008 | 0.238 | 0.971 |
| 15 | 6.817 | 0.591 | -0.056 | -0.388 | 0.969 | 6.111 | 0.653 | 0.052 | 0.152 | 0.971 |
| 30 | 6.889 | 0.576 | 0.050 | -0.247 | 0.971 | 6.266 | 0.624 | 0.243 | -0.207 | 0.974 |
| *Differences* | | | | | | | | | | |
| 2 | -0.007 | 0.120 | 0.328 | 0.977 | 0.027 | -0.008 | 0.119 | 0.201 | 0.642 | 0.001 |
| 3 | -0.007 | 0.123 | 0.349 | 0.834 | 0.020 | -0.008 | 0.121 | 0.316 | 0.746 | -0.013 |
| 5 | -0.007 | 0.123 | 0.214 | 0.627 | 0.013 | -0.009 | 0.124 | 0.178 | 0.600 | 0.008 |
| 7 | -0.007 | 0.122 | 0.264 | 0.593 | 0.019 | -0.009 | 0.120 | 0.282 | 0.592 | 0.013 |
| 10 | -0.007 | 0.119 | 0.188 | 0.410 | 0.043 | -0.009 | 0.118 | 0.233 | 0.353 | 0.040 |
| 15 | -0.007 | 0.117 | 0.304 | 0.393 | -0.024 | -0.008 | 0.114 | 0.348 | 0.319 | -0.015 |
| 30 | -0.007 | 0.106 | 0.445 | 0.545 | 0.018 | -0.008 | 0.102 | 0.415 | 0.528 | 0.033 |

*Notes:* The table presents summary statistics of US dollar swap rates and US Treasury par yields. Mean, Std, Skew, Kurt, and Auto denote, respectively, the sample estimates of the mean, standard deviation, skewness, kurtosis, and first-order autocorrelation. The data are weekly closing mid quotes from Lehman Brothers, from December 14, 1994 to December 28, 2000 (316 observations).

The parameters of the state-space system include those that control the forecasting time series dynamics and the covariance matrices of the state propagation errors and measurement errors $\Theta \equiv [A, \Phi, Q, R]$. We estimate these parameters using a quasi-likelihood method assuming that the forecasting errors of the par yields are normally distributed. (Please see Appendix B for more details.) In our estimation, we assume that the measurement errors on each series are independent, but bear distinct variance. Thus, $R$ is a diagonal matrix, with each element denoting the goodness of fit on each corresponding series.

Table 2 reports the estimates (and standard errors in parentheses) of the state space estimation on both the US dollar swap market and the US Treasury market.

## 5.2. *Model performance*

Table 3 reports the summary properties of the pricing errors on the swaps and Treasury par yields. We define the error as the difference between the market-observed rates and the model-implied rates, in basis points. The fitting is good despite the simple model structure. Overall, the mean absolute error is within a few basis points. The maximum error is only 28 basis points for the swap rates and 41 basis points for the Treasury par yields. An inspection of the error properties across different maturities indicates that the key difficulty of the model lies in fitting interest rates at short maturities (two years). The mean error on the two year rates is −7.5 basis points for swaps and −4.5 for Treasuries, implying that the observed two-year rates are on average lower than those implied by the model.

Figure 1 plots the time series of the pricing errors on the swap rates (left panel) and the Treasury par yields (right panel) at selected maturities: 2, 5, 10, and 30 years. We observe that except at short maturities, the pricing errors are normally within ten basis points. The magnitude of these pricing errors is comparable to those reported in much more complicated models.

## 5.3. *Factor dynamics*

By applying the state-space estimation, we obtain not only the weekly fits on the yield curve, but also the parametric estimates on the dynamics of the three factors. A detailed specification analysis of the factor time series dynamics and the associated analysis of the market price of risk is beyond the scope of this

**Table 2.** Summary statistics of the three factors from swaps and US STRIPS.

| Data | Swap | Treasury |
|------|------|----------|

*State Propagation Equation:* $X_t = A + \Phi X_{t-1} + \varepsilon_t$, $\quad S_\varepsilon S_\varepsilon^\top = \text{Cov}(\varepsilon)$

$$A = \begin{bmatrix} 0.1831 & (0.1233) \\ 3.0572 & (0.6830) \\ 7.9858 & (1.4326) \end{bmatrix} \qquad \begin{bmatrix} 0.2405 & (1.4971) \\ 4.0164 & (2.2390) \\ 4.4539 & (3.9432) \end{bmatrix}$$

$$\Phi = \begin{bmatrix} 0.9761 & -0.0052 & -0.0027 \\ (0.0133) & (0.0307) & (0.0081) \\ -0.0163 & 0.9005 & -0.0110 \\ (0.0081) & (0.0164) & (0.0046) \\ -0.0386 & -0.1895 & 0.9350 \\ (0.0164) & (0.0425) & (0.0115) \end{bmatrix} \qquad \begin{bmatrix} 0.9660 & 0.0018 & -0.0046 \\ (0.1497) & (0.0057) & (0.0051) \\ -0.0358 & 0.9673 & -0.0122 \\ (0.0303) & (0.0123) & (0.0106) \\ 0.0136 & -0.0286 & 0.9299 \\ (0.0490) & (0.0233) & (0.0202) \end{bmatrix}$$

$$S_\varepsilon = \begin{bmatrix} 1.1173 & 0 & 0 \\ (0.0552) & & \\ -0.0634 & 0.7012 & 0 \\ (0.0577) & (0.0413) & \\ -0.7486 & 0.3839 & 1.5043 \\ (0.1723) & (0.1862) & (0.1305) \end{bmatrix} \qquad \begin{bmatrix} 1.1418 & 0 & 0 \\ (0.0726) & & \\ 0.1898 & 2.3490 & 0 \\ (0.2869) & (0.2455) & \\ -1.5145 & 2.3074 & 3.6332 \\ (0.6367) & (0.6562) & (0.3997) \end{bmatrix}$$

*Measurement Equation:* $S_t = h(X_t) + e_t$, $\quad \text{Cov}(e) = \text{diag}\left[\sigma_i^2\right]$, $\quad i = 2, 3, 5, 7, 10, 15, 30.$

$$\begin{bmatrix} \sigma_2 \\ \sigma_3 \\ \sigma_5 \\ \sigma_7 \\ \sigma_{10} \\ \sigma_{15} \\ \sigma_{30} \end{bmatrix} = \begin{bmatrix} 0.1106 & (0.0115) \\ 0.0512 & (0.0051) \\ 0.0114 & (0.0012) \\ 0.0130 & (0.0007) \\ 0.0188 & (0.0007) \\ 0.0295 & (0.0017) \\ 0.0127 & (0.0026) \end{bmatrix} \qquad \begin{bmatrix} 0.1468 & (0.0180) \\ 0.0928 & (0.0112) \\ 0.0314 & (0.0016) \\ 0.0003 & (0.0785) \\ 0.0409 & (0.0021) \\ 0.0498 & (0.0039) \\ 0.0285 & (0.0027) \end{bmatrix}$$

| $\mathcal{L}(\times 10^{-3})$ | 5.6517 | 4.7706 |
|---|---|---|

*Notes*: The table reports the parameter estimates (standard deviations in parentheses) of the state-space system. The state propagation captures the dynamics of the three factors $X_t \equiv [F_t, M_t, T_t]$, where $F_t$ is represented in one thousandth, and $M$ and $T$ are in years. The standard deviation of the measurement error ($\sigma_i$) captures the model's performance in fitting the constant maturity yields or swap rates of the denoted maturities. The standard deviation is measured in annual percentages. The model is calibrated to both the US dollar swap rates (left panel) and the US Treasury constant maturity par yields, both of which are weekly data from December 14, 1994 to December 28, 2000 (316 observations).

paper. Therefore, we use only a simple VAR(1) specification to summarize the properties of these factors. In what follows, we analyze the time series of the three factors. We compare how the three factors relate to one another and how the two markets differ.

**Table 3.**   Summary statistics of pricing errors on US dollar swap rates and US treasury par yields.

| Mat | Swap | | | | | | Treasury | | | | | |
|-----|------|-----|-----|-----|-----|-----|------|-----|-----|-----|-----|-----|
|     | Mean | Std | Min | Max | Auto | | Mean | Std | Min | Max | Auto | |
| 2   | -7.524 | 7.641 | 8.611 | 28.290 | 0.893 | | -4.358 | 13.970 | 12.669 | 41.425 | 0.923 | |
| 3   | -2.681 | 4.053 | 3.948 | 13.102 | 0.751 | | -1.731 | 9.243 | 8.077 | 31.094 | 0.871 | |
| 5   | 0.608 | 1.053 | 0.796 | 5.635 | 0.158 | | 1.327 | 3.400 | 2.602 | 14.568 | 0.531 | |
| 7   | 0.843 | 1.323 | 1.087 | 7.859 | 0.257 | | 0.723 | 1.401 | 0.857 | 8.929 | 0.111 | |
| 10  | 0.022 | 1.837 | 1.279 | 10.430 | 0.245 | | 0.249 | 4.315 | 3.221 | 13.536 | 0.674 | |
| 15  | -0.879 | 2.446 | 2.052 | 8.118 | 0.629 | | -3.423 | 2.983 | 3.947 | 12.308 | 0.434 | |
| 30  | 0.445 | 0.763 | 0.554 | 6.676 | 0.160 | | 1.341 | 2.503 | 1.758 | 17.064 | 0.468 | |

*Notes*: The table presents summary statistics of the pricing errors on US dollar swap rates and US Treasury par yields. We define the pricing error as the difference, in basis points, between the market observed rates and the model implied rates. Mean, Std, Min, Max, and Auto denote, respectively, the sample estimates of the mean, standard deviation, mean absolute error, max absolute error, and first-order autocorrelation. The market observed rates are weekly closing mid quotes from Lehman Brothers, from December 14, 1994 to December 28, 2000 (316 observations). We compute the model-implied rates based on the state space system estimated in Table 2.

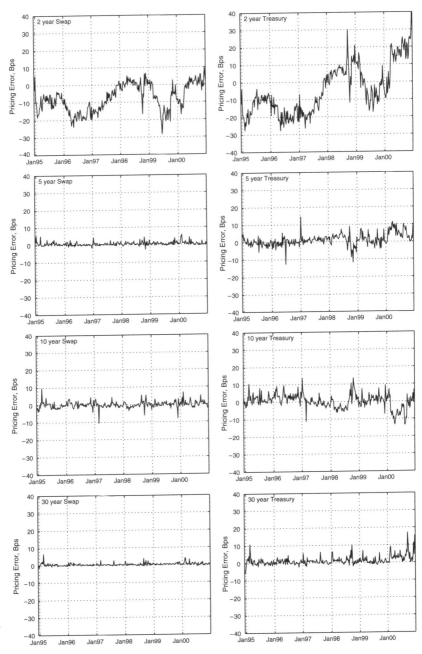

**Figure 1.** Swap rate pricing errors. Lines report the time series of the pricing errors on swap rates and Treasury par yields. The pricing error is in basis points, defined as the difference between the market-observed rate and the model-implied rate. We compute the errors based on the model estimates in Table 2.

The properties of swap spreads, which we defined as the difference between the swap rate and the constant maturity Treasury par yield, are of great interest to both practitioners and academics. The magnitude of the swap spread reflects the difference in the default risk of the financial sector that quotes LIBOR rates and the US Treasury. In addition, the swap spread may also include a significant liquidity component. The swap markets are a purely contract-driven market, but the interest rates in the Treasury market are often driven by the supply and demand of certain Treasury issuance. In what follows, we analyze the two components in the swap spreads based on our model structure.

### 5.3.1. *The dynamic level factor*

Under our model structure, the level of the yield curve can be represented by the instantaneous short rate $r$. The left panel of Figure 2 plots the extracted instantaneous interest rate from the swap market (dashed line) and the Treasury market (solid line). The right panel of Figure 2 depicts the difference (swap spread) between the two short rates. The average spread on the two short rates over this sample period is 34.19 basis points. Overall, the two short rates move very closely to each other. However, the swap spread does change over time. Before 1998, the spread is in general within 40 basis points. The spike in the swap spread in late 1998 and early 1999 corresponds to the hedge fund crisis during that time. The swap spread during year 2000 is also unusually high,

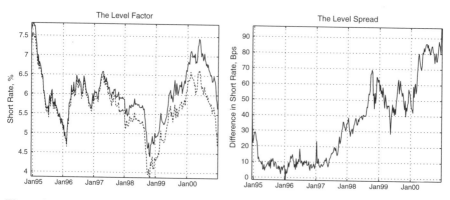

**Figure 2.**    The short rate and swap spreads. The left panel depicts the instantaneous interest rate (in percentages) implied from the US Treasury market (solid line) and the swap market (dashed line). The right panel depicts the spread, in basis points, between the short rate from the swap market and the short rate from the Treasury market.

corresponding to the reduced supply in the US Treasury as a result of the budget surplus at that time. Thus, although the spread spike in early 1999 can be attributed to a credit event, the spread plateau in 2000 is mainly due to liquidity factors.

### 5.3.2. *The slope and curvature factors*

The slope of the forward rate curve is closely related to the drift parameter $\kappa$ of the short rate risk-neutral dynamics. The slope is positive when $\kappa$ is negative. In contrast, the instantaneous volatility $\sigma$ of the short rate dynamics is closely related to the curvature of the forward rate curve. The higher the volatility, the more concave the forward rate curve.

Figure 3 plots the time series of $-\kappa$ (left panel) and $\sigma$ (right panel) as an illustration of the slope and curvature dynamics of the yield curve. The solid lines depict the factors extracted from the US Treasury market and the dashed lines depict the factors from the swap market. The two markets move closely together as their shape (slope and curvature) of the forward rate curves also move together. Furthermore, comparing the time series of the short rate to that of the slope and curvature factors, we see that the slope and curvature factors tend to move in a direction opposite to the level factor. When the short rate is high, the forward rate curve tends to be flat. The two spikes in the slope and curvature time series correspond to the two dips in the short rate.

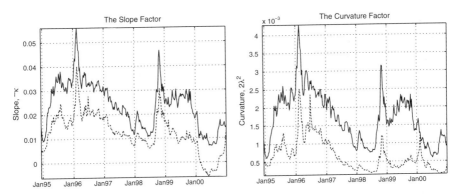

**Figure 3.**   The slope factor $-\kappa$ and the curvature factor $\sigma$. Lines depict the slope factor ($-\kappa$, left panel) and the curvature factor ($\sigma$, right panel) extracted from the US Treasury market (solid line) and the swap market (dashed line).

## 6. Extensions: Jumps in Interest Rates

Our model is derived under three important assumptions: the positivity of interest rates, a finite state representation, and a diffusion state dynamics. We contend that interest rate positivity is a necessary condition to guarantee no arbitrage, as long as we are allowed to hold cash for free. A finite state representation is also necessary for complete hedging to be feasible in practice in the presence of transaction costs. However, the assumption on pure-diffusion state dynamics is more for convenience and tractability than for reasonability. We do see that interest rates move discontinuously (jumps) every now and then. In this section, we explore whether incorporating a jump component by itself violates the assumptions on positive interest rates and finite state dynamics and if not, how jumps can be incorporated into the state dynamics.

We start with the degenerating case that the jump component has zero weight in the state dynamics. Then, our previous analysis indicates that zero prices can be written as

$$-\ln P(r_t, \tau) = c(\tau) r_t, \qquad (34)$$

where the short rate $r_t$ follows a square-root dynamics with a zero mean:

$$dr_t = -\kappa r_t dt + \sigma \sqrt{r_t} \, dw_t, \qquad (35)$$

and the coefficient $c(\tau)$ satisfies a Riccati equation. As we discussed before, this model serves as a special example of a one-factor affine model.

Duffie, Pan, and Singleton (2000) incorporate Poisson jumps in the affine structure. Filipović (2001) incorporates more general jumps in a one-factor affine structure. Since we are dealing with a one factor structure, we consider the more general jump specification in Filipović (2001). Filipović (2001) proves that under the general affine framework, the positive short rate $r_t$ is a CBI-process (Conservative Branching Process with Immigration), uniquely characterized by its generator

$$\mathcal{A}f(x) = \frac{1}{2}\sigma^2 x f''(x) + (a' - \kappa x) f'(x) + \int_{\mathbb{R}_+^0} (f(x+y)$$
$$- f(x) - f'(x)(1 \wedge y))(m(dy) + x\mu(dy)), \qquad (36)$$

where $a' = a + \int_{\mathbb{R}_+^0}(1 \wedge y)m(dy)$ for some numbers $\sigma^2, a \in \mathbb{R}_+, \kappa \in \mathbb{R}$ and non-negative Borel measures $m(dy)$ and $\mu(dy)$ on $\mathbb{R}_+^0$ (the positive real line excluding zero) satisfying

$$\int_{\mathbb{R}_+^0} (1 \wedge y) \, m(dy) + \int_{\mathbb{R}_+^0} \left(1 \wedge y^2\right) \mu(dy) < \infty. \tag{37}$$

We can obtain our current model by setting the jump part to zero and the constant part of the drift of the square root process to zero ($a = 0$). The two Borel measures define two jump components. The jump component defined by $m(dy)$ is a direct addition to the diffusion process. The jump component defined by $\mu(dy)$ is specified as proportional to $x$. Hence, we label the former as a constant jump component and the latter a proportional jump component. In essence, the arrival rate of jumps in the "constant" component does not depend on the short rate level, but the arrival rate of the "proportional" component is proportional to the short rate level. Condition (37) requires that the jump component defined by $m(dy)$ exhibit finite variation and the jump component defined by $\mu(dy)$ exhibit finite quadratic variation.

Under the specification in (36), the zero prices are given by

$$-\ln P(r_t, \tau) = A(\tau) + B(\tau) r_t \tag{38}$$

with $A(\tau)$ and $B(\tau)$ solve uniquely the generalized Riccati equations

$$B'(\tau) = R(B(\tau)), \quad B(0) = 0 \tag{39}$$

$$A(\tau) = \int_0^\tau F(B(s)) \, ds, \tag{40}$$

where $R$ and $F$ are defined as

$$R(\lambda) \equiv 1 - \kappa\lambda - \frac{1}{2}\sigma^2\lambda^2 + \int_{\mathbb{R}_+^0} \left(1 - e^{-\lambda y} - \lambda \left(1 \wedge y\right)\right) \mu(dy); \tag{41}$$

$$F(\lambda) \equiv a\lambda + \int_{\mathbb{R}_+^0} \left(1 - e^{-\lambda y}\right) m(dy). \tag{42}$$

To guarantee that all rates are bounded from zero, we need to set $A(\tau) = 0$ for all $\tau$, which we obtain by setting $a = 0$ and $m(dy) = 0$. The condition $a = 0$ is already known. The second condition $m(dy) = 0$ says that we cannot add a constant jump component while maintaining that all rates are bounded from zero. Nevertheless, we can incorporate a proportional jump component. Since $B(\tau)$ is positive for all $\tau$, all interest rates are bounded from zero. In absence of the proportional jump component, $R(\lambda)$ is reduced to our Riccati equation for the diffusion case. The last term in (41) captures the contribution of the proportional jump component.

## 7. Conclusion

In this paper, we contend that all interest rates should be bounded from below at zero. Such a seemingly innocuous contention, together with the assumption of continuity, results in a dramatic collapse of dimensionality. Such conditions lead to a term structure model that has only one dynamic factor and two static factors. Even more surprising, there are no other parameters in the model that affect the shape of the term structure. Therefore, model calibration becomes a trivial problem and there no longer exists a distinction between out-of-sample and in-sample performance. Furthermore, risks from the three factors can be hedged away easily with only a few instruments. Since there are no more parameters, the model is not subject to any parameter risk.

To put the model into practical application, we cast the model in a state-space framework and estimate the three states via quasi maximum likelihood together with an extended Kalman filter. We apply this estimation procedure to both the US Treasury market and the US dollar swap market. Despite its extreme simplicity, the model performs well in fitting the daily term structures of both markets. A time series analysis of the extracted factors from the two markets provides us with some interesting insights on the evolution of the interest rate market.

A potential application of the model, which can be explored in future research, is to forecast the term structure of interest rates. Recently, Diebold and Li (2003) and Diebold, Ji, and Li (2004) illustrate how the Nelson–Siegel framework can be applied successfully to forecasting the term structure of Treasury yields. Yet, the inherent inconsistency of the Nelson–Siegel model is well-documented in Björk and Christensen (1999) and Filipović (1999, 2000). Our model provides a parsimonious but consistent alternative to the Nelson–Siegel framework.

## Appendix A.  Factor Representation

The term structure is determined by the following ordinary differential equation:

$$c'(\tau) = 1 - \kappa c(\tau) - \frac{1}{2}\sigma^2 c(\tau)^2, \qquad (A.1)$$

with $c(0) = 0$. One solution of this Riccati equation is given in (27). Another way of solving the equation is through the following change of variables:

$$\psi(\tau) \equiv \frac{c(\tau)\sigma^2 + \kappa}{\sqrt{\kappa^2 + 2\sigma^2}}, \quad \lambda = \frac{1}{2}\sqrt{\kappa^2 + 2\sigma^2}, \tag{A.2}$$

where $\kappa^2 + 2\sigma^2$ defines the discriminant of the ordinary differential equation. Then the ordinary differential equation (A.1) is transformed into the elementary problem

$$\psi'(\tau) = \lambda(1 - \psi(\tau)^2) \tag{A.3}$$

with $\psi(0) = \kappa/(2\lambda)$.

The solution of (A.3) is

$$\psi(\tau) = \tanh\left[\lambda\left(\tau - M\right)\right],$$

where $M$ is defined by the boundary condition

$$\psi(0) = \tanh\left(-\lambda M\right) = \frac{\kappa}{2\lambda}.$$

That is,

$$M = -\frac{1}{\lambda}\operatorname{arctanh}\left(\frac{\kappa}{2\lambda}\right).$$

Translating $\psi(\tau)$ back to the bond pricing coefficients $c(\tau)$ gives

$$c(\tau) = \frac{2\lambda}{\sigma^2}\left[\tanh\lambda\left(t - M\right) + \tanh\lambda M\right] \tag{A.4}$$

The instantaneous forward rate is given by

$$f(\tau) = c'(\tau)r = \frac{2\lambda^2 r}{\sigma^2}\operatorname{sech}^2\lambda\left(\tau - M\right) = F\operatorname{sech}^2\lambda\left(\tau - M\right)$$

where

$$F = \frac{2\lambda^2 r}{\sigma^2} = r\left(1 + \frac{\kappa^2}{2\sigma^2}\right),$$

is the maximal forward rate and $M$ is the corresponding maturity.

## Appendix B. Extended Kalman Filter and Quasi Likelihood

The state-space estimation method is based on a pair of state propagation and measurement equations. In our application, the state vector $X$ propagates according to VAR(1) processes specified in (31). The measurement equation is given in (32), which is based on the valuation of the par yield. Let $\bar{X}_t$ denote the *a priori* forecast of the state vector at time $t$ conditional on time $t - 1$ information and $\bar{V}_t$ the corresponding conditional covariance matrix. Let $\hat{X}_t$ denote the *a posteriori* update on the time $t$ state vector based on observations $(S_t)$ at time $t$ and $\hat{V}_t$ the corresponding *a posteriori* covariance matrix. Then, based our OU state process specification, the state propagation equation is linear and Gaussian. The *a priori* update equations are:

$$\bar{X}_t = A + \Phi \hat{X}_{t-1};$$
$$\bar{V}_t = \Phi \hat{V}_{t-1} \Phi^\top + Q. \tag{B.1}$$

The filtering problem then consists of establishing the conditional density of the state vector $X_t$, conditional on the observations up to and including time $t$. In case of a linear measurement equation,

$$S_t = H X_t + e_t,$$

the Kalman Filter provides the efficient *a posteriori* update on the conditional mean and variance of the state vector:

$$\bar{S}_t = H \bar{X}_t;$$
$$\bar{A}_t = H \bar{V}_t H^\top + R$$
$$K_t = \bar{V}_t H \left( \bar{A}_t \right)^{-1}; \tag{B.2}$$
$$\hat{X}_t = \bar{X}_t + K_t \left( S_t - \bar{S}_t \right);$$
$$\hat{P}_t = (I - K_t H) \bar{V}_t,$$

where $\bar{S}_t$ and $\bar{A}_t$ are the *a priori* forecasts on the conditional mean and variance of the observed series and $R$ are the covariance matrix of the measurement errors.

However, in our application, the measurement Equation in (32) is nonlinear. We apply the Extended Kalman Filter (EKF), which approximates the nonlinear measurement equation with a linear expansion:

$$S_t \approx H \left( \bar{X}_t \right) X_t + e_t, \tag{B.3}$$

where

$$H\left(\bar{X}_t\right) = \left.\frac{\partial h\left(\bar{X}_t\right)}{\partial X_t}\right|_{X_t=\bar{X}_t}. \tag{B.4}$$

Thus, although we still use the original pricing relation to update the conditional mean, we update the conditional variance based on this linearization. For this purpose, we need to numerically evaluate the derivative defined in (B.4). We follow Norgaard, Poulsen, and Raven (2000) in updating the Cholesky factors of the covariance matrices directly.

Using the state and measurement updates, we obtain the one-period ahead forecasting error on the par yields,

$$e_t = S_t - \bar{S}_t = S_t - h\left(\bar{X}_t\right).$$

Assuming that the forecasting error is normally distributed, the quasi log-likelihood function is given by

$$\mathcal{L}\left(\mathbf{S}\right) = \sum_{t=1}^{T} l_t, \tag{B.5}$$

where

$$l_t = -\frac{1}{2}\log\left|\bar{A}_t\right| - \frac{1}{2}\left(e_t^\top \left(\bar{A}_t\right)^{-1} e_t\right),$$

where the conditional mean $\bar{S}_t$ and variance $\bar{A}_t$ are given in the EFK updates in (B.2).

## Acknowledgment

We thank Cheng F. Lee (the editor), Yacine Ait-Sahalia, Peter Carr, and Massoud Heidari for insightful comments. All remaining errors are ours.

## References

Ahn, D.-H., R. F. Dittmar and A. R. Gallant, "Quadratic Term Structure Models: Theory and Evidence." *Review of Financial Studies* 15, 243–288 (2002).

Babbs, S. H., "Rational Bounds." Working Paper, First National Bank of Chicago (1997).

Backus, D., S. Foresi, A. Mozumdar and L. Wu, "Predictable Changes in Yields and Forward Rates." *Journal of Financial Economics* 59, 281–311 (2001).

Balduzzi, P., S. Das, S. Foresi and R. Sundaram, "A Simple Approach to Three-Factor Affine Term Structure Models." *Journal of Fixed Income* 6, 43–53 (1996).

Beaglehole, D. R. and M.S. Tenney, "General Solution of Some Interest Rate-Contingent Claim Pricing Equations." *Journal of Fixed Income* 1, 69–83 (1991).

Beaglehole, D. R. and M. S. Tenney, "A Nonlinear Equilibrium Model of Term Structures of Interest Rates: Corrections and Additions." *Journal of Financial Economics* 32, 345–454 (1992).

Björk, T. and B. J. Christensen, "Interest Rate Dynamics and Consistent Forward Rate Curves." *Mathematical Finance* 9, 323–348 (1999).

Black, F., "Interest Rates as Options." *Journal of Finance* 50, 1371–1376 (1995).

Brandt, M. and D. A. Chapman, "Comparing Multifactor Models of the Term Structure." Working Paper, Duke University (2002).

Brandt, M. and A. Yaron, "Time-consistent No-Arbitrage Models of the Term Structure." Working paper, University of Pennsylvania (2001).

Brown, R. H. and S. M. Schaefer, "Why Long Term Forward Interest Rates (almost) Always Slope Downwards." Working Paper, Warburg Dillion Read and London Business School UK (2000).

Chen, R. R. and L. Scott, "Maximum Likelihood Estimation of a Multifactor Equilibrium Model of the Term Structure of Interest Rates." *Journal of Fixed Income* 3, 14–31 (1993).

Constantinides, G. M., "A Theory of the Nominal Term Structure of Interest Rates." *Review of Financial Studies* 5, 531–552 (1992).

Cox, J. C., J. E. Ingersoll, and S. R. Ross, 1985, "A Theory of the Term Structure of Interest Rates." *Econometrica* 53, 385–408 (1985).

Dai, Q. and K. Singleton, "Specification Analysis of Affine Term Structure Models." *Journal of Finance* 55, 1943–2000 (2000).

Dai, Q. and K. Singleton, "Expectation Puzzles, Time-Varying Risk Premia, and Affine Models of the Term Structure." *Journal of Financial Economics* 63, 415–441 (2002).

Dai, Q. and K. Singleton, "Term Structure Dynamics in Theory and Reality." *Review of Financial Studies* 16, 631–678 (2003).

Diebold, F. X., L. Ji and C. Li, "A Three-Factor Yield Curve Model: Non-affine Structure, Systematic Risk Sources, and Generalized Duration." In L. R. Klein, (eds.) *Memorial Volume for Albert Ando. Cheltenham* UK: Edward Elgar (2004).

Diebold, F. X. and C. Li, "Forecasting the Term Structure of Government Bond Yields." Working Paper, University of Pennsylvania (2003).

Duffee, G. R., 2002, "Term Premia and Interest Rate Forecasts in Affine Models." *Journal of Finance* 57, 405–443 (2002).

Duffie, D., *Dynamic Asset Pricing Theory* 2nd ed. Princeton, New Jersey: Princeton University Press.

Duffie, D. and R. Kan, "A Yield-Factor Model of Interest Rates." *Mathematical Finance* 6, 379–406 (1996).

Duffie, D., J. Pan and K. Singleton, "Transform Analysis and Asset Pricing for Affine Jump Diffusions." *Econometrica* 68, 1343–1376 (2000).

El Karoui, N., R. Myneni and R. Viswanathan, "Arbitrage Pricing and Hedging of Interest Rate Claims with State Variables: I Theory "Working Paper." University of Paris (1992).

Filipović, D., "A Note on the Nelson–Siegel Family." *Mathematical Finance* 9, 349–359 (1999).

Filipović, D., "Exponential-Polynomial Families and the Term Structure of Interest Rates." *Bernoulli* 6, 1–27 (2000).

Filipović, D., "A General Characterization of One Factor Affine Term Structure Models." *Finance and Stochastics* 5, 389–412 (2001).

Flesaker, B. and L.P. Hughston, "Positive Interest." *RISK* 9, 46–49 (1996).

Goldstein, R. and W. Keirstead, "On the Term Structure of Interest Rates in the Presence of Reflecting and Absorbing Boundaries." Working paper, Ohio-State University (1997).

Gorovoi, V. and V. Linetsky, "Black's Model of Interest Rates as Options, Eigenfunction Expansions and Japanese Interest Rates." *Mathematical Finance* forthcoming (2003).

Heath, D., R. Jarrow and A. Morton, "Bond Pricing and the Term Structure of Interest Rates: A New Technology for Contingent Claims Valuation." *Econometrica* 60, 77–105 (1992).

Heidari, M. and L. Wu, "Are Interest Rate Derivatives Spanned by the Term Structure of Interest Rates?" *Journal of Fixed Income* 13, 75–86 (2003).

Jacod, J. and A. N. Shiryaev, *Limit Theorems for Stochastic Processes*. Berlin: Springer-Verlag (1987).

Jamshidian, F., "Bond, Futures and Option Valuation in the Quadratic Interest Rate Model." *Applied Mathematical Finance* 3, 93–115 (1996).

Jin, Y. and P. Glasserman, "Equilibrium Positive Interest Rates: A Unified View." *Review of Financial Studies* 14, 187–214 (2001).

Kalman, R. E., "A New Approach to Linear Filtering and Prediction Problems." *Transactions of the ASME—Journal of Basic Engineering* 82, 35–45 (1960).

Knez, P. J., R. Litterman and J. Scheinkman, "Explorations Into Factors Explaining Money Market Returns." *Journal of Finance* 49, 1861–1882 (1994).

Leippold, M. and L. Wu, "Asset Pricing Under the Quadratic Class." *Journal of Financial and Quantitative Analysis* 37, 271–295 (2002).

Leippold, M. and L. Wu, "Design and Estimation of Quadratic Term Structure Models." *European Finance Review* 7, 47–73 (2003).

Litterman, R. and J. Scheinkman, "Common Factors Affecting Bond Returns." *Journal of Fixed Income* 1, 54–61 (1991).

Longstaff, F. A., "A Nonlinear General Equilibrium Model of the Term Structure of Interest Rates." *Journal of Financial Economics* 23, 195–224 (1989).

Longstaff, F. A., P. Santa-Clara and E. S. Schwartz, "Throwing Away a Million Dollars: The Cost of Suboptimal Exercise Strategies in the Swaptions Market." *Journal of Financial Economics* 62, 39–66 (2001).

Norgaard, M., N. K. Poulsen and O. Raven, "New Developments in State Estimation for Nonlinear Systems." *Automatica* 36, 1627–1638 (2000).

Pan, E., "Collpase of detail." *International Journal of Theoretical and Applied Finance* 1, 247–282 (1998).

Rogers, L. C. G., *Mathematical Finance.* vol. IMA, Vol. 65. New York: Springer (1995).

Rogers, L. C. G., "Gaussian Errors." *RISK* 9, 42–45 (1996).

Rogers, L. C. G., "The Potential Approach to the Term Structure of Interest Rates and Foreign Exchange Rates." *Mathematical Finance* 7, 157–176 (1997).

# INDEX